Echo and Reverb

PETER DOYLE

Echo and Reverb

FABRICATING SPACE IN POPULAR
MUSIC RECORDING, 1900–1960

WESLEYAN UNIVERSITY PRESS

Middletown, Connecticut

Published by Wesleyan University Press, Middletown, CT 06459
www.wesleyan.edu/wespress
© 2005 by Peter Doyle
Printed in the United States of America
5 4 3 2 1

Library of Congress Cataloging-in-Publication Data
Doyle, Peter, 1951–
  Echo and reverb : fabricating space in popular music recording,
1900–1960 / Peter Doyle.— 1st ed.
    p. cm.
  Includes bibliographical references (p.   ), discography (p.   ), and index.
  ISBN-13: 978-0-8195-6793-2 (cloth : alk. paper)
  ISBN-10: 0-8195-6793-0 (cloth : alk. paper)
  ISBN-13: 978-0-8195-6794-9 (pbk. : alk. paper)
  ISBN-10: 0-8195-6794-9 (pbk. : alk. paper)
  1. Popular music—History and criticism. 2. Sound recordings—
Production and direction—History. I. Title.
  ML3470.D69 2005
  781.64'149—dc22   2005013310

The author gratefully acknowledges permission to reproduce the following:

"Catfish Blues a/k/a Rollin' Stone" (Muddy Waters)
© 1959, 1987 (renewed) WATERTOONS MUSIC (BMI)/Administered by BUG
All Rights Reserved. Used By Permission.

"My Blue Heaven" (Walter Donaldson/George Whiting)
Donaldson Publishing Co. (ASCAP)/George Whiting Publishing

"Swing, Brother, Swing" by William E. Cantrell, Quinton M. Claunch
© 1936, 1961 (renewed) by Universal Music Corporation / ASCAP
Used By Permission. International Copyright Secured. All Rights Reserved.

"Voice of a Fool, The" by William E. Cantrell, Quinton M. Claunch
© 1958 (renewed) by Irving Music, Inc. on behalf of Jec Publishing Corporation / BMI
Used By Permission. International Copyright Secured. All Rights Reserved.

"When the Lights Go Out" (Willie Dixon)
© 1954, 1982 (renewed) HOOCHIE COOCHIE MUSIC (BMI)/Administered by BUG
All Rights Reserved. Used By Permission.

Every effort was made to contact the current copyright holders of the works cited in this volume.

Contents

Acknowledgments

Ross Gibson, Noel King, Phil Hayward, Jon Fitzgerald, Rob Bowman and Neil V. Rosenberg generously commented on early versions of this manuscript. Susan Fast offered detailed and knowledgeable responses to successive later drafts, and Tony Mitchell gave sound advice and encouragement. Anne Bickford, Bruce Bongers, Robert L. Campbell, Michael Finucane, Phil Hayward, Bruce Johnson, Richard Ruhle, Neil V. Rosenberg, John Whiteoak and others helped with many elusive facts and references and offered important corrections. Raymond Devitt provided an uncannily accurate on-call reference service for all matters related to twentieth-century popular music. Sue Doyle cast a knowing eye over numerous drafts, and Bridie Doyle offered invaluable assistance with the proofing. My deepest thanks to them all. Any errors of fact or interpretation, of course, remain entirely mine.

I would also like to gratefully acknowledge the financial assistance given this project by both the Media Department and the Division of Society, Culture, Media, and Philosophy at Macquarie University, Sydney.

CHAPTER 1

Introduction

Sometime in the late 1940s, Foy Willing and the Riders of the Purple Sage, a Los Angeles–based western band recorded the song "Blue Shadows on the Trail" for the Teleways radio transcription service. The recording begins with two bars of accordion and vamped rhythm acoustic guitar, after which three male voices sing "Woo-woo-woooo" in falsetto, the voices coming in two beats apart, with each singing a little lower than the preceding one, and each progressively more off-microphone. The last voice seems to be coming from far off. The voices cease and an electric steel guitar comes in, further still off-mic and featuring a slow vibrato. The lyric begins with all the voices singing a close-knit, Tin Pan Alley–style harmony, with carefully controlled swells and diminuendos. Each line is punctuated by a steel guitar lick that recalls the male voices' "woo-woo-wooo" in the introduction.

> Blue shadows on the trail
> Blue moon shining through the trees
> And a plaintive wail from the distance
> Comes a-driftin' on the evenin' breeze.

For listeners with even a slight acquaintance with "dime novels," western comic books, radio serials or cowboy movies, the song readily suggests the spaces and places of the popularly constructed American West: the strummed guitar might be akin to the sound of the singer's horse ambling across the prairie; the "woo-woo-wooos" are creatures calling out in the distance, perhaps whippoorwills, or (as a devotee of wagon-train westerns would suspect) unseen Indians signaling to one another as they secretly observe the singer. The far-off steel guitar suggests a creature of the night— perhaps a coyote howling eerily from atop a butte or mesa (no doubt silhouetted against a rising full moon). The combination of lyric content, vocal harmony, instrumentation and studio contrivance here sets up a virtual geography, a coherent, highly specific sense of place and space.

In part, the polished, professional, unhurried feel of "Blue Shadows" might derive from the support the song gets from extrinsic, nonmusical traditions: widely disseminated preexisting representations of the "cowboy" west in comic books, dime novels, western movies, sheet music covers, popular landscape art and so forth, as well as other, newer traditions of the sonic representation of space in radio serials and on movie soundtracks. When the producers decided to place the steel guitar off-mic, they were apparently satisfied that the record's listeners would be cued to imagine the appropriate "western" image.

Compare this with Elvis Presley's version of "Mystery Train" (1955), recorded at Sun Studios on the eve of the singer's move to RCA (and consequent megastardom). The first sound heard on the recording comes from Scotty Moore's electric guitar, a "hammering-on"[1] on the low strings, followed by a brisk repeating figure located around the middle register. The guitar sound is highly "echoic." These ingredients, the use of reverberation (reverb), the low pitch of the guitar and the brisk shuffle feel combine to evoke something of the sound of a train in the distance, an effect much compounded when Presley starts singing, "Train I ride, sixteen coaches long." Again, recording contrivance complements lyrics and musical sounds in manufacturing a sense of near and far, a sense in the listener that the musical sounds are emanating from different "locations" within a musical field.

And the singer here is ambiguously "located." He is at one moment on the train, at another apparently watching the train leave, and yet another waiting for it to bring "his baby back." While the echoic guitar maintains a constant "background" sense of locomotive urgency, the reverb and echo delay around the singer's voice in concert with the moments of deliberately "jerky" phrasing gives rise to a sense of nervousness, of simultaneous dread and jubilation. A runaway train, perhaps. The place of the voice in the mix, reverberant, yet "up front," compounds the ambiguities, setting up a simultaneous nearness and remoteness.

While it is difficult to "make sense" of this spatiality in the same way that one can interpret "Blue Shadows," it is no less effective for that. Where "Blue Shadows" employs aural spatiality in a clever but nonetheless realist way to create a coherent, pictorial sense of place, "Mystery Train" uses its spatialities in order to evoke a sense of disordered space, of Dionysian abandon. "Blue Shadows," for all its technical mastery, presents as being very much the product of a largely obsolete aesthetic regime—open-throated voices singing close harmony, the use of strict, unsyncopated tempo—whereas Presley's "Mystery Train" has enjoyed a steadily growing status since the time of its recording. The track has been permanently on RCA's catalogue since the late 1950s, and is a particular favorite among Presley fans and devotees of rock 'n' roll music. It has lent its name to a much-reprinted critical work by Greil Marcus[2] as well as to Jim Jarmusch's film.[3] The particular guitar sound Scotty Moore employed on that track has been much emulated, the riff much quoted.[4]

Consider also Robert Johnson's recording of his own composition "Come on in My Kitchen" (1936). The track is composed solely of Johnson's voice and acoustic slide guitar. Johnson sings a couple of verses in his more usual singing voice, then breaks for a few bars to insert some sotto voce murmurings, matching each utterance with guitar lick of increasing subtlety.

> [Guitar lick.]
> Baby can't you hear that wind howl? [*spoken*].
> [*Different slide lick, softer.*]
> Oh, can't you hear that wind howl? [*spoken*].
> [Slide lick repeated, followed by barely discernible rattling
> of bottleneck on string as last note is held.]

This recording too is concerned with place and space. As in "Blue Shadows" and "Mystery Train," the listener's attention is directed to a real-world physical phenomenon (in this case, the howling wind) that is represented by musical means, the delicately picked slide guitar. Yet the "landscape" spatiality is overridden here by a more arresting sense of a different place: the actual physical space occupied by the singer and his guitar at the moment of the recording. Although we do not have any strong pictorial reference to aid us in visually imagining *this* space, the close miking of the voice and guitar, the singer's deliberate use of barely audible utterances and extremely delicate guitar figures, plus the inclusion on the recording of other "intimate," nonmusical sounds (such as the "accidental" rattle of the slide against the strings of the guitar)—all serve to create sense of moment, and create a sense in the listener of proximity to the singer. The listener is afforded a kind of aural glimpse, a private sonic close-up of the singer in action.[5] When the singer invites us to "hear the wind howl" he is working near the limits of what was possible in recorded dynamics at the time, drawing his listeners in, inviting them to pay even closer, more concentrated attention to the music.

In visual terms, listening to "Blue Shadows" might be likened to the experience of looking at a large, romantically rendered work of landscape art, while Presley's "Mystery Train" might be imagined more as an expressionist or cubist painting, in which the viewer might encounter the real in an exhilaratingly re-formed, nonrealist configuration. Listening to the Johnson song then would be like being *inside* an installation. In their different ways these recordings each use sonic means to contrive a sense of space and place, and in each case this spatiality is critical to the recordings' musical effects. It is with these and other kinds of sonically created spatiality that this book is concerned.

My original intention was to answer what seemed to be a simple enough question, or series of questions concerning the use of the echo and reverb production effects that so typified many "classic" rock 'n' roll and rockabilly recordings—from the reverberant voice effects used by Elvis Presley and others, to the echo and reverb effects used most notably on electric guitars, but also found applied to saxophones, drums, harmonicas and other instruments. I was particularly interested in the "big echo" sound of much early rockabilly music of the mid-1950s and guitar instrumental music from the late 1950s and early 1960s. The questions basically were, In what ways do these echo and reverb effects accomplish their task? Whence did they come? Why should they be present at all?

The questions partly arose from personal experience as both a dedicated listener to live and recorded music and as a semiprofessional electric guitarist. Experience in the latter role had taught me that the merest touch of echo and reverb could greatly alter the emotive impact of sounds produced, and the affective change often seemed to be out of all proportion to the purely sonic changes wrought by the effect. By flicking the switch on a tape echo unit, suddenly low notes played on my guitar took on a menacing presence, or a slow, lazy shimmer. The high notes became more piercing, and previously indifferent riffs and figures (sometimes) took on a rich, haunting fullness. Why should this be so?

Although there now exists a quite considerable body of scholarly, semischolarly and mass-market literature dealing with rock 'n' roll music in musicological, social, historical and/or anecdotal terms, there have been few serious attempts specifically to address the question of why one of the primary characteristics of the music, the use of echo and reverb, should be present at all. Similarly, the last ten or twenty years has seen the growth of a culture of fetishization of "classic" production sounds among many musicians, which has seen the reissue of a number of 1950s- and '60s-styled amplifiers, guitars and ancillary devices, including echo and reverb units. When I started out playing guitar in the early 1970s, what knowledge there was circulating about "the Sun Sound," and "the Chess Sound" was anecdotal and fragmentary, and snippets of information about guitar sounds used by players like Scotty Moore, Les Paul, Muddy Waters or Dick Dale were rare. Nowadays magazines such as *Guitar Player* provide a great deal of information about how particular sounds were achieved, what devices were used and so on. Similarly, worldwide networks of keen amateurs exist, whose members communicate via websites and e-mail, or meet at workshops conducted at blues and roots music festivals. The coming on line of digital signal processing technologies such as the Quadreverb, Lexicon, and computer packages such as ProTools have made available to both institutional and home-based producers a great range of effects. At the lower end, a wide range of relatively cheap "black boxes" and foot pedal effects units that offer a range of echo and reverb effects are available to musicians. Reverb and echo effects are ubiquitous in contemporary popular music making. All this notwithstanding, questions of how these sonic variables might bring about an affective outcome in listeners have gone largely unasked.

Returning then to the backstory to this current project, the echo and reverb effects I was hearing on classic rock 'n' roll recordings sometimes seemed to suggest (to me) something to do with the supernatural; in combination with certain lyric styles, instrument mixes, certain pitches and tempos, the echo was in some way suggestive of hoodoo powers and magical forces. (Indeed, one of the most common adjectives encountered in writings about echoic guitar and vocal music is "haunting.") But at other times reverberant and/or echoic sonics suggested desolate, wide-open landscapes, depopulated but for a single wayfarer (later notable examples being Ry Cooder's slide guitar pieces for the soundtrack to *Paris, Texas* (directed by Wim Wenders, 1984) and Ennio Morricone's western soundtracks), or deserted streets late at night. Sometimes dark, subterranean spaces were evoked; at other times this listener was put in mind of grand mountains and canyons. Then again, the echo effect on the "surf guitar" music of Dick Dale or the Atlantics readily suggested tiny figures on Malibu surfboards dwarfed by murderously large waves. Or echoic electric steel guitar in some *hapa haole* Hawaiian music conjured up a notion of waves lapping lazily on palm-fringed beaches, of dreamy, sensual tropical evenings. But then the echo and reverb-laden voice and electric guitars on, say, Gene Vincent's "Be Bop a Lula" (1956) suggested to me the ambience of a Saturday night scout hall rock 'n' roll dance. And so on. Echoicity was highly evocative, but there was no one-to-one relationship between the effect and what was signified by its deployment.

Echo and reverberation made it seem as though the music was coming from a somewhere—from inside an enclosed architectural or natural space or "out of" a specific geographic location—and this "somewhere" was often semiotically highly volatile. On reflection it became clear that with the addition of echo and reverb, "place" and "space" had become part of the larger musical equation, a new component in the musical totality. To understand how and why echo and reverb "did something" to the music then, it would be necessary to investigate these sonically represented spaces.

The spaces ranged from the decidedly concrete to the mythic and/or purely imaginary. Furthermore, some of these sonic spatialities were "pictorial," somehow referring me back to my own learned preconceptions of, say, the American West or the beach at Waikiki (neither of which I have actually visited). At other times this musico-sonic spatiality was less explicitly pictorial, even tending toward the hallucinatory, in some way evoking in me a sense of strangeness or disquiet. Yet another type of less pictorial spatiality was to be found, in say, the music of Bo Diddley, Little Walter, or early Elvis Presley recordings, in which everything seems to be vibrating, echoing, reverberating in an out of control, manic, "atomic" kinesis, suggesting movement in space but without any special reference to specific real-world spaces or places.

These preliminary musings were made in relation to recorded rock 'n' roll, rockabilly and electric blues music that had an unmistakably "echoic" character, in which a producer had apparently deliberately added synthetic echo, either by manipulating magnetic tape record and playback heads to achieve a "slapback" effect[6] or simply through placing a second microphone in a reverberant space—most commonly the studio toilet. But "virtual spatiality" was not merely a product of the deliberate, sometimes heavy-handed use of studio effects. Clearly the actual acoustic regime of the studio itself (not just the studio bathroom) was crucial; so too were the specific deployments of the recording apparatus and the placements of voices and instruments within that space. Also to be factored in were the many acoustic adjustments and accommodations, both small and large, made by performers to their instruments, to each other, to the studio space and to the recording apparatus.

To be considered as well were the complex sets of interpersonal accommodations—especially important in the southern U.S. studios where most often white producers recorded itinerant or déclassé African American artists or poor whites. Indeed, these interpersonal considerations are arguably crucial to any recording studio, anywhere; typically the performers, isolated in the spotlight, are watched, monitored and directed by unseen engineers and producers. In such situations potentials simultaneously exist for everything from the crassest form of bullying and intimidation to the most intimate creative synergies.

Thus I concluded that the spatialities set up by the use of echo and reverb as musical effects cannot at any certain point be separated from larger issues of "production" and production values; these in turn involve matters of proxemics and interpersonal relations, which in turn involve powerful social forces from beyond the studio—in particular, tensions around class, racial and sexual politics.

It became clear that to understand the workings of the echo and reverb effects used in 1950s rock 'n' roll it would be necessary to go beyond a synchronic musico-semiotic analysis of the recordings themselves and to locate the recordings in relation to earlier intersecting and overlapping traditions of musical performance and recording in which spatiality was key. Accordingly, certain emblematic recordings will be discussed, going back to recordings of "hillbilly" music of the early electronic period of sound recording (that is, roughly post-1925), southern country blues recordings of the 1930s, big band, western swing, *hapa haole* Hawaiian guitar music of the 1940s, postwar country music, "singing cowboy" music and (some) early electric southern blues, as well a series of influential and commercially successful highly spatialized pop, country, blues and novelty recordings produced in postwar Hollywood.

It will be argued that in pre–magnetic tape popular music recording, especially southern U.S. blues and country recording, questions of place and space (at both the personal and collective levels), were crucial, and that many of what are now widely regarded as the most idiosyncratic and valuable "roots music" recordings (such as Robert Johnson's "Come on in My Kitchen") derive much of their affective power from spatial tensions, traces of which, I shall argue, are detectable in the recordings themselves. A number of key artists knowingly made use of spatio-acoustic conditions in order to present uniquely their own "sense of self." The social, the personal, the geographic, the demographic, the physico-spatial conditions of their lives (and of life in general) were rendered into aesthetic effects.

This particular translating of the "lived" into the musical recording, while not exclusive to them, was a defining feature of much southern country blues and hillbilly recording, and this tradition of the highly individual, very personal sense of "self-in-place" was readily available, geographically and culturally for adoption by the very artists and some of the producers who created rock 'n' roll and rhythm and blues music in the 1950s. The echoic voice, the echoic electric guitar, harp or tenor sax, were new enactments of prior traditions of self-representation.

In making sense of 1950s echoic recording, it will also be necessary to go outside the strict domain of music recording to examine other related sound production and recording practices, including deployments of "echoicity" and reverb in Hollywood movie sound. Not surprisingly, some of the most telling uses of the devices are to be found in Hollywood westerns, crime, and horror films of the 1940s. By the late 1940s performers as unalike as pop singer Vaughn Monroe and blues singer John Lee Hooker were using echo and reverb, albeit in different ways, to signify uncanny presences. Presumably audiences readily understood what was intended by the effect. It is difficult to account for this relatively sudden appearance without reference to the prior semiotic listener training groundwork done by Hollywood movies, in which these same acoustic effects are explicitly linked to stories of terror and the supernatural, and moments of mystical transformations. Accordingly chapter 4 deals with some key, nonmusical cinematic uses of echo and reverb effects.

I shall then go on to argue that by the late 1940s and early 1950s, a repertoire of "spatial" sonic production practices, musical and nonmusical, had become available, and in theory these were easily reproducible for anyone with basic magnetic tape recording equipment. Through the late 1940s a subset of spatialized popular songs began to appear that relied on reverb effects (in league with lyrics and musical effects) to set up "pictorial" spaces. These earlier overt uses of spatial production devices were in the main realist and singular in their reference. The sonic "3-D" of Foy Willing's "Blue Shadows on the Trail," for instance, seeks to replicate the acoustic conditions of a western landscape at sundown; the ghostly voices on Vaughn Monroe's "Riders in the Sky" (1949) or the sirenlike calling of the off-mic steel guitars in pop Hawaiian music, while flirting with the supernatural, nonetheless sought to trigger in the listener mental images of coherent, "imaginable" physical spaces. In the hands of the artists and producers at Sun, Chess and elsewhere, these same devices were put to uses that saw an "explosion" of contradictory, realist and nonrealist signification.

It will be further argued that these spatial production characteristics were much more than an interesting gimmick; they both paralleled and to some extent enacted the global breakout of rock 'n' roll music. These spatialities, as much as any intramusical features (such as twelve-bar structure, backbeat drumming), served to typify and sometimes even define music as rock 'n' roll.

As well as investigating the "supply side" of the equation, we shall also be obliged to look at listening practices in relation to recorded and live music, and give some consideration to the various spaces and spatialities in which music is consumed and used. Many of the foregoing remarks and indicated complications might equally be applied to this consumption side of the music contract: for instance, we should consider some of the many different architectural spaces and acoustic regimes in which music is listened to as well as changes over time in playback apparati. It will be necessary to consider the interpersonal complexities operating at the sites of production *and* the interpersonal configurations among music listeners, both actual (if temporary) communities of listeners in the one architectural space and notional communities of geographically disparate listeners. With regards to solitary listeners, some consideration must be given to different modes of listening, differing degrees of "distractedness" and focus with which listeners address recorded music.

In other words, recorded music will need to be considered in both its most collective and most individual consumption modes. This work asserts that it was in recorded southern blues, rock 'n' roll and rhythm and country music of the late 1940s and early 1950s (located as these were outside but still close to the mainstream of the American popular music industry) that many of the ground rules of rock music production and consumption were laid down, and that the fabricated "virtual spaces" that typified so many of these recordings provided an imagined "shared" space, occupied by both listeners and performers. In this "space," listeners could choose to engage and interact with the music in a most intense, solitary way or in ways that were wholly collective and community-forming.

The following chapters are arranged according to a rough chronology. Chapter 2 examines ancient and medieval acoustic histories and mythologies, tracing them through to the nineteenth-century beginnings of sound recording and the establishment of a popular music recording industry. Chapters 3 to 7 trace the subsequent emergence of spatial music and sound recording practices up to the early 1950s, while the remaining chapters examine in more detail how the makers of early rock 'n' roll recombined these practices and effects. Before proceeding with that story, however, I shall survey here some of the broader critical, scholarly and theoretical territories into which this study wanders. Readers who proceed directly to chapter 2 may feel a need to refer back to this section, at least for an explication of the Deleuze/Guattarian terms *territorialization, deterritorialization* and *reterritorialization,* which are used throughout this book. Unlovely though these neologisms may be, they reference a set of ideas that provide a practical analytical tool, yet remain sufficiently open-ended to allow for and suggest freer, more imaginative speculations.

Literature

Since the beginning of the twentieth century, writings about popular music—reviews of performances and recordings, biographies, "star" profiles, histories, music trade news, fan literature, and, since the late 1960s, high-flown "think pieces"—have been a steadily increasing presence in popular and specialty presses. Within the academy, studies of popular music have emerged (generally as a minority practice) within such diverse disciplines as sociology, literary studies, psychology, ethnography, anthropology, cultural history, architecture, physics, engineering, geography, archeology, leisure studies, gender studies, postcolonial studies, diaspora studies and musicology. In these fields, with the exception of the last, the primary focus is not on the musical object itself—its internal structures and relationships, the various aspects of its sonic constitution, its connections with its own "outside"—but rather with the social, cultural and physical contexts in which music resides. Sociologists studying popular music, for example, may use popular music to exemplify social and cultural formations, or may examine social formations arising around certain music practices, or may be mainly concerned with furthering discussion of competing analytical models and theories. Although the extent to which they attend to the specifics of the music in question varies, their primary concern will by definition generally remain extramusical. The discipline of musicology, on the other hand, has been frequently criticized for its resolutely intratextual focus, and for its general indifference to broader cultural contexts.[7]

Theodore Adorno's work on Tin Pan Alley popular music of the 1920s linked certain intratextual characteristics—particularly lyrics and textural qualities—to politics in the larger social world. Adorno damningly locates the music industry and its products within a larger mass culture operation serving to manipulate, infantilize and silence subjects, and generally deaden political will. Although subsequent writers have generally not fallen in step with Adorno's wholly pessimistic view of popular music,[8] his broad approach of seeking and seeing both the text within the culture, and the culture within the specificities of the text has informed various (minority) strands of popular music studies since, exemplified in the work of writers as diverse as Alan Lomax (1968), Phillip Tagg (1979, 1982), Richard Middleton (1990), Theo Van Leeuwen (1991), Susan McClary (1991), Robert Walser (1993), Paul Theberge (1997), Steve Waksman (1999), David Brackett (2000), Susan Fast (2001) and others.

Susan McClary and Robert Walser[9] have outlined some of the problems specific to writing "pop musicology." They refer to rock criticism's and academic writing's tendency to "vague pretentiousness" and chronic failure to address what is really at stake in the tunes. The alternatives in writing about music are either to write impressionistically (and thereby fail to address the details) or to address the details in technical terms (and risk mystifying readers). In addition, there are severe problems specific to pop musicology. Pop musicologists need to dispense with established musicology's notions of the inherent, self-evident "greatness" of certain musical texts and the discipline's indifference to the social grounding of those texts (they are transcendent; ergo, their social grounding is largely irrelevant). Yet in looking beyond purely formal intramusical considerations, a huge range of multidisciplinary approaches are suddenly called for:

One of the extraordinary ironies of contemporary musicology is that the intellectual apparatus required of those studying 'serious' music . . . is practically nonexistent . . . while that required of those studying popular music—where reception, social context, and political struggle are regularly regarded as central issues—is vast.[10]

Moreover, musicology's eschewing of purely affective responses to music as being somehow childish or naïve has left modern popular music analysts with a difficult task:

to try to make the case that a particular configuration sounds mournful (something that may be obvious to virtually all listeners . . .) is to have to invent a philosophical argument for meaning in music and try to reconstruct forgotten codes out of centuries of music. At first glance, for instance much of Philip Tagg's work appears bogged down in what seem to be irrelevant issues (why semiotics?) and irrelevant repertoires (what has a Bach passion got to do with ABBA's "Fernando"?). If Tagg were in a context in which semiotics existed as a matter of course, he could simply refer. But unfortunately most of his steps are absolutely necessary—he has to rebuild the whole of Western musical semiotics before he can unpack the theme from Kojak.[11]

In contrast to his earlier broad endorsement, Walser (1993) takes issue with Tagg's work in his *Running with the Devil* for too often ignoring or marginalizing both the political economy of popular music and its actual operations in social contestation. The scientific rigor and objectivity for which Tagg strives, argues Walser, manifest in his elaborate taxonomies and extensive acronymic abstractions, has produced often excessively complex, cumbersome and even artificial analyses. The steps Tagg takes to so carefully guarantee accurate delineation of meaning ultimately serve to inhibit the attribution of the social meanings he is seeking. There are no people in Tagg's analytical world, where musicians and fans are reduced to "Emitters" and "Receivers," thereby reinforcing the flawed model of art as a conduit for delivering meaning, "rather than as a social field for constructing, negotiating and contesting it."[12]

Walser's remark that "you have the problem of connecting art and society only if you accept the assumptions that separate them,"[13] does much to point the way to a meaningful, yet accessible, socially grounded musicology. Popular music recordings are objects of material culture, and reflect (albeit in complex and not necessarily obvious ways) aspects of the cultural conditions obtaining at the places of their production and reception. These objects in turn participate in the processes by which subjectivity is constructed;

they determine, in their own ways, the cultural fields from which they spring. The repeated, more than slightly anxious quest for ironclad, positivist legitimacy perhaps serves, albeit unwittingly, to revive the discredited and simplistic assumption that the art object *is* hermetically separate from the social. On the other hand, "legitimacy anxiety" might also stem from residual reservations concerning the validity of the popular music artifact itself, as though there was a need to justify (again and again) its study, in answer to antique prejudices concerning high and low art, and in particular to dispute or compensate for the perceived triviality of the pop artifact.

In reviewing methodologies of pop musicology, David Brackett (2000) alerts us to the pitfalls of studies that assume the stability of musical codes and the "material immanence" of the pop music text. "The recourse to 'immanence,'" he writes, "relegates the discussion of a musical text to an ahistorical, noncultural vacuum, a vacuum without perceiving subjects." If we accept that musical meaning is conveyed through a code that is "sent" by a somebody, then we must assume a receiving or consuming somebody as well, and thus we need to consider parallel codes relating to listener competency.[14] Codes are no more static, argues Brackett, than are the types of competence that listening subjects may bring to bear on them; furthermore, "the way in which we 'decode' a piece may change our sense of the piece we are hearing, necessitating an infinite series of new perspectives in the act of listening" (13).

Degrees and types of competence may indeed vary greatly between listeners, and even for a single listener. We may listen to a recording one day, and, for no special reason, experience a near magical awareness of the sounds and musical relations, intuit the inner codes as they are being simultaneously acknowledged and refigured, feel the "three dimensionality" of the recording as though we and the music are copresent in a single, fluidly gridded zone. The same recording heard the next day might offer no more than background static. And these huge variations in the nature of the encounter, to this listener at least, do not seem to depend on the quality of the playback device or on the acoustics of the playback space: pieces of recorded music heard "accidentally" on a store radio, or on a pub jukebox, or on a lo-fi car stereo may produce surprisingly intense listening experiences, while more deliberate, purposeful listenings may leave us strangely unmoved. Or may not, according to the complex and mysterious workings of various sets of personal and collective, internal and external, affective and physico-acoustic variables.

The issue of competence raises questions as to the stability and "readability" of the musical object, especially in relation to the more connotative layers of meaning. If we identify connotations, especially of the more ephemeral kind, how can we be sure that they are indeed present in the text and "working" on listeners? The present work assumes that there may well be a great number of possible listening positions and "competency profiles" for any popular music recording. Indeed, the three-minute pop recording, designed to sell itself in a single hearing, easily repeated on the home player, jukebox, dance hall or disco turntable, allows for particularly easy access; nearly anyone can become an expert, of sorts, on a particular recording, and on entire genres and styles. One important assumption I make is that, while it may not be universal, high-competency listening is sufficiently ubiquitous to underwrite, in principle, the idea of a semiotic reading of the pop recording. A common feature of many of the recordings surveyed here is that they were made by musicians and technicians who, as their biographers note, were themselves obsessively close, knowledgeable listeners to the recorded popular music, both of their time and earlier. Furthermore, many of the hillbilly, "Hawaiian," jazz, country blues and early rock 'n' roll records talked about here inspired widespread "do it yourself" copycat practices among their audiences, practices that involved extremely close (yet frequently amateur, musically unlettered) engagements with the recorded artifact, and these engagements occurred both at the individual level and within larger listening formations.

For other listeners—or for high-competency listeners during their more distracted moments—the engagements may occur at more unconscious levels. Listeners may have very strong feelings for a certain recording, for example, but may have only the vaguest awareness of its sonic specificities, its textures, structures, its location within a generic history, and so forth. Furthermore, many of the spatial effects traced in the pages that follow, effects that notionally "locate" the musical objects and listeners, frequently do so covertly. Effects that might have aroused conscious notice and comment when they first appeared (and many did) might go quite unremarked later, but this is not to say that those effects do not continue to "work on" listeners, regardless of whether or not individual listeners closely interrogate their precise responses to the music. An example: a number of "pop western" recordings of the 1940s and 1950s, as already noted, used reverberant guitar or vocal sounds to sonically represent "western" landscapes (a relatively simple denotative device borrowed in part from radio dramas, and movie soundtracks) and on occasions to further represent numinous moments experienced within the western landscape (well exemplified in Vaughn Monroe's hit record of "Riders in the Sky"). Yet Ry Cooder's version of the slide guitar piece "Dark Was the Night" on the soundtrack to *Paris, Texas,* elaborately treated with echo and reverb, and appearing more than thirty years after these more commonplace uses of echo and reverb, is not infrequently described by listeners in adjectival terms (mysterious, atmospheric, haunting). In other words, a spatiomusical effect more or less unproblemmatically present in pop music in the 1940s and 1950s as denotation, resurfaces to later audiences, less *consciously* aware of its semiotic history, as connotation. This work is thus much concerned with the semiotic history of such spatializing effects, and the contexts in which they first appeared, as well as their later appropriations.

Certain of the thornier methodological problems attending cultural interpretations of music—such as what different musical scales and intervals, harmonic relationships, timbral characteristics and combinations might "mean"—will thus be less at issue here. In the first instance, paramusical acoustic spatial indicators like echo and reverberation might be seen, according to the schema derived by C. S. Peirce, as "indexical signs": indices of the physical conditions that produce them, like footprints in snow, or smoke from a fire. The reading of such effects, even when they are used "fictitiously," as in pop western recordings, requires some minimal interpretation, but not generally of a contentious kind. Reverberation and echo simply *are* sonic attributes of physical space. When discussing the nature of the space(s) inferred by the use of echo and reverb on recordings, however, especially when lyrics do not cue us to imagine specific space(s), we move further into the area of connotation; in teasing these meanings out, we run the risk of interpreting idiosyncratically, of overinterpreting, or of misreading. In regards to this study, the risks of over- or wrongly interpreting becomes greater the further we move along the time line: generally speaking, the earlier we are in the history of sound recording, the more denotative the uses of spatial effects tend to be, making the task of interpretation relatively more straightforward. By the late 1940s, however, a much wider range of possible meanings was available to record makers and listeners, and many of these are at odds with others (such as the use of reverb or echo to locate a voice at a marked physical distance from the imagined "center stage" and also to suggest the inner voice or conscience of the singer).

The safeguards against obsessive and overheated interpretations include, along with the usual highly modalized language of scholarly caution ("suggests," "might be seen as," "could be," "implies"), the accreting of multiple examples in which domains of broadly similar meaning can be identified. Up until the coming of rock 'n' roll—which represents a decisive break in the tradition—spatial constructs in pop music recording can be seen emerging in a more or less orderly way, as "banks" of possible signification are gradually built up in a number of genres, across the major sound technologies: radio, movies and music recording. Thus this study is organized on a roughly historical basis; when viewed in this linear context the emergence of spatializing recording practices up to the coming of rock 'n' roll at least, reveals itself as often surprisingly clear and even orderly.

Concerned as it is with the emergence of a "virtual space" tradition in popular music recordings, this work makes repeated use of terms such as "spatial," "spatiality," "place," "location," and is especially concerned with the ideas of (virtual) movement, "emplacement," centrality and peripherality as enacted "within" the popular music recording. Of recent years such terms have become central to much writing in the humanities and social sciences. Indeed, in "The Space of Culture, the Power of Space," Lawrence Grossberg (1996) voices reservations about the recent proliferation in cultural studies of the poetic language of travel, homes, voyages and destinations "to describe discourses, power and the Imaginary." Grossberg cites the terms "margins," "boundaries," and "positions"; to these might be added "borders," "migrancy," "mapping," "terrain," "location," "routes," "tracks," "lines," "movement," "horizons," "crossing," "crossing-over," "in-betweenness," "landscape," "soundscape," "songlines" and of course "place," "space" and "spatiality." Popular music studies in particular has enthusiastically adopted these vocabularies, and geospatial tropes and terms have become staple themes for scholarly conferences and published anthologies.

Generally speaking, such works have tended to invoke their musical examples in the main only glancingly, and have not much concerned themselves with the specifics of how recordings might replicate or fabricate conditions of actual acoustic space, nor how such fabricated spatialities might relate to or enter into dialogue with real-world physical or metaphoric spaces. Cultural geographers performing interventions in the field of music studies in particular have adopted spatial lexicons, using the terminologies in both literal and highly metaphoric senses. Such studies have also in the main little concerned themselves with specifics of the musical texts they invoke. Of the dozen contributions to Leyshon, Matless and Revill's (1998) collection *The Place of Music,* for example, only five address intratextual qualities (structural features, actual sounds) of the music they discuss, and two of these confine their analyses to lyrics alone. Swiss, Sloop and Herman's (1997) *Mapping the Beat* similarly contains few examinations of actual sonic-musical fabrics, while Connell and Gibson's (2003) *Sound Tracks* confines its discussion of *intra*textual space to little more than passing mention of place names in certain popular songs. Notwithstanding their heavy reliance on spatial rhetoric, it could be said that these works have generally regarded the music text as a given, concerning themselves more with the ways popular music is located within or helps to delineate larger physical and cultural spaces and identities, rather than with how space and acoustics signify *within* the musical text.

Spatial understandings of more immediate use to the present project are to be found in the work of French philosopher/theorists Giles Deleuze and Félix Guattari, who have theorized complementary relationships between music and space(s).

I. A child in the dark, gripped with fear, comforts himself by singing under his breath. Lost he takes shelter, or orients himself with his little song as best he can. The song is like a rough sketch of a calming and stabilizing, calm and stable, center in the heart of chaos . . .

II. Now we are at home. But home does not pre-exist: it was necessary to draw a circle around that uncertain and fragile center, to organize a limited space . . . the forces of chaos are kept outside. . . . Radios and televisions are like sound walls around every household and mark territories . . .

III. Finally one opens the circle a crack . . . lets someone in, calls someone, or else goes out oneself. . . . One launches forth, hazards an improvisation . . . one ventures from home on the thread of a tune.[15]

These are not, the authors point out, three successive moments in an evolution but rather aspects of a single thing they call the Refrain. They posit that music, through the agency of repetition and the refrain, is part of a larger process of the continual creation and dissolution of space, or "territory." They use the terms "territorialization," "deterritorialization" and "reterritorialization" to describe this constant making, unmaking and remaking of "territory," and the concepts are integral to Deleuze-Guattarian thought. The refrain is a particular "territorial assemblage."[16] Birds mark out their territory by means of their song. Greek modes and Hindu rhythms are territorial, provincial, regional.[17] "The refrain is rhythm and melody that have been territorialized because they have become expressive—and they have become expressive because they are territorializing" they say.[18]

Murphie has applied Deleuze-Guattarian notions of territory and the refrain to modern popular music (Deleuze and Guattari's musical examples are in the main from the Western classical music canon), addressing the music of Nick Cave, as used in the film *Wings of Desire* (directed by Wim Wenders, 1988).[19] In order to realize a Deleuze-Guattarian understanding of popular music, Murphie argues that the term *territory* should be given as wide a definition as possible, just as it should also be taken in its most literal senses. Territory must include the broad connotations deriving from standard dictionary definitions such as "a tract of land; region or district," "ideas of state or sovereign jurisdiction," or "field of action, thought" and so on. Furthermore, says Murphie,

[When] speaking about territory in Deleuze-Guattarian terms one is not speaking about pre-existent and permanent arrangements but about territory as a constant process of formation and dissolution . . . the dissolution of territories becomes just as important as the production of them.[20]

All is process, "machinic heterogenesis." Territories make, alter and un-make subjects, while subjects in turn make, alter and unmake territories. The process is as political as it is "natural," liberatory as it is repressive.

It is above all a question of what processes (which they call "lines of flight" . . .) are available for the formations of desired territories and their maintenance. . . . Cou-pled with this is the necessity for the unmaking of despotic or undesirable territo-ries (. . . formed by "apparatus of capture").[21]

Popular music events are to be understood within this interactive ecology. The refrain, music's repetitions and progressive variations make territory (to the same extent that Deleuze and Guattari's prime examples—the bird's singing, the child's whistling in the dark—do). And stereos, dance floor public address systems might just as easily stand in for Deleuze and Guattari's territory-making radios and televisions. For Deleuze and Guat-tari, the creation of territory is the very function of the refrain, and the dis-connection of refrains from their territory—their deterritorialization—is what they call music.

This territory-making, says Murphie, is itself a portable process: bands go on tour, people carry radios, birds migrate. Musical sound events—discrete rhythmic beats and individual sounds—might be seen then as ter-ritory markers, like surveyor's pegs newly placed on a tract of land. The processes of repetition and reiteration further mark out and make famil-iar the territory, just as they erase the residual traces of earlier territorial-izing processes.

This Deleuze-Guattarian notion of territory-making through music does not specifically refer to the sort of deliberate, synthetic sonic spatial-ity created by reverb and delay devices. Indeed, given one particular read-ing, the question arises, why bother with echo and reverb hyper-spatiality at all, if music is inherently spatial anyway? One possible answer might be that by including overt spatial traces and tropes of spatiality within the recording text, the producers are signaling the territorializing work of the musical text, making the territorial project fully explicit, even attempting to specify and delineate the territories that are being made and unmade by the recording, to fully control the process. At the same time, the render-ing of explicit spatialities within a larger field of territoriality might be viewed as a signalling that the space-making work also carries a powerful (if secondary) reference to "inner space," to zones of the psyche, to spaces within spaces.

Synthetic echo and reverb might also be seen as the paradigmatic in-stance of the (de)territorializing refrain. A sound emitted here is repeated there, the space in-between thus is delineated, mapped, known, possessed.

Or perhaps the opposite occurs; the echo is diminishing, retreating, irretrievably other. The echo and the space between here and there is alienated, lost, unknowable. The refrain is spread too thinly to "hold" the territory.

While it is not proposed to systematically work through and apply Deleuze-Guattarian notions to the whole history of early recorded spatiality, the notion of territory-making and -unmaking will have general relevance to discussions below of mythic echo (chapter 2), echo and reverb in singing cowboy music (chapter 4), and in explorations of the utopian, deterritorialized moments of early rock 'n' roll (chapter 8). At the same time, the paired notions of territorializing and deterritorializing might broadly be equated with, and might serve to amplify Keil's notion of participation, and his characterizing of the tensions between the live and the recorded as a contest between the Dionysian and the Apollonian.

Charles Keil talks of a number of constants in what he calls "peoples' music." "A vital music," he says, "always has Dionysian and Apollonian aspects competing for primacy."[22] The Apollonian principle in art refers to the "frozen moment of dreamlike perfection, the illusion of ideal or perpetual life in separation from nature," contrasted to the Dionysian yearning for dissolution, "for immersion of self, in fellow man and in nature."[23] Blues music and American polka, argues Keil, in their live performed aspects involve powerful enactments of the Dionysian: wild, often acrobatic performances, Bacchic, abandoned behavior on the part of audience. He cites the "classic, dreamstate" recordings of T. Bone Walker as being in total contrast to the legendary frenziedness of his live performances:

All recordings are inherently Apollonian, just as all live performances tend toward the Dionysian. . . . [E]arly on . . . all participants in the rites of blues and polkas heard the recordings not as mere echoes but perfected echoes of their live experience. . . . I suspect that the perfectionism in blues and polka recordings is an expression of . . . musicians and their audiences wanting the cleanest and most sophisticated versions of their music in public space. . . . Once norms are established, recorded blues and recorded polkas take on a perfectable dream life of their own.[24]

Keil specifically locates the peaks of Apollonianism in blues and polka recording as occurring in the late 1920s and in the 1950s (both of which periods are key to this present study); paradoxically, however, the "resurgence of 'delta' blues and 'village' polka [represents] a resurfacing of Dionysian forces . . . in periods of marked political conservatism."[25]

Keil's dichotomy is useful in that it lays stress on the relative autonomy of recorded music from live, leaving the way open for a specific theorizing of the recorded, with special reference to the sonic category of production. His dichotomy, however, implicitly cuts across the suggestion made above (and amplified later herein), that slapback and reverb-laden recordings such as Presley's "Mystery Train" enact the Dionysian on record, in a way specific and unique to recording. Keil, however, is not attempting to set the dichotomy up as a simplistic, rigid formulation characterizing all recorded and live music; rather, he puts forward the Apollonian and the Dionysian as inherent *tendencies* only. Indeed, much of the power of Presley's "Mystery Train," and of, say, Bo Diddley's early recordings (which are also of special interest to Keil) derives from the extent to which they stood in opposition to then current recording "best practice." The creation of the Dionysian by use of production devices, in the otherwise largely repressive Apollonian domain of 1950s American popular music recording thus assumes even greater significance.

Elsewhere in the same work, Feld also addresses the dichotomy between sounds in their "natural," worldly setting and sounds as recorded artifact by employing R. Murray Schafer's notion of "schizophonia," which "refers to the split between an original sound and its electroacoustical transmission or reproduction."[26] Feld summarizes Schafer's formulation:

> Schafer laments a deterioration in world acoustic ecology from hi-fi to lo-fi soundscapes, a proliferation of noise corresponding to the increased separation of sounds from sources since the invention of phonograph recording. . . . Early technology for acoustic capture and reproduction fueled a preexisting fascination with acoustic dislocations and respatialization. Territorial expansion, imperialistic ambition, and audio technology increasingly came together, culminating in the invention of the loudspeaker.[27]

Feld compares Schafer's formulation of "sounds split from their sources" with Walter Benjamin's celebrated essay "The Work of Art in the Age of Mechanical Reproduction,"[28] with Attali's notion of "repeating,"[29] and with Baudrillard's conception of the "signature."[30] The connotations of the term *schizophonia* are intentionally negative, suggestive of the personally and collectively dysfunctional: recorded sound is characterized as inherently alienated, commodified; the "lo-fi soundscape" is a dystopic, hegemonic space, encouraging of passivity. As a counter to Schafer's wholly pessimistic notion, Feld poses a construct involving complementarity, borrowing from Gregory Bateson the term *schismogenesis,* which refers to "patterns of progressive differentiation through cumulative interaction and reaction."[31] He quotes Bateson's formal definition: "Schismogenesis refers to 'classes of regenerative or vicious cycles . . . such as A's acts [are] stimuli for B's acts, which in turn [become] stimuli for more intense action on the part of A.'"[32] In complementary schismogenesis, "the mutually promoting actions are essentially dissimilar but mutually appropriate, eg in cases of dominance-submission, succoring-dependence, exhibitionism-spectatorship."[33] While Feld's formulation is essentially extratextual, in that it refers to structural constraints within which musical texts are located without specifically theorizing or addressing intratextual events, it nonetheless is of some value here as a counterformulation to the implications of unredeemable alienation implicit in the "sounds split from their sources" models of recording.

There is one other key concept in Keil and Feld of specific relevance to this study, Keil's resuscitation of anthropologist Lévy-Bruhl's notion of "participation," later refined by Barfield. Keil quotes Lévy-Bruhl:

> The Bororo . . . boast that they are red araras (parakeets). This does not merely signify that that after their death they become araras, nor that araras are metamorphosed Bororos. . . . "The Bororos" says Von den Steinem . . . "give one rigidly to understand that they are araras at the present time, just as if a caterpillar declared itself to be a butterfly."[34]

Implicit in the formulation is the idea that participation is a prior, Edenic, "golden age" state or activity. Participation is preindustrial, prelogical and even premythical.

> All humans were full participants once upon a time, and I believe we still experience much music and perhaps some other portions of reality this way. . . . Participation is the opposite of alienation from nature, from society, from the body.[35]

This important idea will bear on the present study in a number of ways. First, it is of pointed relevance to the Western myth of Echo in particular (discussed in chapter 2). Second, it further relates to and illuminates the nexi between actants in a number of separate dualist structures that will emerge in this study: sound sources and their echoes, man and environment, "real" sounds and their recorded counterpart, the interrelationships between musicians and audiences, between "lead" musician(s) and (secondary) obbligato player(s), and lastly, between the phonograph recording and its listener(s). One of the developments traced in this study will be the way in which (virtual) spatial characteristics allowed ever greater, ever more complex varieties of participation in music, by listeners and performers. The "coming on line" of an ever wider range of recorded spatial possibilities in the post–World War II period afforded audiences new and greatly extended modes of participation, and these, I shall argue, were a major factor in the global diaspora of rock 'n' roll.

The broad factual information underpinning the arguments that follow is drawn from disparate sources. Colin Escott,[36] Charlie Gillet,[37] Peter Guralnick,[38] Alan Lomax,[39] Bill C Malone,[40] Charles Shaar Murray,[41] Paul Oliver,[42] the late Robert Palmer,[43] Nick Tosches[44] and Tony Russell[45] provide much insight and hard historical information surrounding the circumstances of southern roots music making, its origins, its history as a recorded form and the circumstances under which it was and is consumed. With the exception of Lomax (and to a lesser extent, Malone and Oliver) these researcher/journalists might be typified as being of the "rock generation." Writing works directed at a predominantly rock-fan audience, all came to prominence in the 1970s and 1980s. Generally speaking, their project was to elevate American "roots music" to be at least on a par with rock music, which in the late 1960s and 1970s was beginning to receive "serious" critical attention in magazines such as *Rolling Stone* and *Creem*. Tosches wrote a series in the latter magazine, beginning in 1979, entitled "The Unsung Heroes of Rock 'n' Roll,"[46] that, like most of his work, examined what he saw as the looser, more exuberant, disruptive and wholly uncompromising antecedents to what became rock 'n' roll and (for him, the vastly inferior) rock music. Tosches is constantly alert to the passionate, the anomalous, the absurd and the transitory in recorded music, especially (but not exclusively) of the southern United States. Tosches's favorite theme of cultural mixings and meldings, his interest in white musicians who sounded "black," and African American musicians who sounded "white," his focus on the Dionysian in southern "roots" music generally informs much of what follows here. Although non–academy-based (even antiacademic), Tosches is a notable, diligent field researcher, and he provides much solid factual information about southern music, including the specifics of actual recording sessions.

Similarly, Peter Guralnick provides much thoroughly researched basic information about pre–rock 'n' roll and "counter-rock" music: Chicago blues (*Feel Like Going Home*),[47] soul music (*Sweet Soul Music*),[48] southern music in general (*Lost Highway*),[49] as well as the definitive biographies of Elvis Presley (*Last Train to Memphis*[50] and *Careless Love*).[51] Like Tosches, Guralnick does not privilege theoretical approaches, whether of music or society, but (like all the writers cited above) employs essentially scholarly research methodologies in his work. Greil Marcus's comments on Guralnick's *Lost Highway* might apply to the entire Guralnick/Tosches/Escott/Palmer/Gillet strand of "serious" roots journalism and rock historiography: "For all its stylistic groupings, *Lost Highway* is less a study of musical genres, or even of individual performers, than a very closely observed and broadly applied study of vocation: an attempt to define the most valid form of music as work, and as cultural politics."[52] Although the scholarly Lomax and Malone have weaker allegiances with the "alternativeness" of the rock counterculture, they share with the rock writers generally progressive, liberal and/or libertarian politics. This group of writers/researchers are generally drawn to the liberatory potentials of "minority culture," just as they take as axiomatic that such cultures are fragile and that the liberatory moments they produce remain all too transitory.

This underlying interest in the cultural politics of their object of study has meant that these writers are occasionally (but not always, and rarely systematically) attuned to interpersonal dynamics in music recording: what precisely happened, for instance, when Presley (or the Carter Family, or Howlin' Wolf or Robert Johnson) first entered the studio, how did they behave, how were they treated, and so on. Their interest thus frequently focuses on (and sometimes fetishizes) the precise time and place at which the recording was made. The recording itself becomes a means by which the modern-day listener might be vicariously present at that long gone moment, a text that contains a coded record of a complex and highly charged cultural and political encounter, simultaneously manifest at collective and personal levels.

Yet the mostly white, liberal "goodwill" agenda of this group of writers also sometimes acts as a limitation to analysis. Underpinning their writing is the aim of elevating the work of a number of minority musicians to the rarefied class of "great American music." Implicitly, the "art" of such musicians is rendered as essentially transcendent and ineffable. While such canon making may be politically and socially justifiable, it frequently has the unintended effect of foreclosing on discussions of exactly what is present in the recording. Recordings themselves often become lesser "emanations," secondary to the presence, the actuality of the great man or woman in performance.[53]

Just as the physical presence of the great performer assumes priority over the product, so does the place of the performance assume a sacredness, as evidenced by the latter-day fetishization of the Mississippi Delta region for example, as a kind of holy land of country blues. Thus are produced narratives of place, and "lives of the saints"–type anecdotes about the great southern musicians. Much of the writing about southern music, for all its insight, is in the end subject to many of the same shortcomings as traditional musicology's approach to the musical text, as outlined by McClary and Walser (discussed below, this chapter).

So, with few exceptions then, the increasing importance of spatiality in minority culture, or "roots" recording goes largely unremarked and, when mentioned, remains largely unexplored. Even when mention is occasionally made in passing of spatial characteristics (it is difficult to talk of the contribution of Sun Records, for instance, without at least referring to the use of the "echo chamber") none question why it should be present in the first place or investigate how it operates, either aesthetically or semiotically.

In his book about Jimi Hendrix, Charles Shaar Murray[54] almost breaks with the tradition by constructing a (partial) history of recorded music sounds. He places Hendrix's music in the context of earlier guitar music recording traditions. Intertwined with a broad history of postwar popular music and a biography of Hendrix is an investigation of the complex voice-instrument relationships in rock 'n' roll and rock music. He talks of the "one man with a guitar" formulation of prewar country blues and hill-billy music on the one hand, and then stands this against the big band and later the R & B jump band traditions in which the guitar was a much lesser voice but still integral to the musical totality. For Murray, these two strands coalesced in 1960s soul bands, and it was from this specific mo-ment and aesthetic regime that Hendrix emerged as an R & B electric gui-tarist. Hendrix, for Murray, went on to broaden immeasurably the sonic scope of electric guitar. With Hendrix, the electric guitar was not simply a discrete presence in a larger mix; it came to set the sonic parameters of the recorded music, and bass drums and voice became in a sense smaller ele-ments within the field defined primarily by the sounds of the guitar itself. The work of British-based, baby boomer Murray is notable in that, while the book has been marketed (successfully) as a biography of Hendrix, more space and concentrated analysis is given over to close examination of the music as it exists on record. Although Murray stops short of systemati-cally locating sonic elements in terms of spatialities, his work is significant for the way it closely engages with the recorded sound objects—without, however, losing sight of the historical, social and aesthetic extramusical contexts in which those objects are located.

A number of writers make specific reference to spatializing devices—in-cluding echo and reverb—in discussions of record making, and a few of these attempt, in the main very briefly, to "read" these effects for social meanings. Albin Zak's *Poetics of Rock* reminds us that modern pop music is primarily a recorded form. When we talk about rock music, he says, we usually mean recorded songs, artifacts that may be encountered over and over again, until words, riffs, solos, sounds, nuances of pronunciation and instrumental timbre are known intimately, a process very much in contrast to our fleeting encounters with live performed music. Furthermore, echo-ing a point made by Evan Eisenberg, Zak argues that much of what con-stitutes the conventions of modern pop music evolved out of the exigen-cies of the recording process and marketing requirements of the recording industry: "recording moved almost inevitably from a process of collect-ing, preserving, disseminating to one of making. The aesthetic criterion shifted from the sound of the actual performance to the sound of the re-cording."[55] Zak goes on to discuss specifically both echo and reverb (which he calls "ambience"). Although his account is informed by a subtle insider sensibility, he does not generally discuss possible social meanings of the sonic devices he examines, nor is he especially concerned with their early history, nor with how spatial "vocabularies" emerged over time.[56] However, Zak's unstated but recurrent underlying point—that the most powerful musical effects may arise from the most exquisitely fine sonic differences in the musical text (which may themselves result from equally subtle production decisions) is important, and a similar axiomatic understanding informs this work.

One of the more systematic treatments of spatiality in recording is to be found in Allan Moore's *Rock, the Primary Text*.[57] Breaking with the sociological tradition in popular music studies, Moore's project is to describe and discuss "what really is at stake" in the recordings, deliberately locating his study intratextually:

Simon Frith (1983:53–54) suggests that the aesthetic question ('how does the text achieve its effects?') is secondary to the interpretation of the text's generalized social meaning: 'Is it repressive or liberating? Corrupting or uplifting? Escapist or instructive?' I . . . would suggest that what Frith cites as the aesthetic question is secondary to at least two others, which are 'what precise effects can the text achieve?' and even more fundamentally, 'what does the text consist of?'[58]

Later he says:

The mediation of rock through social and cultural formations has received a great deal of attention in recent years—likewise its historical mediation is frequently addressed. However there is a further set of mediatory factors that tend to be overlooked, and they are the technology involved in the production of the music itself. Indeed, consideration of these factors is frequently ignored in the discussion of any music, no matter what the style.[59]

Moore's own analysis, however, ends up being in the main so solidly intratextual, with so little reference to the social and psychic extramusical groundings of his texts, that he arguably "fails" the McClary and Walser test, at least partly reinstituting a version of classical musicology's axiomatic belief in immanence, in the inherent greatness of certain musical works regardless of their social groundings. Moore's major methodological departure from the methods of classical musicology (as outlined by McClary and Walser) is that he does not take this greatness to be self-evident. Rather, he attempts a rigorous and thorough description of textual events and effects, and makes his own judgments of value or otherwise a fortiori, based on his analysis.

On the other hand, Moore's dogged intratextuality affords him the space to explore and describe the musical text with an admirable, and largely unprecedented thoroughness. In his analyses, Moore specifically addresses the fact of spatial location of sounds on recordings, which he sees as a product of multi-tracking.[60] Moore cites "texture" as the category of analysis into which a study of spatiality should rightly fall: "the control over spatial location is strongly related to the use of musical texture as a separate domain, and gives rise to two virtual concepts, of time and space."[61] He goes on to build a model for textural analysis appropriate to rock music, in which spatiality is included as a musicological subcategory.

For rock the 'strand' of texture is often equivalent to 'instrumental timbre.' It can best be conceived with reference to a 'virtual textural space,' envisaged as an empty cube of finite dimensions, changing with respect to real time (almost like an abstract three-dimensional television screen). This model is not dissimilar to that employed intuitively by producers, but I shall refer to it as the 'sound-box' rather than the 'mix,' to indicate that my analysis privileges the listening, rather than the production process. All rock has strands at different vertical locations, where this represents their register. Most rock also attempts a sense of musical 'depth' (the illusory sense that some sounds originate at a greater distance than others), giving a sense of textural foreground, middleground and background. Much rock also has a sense of horizontal location, provided by the construction of the stereo image. The most important features of the use of this space are the types and degrees of density filling it (whether thin 'strands' or 'blocks'), and the presence of 'holes' in this space, i.e. potential areas left unused. In this respect, earlier styles can seem almost one-dimensional, while more recent styles can make fuller use of the potential, which, of course, has to be set up by and for each individual style.[62]

Promising though Moore's sound-box is, its usefulness to this work is limited by its implied specificity to stereo and/or multi-tracked recordings. Moore derives his sound-box as a tool for the analysis of progressive rock music; that is, that body of recorded music which had its beginnings, for Moore's purposes, in the Beatles' *Sgt. Pepper's Lonely Hearts Club Band* of 1967.[63] By that time virtually all album tracks and many singles were recorded and issued in stereo, and Moore's construct inevitably privileges stereo spatiality.[64] Indeed, to remove the stereophonic aspect from the sound-box formulation would be to dismantle the sound box, as monaural recorded music would have no horizontal, left-right axis at all. A mono sound-box would be reduced to a two-dimensional vertical plane.

This present study will focus, although not exclusively, on spatiality in pre-stereo recordings. The lack of left-right axis in mono sound reproduction has been typically seen as a limitation to the fabricating of spatiality, and mono sound in general seen as a manifestly primitive precursor to stereo sound. At the same time, however, certain moments in late mono spatiality might be seen as highly deterritorialized (liberatory, Dionysian), answered by stereo's rigidly territorializing fixity. The absence of the left-right variable axis, rather than being a limitation, might in fact provide an inherent counterterritorializing tendency. Mono spatiality is, in a sense, "unmappable," providing a potentially wilder, uncharted sound ecology. Mono spatiality, of course, may also operate in the opposite way: it would be difficult to find more ambitiously territorializing musical texts than, say,

Slim Whitman's highly spatialized mono recordings "Love Song of the Waterfall" or "Indian Love Call" (both 1952). The point remains, however, that stereo "grids out" the whole sound space and, regardless of how sounds are deployed within, the very act of gridding is of itself an act of despotic territorializing.

Another problem arises from ambiguities in the sound-box construct in regard to the notion of depth. Moore's definition—"the illusory sense that some sounds originate at a greater distance than others"[65]—actually conflates two completely separate variables: the amount of reverberation present and the amplitude of each voice relative to others. Reverberation itself can be further broken down. The "position" of an element in fore-, middle- or background will partly be determined by the amount of "real" or synthetic reverberation present, and/or by the degree to which that sound is on- or off-mic. On-mic sounds (that is, sounds recorded relatively near to the microphone) will contain relatively more of the original, direct-from-the-source signal and less "secondary" or ambient sound reflected off walls and objects within the space (that is, relatively less reverberation). The further off-mic the sound, the relatively greater the proportion of reflected sound. From the listener's point of view, there is no *necessary* intrinsic difference between sound that has been actually recorded off-mic and sound recorded on-mic and to which synthetic reverb has been added later. The primary variable is the degree of reverb, be it naturally occurring or fabricated. The other variable is simple volume; louder equals nearer, softer equals further away.

In talking about the acoustic guitar harmonics in Yes's "Roundabout" as "(appearing) louder" and therefore relatively foregrounded[66] or in discussing Fleetwood Mac's "Little Lies,"[67] the variable of depth seems to be at least partly if not wholly dependent on relative amplitude, regardless of the presence or absence of reverb. At other times, such as in Moore's discussion of Def Leppard's "Love Bites" and Wishbone Ash's "Throw Down the Sword"[68] and elsewhere, reverb appears to be the major depth-creating effect (although these instances do not find favor with Moore, because the reverb "[puts] up a subtle barrier between the listener and the hitherto immediacy of the sound.")[69] Other writers too have tended to conflate these two variables: Wishart for instance has depth "represented by decreasing amplitude and increasing reverberation," with the additional variable of a rolling-off of treble tones to denote distance.[70]

Of central importance to this present study, however, are recordings in which the loudest element is also the most reverberant: the guitar in Link Wray's "Rumble" (1958), Elvis Presley's voice in "Baby Let's Play House" (1955), for instance. Moore's notion of depth would have difficulty negotiating these tracks, and the great many "classic rock 'n' roll" and R & B recordings that make use of this particular textural feature. Problems also arise from the collapse of all variables into a single, general notion of spatiality. When register is included as an axis, then notions of "space" necessarily become at least partly metaphorical. Pitch has no absolute, intrinsic "highness" or "lowness," no apparent or virtual location in space of itself. To call shorter wavelength, higher frequency sounds "high" is mostly convention.[71] But the apparent location in space of sound sources, near or far, left or right, *does* refer to the simulation of actual spatial dispositions.

Furthermore, Moore's sound-box is a tool derived to investigate progressive rock and by its very nature will tend to privilege that body of styles while (at least inadvertently) casting everything that predates them as primitive, unfinished. As Moore says after just having described his "sound-box": "The most important features of the use of this space are the types and degrees of densities filling it . . . and the presence of 'holes' in this space. . . . In this respect, earlier styles can seem almost one-dimensional."[72] Although Moore makes good use of the sound-box model in his analyses of individual rock recordings, its ambiguity and inherent mono-unfriendliness limit its usefulness to my investigation. Perhaps the best that can be taken from Moore for this analysis is his statement that "the history of Western musical, let alone rock, textures has yet to be written."[73]

Although not a history of rock textures as such, Cunningham's *Good Vibrations*[74] brings together disparate factual information on the development of rock recording and to some extent fills the "production gap" left by earlier rock writing. By devoting his first chapter, of some forty pages, to an outline of the pre-stereo production contributions made by Les Paul, Sam Phillips, Lieber and Stoller, Steve Sholes, Owen Bradley, Frank Guida, Norman Petty and others, he goes a good way toward correcting many of the biases and incorrect truisms of earlier rock journalism. Disappointingly however, Chess is again omitted; in focusing on technological change in a strictly linear fashion, the book inevitably ends up treating later as being automatically better. Thus pre-stereo again is implicitly cast as little more than an interesting stop along the way to the more glorious present.

Tom Lubin[75] also looks at certain key aspects of the development of studio production devices, including echo and reverb. He locates the latter within the domain of signal processing, which he divides into four types: delay, reverb, equalization and variable gain amplification.[76] In the first few decades of electric recording (roughly from 1925 onward), signal processing amounted to little more than the equalizing of microphone input. In the late 1940s reverb "chambers" were developed to enhance the sounds of voice, horns and strings. Lubin links the development of echo (that is, distinct, regular repeats of the source sound) with the invention of the tape recorder. Lubin's primary concern though is with later uses of the devices: "Over the past few years, signal processing has become significantly more elaborate, diverse, and much more than merely an enhancement or surrounding."[77]

Lubin does not consider, however, "accidental" spatialities (such as varying unintended traces of room ambience) as well as other spatial and near spatial effects employed spontaneously or otherwise by performer (rather than by the engineer/producer). Speaking primarily as a studio professional, Lubin later describes in general terms the effect of the use of delay:

Reverb brings sound to life. It gives the impression of power, adds drama, size and depth. It changes the edges of the sound and identifies the boundary of the image. It provides depth in the sonic picture, and constant contrast and comparison of the direct sound to the surroundings in which the music is played. . . . Reverb is an organic phenomenon that provides a locality of the general sonic scene.[78]

The questions implicitly raised by this—such as, Why should reverb give the impression of power and add drama? What exactly are the "image" and the "locality"? What constitutes the "sonic scene"?—remain unanswered.

The late Robert Palmer, a professional musician as well as leading music researcher investigates electric guitar tonalities in his "Church of the Sonic Guitar,"[79] in which he touches teasingly on production spatiality as a domain, a category of musical device. "To attend a show by [Velvet Underground, Television, Sonic Youth]," he says,

is to immerse oneself in a clanging, droning, sensurround of guitar harmonics, within a precisely demarcated, ritually invoked sonic space. This is the movable Church of the Sonic Guitar, a vast and vaulted cathedral vibrating with the patterns and proportions of sound-ratios tuned precisely enough to have pleased Pythagoras.[80]

Palmer traces a tradition of loud, distorted electric guitar playing back to certain electric blues and western swing guitarists of the 1930s through the 1950s, such as Bob Dunn, Pat Hare, Willie Johnston, Clarence Gatemouth Brown and Guitar Slim. These musicians played (and recorded) at, for the time, very high volume and, counter to the industry standards of the day, consciously employed highly distorted, overdriven valve amplifier tonalities. Hendrix and modern electric guitar bands like Sonic Youth are located squarely within this tradition, says Palmer:

an electric guitar, properly tuned to resonate with everything from the hall's acoustics to the underlying 60-cycle hum of the city's electrical grid, is forming its massive sound textures from harmonic relationships that already exist in nature. . . . In electric music—rock 'n' roll—one of the first proofs of this theory was the engineering experiments conducted at Chess Records in the late 1940s and early 1950s. A tile bathroom adjacent to the studio was chosen as a resonating chamber for guitar amplifiers, resulting in sounds on early records by Muddy Waters that can still raise the hairs on the back of your neck.[81]

For Palmer the "big" textures possible from the overdriven, richly distorting electric guitar have a mystical, archetypal quality that brings together the acoustic properties of medieval Christian, Muslim and Indian religious architecture, ancient Pythagorean notions of fundamental, cosmic "vibration," Chinese and Indian metaphysical traditions as well as African American hoodoo beliefs in "the Devil or Legba, the Yoruba/hoodoo god of the crossroads, the opener of paths between worlds."[82]

This particular essay of Palmer's covers some of the same historical ground—early western swing electric guitar, the role of Les Paul, the pivotal significance of production practices at Sun and Chess studios—as my premise and his notion of a "precisely demarcated, ritually invoked sonic space" is broadly consistent with what follows here.[83] Palmer in his music writings is usually admirably painstaking in making his meaning explicit when discussing music and intramusical figures, and is particularly sensitive to the extramusical influences of site, geography, physical movement and "spirit of place." However, Palmer does not in the end further unpack his own highly suggestive notions of "sonic space," nor is he concerned with how these spaces might have first appeared and later evolved and mutated within sound recording traditions.

Serge Lacasse on the other hand has offered the most thorough treatment of recorded space to date. He locates his notion of sonic spatiality within a wider discussion of "the evocative power of vocal staging in recorded rock music and other forms of expression."[84] For Lacasse, "vocal staging" refers to

any deliberate practice whose aim is to enhance a vocal sound, alter its timbre, or present it in a given spatial or temporal configuration with the help of any mechanical or electrical process, presumably in order to produce some effect on potential or actual listeners.[85]

Thus exploiting the purely acoustic properties of a building (a cathedral, say) while speaking or singing, or using an electrical reverb unit to alter sound qualities would both constitute cases of vocal staging, while simply altering the pitch of one's voice without external acoustico-mechanical aids would not. Lacasse uses the expression "vocal setting" to refer to a specific configuration of vocal staging, whose characteristics are described in terms of loudness, timbral quality, and spatial and temporal configuration.[86] He likens the concept of vocal staging to the broad theatrical notion of mise-en-scène, and that of setting to a particular effect of mise-en-scène occurring at a given time or lasting for a given duration.

Although the stated focus of Lacasse's work is the "staging of the voice" in recorded rock music, he ranges much further afield, touching on the uses made of resonance, echo and reverberation in Paleolithic and Neolithic times (with particular reference to shamanistic practice); the acoustic properties of temples in European, South American and Levantine antiquity; vocal traditions of the Greek and Roman theaters; the importance of reverberation in medieval sacred music; to the use of spatial effects in early European opera and court music. He also surveys various vocal effects used for musical and sacred purposes in non-Western contexts: Africa, Asia, Melanesia, Polynesia and pre-Columbian North America. Similarly, he identifies some key enactments of vocal staging in twentieth-century radio broadcasting, cinema, theater and avant-garde sonic art. With regard to non-Western and/or premodern vocal stagings, Lacasse draws few conclusions, noting that "the contexts in which the practice [of staging voices] generally occurs are related everywhere with ritual and/or spectacle."[87] In summarizing his survey of vocal effects in theatre and cinema, he hazards some broad conclusions:

In some of the examples discussed [in cinema and theater] . . . spatial signature seems appropriate to the objectification of some 'inner space' (a character's imagination; drunkenness etc). . . . In radio . . . added reverberation might be used to provide some contrast between discourses (for example, two aspects of the same character). In other words, it is not the reverberation itself that 'means' something: rather it appears to be the conflict raised from the way the affected sound source actually sounds within the film/drama compared to the way it *should* sound within the visualized/suggested environment. . . . [N]otwithstanding what has just been said, there seems to be quite a high degree of cohesion in regard to the use of effects like reverberation, sound level manipulation, filtering etc.[88]

Similarly, in a discussion of Patti Page's recording of "Confess," (1947/1948) which features both the double tracking of Page's voice and the overt use of reverb effects, Lacasse writes:

it is possible that the reverb brings a 'religious' connotation to some listeners, enhancing the metaphorical figure already exploited by the lyrics (confession). On an even more abstract level, it is also possible that some listeners hear the reverberated voice as an inner thought.[89]

Generally, however, Lacasse does not attempt to uncover social meanings for the effects he so carefully describes. Neither is he concerned with what the relationship between the changes in the specifics of the recorded text over time and broader cultural changes might be. His reserve in ascribing cultural meanings is in one way understandable. After all, how can we know with any "legal" certainty how different listeners might have encountered different recordings and their spatial effects twenty, fifty or seventy years ago? Given the existence of broad consistencies in popular music "space-making" practice, however (certain effects, repeatedly used with certain lyric, melodic, harmonic and/or time structures) and broad, clearly evident, "orderly" changes to these practices over time, a circumstantial case—I believe a strong one—can be made for the existence of a coherent spatial semiotics operating in popular music recordings.[90] So the issue is not simply, I would argue, that recorded voices are "staged" (they clearly are) but rather, what might be the nature of that staging? What characterizes these ancillary, sonically rendered but implicitly visual representations? And how might the two domains, the music and the effects (the actors and the scenery perhaps) interact?

William Shea's dissertation on technology in American popular music looks closely at production practice in the postwar period.[91] Drawing on an apparent insider knowledge, Shea identifies a number of broad domains of record production practice, in the pop mainstream, in rhythm and blues and rock 'n' roll, and is alert to many finer points of mixing and microphone placement. He also interviews both Mitch Miller, who oversaw important early pop recordings by Patti Page, and Milt Gabler, who, after a long career recording jazz and swing bands produced Bill Haley's "Rock Around the Clock." When information is harder to come by, Shea speculates, convincingly, as to how various effects were achieved. Although he does not explicitly theorize spatiality, Shea is keenly aware of the presence (or absence) of reverb and echo in his examples, and makes considered generalizations about reverb as an aspect of production in pre–rock 'n' roll rhythm and blues recording. Shea is, however, even less willing than Lacasse to speculate on how or why echo and reverb should produce such powerful subjective effects in listeners.

Much of the larger, general story of phonograph development, particularly in regard to the early, pre–electric recording stage is drawn from Gelatt's *The Fabulous Phonograph*[92] and Read and Welch's *From Tin Foil to Stereo*.[93] Both books, however, are little concerned with popular, or "low" recording, taking it as axiomatic that the phonograph device only truly justifies its existence by capturing high moments in the Western classical music canon. Thus the important and vibrant histories of "race," "hillbilly" and "ethnic" recording are completely ignored by both books, while early sacred, "coon" songs, parlor and vaudeville blues scarcely rate a mention. Rock 'n' roll music is completely absent from Read and Welch, treated offhandedly in Gelatt. Some of these biases, particularly in regard to pre–magnetic tape recording of 78s are being addressed by a number of contemporary writers, especially those centered around the collectors' magazine *Victrola and 78 Journal*, edited by Tim Gracyk, and *78 Quarterly*. The former, while primarily dealing with the generalities of Victrola and early 78 collecting and with the finer points of the repair and maintenance of old machines, nonetheless combines detailed knowledge of early recording practices; thoroughly researched biographies of early, but often now largely forgotten stars; as well as discographies, graphics, record catalogues and so on, all dealt with in a refreshingly cross-generic way. Opera singers, hillbillies, dance bands, blues singers and vaudevillians get equal treatment.[94]

Despite its shortcomings, a theoretical discussion of relevance to this inquiry is to be found in *From Tin Foil to Stereo*. First published in 1959 and later revised, the work aims to be an authoritative treatment of the history and aesthetics of the recording medium. While much of Read and Welch's long work is concerned with debates irrelevant to this study, they do at a number of points directly and indirectly address and even attempt to resolve aesthetic questions related to recorded spatialities. Speaking of recording practices in the early electric period in the United States (roughly, from 1925 on) they describe two contending recording "philosophies" that had their origins in radio broadcasting.

One of these derived from exposure to the 'close-up' radio broadcast, where small groups of singers or instrumental ensembles would use a small dead studio and work close to the microphone. Carried to its ultimate end, this technic resulted in the popularity in the vocal distortions of the 'crooner' and the heavy lush background music. The effect of this was to provide an effect of intimacy, the orchestra and soloist being transported into the living room, the singer or soloist singing just for you. The contrary philosophy was based on the conception of bringing the listener into the studio or auditorium. In this method, the natural room resonance of the studio or acoustical reflections of the auditorium, were broadcast along with the sounds directly received by the microphones to give that illusion to the radio audience.[95]

The influence of the former group, according to Read and Welch, led to the emergence of crooners and PA-dependent artists such as Whispering Jack Smith and Little Jack Little. Rarely slow to pass judgment on such matters, the authors declare: "Obviously this sort of thing may be enjoyable, but it does not constitute accurate sound reproduction. It may do no harm but it should be recognized for what it is, an unnatural distortion."[96] Read and Welch lengthily quote other commentators on questions of recording aesthetics; in some of these, similar concerns arise regarding "distortions," trickery and such. Much of the discussion of recording aesthetics is taken up with the rightness or otherwise of introducing these "distortions" into recording:

reproduction has become so standardized that it is not an easy matter to even recognize a singer's voice; and further that the technique of the recording studio makes it possible for almost anybody who can give tongue, however crudely, to have his or her voice so dressed up with overtones and resonances so as to produce the sort of noise that today is such a commercial success.[97]

The authors locate this discussion within an older opposition in sound recording and broadcasting: realism versus romanticism. They quote a writer in the magazine *Gramophone* to define the terms: "The Realists stood out strongly for as accurate a reproduction as possible of the actual sounds recorded, but the Romantics held that a certain sacrifice of accuracy was permissible, nay, even desirable, if it induced a quality more pleasing to the ear."[98] This opposition between "realist" and "romantic" schools will be of particular importance to the discussion in chapter 2 of certain (inadvertently) spatial and "placed" recordings of the early electric period.

Read and Welch then move on to discuss the experiments of Les Paul and "the purposeful distortions of the recorded groove" created by what Paul called, in the 1950s, the "New Sound." From there they raise the matter of (but withhold final judgment on) "distortions purposely created by the use of echo chambers and electrical circuits which accomplish the same end," as well as "dubbing" and splice editing to remove imperfections in a performance.[99] Interestingly, the authors then quote from an article by Potamkin published in the *Phonograph Monthly Review* as early as 1930, which in turn speaks of remarks made in the *Nouvelle Revue Française* by Paul Deharme:

Deharme believes that the contemporary intelligence is in need of imagination, of lyric transformation such as is not offered by the classic forms, nor even by the new forms, and which radio may satisfy. Among these prime necessities he places "the taste for the unreal," as is evinced by the willingness of the popular mind to believe in a succession of images lacking color projected on a screen lacking relief and in such a contradiction of ordinary logic as the animated cartoons of Max Fleischer, where real personages participate with designs. He believes that the radio can create its analogy to these visions, by putting in place of a spectator of images an auditor of images.[100]

The notion here that sound qualities alone might be used to construct analogies to vision, with the potential freedom to move between the real and the fantastic indicates an early awareness of radio's (and by implication, sound recording's) deterritorializing potentials, which accords with the main thrust of this book. The further implication that this "taste for the unreal" resides with the mass market, and that culturally "low" forms such as the animated cartoon might be leading the way is wholly in accord with the argument following here: that it was in "low," marginalized, little-respected and thus largely unmonitored musical recording domains ("race" and "hillbilly" music in particular) that some of the most radical and influential production innovations took place, and that the listeners to these forms were indeed increasingly, if unwittingly, learning to be "auditors of images."

Echo, reverberation and resonance are of major concern to the practitioners and theorists of "sound art." Densil Cabrera, for example, both surveys practices within the genre of what he calls "resonating sound art," and reports on his own research into acoustic and psychoacoustic aspects of room resonance.[101] The latter he bases upon listening tests he administered aimed at eliciting descriptive, evaluative and emotional responses from thirteen subjects. Cabrera carefully distinguishes resonance (and thus resonating sound art) from reverberation. Tank-piece musicians, for example, have explored extremes of reverberation—up to forty-five seconds in some cases—but resonating sound art places emphasis "solely on the sound of reverberation, rather than a sound source within a reverberant space."[102] The split-off, inherently "schizophonic" nature of Cabrera's experiments (his object of study is the pure resonance of spaces, wholly divorced from their source sounds) limits the applicability of his aesthetic and psychoacoustic findings to this study, however, where it is precisely the interactivity between source and echo/reverberation that delineates the virtual spaces of the recording. Furthermore, the subjective responses Cabrera elicits from his trained listeners[103] focus primarily on permutations to recorded resonances over successive generations of rerecording, and this too is not frequently replicated in popular music recording practice, certainly not since multi-tracking on magnetic tape became possible.[104]

Echo and reverberation as physical phenomena are the subject of a substantial body of works in the field of architectural and acoustic design. Indeed, the project of psychoacoustics could be seen largely as an attempt to deal in a technical way with the affective aspects of particular sound properties, especially reverberation and echo. Architectural decisions regarding room dimensions and building materials used will obviously produce differing acoustic regimes in constructed spaces. In the literature of acoustic design, typically certain configurations are discussed in relation to the design of spaces for music production, for business, industrial or domestic uses, etc. In texts that deal specifically with the design of concert halls, drama theaters and studios, issues of echo and reverberation attain prime importance.

Beranek, whose primary concern is the design of concert halls and opera houses, discusses the impact of physical-acoustic room properties on musical sounds.[105] He goes to some pains to build a vocabulary that might bridge the differing linguistic domains of engineers, musicians and critics, in each of which such words as "echo," "reverberation" and "resonance" often have quite different meanings. Beranek's project is to render subjective, aesthetic sensations of music into technical formulations that engineers, architects and acousticians might find useable. Beranek's concern, however, is primarily with the production and consumption of "live" Western classical music and he takes as given the aesthetic desirability or otherwise of specific musical sounds and sound regimes; thus ultimately his work has little direct bearing on this study. Indeed, the evolution of the "virtual spaces" of the echoic southern recordings herein addressed largely arose out of musicians' and producers' need to deal with, to "rise above" the acoustic shortcomings of the spaces in which they worked: for musicians, it was bars, dance halls, tent shows, ramshackle juke joints and "chicken shacks"; for producers it was cheap, often cramped, undercapitalized studio spaces, or hastily adapted hotel rooms, public meeting halls and so forth.

Beranek cites two specific attempts to assess the subjective effects of echo and reverb on listeners. Although he has no special concern with recorded music as such, in order to simulate a range of differing acoustic conditions, the experiments used magnetic tape recordings with added delay, and so are of incidental interest here. The first experiment was conducted at the University of Göttingen in 1951 and the other was carried out a little later in Australia, by the Commonwealth Scientific and Industrial Research Organization (CSIRO). Beranek describes the latter:

[The scientists] presented music through loudspeakers, to a group of 20 listeners. In order to produce the equivalent of a reflection from a surface in a room, they used a magnetic tape recorder that added to the original transcription of the music the same music delayed by an amount of time of up to 1000 milliseconds. The amount of the delay could be varied and the intensity of the delayed or 'reflected' music could be adjusted. . . . Each passage took 14 seconds to play. The music was recorded by a string quartet playing outdoors.
During the period of silence between repetitions, the listeners were asked to report whether they were disturbed by the added reflection, not just whether they could perceive it.[106]

It is noteworthy that these formal experiments were roughly contemporaneous with the hit-and-miss experimentation being conducted by Les Paul, Sam Phillips, Bill Putnam (who engineered the early Chess sides) and others. Other than as passing curiosity, however, the CSIRO experiments add little to understanding of the workings of echo and reverberation on recorded music, treating as they do questions of what constitutes aesthetic desirability as unproblematic. Indeed when R & B and rock 'n' roll music started gaining wide airplay, the presence of echo and reverb on the records was one of the features most noted (and despised) by "establishment" commentators, although it was at the same time perhaps the single most replicated feature.[107]

It is worth noting that participants in the CSIRO experiments, laboratory staff in the main, cited 100 millisecond delay as "disturbing,"[108] while Les Paul used roughly that same delay in his first highly successful experiments with tape: "The repeating of the delay was a matter of choice, as to how much delay you wanted and how much repeat you wanted, although the timing of the delay was about one tenth of a second to avoid a reverb effect."[109] It was with this configuration that Paul produced his influential hit "How High the Moon." As with so many later production-related and musical innovations of R & B and rock 'n' roll music, the musicians and producers were most successful when they worked in the shadow of then current industry "best practice."

To make sense of why some listeners should be attracted, and others repelled by the same inclusion needs more than a simple technical description of the effect. Clearly some awareness of the social and cultural contexts of music production and consumption is called for, and a number of writers in the field of popular music studies have attempted this. Academic writers who deal at all with "production sound" in 1940s and 1950s popular music have tended to do so briefly, dealing with the period as an early, crudely experimental stage whose main importance (in terms of the history of production values, at least) lies in it presaging the more important and more interesting rock productions of the 1960s and after. When spatiality is addressed, it is often seen as beginning in earnest with the coming of stereo hi-fi sound in the late 1950s.

But writers have on rare occasions attempted to address specifically the social meanings of echo and reverberation in popular music recordings and in film. Richard Hoggart remarked in passing on the sociological implications of magnetic tape echoicity in mainstream mass-market popular recordings, talking of a class of "sentimental" popular songs, either overtly religious or secular but delivered with quasi-religious feeling: "They are vulgar it is true [but] they deal only with large emotional situations: they tend to be open hearted and big bosomed. . . . They are not cynical or neurotic."[110] He goes on to talk about the blurring of dividers between hymns such as "Abide with Me," "The Old Rugged Cross" and "Ave Maria," and songs such as "Danny Boy" and "Now is the Hour":

the same kind of emotion floods through them all. It is not difficult to understand why the films' aerial massed strings and the huge angelic choirs, singing in the vaulted upper regions 'I'll Walk Beside You,' 'You'll Never Walk Alone,' 'I Believe, My Friend' or 'I'm Walking Behind,' are so easily accepted; or why the echo chamber has become so popular—since it suggests something both out of this world and the intimacy of that singing in the bath which makes us all feel that we have fine voices.[111]

Hoggart continues the idea:

there is an extension; from home-family-love-neighborliness to Our Father in Heaven, where the values of Our Father in Heaven are felt to be similar to those of a loving home . . . the 'we two only' or 'just the two of us' idea of love can be given all the trappings of religious feeling—for itself and of itself: there is nothing out-side. Then follow quickly all the celestial choirs roaring out against a hollow back-ground suggestive of infinite height and space. For the love song sung in the reli-gious manner the two main styles seem to be the 'elevated celestial' or 'Sweetheart of the Universe' for women.[112]

R. Murray Schafer talks about the sound properties of natural spaces and the reverberant properties of the built environment; while he goes to considerable lengths, however, to catalogue the world soundscape soni-cally, he is dismissive of recorded music (surely one of the most ubiquitous nonnaturally occurring sounds on earth) and only very briefly addresses *re-corded* echo and reverberation—and then only as an afterthought to a com-ment made by Blaukopf:

'[in a gothic church] the loss of high frequencies and the resulting impossibility of localizing the sound makes the believer part of the world of sound. He does not face the sound in "enjoyment"—he is wrapped up by it' (Blaukopf).
  The experience of immersion rather than concentration forms one of the strong-est links between modern and medieval man. But we can look back farther still to determine a common origin. Where then is the dark fluid space from where such experiences spring? It is the ocean-womb of our first ancestors: the exaggerated echo and feedback effects of modern electronic and popular music re-create for us the echoing vaults, the dark depths of ocean.[113]

But ultimately, to attempt to "read" echoic and reverberant sound effects back to a single stable, bedrock meaning—the actual maternal womb or the prehistoric oceanic home of our evolutionary ancestors—is to miss the fun-damental fluidity and variability of listening in the modern, schizophonic world. Like anyone else in the lo-fi schizophonic industrial world, I neces-sarily remain mostly distracted, oblivious to the oceans of sound around me. And the harder I try to listen, sometimes the less I hear. As I review again and again the sound examples used in this study, for instance, I gener-ally experience a progressive desensitization to the recordings: Is there really discernible reverb on that voice? Is that really delay there? And yet I can walk into a shop and hear an old Little Richard record playing over low-quality store radio and be stopped in my tracks, as the imaginary coor-dinates of that sonic field for a brief moment completely overwrite the sound and space of my real world. This book is an attempt to acknowledge the whimsical, elusive, inexhaustible ability of the song to remake space.

CHAPTER 2

Harnessing the Echo

⊢◇⊣

Mythic Echo, Echo in Antiquity

Can architecture be heard? Most people would probably say that as architecture does not
produce a sound it cannot be heard. But neither does it radiate light, yet it can be seen.
—Steen Rasmussen[1]

suave locus voci resonat conclusus
(How sweetly the enclosed space responds to the voice)
—Horace, *Satires*, I, iv, 76, speaking of people
who recite their works in the Roman Baths[2]

Already the microphone has crossed the threshold of the lips, slipped into the interior world
of man, moved into the hiding places of the voices of consciousness, of the refrains of memory, of the screams of nightmares and of words never spoken. Echo chambers are already
translating not just the space of a set but the distances within the soul.
—Jean Epstein[3]

Both reverberation and echo are reflected sound. Echo occurs when a
sound is reflected in such a way that the source sound is distinctly reproduced, as when a shout bounces off a distant, relatively flat wall, for instance. Echo might be single or multiple, depending on how many times
the sound bounces. Reverberation, on the other hand, occurs when sound
is reflected either so many times that no single, discontinuous repeat of the
source sound is heard, or when the reflective surfaces are too near the listener to allow subjective aural separation (as in, say, a tiled bathroom)

Reverberation does much to define what we perceive as timbre, volume
and sound coloration, and largely determines our perceptions of how particular sounds are located, whether they are near or far. If all real-world
sounds were to be somehow stripped of their cloaking of reverberation, it
would be a wholly disorienting, dead, almost spaceless and depthless world.[4]
Lower amplitude reverberation though, like much of the totality that composes "hearing," is something of which we are frequently not conscious,
however much it may affect our subjective experiencing of place and space.

Echo, which, scientifically speaking, is merely a specific type of reverberation, is more readily noticed. To hear one's own voice "emanating" from the chasm, cliff or mountain, or even to hear one's footsteps bouncing off a distant wall—such phenomena have long been found intriguing, in the ancient and modern worlds, in both pre- and postindustrial cultures. That which is not the self seems to talk to us with our own voice, using our own sounds. The obvious atavistic suggestion posed by the phenomenon of echo is animist: that the nonhuman world "talks," that it possesses human characteristics. But other questions then arise: Does the world resemble the self or is the self simply a much lesser, relatively inconsequential emanation of the world? So where am "I," really—here or there? And is there really an "I" to ask the question? The phenomenon of echo is profoundly ambiguous: it suggests on the one hand an irreconcilable dualism, while simultaneously hinting at a transcendent monism, that all in fact may at base be one. Yet even in this latter lurks the suspicion of total alienation, that the "one" might be the universal prison of the narcissistic self.

And this is before we get to the added degree of abstraction that recorded reverb and echo entail. Before investigating concrete instances of sound-recorded reverberation, it is illuminating to look at some preexisting traditions of understanding, deploying and manipulating echo and reverberation.

In a culture that privileges the visual sense over all others, materiality is most commonly mediated in visual terms. We rely on visual representations to gain any sort of notion of "what things are like." Photographs, drawings, blueprints, floorplans, artists' impressions, maps—diagrams all translate the material world primarily into visual images. Written and verbal descriptions of place and space, of building and architecture also rely primarily on the invocation of images in the reader's mind, in the "mind's eye." Yet as writers such as Rasmussen, Schafer and Lamb attest, and as the whole practice of "sound art" seeks to demonstrate, although culturally undervalued, sound is also a semiotically rich attribute of physicality. Physical forms might just as well be described and catalogued in aural, tactile or olfactory terms. If place, space and physical form were to be perceived or described in terms of their acoustic and aural properties, a rich substratum of signification might be accessed. This layer of meaning might contain, in surprisingly unproblematic form, many of the attributes of place that lie just below the surface of conscious perception.[5] The discourses of architectural criticism, for instance, make frequent use of nonspecific, aestheticist terms such as "atmosphere," "mood," "charm," "grace" and so forth, that upon closer sonic investigation might be much more closely and specifically described.

It is unlikely, however, that sound taken alone could equal the almost limitless extent and depth of significations afforded by the visual sense, and it is no part of this book to claim such. Operating as a counterpart to the visual, tactile and olfactory, however, as a neglected, often only dimly registered aspect to physicality, sound and sound qualities might act as a kind of other, a commentary upon, a subtext to that which is primarily perceived.

Some of the mythological formulations of the phenomenon of echo construct it precisely in this binary, dualistic way. Echo appears as a minor but significant character in Greco-Roman mythology, sometimes as a daughter of the earth goddess Gaia.[6] In Ovid's account,[7] Echo is a beautiful nymph, fond of woods and sports, and a favorite of Diana. She is, however, inclined to ceaseless chatter and always seeks to have the last word in any exchange. Zeus (or, romanized, Jupiter) has Echo detain his wife Hera (Juno) in ceaseless small talk, while he adulterously cavorts with nymphs. Hera comes to suspect Echo's role in the deception and decrees that the nymph may henceforth speak only when spoken to, and then may only repeat the last few syllables uttered to her by others.

Later Echo observes and falls in love with the beautiful and vain Narcissus, and follows his footsteps, longing to address him, but is obliged to wait until he chooses to address her. He eventually calls on her to show herself, but when she does he spurns her.[8] Heartbroken, she hides herself away in the recesses of the woods, living in caves and among mountain cliffs. Over time her flesh wastes away, her bones change into rocks until nothing is left of her but her voice. She remains however ever ready to reply to anyone who calls her. Narcissus goes on to the reflexive exploits for which he is better known. His record of overweening self-regard, however, is first evidenced in his encounter with Echo.[9]

The Ovidian version of the myth suggests a fundamental dualism: by the end of the story the human self, the masculine Narcissus, is alienated from his complement, the female Echo. As a result of this neglect, Echo is subject to a kind of atrophy. The remnants of her existence are eventually displaced into the landscape. All that remains is the residual aural effect (although Echo is still sentient). Echo and Narcissus are both losers here. The underlying thematics are of splitting, of reduction, of loss of the self. The Echo and Narcissus myth is in some ways a "fall" story, although, unlike other golden age narratives, Narcissus and Echo never enjoy a prior state of wholeness from which they fall. What is lost is the *chance* of wholeness, rather than the actuality. Recalling the notion of participation from chapter 1, while the myth of Echo and Narcissus speaks of the alienation of the physical world from the human subject, it also signals a residual participatory possibility. Full participation may no longer be possible; we cannot,

like the Bororo (as cited in Keil 1994) *be* parakeets. But a potential participatory nexus remains; Echo waits to answer any who may call her. A limited reunification with nature is possible, but only in the sonic realm.[10]

Other accounts place Echo as the focus of violent and traumatic events.
Earlier Greek versions, for example, have Echo as a musically inclined
nymph who inhabits deep woods. Although very beautiful, she denies the
love of any man or immortal, thus attracting the resentment of many. The
god Pan, a rejected suitor, has the shepherds (his followers) tear Echo's
body to pieces and then scatter the remains far and wide. Gaia, the earth
goddess receives the pieces into her bosom, and retains Echo's voice and
talents for answering and imitating sounds and voices.[11] In yet another telling, Pan strikes Echo dumb, save for the power to repeat utterances. The
shepherds become infuriated by this habit of hers and eventually tear her to
pieces of their own volition.[12]

In one western Australian Aboriginal account, echo is personified as a
malevolent child-stealing personage named Balyet (alternatively named
Marali). Originally a beautiful girl, whose beauty caused two blood brothers to fight to the death, Balyet has been made a complete outcast, so much
so that not even death will accept her. Like the Greco-Roman Echo figures,
Balyet's body wastes away over time (although she remains technically a living woman and not a ghost). She haunts high rocky gullies, visible only at
night, and then only as a mist. Lonely and painfully childless, she calls to
children, seeking to lure them away from their homes. Those who respond
are led away from family, and taken in Balyet's cold, killing embrace. When
Balyet realizes the child is dead, she retreats screaming into the mountain
gullies. Those children who manage to escape usually become ill and die.
Young girls are especially at risk from Balyet.[13] Whereas Greco-Roman
Echo is very much a secondary character, sentient but incapable of initiating dialogue, Balyet retains autonomy. Even in her final reduced form she
initiates action, albeit action antagonistic to humans.

At this point explorations of mythic echo and its semiotic implications
must desist, although some of the tensions and dualities briefly indicated
here will be revisited when the emergence of "distant," secondary and
echoic voices in sound recordings are looked at. Indeed, although they may
seem to be at a great remove, certain echoic slapbacks, synthesized reverb
and electric guitar effects employed on a number of blues and country recordings in the mid-twentieth century directly relate to and play out the
same questions of the self and the occupation of spaces that so concerned
the ancients. Not only that, but these twentieth-century low-art forms employed precisely the same trope—echo—to continue and in some cases
partly to resolve the investigation.

While echo is largely a phenomenon of the natural world, the phenomenon of reverberation figures in human history more as a secondary (although frequently a key meaning–fixing) quality of the built environment. Echo is often mythologized as a disempowered (though mocking) female voice. We also find reverberation to be gendered (as male); rather than dispossessed and mocking, it is associated with seats and sites of power, with pomp and circumstance.

Reverberation is produced when sounds are emitted inside a space enclosed by hard surface materials. This production may naturally occur in a cave dwelling, but less so in a hut, tent, cabin, lean-to and so forth. Reverberation acts as an amplifier of sounds, both by causing sound events to last longer and through "consonance"—the reinforcing of midrange frequencies. The temples, mausoleums, palaces, ziggurats, and legislatures of antiquity were highly reverberant spaces, and this quality provides specific acoustic "framing" of utterances made within them. In the preindustrial soundscape, where human cries and shouts, the bleatings of herd animals, the clatter of hooves on stones, the pounding of grain, the rattling of armor were among the loudest of everyday man-made sounds, the architecturally amplified voice must have held special connotations. Certainly, we have only to consider how reverberant modern-day public buildings—churches, war memorials, law courts, art galleries, public libraries—seem to "naturally" produce in us a hushed awe (despite our being relatively inured and desensitized to sonic effects). It is more than likely that the "aura" of reverberation in the ancient world was a quality much associated with the pronouncement from on high, be it from pharaoh, emperor, king, priest, governor, satrap or magistrate.

Just as there exists a correspondence between the reverberant utterance and secular power, so too is there an ancient nexus between the reverberant spaces and the sacred or magical. This is exemplified in the sacred grottoes and caves of preurban societies, and later by the acoustic properties present in temples, shrines, mausoleums, right down to the modern church, mosque, temple, synagogue or wat. Schafer cites instances of "magical" acoustics in the ancient world: the Neolithic cave of Hypogeum in Malta with a resonating cavity in the wall that gives an amplified "oracular" quality to the male voice;[14] a mythical room in a Babylonian ziggurat where whispers were reputed to last forever (a precursor of the sound-recording apparatus); an actual room in the Ali Qapu in Isphahan, whose highly polished walls produce extremely long reverb; the Chinese legend of a black box, into which a king may speak orders and send them around the kingdom[15]—another mythic precursor to the recording device. (Indeed, at its moment of invention, Edison's first tinfoil recording device more resembled natural echo than it did the mass-produced phonograph record: "One minute Edison was shouting 'Mary had a little lamb' and the next minute, with his mouth shut, he was shouting it again," thereby fulfilling "Emerson's prediction that we would 'harness the echo.'"[16]

There is an integral and enduring connection between what might be called "reverberancy" and the sacred. The ancient mystery cults of the Eastern Mediterranean—the mysteries of Eleusis, Dionysus, Orpheus and Isis— had as their focus the death and rebirth of a god, with an entombment often at the very center of their respective mythologies. Enclosed spaces—both natural and constructed—were used by these initiatory cults for their rituals, wherein the postulant might undergo his (symbolic) death and ecstatic rebirth as an initiate.[17] Shamanistic practice likewise makes use of the sacred cave, wherein the shaman might have his visions (just as Christian mystics would later make similar use of the bare cell, as site for contemplation, spiritual practice and in time, possibly, mystical transformation).[18]

The Roman cult of Mithraism also used specially constructed vaults for its rituals, and like other Mediterranean mystery cults used symbolic death and rebirth experiences to engender ecstatic states in its practitioners.[19] Mithraic ritual practice had a direct influence on early Christianity, as did its architecture, exemplified in such things as the central placement of the altar, the use of faced-stone building materials, the maintaining of an ambience of institutionalism and high solemnity.

Instead of being a place of private and privileged experience (as were the sites used by the mystery cults), however, the Christian church building enclosed an entire collectivity, the Christian community, and offered, rather than ecstatic experiences, the simultaneously more democratic but more diluted promise of salvation to any who might seek it. Architectural decisions made by early Christians had direct acoustic outcomes, and the specific acoustic properties of these spaces, especially their high degree of reverberance, played a key role in determining and shaping the practices conducted within, sonic and otherwise. During the Constantine period, Christians began to adopt the basilica type of building to house growing congregations. Krautheimer describes the history of this building type:

[A] basilica was but a large meeting hall . . . a hall to transact business. . . . On a dais, the tribunal, the magistrate and his assessors would sit in court ; surmounting it, a shrine sheltered the effigy of the Emperor in whose presence alone law could be dispensed and business contracts validly concluded . . . a number of basilicas might be assigned different functions: stock and money exchanges, clothing bazaars, florists arcades, special law courts. . . . Army camps had their riding and drill basilicas, opening on a sanctuary where the eagles of the legion and the emperor's effigy were kept. . . .
. . . [S]acred overtones grew stronger with the growing import of the cult of the Emperor's divinity. The palace basilica in which he sat enthroned was ipso facto a

religious building. The drill basilica of a barracks became religious ground as the garrison paraded and swore loyalty before the emperor's bust. In forum basilicas, his effigy consecrated official and private business.[20]

The basilicas of the early Middle Ages operated acoustically in two key ways. Drawing on the ancient traditions of the "speaking" of secular power, the cathedral acoustics served to amplify and give substance and import to the utterances of the priest, both ritual and sermonizing. The priest himself derived his authority as a kind of local delegate for the pope in Rome, who derived his authority from Saint Peter by apostolic succession from Christ. The utterances of the priest, while not underwritten by any supernatural guarantee of certainty (priests are neither soothsayers nor oracles, nor even adepts in the gnostic or magical sense of the word) are backed by the institutional power of the Christian church, representing in the Middle Ages immense centralized political power, as well as spiritual authority. Church acoustics both enabled the priest to be heard by a large congregation, and gave his voice a quality of singularity, strength and authority. In the very early days of the church the sermon was of prime importance in winning converts, but by the Middle Ages in central and western Europe, where church Latin was not the vernacular language, the homily became less important than the ritual of the Eucharist itself.

The medieval cathedral did more acoustically, however, than simply enhance the priest's performance to the congregation. Cathedrals, says Schafer, are "acoustic machines" whose purpose is to get the attention of the deity and make Him listen.[21] The most notable acoustic property of cathedrals and large basilicas is the extremely long duration of sound reverberation inside them. Bagenal and Wood demonstrate that these buildings are indeed sophisticated resonating machines, producing reverberations of up to twelve seconds' duration. Furthermore many cathedrals are said to possess a "sympathetic note": a tendency to particularly favor certain frequencies, usually around A or A-flat. These acoustic qualities discouraged the use of vernacular speech patterns, as the long duration of reverb muddies the sounds. If vowels are intoned slowly, however, and spoken around the pitch of the "sympathetic note" they will possess great carrying power and amplitude. Thus over time the delivery of sermons and the recitation of prayers, according to Bagenal and Wood, evolved into chant. Plainsong began as simply spoken psalms.[22] Indeed, the very development of polyphony, they argue, could be seen as a by-product of medieval church architecture. In a sense, everyday speech is here being turned into a specifically stylized verbal form: song. And, as Bagenal and Wood point out, the architecture itself is acting as a musical instrument: "It was found that so great was the unifying tone effect of the church as an instrument that more than one tune could go on at the same time and if certain musical rules were kept, the result would be pleasing. . . . [Polyphonic music] depended on human voices using the church as their major instrument."[23]

This notion would later find an important direct rhyme in twentieth-century practice, when Brian Eno (and others) would come to see the recording studio as a kind of musical instrument.[24] Later, I shall argue that some of the "religious" intensity and monastic inward focus of the church was also to be re-created in the recording studio, sometimes knowingly. But to return to the medieval church, not only was it a resonating musical instrument; sometimes it also possessed apparently "magical" properties that were a direct result of its reverberant character: "a mass by Fairfax—the mediaeval organist of St Albans—was composed with *a fourth part supplied by the church*. Even if this is no more than legend, it shows that the building was recognized as an instrument."[25] The church building is a kind of communication exchange, with messages moving from the deity through the agency of the priests to the faithful and from the faithful to God. The acoustic "animating" of the building interior provides a kind of theatrical effect that enables the cathedral to represent simultaneously both heaven (God's home) and "the world" (humans' home). The long reverberations of the church building echo the workings of political power, spiritual authority, human sociality and individual transcendence all at once, while the appearance of the "fourth voice" hints at the lingering presence of a residual paganism.

The church then is a kind of conduit linking the congregation with two remote seats of power, heaven and Rome. The churches of the Reformation on the other hand were built to accommodate more immediate communications, between minister and flock, and among church elders, municipal officials, deacons, and so on.

The Reformation was the culmination of a long reform movement between opposite temperaments as to whether the true source of Authority was Christ's body, as presented in the central office of the Church, or in God's Word—the Scriptures. . . .
. . . The pulpit in the reformed church took on a special importance, for the scriptures once established, required ceaseless expounding and explaining.[26]

Generally speaking, Protestant churches of the Reformation were built or modified so that the ratio between the number of the congregation and the volume of air in the building lessened, so that reverberation became less, thus allowing the use of vernacular speech from the pulpit (and incidentally the development of new styles of music). The church interior was "desacralized," rendered much less reverberant, as the institution of the church itself was demoted in relative importance, and the authority of local church councils was correspondingly enhanced. As well as housing the meetings of the faithful, the church now had to provide a meeting place wherein governing bodies might discuss church business, argue and make decisions.

Bagenal and Wood link the development of the cantata form to the specific acoustics of the reformed church. They describe the Lutheran church of Saint Thomas's at Leipzig, where for a time J. S. Bach was the organist. The church featured numerous staircases, wooden galleries and "swallow's nests"—family "theater boxes" for the town burghers. Acoustically, these furnishings greatly reduced the reverb duration, down to perhaps two seconds. Furthermore the church has no "note," or region of response. Thus Bach was able to compose a "busier," often rapid tempo music: fugue, cantata, passion music and set pieces in any key he chose. The church was in some ways then nearer in acoustic character to a later concert hall than a cathedral.[27]

Indeed, as Bagenal and Wood point out, it was only at this time that purpose-built music halls and opera houses began to appear in Europe.[28] Hitherto college halls, churches and even large rooms in houses were the main sites of formal music performance (although "low" music, then as now, was made in taverns, brothels, shebeens, camps, farmhouses and the like). Following on from the Protestant church tradition, these purpose-built halls were designed to produce much shorter reverberation times.

It has been suggested that with the rise of rationalism and the retreat of religion, first during the Renaissance and later during the Enlightenment, the notion of "high art" emerged as a secular replacement for religion. Certain pseudoreligious trappings began to adhere to "high art": the "correct," cultivated mode to be employed when approaching Art became one of respect, reverence and awe. So too emerged the romantic notion of the artist as fundamentally different, as the singularly privileged bearer of "vision," as a kind of secular mystic.

The impact this notion had on the production and consumption of music was to foster a growing split between music makers and audiences, as reflected in the spread of concert halls and opera houses as temples to high culture. As Lawrence Levine has demonstrated, the "sacralization of culture" was associated with the appearance of strict behavioral codes, both statutory and informal, imposed on the erstwhile heterogeneous public spaces of libraries, art galleries, public parks, theaters, concert halls and opera houses.[29] Parks for instance became "didactic landscapes" and "moral spaces."[30] The spirited audience participation that had characterized musical performance earlier in the century was rigorously stamped out. "Low" and vernacular elements (such as minstrelsy or "singalong" material) were increasingly excluded from "good" music programming, in favor of a shrinking canon of predominantly European-composed works. The character of the music theater changed drastically over a relatively short time:

Concertgoers were increasingly lectured on the elements of proper behavior. In 1892, Edward Baxter Perry told them they had "no right" to sit through a concert "stolid and indifferent," to think about business or domestic affairs, to read the old letters accumulated in their pockets, to trim their fingernails, to crunch peanuts, "or even to take a nap." Attention, he announced, "is a rigid rule of the concert room." Silence, he reminded them, "is to music what light is to painting." . . . Gradually such injunctions became an integral part of the rules governing audience behavior. Intermissions were introduced to allow the audience to stretch, talk, promenade and then presumably subside into reflective quiescence when the music resumed. . . . [L]ights were dimmed in concert halls to further focus attention on the performers rather than the audience.[31]

The new emporia of the emerging mass culture—movie houses, music halls, vaudeville theaters—began to ape the trappings of high culture, imposing policies of "cleanliness and order," and seeking to banish "vulgarisms and coarseness."[32]

This behavioral disciplining of fin de siècle audiences was part of the larger development, Levine points out, of the long-term split between the private and public spheres of life described by Norbert Elias.[33] Levine has traced the growing differentiation of social functions during the late nineteenth century, which finds pointed expression in the cult of etiquette and the slew of etiquette manuals published in the United States. Decorum, circumspection, strictly controlled bodily carriage, meticulously, even obsessively monitored personal appearance, the suppression of affectivity— all became de rigueur for the bourgeoisie and "respectable" working class in public. Levine talks of the impact this had on public entertainment:

Reactions and emotions had to be carefully governed. In the sense that opera houses, symphony halls, and art galleries, as well as the larger movie theatres and vaudeville houses reflected this process they were mirrors of society. But they were more than that; they were active agents in teaching their audiences to adjust to the new social imperatives, in urging them to separate public behavior from private feelings, in training them to keep a strict reign over their emotional and physical processes.[34]

These two independent processes—the growing splits between "high" and "low" culture, and the further separation of life into public and private spheres—were both at their peak at the precise moment that the phonograph[35] came onto the scene in Western societies. Its uses were to an extent shaped and determined by these factors, as well as by the inherent physical and technical attributes, and limitations, of the apparatus itself. In the acoustic period of sound recording (up to about 1925) practices emerged to which the spatially disruptive recordings of early hillbilly and blues present a kind of counterpractice—which itself became a continuing practice, a tradition even. Thus, although this is not a history of the phonograph and gramophone, least of all in the acoustic period, we must look briefly at some of the early spatial characteristics pertaining to both devices, in both their production and reception aspects.

"Whispering": Early Phonograph Recording

The early phonograph and later the gramophone were subject to strict technical limitations. Even at its best, acoustic gramophone recording could not achieve a frequency range greater than 168 to 2000 Hertz (Hz).[36] (The audible range of frequencies in a concert hall, by comparison, is about 20 to 20,000 Hz.) Early forms of the apparatus, such as Edison Cylinders, recorded within an even narrower frequency range, greatly restricting what could and could not be satisfactorily recorded. The male human voice, if kept steadily modulated, might register on the apparatus, and so might midrange musical instruments. Larger orchestras were problematic, as were instruments in the higher or lower frequency ranges. Particularly well suited were brass instruments and brass bands, and single male voices.

In the earlier phases of the phonograph recording industry, there was no suitable way of duplicating cylinders; players would perform a piece simultaneously into a maximum of ten recording machines lined up around them, producing ten cylinders. When the "take" was completed the machines would be reloaded and the process repeated, for hours on end.[37] With disc recording came greater efficiencies in duplication, but performers were still obliged to crowd around the acoustic recording horn. And despite steady improvements in frequency range, the same midrange instruments—pianos, brass, banjos, etc—were generally favored throughout the pre-electric recording period.

Early sound recording and playback was ambiguously situated in relation to then reigning notions of high and low culture, and displayed a slightly schizoid nature as a result. Edison originally saw the device mainly as an aid to commerce and education;[38] others saw it as a means of archiving and distributing the finest in culture. But when commercial recording got under way in the United States in the 1890s, the great bulk of material was produced for coin-in-the-slot machines, the prototype to the jukebox.

With the playback device still cumbersome and requiring acrid storage batteries to run, its major use was as a machine of public entertainment.[39] Coin-operated machines, located in taverns, bars, diners, railway stations, amusement parks and arcades, ferry houses and the like, returned owners up to fifty dollars a week,[40] but required a steady supply of fresh cylinders.[41] Material recorded during this period included Sousa marches, polkas and Stephen Foster melodies, spoken sermons, jokes and recitations, cornet, clarinet and piano pieces, whistled melodies, bird calls, short orchestral pieces and anthems. Catalogues listed musical selections under categories such as "Sentimental," "Topical," "Comic," "Negro" and "Irish." Musical comedy was also very popular.[42]

Yet another well-established category was the "Descriptive Record." Gelatt describes one such recording, "Down on the Suwannee River." Over its two minutes' playing time, says Gelatt, "it spun out the excitement of Pulling in the Gang Plank, Steamboat Bells, Whistle, and Dance on Board with Negro Shouts and Clogs."[43]

The cultural product that found its way onto the early Edison Cylinders and gramophone discs, was then in the main "low":

[H]owever much the advertisements prated of a 'musical education of the young' . . . the phonograph still showed all the earmarks of a cultural pariah. Columbia and Edison had made a few tentative infiltrations into the giant domain of great music that was supposed to envelop the American home in the aura of uplifting art, but the bulk of their efforts pointed in the direction of pure home-grown 'corn.'[44]

But while the recorded material in the cylinder period might have been low or middlebrow, there is little to indicate that it was generally anything but professional and disciplined in its arrangement and execution. The requirement that recording artists spend day after day making multiple copies of the same piece was an obvious barrier to quirky amateurs, and undisciplined "folk" performers, as it tended to discourage improvisation and spontaneity.

The recording apparatus itself imposed strict spatial disciplines on artists. Richard Jose, a singer of sentimental ballads described the recording process in 1907:

It's the most secret thing in the world—for the singer. You're locked all alone with a band in a big bare room. Your back is to the musicians and your face to a bleak blank wall through which protrudes a solemn horn. A bell rings—one. That is to get ready, for the receiving instrument is so sensitive that if you moved your sleeve against your coat the sound would register. Somebody outside presses the button—two. The band starts the prelude, then you sing, turning neither right nor left, always looking and singing into that protruding horn. And you can't even let your breath out after your last note; you must close your lips on it and wait for the little whir within the horn to cease.[45]

These production constraints thus favored seasoned troupers: musicians, raconteurs, singers and comedians from the vaudeville circuits and highly disciplined, professional brass bands such as the immensely popular John

Philip Sousa and his United States Marine Band.[46] Such performers were able to produce on call carefully controlled, calibrated and thoroughly "road-tested" performances of favorite songs, recitations and orations, which might have already been performed thousands of times onstage.

Regardless of whether the records were played back in private or public space, the performance itself was generally located firmly within the public sphere. It "minded its manners." "Vulgarities," if used at all, were carefully pitched to stay firmly within the realm of the acceptable; voices were modulated just so, even when clowning (*especially* when clowning). Scarcely for a moment did the professional entertainer let slip the veneer of the performance, of controlled proximity to (or distancing from) the audience. Despite gestures of the spontaneous in the content, the mark of the professional was, and largely remains, unbroken control, seamless delivery and unfailing self-awareness. Recordings made by the professionals came imbued with their own spatial codes; they constructed their own virtual proscenium arch.

While the performances then were located firmly in the public sphere, the disposition of the playback apparatus itself—whether in public or domestic space—created certain new local juxtapositions of (and apparent anomalies between) the public and private. To play a descriptive record such as "Morning on the Farm," for instance, in one's own parlor was, according to the blurb in the catalogue, to open an imaginary window on a farmyard scene: "so real and exact that it requires but a slight stretch of the imagination to place one's self in that delightful position, the result of which is the drinking in of copious drafts of fresh air and numerous other pleasures attainable only on the farm."[47] This "sound picture" overlays the fictive spatiality of the "picturesque farm" onto the actual space of the "parlor," without challenging the integrity of either space. The descriptive record's pictoriality might be seen as an aural extension of, say, a framed picture of a rural scene hanging on the wall in the same parlor. Although the space "depicted" on the recording may be nominally "other," like the painting, the spatiality of the recording is largely coded, controlled and stabilized within and by the bourgeois domestic space in which the record is played.[48]

With the advent and rapid ascendancy of flat disc recording in the early 1900s, recording expanded in quantity and scope.[49] Both recording activity and sales of players and records expanded into Europe, Australasia, and Asia. Companies sought to expand markets by widening the range of material on catalogue. The most influential and active of the first-wave recording producer-engineers, Fred Gaisberg also conducted recording trips throughout Europe and the Far East, recording a wide range of material:

Gypsy singers, professional tenors and baritones, "romance singers," tavern musicians, court musicians, "traditional music," orations, military marches, soldiers' songs, synagogue cantors and church choirs, "negro ditties" and so on.[50] The Gramophone Company published separate catalogues in English, Scotch, Irish, Welsh, German, Italian, Spanish, Viennese, Hungarian, Russian, Persian, Hindi, Sikh, Urdu, Arabic and Hebrew records. Unlike the southern United States field trips of the early electric period twenty years later, which produced a virtually worldwide appetite for "hillbilly music," the material recorded on the Gaisberg field trips did not "travel" back to the hubs of distribution in England or the United States. Rather, the recordings were seen as being suitable only for the markets local to where they were recorded: recordings of Japanese musicians for sale only in Japan, Burmese recordings only in Burma, and so on.[51]

Despite the overwhelming technical difficulties faced, record companies also sought to exploit the worldwide craze for operatic arias by offering abridged operatic selections (records were generally limited to two minutes' playing time) with minimal piano accompaniment (orchestral recording was still, in the early 1900s, extremely problematic). In general, recording producers sought professional members of prestigious opera companies—singers with local standing, but without international reputations.[52] One such of these opera singers was Enrico Caruso, first recorded by Gaisberg in 1902, to immediate commercial and artistic success. Recordings were subsequently made (by Gaisberg and others) of some of the most famous opera singers, those with the international reputations. Histories of recording recount numerous anecdotes of the encounters between these great stars and the recording apparatus. "Looking back," writes Gaisberg,

it is hard to realize my state of nerves at the responsibility of recording Patti, Melba, Caruso, Paderewski and other stars in those pioneering days. . . . In those days of star worship, an artist's patience with us was short, and to ask one to repeat an aria because of any fault other than her own would probably send her off into a tantrum that would ruin the session.[53]

Gaisberg recounts long, prerecording negotiations with the tenor Francesco Tamagno, after which Gaisberg's brother went to the singer's mountain home, and set up the recording machinery in the house's music room. Over the three-week period, nineteen release-quality recordings were made.[54] Later Gaisberg and his brother went almost as supplicants to the castle home of the famous diva Adelina Patti, where they were received by underlings, put up as guests and, having set up the apparatus, were then made to wait two days until the diva was prepared to sing. It took an entire week to record a few selections.[55] This stands in contrast to the businesslike two hours in which the not yet famous Caruso's first ten selections were recorded. Significantly, for this latter session, Caruso visited Gaisberg's studio, rather than the reverse.[56]

It is not difficult to see a spatial micropolitics at work in these anecdotes. The "personal space" of the famous singer is a privileged, hierarchically coded zone. The recording engineers are "received," as though by royalty, and they are careful to demonstrate by their behavior that they recognize the underlying royalty/artisan relationship.[57] Given the immense popularity of opera singers at the time, and the unique social status they enjoyed, this is not wholly surprising. "At the turn of the century," writes Gelatt, "the opera singer was at the peak of his glory . . . [the great stars] were objects of adoration, [inhabiting] an exhilarating and resplendent society."[58]

The famous opera singers of the day were favorites with European royalty, and were frequent guests at royal courts, summer houses, ski lodges and so on. Thus by a kind of virtual "one degree of separation," the gramophone owner who bought and played these recordings was granted a vicarious audience with the singer, which in turn meant a proxy admission to the highest social circles possible: European royalty. The gramophone was a medium notionally linking the home listener to the hitherto unimaginably remote complexes and ensembles of European royal power. Conductors and opera singers who rubbed shoulders with the aristocracy of the Old World might be intimately (if only virtually) present in the domestic bourgeois parlor, via the agency of the gramophone apparatus. The territorializing force these virtual presences exerted on the etiquette-obsessed middle classes of the early twentieth century is not hard to imagine.

Certainly, some compensatory (de)territorializations might also operate; the opera singers' intimate space too, has been invaded, and the subsequent mass reproduction and distribution of the "log" of that spatial invasion—the sound recording—enables a mass audience to "get closer" in a sense to the singer than any listener in any opera house ever could have. Given the narrow frequency and amplitude range recordable in the acoustic period, however, the degree of vicarious intimate invasion was necessarily severely limited. In balance, the power in the case of early acoustic operatic recording operates "centrifugally," from the centers out. Once the recording reaches the domestic sphere, although it might in theory be subject to any number of indignities and disrespectful behaviors, the then current strictures of "polite behavior" ensured a transmitting and replicating of codes of social class, of high and low, right into the space of the parlor.

To further establish the "high" credentials of the gramophone and to remove the stigma of saloon and barroom novelty, manufacturers began to design players "that would be accepted, like the piano, as a fine piece of furniture."[59] In late 1906 the Victrola went on the market in the United States and quickly became ubiquitous in the American domestic parlor. Sales of Victor's highbrow Red Seal Records, priced on a scale according to the records' "eminence," rose accordingly:[60]

A collection of Red Seal Records established one as a person of both taste and property. Along with the leather-bound sets of Dickens, Thackeray and Oliver Wendell Holmes, Victor Red Seals became a customary adjunct to the refined American parlor, to be displayed with pride to impressionable guests and relations.[61]

Rival companies followed suit, building more and more ornate Victrola-like parlor phonographs, such as Columbia's Grafonola. Meanwhile the Edison cylinder player, for which a mass-producing duplicating procedure had been devised, continued to service the "low" end of the market, still providing the humorous orations, marches and vaudeville songs, as sales gradually leveled off, and then began to decline.[62]

In England, the Gramophone Company had long been recording, to general commercial success, leading music hall entertainers, such as Dan Leno, and Victor in the United States followed suit around 1910 by recording famous U.S. vaudeville entertainers such as Sophie Tucker, Al Jolson, Stella Mayhew, Nora Bayes and others. These artists were generally backed on record by theater pit orchestras; thereafter a combination of two cornets, two clarinets, trombone, oboe, flute, tuba, percussion, two Stroh violins and viola became the basic standard recording ensemble for popular selections.[63]

In the years following 1911, a craze for "hot dance" swept America and then Europe, evoking a further dramatic effect on recording—on how (and what) records were made, and on how they were consumed. A wave of new dances—Tangos, One-Steps, Hesitation Waltzes, Bostons and Turkey Trots—which shifted natural accents to the off-beats, appeared among upper-class Americans and, largely via phonograph records, spread through the social classes. The dance craze ended the reliance of the record companies on military bands and had a sudden deterritorializing effect on the acoustic spaces in which records were played:

the turkey trot and other hurry-up dances had been inspired by Afro-American theatrical and sporting figures . . . freed ragtime couples from the strait jacket of the nineteenth century's figure and set dances. Irving Berlin's "Everybody's Doing It," "Snooky Ookums," and "Alexander's Ragtime Band" . . . and other Tin Pan Alley hits in this new manner, set feet to moving, even in the world's finest social circles. People danced to lose weight or to be rejuvenated, and some of the best medical minds believed that dancing aided digestion . . . dancing made people, whatever their origins, feel the equal of anyone in society.[64]

The production side of the process was also being deterritorialized. The popular figureheads of the dance craze were the famous ballroom dancing couple, Vernon and Irene Castle, backed by the multiracial Syncopated Society Orchestra, under the leadership of James Europe. The Castles and Europe supervised Victor recording sessions for the new dance records, to ensure that the music was sufficiently "hot" for dancers. The persona of Irene Castle, in particular, played a major part in determining how these new dances and new social behaviors were received by mass audiences: "A free spirit, who served as the embodiment of the liberated woman, Irene smoked cigarettes, was among the first to have her hair bobbed."[65] Columbia made dance records led by their own expert, who, rather than standing stock-still in front of the recording horn, danced the new steps to the music of the studio orchestra while speaking instructions into the horn.[66]

By a kind of participatory complementarity, a similar "loosening up" of decorum occurred on the reception side of the recording apparatus. The parlor phonograph, playing hot dance recordings for domestic social gatherings reconfigured domestic space, predicating extravagant and libidinous movements of bodies, marking out new and, to some extent liberatory, territories.

If the hot dance and later the jazz craze that followed it then undermined some of the more stringent etiquette restrictions of late nineteenth-century gentility, and took recorded dance music away from the rigid territorializations of the military brass bands, it nonetheless instituted new territorial regimes. In one sense the fox-trot and hot dance crazes represented an *embourgeoisement* of the phonograph audience; any phonograph listener might become a vicarious participant in the Castles' glamorous social world, a temporary member of the "make believe ballroom." In contrast, the listener to an operatic phonograph record had only been "allowed" to appreciate and witness, mutely and passively, the supreme talents of the aristocratically connected grand opera singers. The persona of the opera singer on record was too aloof to notice or care how the lowly listener behaved. But the new hot dance record "cared"; it invited listeners to participate, to make precise spatial appropriations within the listening space. It treated the domestic space as though it were a public space, a ballroom. The instructions being spoken out of the phonograph speaker, the syncopated, percussive rhythms, the swaying and swirling strings and clarinets—for all that they may have been liberating, so were they limiting, as if to say, "You may go this far, but no further."

And the new bands that enjoyed the greatest commercial success, similarly, were often those best able to enact simultaneously liberatory and "despotic" elements into their performance. The strictly disciplined, formally dressed, brilliantined "lounge lizard" look of the Paul Whiteman Orchestra well typifies the simultaneous containment and release rituals of the dance-era bands. Although the supper club / cabaret look of the new orchestra might have contrasted with the parade-ground punctilious-ness of the military band, the level of discipline within each was not neces-sarily dissimilar.

Contemporaneous with the dance crazes of the acoustic recording period was a shift in "fine music" recording from opera singers to symphonic re-cordings. Unable to compete with Victor/HMV's opera catalogue, which featured such unassailable luminaries as Caruso, Melba, Tetrazzini and McCormack, British companies signed contracts with famous conductors such as Thomas Beecham and Sir Henry J. Wood, and recorded selections from Tchaikovsky, Stravinsky, Grainger, Richard Strauss, Wagner, Beetho-ven and others.[67] Abridged movements of string quartets were also re-corded. Gelatt writes: "In England and on the Continent, orchestral records had 'arrived' by the end of World War I. Acoustically they were good enough to afford at least moderate satisfaction to critical listeners; commercially they were on a par with the old-style celebrity vocals."[68] He continues: "The pho-nograph was attracting a new kind of listener—the serious intellectual con-noisseur of the arts who collected records with the same gusto as the novels of Virginia Woolf or the poetry of Ezra Pound."[69] In 1923, British novelist Compton Mackenzie and Christopher Stone (very much Gelatt's "new kind of listener") founded the magazine *Gramophone,* with the aim to "review . . . records in the way a literary magazine reviews books."[70]

In keeping with its new domestic importance, as purveyor of hot dance music or classical orchestral selections, the phonograph became larger and ever more elaborately finished: there was a minutely curlicued "Louis XVI" Victrola; a Columbia "Donatello," five feet high and featuring paintings of symbolic figures (Intelligence, Justice, Temperance and Peace); or the "Queen Anne No. 5," finished in Chinese Chippendale. The highest priced domestic units sold for up to two thousand dollars in the United States.[71]

It was into this regime, with its distinct high and low recording cultures, each with its own relatively stable spatial codes, that the electrical recording emerged in the middle of the 1920s. This emergence roughly coincided with the sudden, almost accidental opening up of the "race" and "hillbilly" markets, the former mainly in the U.S. south, the latter worldwide. These happenings in combination set in train whole new spatial codes, both in record production and consumption.

In the mid-1920s two crucial but separate developments in sound recording coincided. The first was the development at Bell Laboratories of a fully electrical recording process. Under the new process, audio input was picked up by condenser microphones (replacing the large fluted horns of the acoustic process), amplified by means of vacuum tubes and recorded using an electromagnetic recording head.[72] At the same time Bell Laboratories developed a much improved acoustic playback device, which used a nine-foot exponential-horn, segmented so as to fit in a domestic phonograph cabinet.[73]

These two separate developments combined to alter dramatically the qualities of recorded sound in three significant ways: gramophone records now played back much louder than before; the recordable frequency range was immediately extended by two and a half octaves, to 100–5000Hz (the very best acoustic recordings had never broken the 168–2000 Hz frequency range); and lastly, recordings became capable of picking up room ambience—of carrying, in other words, significant sonic information about the spaces in which they were made. Of this last point Gelatt says, "the 'atmosphere' surrounding music in the concert hall could now be simulated on records. Musicians were no longer forced to work . . . directly before a recording horn but could play in spacious studios with proper reverberation characteristics."[74]

It was at this point in the mid-1920s that the opposing recording philosophies of "realism" and "romanticism" began to assume major importance. By the time the major recording interests in the United States and Britain began to adopt electrical recording methods, radio broadcasting had already been using microphones for some years. (In the United States, regular live broadcasting of big-name dance bands and orchestras had started as early as 1921.)[75] Much of the technical expertise for early electrical phonograph recording then was provided by technicians already schooled in radio broadcasting, who brought with them the methods, aesthetic premises and prejudices extant in that medium.

The so-called realist school derived from radio practices associated with broadcasting smaller ensembles. Sound sources, whether human voices or musical instruments, were recorded on-mic, in an acoustically dead studio, with all voices[76] then carefully balanced to create an effect of evenness. As one sound engineer wrote in 1930: "In radio broadcasting it usually is desirable to present all sounds as coming from approximately the same plane—that of the microphone. And so levels are raised and lowered to bring all sounds out at approximately the same volume."[77]

Yet another technique, also from radio, arose out of the difficulties engineers had in miking larger orchestras. The use of single microphones led to badly out of balance sound. In response a multiple miking system was devised whereby a number of microphones were so placed as to pick up all parts of the orchestra more evenly. The various inputs were then mixed down into one signal. An inevitable by-product of multiple miking was the intrusion of more "room" into the recording, as more reverberation, echoes and incidental noise were picked up. Separately placed microphones also tended to pick up "spill": the same sound signal recorded by differently placed microphones fractionally apart, creating an out of phase effect, or if far enough apart, an echolike effect. Yet another radio technique derived from radio drama involved slightly off-miking to produce the effect of aural depth. Given the narrow pickup range of early microphones, sounds recorded relatively off-mic tended to sound much "further away" than in fact they were.[78]

With electric recording, suddenly it became possible to represent space in a wholly new way. Earlier "descriptive recordings" such as "Morning on the Farm" had lined up sound effects and provided elaborate verbal cues in order to construct an almost comic-book spatiality. But with electrical recording, suddenly a real sense of spatial depth was possible: the sounds coming out of the phonograph had some of the same sensory qualities as real sounds in a real physical space. Small, varying degrees of reverberation "attached" to separate voices imparted a sense of actual dimensionality, a lifelike roominess in recording. A listener might now apprehend a recording and experience a sense of a physical space, other than the one he was actually occupying.

The potential to record either with or without "depth" then presented record makers with a serious technico-aesthetic problem. A split soon arose whereby it became broadly acceptable to record classical orchestral music so as to include room ambience (and thus aural depth), while "popular music" was in the main recorded "dry," with little or no discernible depth and minimal reverberation. The voices and sounds of high art were accorded virtual sonic space, while low art was denied it. To reprise Read and Welch from chapter 1, the realist approach (that is, depthless recording) provided "an effect of intimacy, *the orchestra and soloist being transported into the living room,* the singer or soloist singing just for you" (my emphasis).[79] Romanticism conversely had the effect of seemingly "bringing the listener into the studio or auditorium."[80]

Classical recording was quick to take advantage of the new capability for aural "largeness." Electrically made recordings of massed choirs were released—led by Columbia's live recording of a choir of 850 singing "Adeste Fideles" (1925).[81] Some commentators like Compton Mackenzie continued to claim a preference for acoustic recordings. This stance was countered by a technical writer at *The Gramophone* who wrote about his disc of "Adeste Fideles": "I brought it home and put it on my . . . gramophone and the result overwhelmed me; it was just as if the doors of my machine were a window opening on to the great hall in which the concert was held."[82] The development of electrical recording, then, with its dramatically increased "fidelity," closed a loop. The spatiality of the concert hall was virtually overlaid upon the space of the home; in a sense, it obliterated the domestic space. The home listener was granted a virtual access to the acoustic regime of the concert hall, an acoustic regime that had already embedded in it whole ensembles of history and class and race politics, highly ordered codes of privilege and exclusion. The aura of sacralized "high art" carried a pointed implication: it was incumbent upon the listener to prove himself worthy of the art, rather than vice versa.

But the spatialities were not necessarily all simply metaphoric codes of class and exclusion. Apart from extrinsic political territorializations, there were intrinsic, prior musical spatialities, best typified by the steadily increasing "pictoriality" in Western orchestral music. In a development that roughly corresponded with the rise of landscape painting, eighteenth-century European composers such as Vivaldi, Handel, or Haydn used musical means to denote events (and sites) in nature: the trilling of piccolos and flutes to represent birds, crescendos to denote the storm and so on. "The descriptive piece of music [of Handel, Haydn and Vivaldi]," says Schafer, "turns the walls of the concert hall into windows, exposed to the country."[83]

As discussed in chapter 1, dynamic variations may have a strongly spatial subjective effect: an orchestra instrument voiced softly might suggest relatively greater distance from the listener; higher amplitude, nearness. Furthermore, the rises and falls in melodic lines might suggest the existence of a vertical spatial axis—we speak of "high" and "low" notes. Purely scalar effects might then suggest movements through space, ascents to the heavens or descents to the underworld. By the nineteenth century, scalar renderings of vertical space, the use of amplitude dynamics to suggest horizontal space, and the use of particular instrument timbres to imitate "real world" sounds all combined to create in European orchestral music a new, much heightened sense of "dimensionality." Even the most nondescript, abstract music, music that did not seek to suggest actual space or to "be about" anything, was nonetheless constructed within the same dynamic spatial planes.

Thus orchestral music came to have a kind of world-making capability. With the coming of romanticism, these worlds became in turn emblems or externalizations of the composer's (and, to an extent, the conductor's) inner state; the musical landscapes (and by implication actual landscapes) became a "screen" onto which was projected the inner state of the composer. The imagined world was an emanation of the soul. Under romanticism, the "great artist" became a world-creating demiurge, singularly empowered to fabricate the sublime dreamed world—be it rendered in musical, visual or textual terms. The represented outer world thus is turned inside out, the chain of reference moving back one remove: the orchestra "refers to" outer, natural spaces (or something like them), which in turn refer to, or are contained within the inner world of the composer.

As a number of commentators have pointed out, the increasing discipline and complexity of the symphony orchestra roughly paralleled the increasing complexities and disciplines of the nineteenth-century factory.[84] The composer might be seen as the entrepreneur, the controller of the productive forces, while the conductor is a kind of plant manager.[85] The members of the orchestra must remain attached to their instruments, in their respective sections of the orchestra, their bodily movements restricted to only those required to operate their instrument (not unlike the requirements put upon factory workers). The audience members listen reverentially, sitting stiffly in their seats, held in place by the strictures of "good manners," of correct public behavior. The conductor alone is allowed freedom of movement; he may gesture extravagantly, his face may contort and his hair may become disheveled as he is transported by his musical passions. He may chide members of the orchestra, or even the audience; he may even refuse to play if all is not to his satisfaction.[86]

The composer and conductor then have dominion over the spatiality; they oversee and direct its construction, and they alone are privileged to range across it. The private ownership of the playback apparatus and expensive orchestral recordings imbued the gramophone owner with a sense of reverence and duty toward the apparatus. The spatial constraints of the concert hall were "transmitted" via the recording, to the listening space. The territorializing power of the concert hall (itself an enactment of haute bourgeois hegemony) was to operate, via the apparatus, within the listener's very parlor.[87]

But the parlor was nonetheless private space, and an artistically literate and socially empowered bourgeois gentleman such as Compton Mackenzie specifically opposed the territorializing force of the apparatus. The power codings of the symphonic gramophone record conflicted with his own class- and gender-based sense of dominion over private space. Indeed, his aim in founding *The Gramophone*, to "review records in the way a literary magazine reviews books" was a kind of taking back of dominion over space, a reassertion of autonomy; his and his associates' aim was to "talk back" to the apparatus. In the founding issue, Mackenzie thus irreverently suggests that chamber music might be played in the morning as an accompaniment to the listener's preparations for the day, the first couple of movements played while the listener has his morning shave.[88] The joke's mild roguishness is predicated on an awareness of the gramophone's domestic spatial "laws." Mackenzie and his ilk, it implies, as privileged, musically literate listeners are above the petit bourgeois, proxemic dictates that the apparatus would seek to impose. While the apparatus is in his possession, in his house, he will use it as he sees fit.[89]

High-art performers were generally shrouded in a pseudoaristocratic mystique that rendered their audiences as little more than humble supplicants. Dance orchestras, vaudeville artists, humorists, reciters and whistlers, on the other hand, played the part of humble supplicants to their audiences. High art might have been seen as bettering and uplifting its audiences but the sole benefit that more quotidian entertainments were seen to be offering was at best a temporary diversion for the duration of the performance and no longer.[90] The contract in the latter case is quite straightforward: the audience member has paid someone who really is "no better than them" (indeed perhaps of considerably lower social status) to provide a service. The relationship more resembles that between a tradesperson and a client.

The mere entertainer (as opposed to the "artist"), approaches his audience humbly, with elaborate courtesy, begging its indulgence. In requesting the audience's close attention, the entertainer is in effect intruding on the audience's psychic "space," appropriating *its* time. In the case of the dance orchestra, the contract is even more specifically "trades": the musicians are paid to provide a highly proscribed musical program. In a cabaret or ballroom setting, the musicians' role and status might most resemble that of the waiters, doormen and so on; they are, at base, paid functionaries. In the dance orchestra boom of the teens and 1920s, however, leading bands commanded high fees, and bandleaders such as Paul Whiteman, Leo Reisman and Fred Waring were clearly high-status individuals. Nevertheless, it is unlikely that they would have been talked about then as bearing any kind of immanent "greatness." Underlying their success was the clear understanding that their high status was dependent on their being able to provide high-quality service to their audiences, to "deliver the goods."

Pre-electric recordings, made before any significant spatiality was even possible, fell in with these existing social codes. The recording was always "on its best behavior," even in its most apparently informal manifestation: the frantic "hot dance" rhythms might have parodied the martial correctness of the brass band, but the lines of discipline within the orchestra held nonetheless. With electric recording and the possibility of aural "space" being included on the recording, it is not difficult to see how (relative) depthlessness became the rule.

The electric-era popular recording might also be typified as a kind of skilled tradesman, visiting the home in order to perform a service. Such a visitor would be expected to mind his manners, to not take liberties. Sonically, the aural regime of the house, the "rules of the house" perhaps, take precedence over the whims of the self-effacing visitor. The high classical recording might enter the humble abode rather more grandly, more like an aristocratic visitor. The householders make special allowances. The most comfortable chair is made available, the good china brought out. The visitor's whims are indulged. He is allowed to territorialize the space. The high classical recording's own (virtual) spatial codes "trump" those of the actual space in which it is played. But the popular music recording was there for the buyer's benefit, rather than vice versa.[91] It was "product" rather than "art." It was without "aura."[92]

As a commodity, the phonograph sound recording strove to present a closed seamlessness, a "gloss" that excluded negatives, contraries and misgivings. In audio production terms, this effect was realized through the "single plane" aesthetic, the conceit that all sounds were emanating from the one plane (even though the amplitudes might vary between voices). The mainstream Western popular recorded music of the period 1925–1935 demonstrates in the main a notable degree of relaxed professionalism in the work of the singers and vocal groups, and a high-level, unhurried, unfussed combinatory competence in the work of ensemble instrumentalists. Tin Pan Alley popular music of that time by and large seems to fully and nearly perfectly "occupy its territory," so much so that there is generally little or no sense of territory. The sound just is. There is little reverberation or echo to suggest a space incompletely or ambiguously occupied. The insouciant, nagging, disquieting voice of the mythical Echo has here been all but excluded. There is no "other" lurking just out of sight, just offstage.[93]

This new textural closure was achieved in a short time. The differences between, say, Paul Whiteman and His Orchestra's acoustically recorded "Whispering" (1920) or Isham Jones Orchestra's "Swingin' Down the Lane" (1923) on the one hand and such early electric recordings as "Three O'Clock in the Morning" or "Changes" (both by the Whiteman band, 1926 and 1927 respectively) are particularly marked. The electric recordings with their greatly increased frequency response demonstrate a much enhanced warmth, or swelling of the lower frequencies, that both enables low-register instrumental harmonies and "rounds out" the timbre of mid- and higher register voices.

But the effect is much more than strictly timbral. The rich, warm, lower register harmonies that electric recording enabled were best shown off at less frantic tempi, and bandleaders, arrangers and producers were quick to experiment with the new sonic potentials. The result was a sudden loosening in feel, an easing of the mechanistic, "crazy clockwork" sound of the earlier hot dance records.[94] The early electric recordings often suggest a certain louche, indolent quality, perhaps best and most famously demonstrated in the emergence of the crooners in the late 1920s.

Recording engineers and musicians of the early electric period nonetheless were able to achieve remarkable consistency and evenness of texture. Indeed, the flowing, graceful parallel lines of the instrumental voices and vocal harmonies, the warm, smooth-toned clarinets and cellos and the closely synchronized reeds—all combined to create a kind of sonic analogue to the molded chrome, lacquer and Bakelite look of art deco consumer products and architecture.[95] The relaxed, polished ambience of early electrical recording, however, was paradoxically dependent on stringent internal disciplines. While realist recording practice sought to locate all voices on the one imaginary plane, it did not in the case of the big orchestras accord equal value to all voices. Indeed, ensemble voices are so compressed that individual sonic identity is frequently effaced. Strings, for example, are so blended that most listeners would not be able to discern individual voices within the harmonies. Vocalists and soloists on the other hand are selectively forefronted; not through the deployment or particular absence of reverb but simply through the use of amplitude differentials— louder rather than softer. The popular ensemble in the Whiteman, Waring, Lombardo style is typified by this strict (though variable) sonic hierarchizing. Every voice had to "know its place."

Which is not to say that depthless recording was necessarily inherently repressive. Mainstream realist recording practice was able to, at times, produce "democratic" refiguring of sonic hierarchies. A notable feature of the recordings of the various Count Basie–led bands, for instance, made from the mid-1930s through to the 1950s, is the ever present vamped guitar strumming of Freddie Green. Regardless of how "hard driving" the front line is, the guitar is almost continually up front—at the very least, present—in the mix. Green played a relatively quiet f-hole–type acoustic guitar, which he strummed in a steady, controlled style. During the thirties, the steel string guitar in a band setting was still most often regarded as a member of the rhythm section, part of the "second line"; guitarists rarely took solos. But here the second-line voices are accorded an importance on par with the front-line voices—directing equal attention to the "engine room" of the band and undermining the privilege of the front line. The rhythm section is doing much more than simply providing the beat. It is adding enhanced harmonic qualities to the rhythm, adding greatly to the complexity and subtleties of the rhythm, providing whole new complexes of what Keil calls "participatory discrepancies": microtonal and microtemporal "out of tune" and "out of time–ness" that serve to involve the audience and create what might be called "color," "drive," "swing," "groove."[96] Whereas the strictly arranged, strictly disciplined Whiteman/Waring/Lombardo bands "deproblematized" relationships between voices by hierarchizing all, in the recorded music of the Basie band (and many others) whole networks of relationship—and new potentialities for discord—are opened up. The number of musical relationships between voices grows exponentially. But rather than producing cacophony (in the case of the Basie band at least) the big band sense of grace and ease was combined with the drive and spontaneity more usually associated with smaller jazz group recordings, the influential recordings of Louis Armstrong and the Hot Five. The effect is of an energized but comfortable, dehierarchized relationship between figure and ground.

Perhaps not surprisingly, the Basie band is regarded by many as the single most evolved exponent of "hard-driving" swing music. It laid the stylistic basis for the Benny Goodman, Artie Shaw and Glenn Miller big bands that so dominated the popular music industry through the late 1930s and 1940s, as well as for both bebop and the jump boogie rhythm and blues of the postwar period. The Basie band's "combinatory democracy" production philosophy stands in sharp contrast to the "combinatory despotism" of the Whiteman/Lombardo/Waring–style bands. But both effects were enabled by the so-called realist production methodologies.

CHAPTER 3

"Way Out There"

Hillbilly, Blues and Jazz

⊢◆⊣

Echoes from the Hills

"All right, boys, this is Frank Hutchison, setting back in the Union Square Hotel, just getting right on good red liquor. All right, Frank, step on it!" So interjects hillbilly singer/guitarist Frank Hutchison one minute and thirty-five seconds into his 1929 Okeh recording, "KC Blues." Other than that single utterance, the recording is wholly instrumental, played finger-picking style on slide guitar. The recording is one of the last of a handful made by this Kentucky / West Virginian performer between 1926 and 1929.

If "realist" recordings, as discussed in the previous chapter strove for a depthless character, they were also "placeless." The exact location of their origins, the place in which the music was performed and recorded was not normally part of the surface of the product. New York, London, Berlin, Hollywood or Shanghai—the location of the recording was rendered as no more important to buyers than the location of the factory where it was pressed, or the mill where the paper for the label was processed.[1] The valences of the popular recording were directed outward, toward listeners rather than "backward," toward the recording's own origins. The actual place, the actual personalities and circumstances of its manufacture were repressed. What was presented instead were professional personae, hovering in no place, other than the place where the record was played.[2]

Hutchison's seemingly spontaneous interjection undermines the conceit of free valency, of total availability to the consumer. He declares precisely where he is (the Union Square Hotel) and gives gratuitous though significant information about his exact circumstances at that moment (the fact that he has been "getting right on good red liquor"). When combined with other paralinguistic and musical signifiers on the recording—in particular, Hutchison's unforced, "conversational" southern accent, and the sly, bluesy insouciance of the delicately picked slide guitar licks—a complex presence is denoted, one that is specifically nonurban, nonnorthern, non mainstream, nonbourgeois, but knowing and self-determining. Deterritorialized. Suddenly the recording has "character," "backstory." Rather than simply being music, this recording is about a specific person, a specific personality at a precise time and place.

And when we know that the Union Square Hotel was in New York City where the recording was made, but that such recordings were produced for sale in regional markets (the southern United States, in this case) then Hutchison's utterance takes on further resonances: he is talking, winking in a sense, to the "folks" back home, perhaps "showing off" about being in New York City. We cannot know who Hutchison had in mind when he addressed the "folks"—whether he imagined a corps of dedicated record buyers and radio listeners from his own hometown in Kentucky, or the much broader (by 1929) global municipality of listeners to hillbilly music. His cavalier refusal to be daunted by the potential enormity of his audience itself enacts a powerful reversal of territorializing flows, but one that had by then become not unusual in "hillbilly" and "race" recording.

While not especially reverberant in production terms, the recording nonetheless demonstrates a playful disregard for the "rules" of realist popular recording. Rather than conforming to the standards of slickness and performer anonymity, it carries its own set of idiosyncratic "backward" attachments, its own cathexes with the real. Rather than a "pitch" delivered by a stage/recording persona, this recording declares, "actual person—real place." Which is not to say it is not "constructed."[3] It is, but in "KC Blues" idiosyncratic traces of the actual are integral inclusions in the construction.

"KC Blues" was made at the height of the hillbilly music craze, which is generally considered to date from 1923, with Okeh's recording of Fiddlin' John Carson (or alternatively, from 1924 with Victor's million-selling recording of Vernon Dalhart's "The Prisoner's Song" / "Wreck of the Old 97") until the beginning of the Depression, when record sales fell into a major slump.[4] At its peak in 1930 it was estimated that in the United States, a quarter or more of all popular records sold fell into the hillbilly / "Old Familiar Tunes" category.[5]

Measured against the standards of aural decorum manifest in mainstream popular recordings of the 1920s, Frank Hutchison's record of "KC Blues" clearly transgresses. Hutchison's claims for spatial autonomy, however, are by no means unusual when seen in the context of the large corpus of "hillbilly," "race" and other ethnic and fringe-market recording carried out by major U.S. labels, notably Columbia and Victor, in the 1920s. Researcher Pat Conte describes the period:

[The] most marvelous decade of recorded music—the 1920s—came about in a natural progression from the days of 'experimental marketing' (where recordists and their equipment toured the globe's centers and niches in vigorous pursuit of the saleable) to the days when such an uncanny savvy for preservation, accidental or not became almost commonplace. . . . [At] the height of the fever brought about by a new technology, and in the ensuing years as the microphone art neared perfection, 'aural oddities,' which could very well have included examples of 1,000-year-old musical styles, were gathered up for the amusement of a most often undefined audience. . . .

Brought back in hopes of profit were examples of nearly every land imaginable, of ritual and social dance, balladeers and bards, court music for royalty, music of secret societies and ceremony, street comics and beggars, puppeteers and a myriad of non-western art-songs, opera, classical and so on.[6]

The global recording expeditions of the 1920s were in many ways a continuation of the exploratory sound recording and market-defining work done by Fred Gaisberg earlier in the century (see chapter 2), and the range of impacts this fringe recording activity had back on mainstream practice is yet to be fully examined. Similarly, the micropolitics of the various exchanges and interactions surrounding local sound recording and the regional marketing of records remains largely obscure, and outside the scope of this study. As Conte points out, sometimes "ethnic" recording "froze" in time music that was never intended by its makers to last; at other times, near extinct preindustrial musics were "captured" and "preserved." Sometimes this niche-marketing recording product remained, to larger markets at least, impossibly exotic, esoteric and marginal.[7]

Within the United States, the project of recording obscure singers and instrumentalists from the southern states was part of a larger project to record and market the musics of Yiddish, Russian, Czech, Irish, Mexican and other émigré subcultures. The significant difference with hillbilly and race recording was that at least some recordings and certain artists spectacularly broke out of their subcultural confines. Some "race" recordings, originally targeted at African American markets (for example, the recordings of such people as Bessie Smith, King Oliver, Louis Armstrong, Fletcher Henderson and Duke Ellington) had a profound and near immediate worldwide musical impact. Similarly, some hillbilly recordings, most famously those of Jimmie Rodgers and the Carter family, also rapidly achieved wide distribution in England, Europe, India, Oceania and Africa. Thus, unlike most other "ethnic" recording, at least some race and hillbilly recording fed directly back into the urban cultural hubs and became itself part of intercultural export "packages." While the bulk of regional race and hillbilly recording output remained in the regions, serving local markets, at least some product became part of the larger dialogues, and the often "accidental" and idiosyncratic recording and production practices evidenced therein were transmitted back to the cultural centers, and were to exert major influences on mainstream production practice.[8] At the same time early southern race and hillbilly recording quickly achieved a semiautonomous life of their own, and formed a large part of the stylistic ground from which the makers of postwar southern music—R & B, blues, rockabilly and rock 'n' roll—sprang.

More specifically, practices such as Frank Hutchison's impromptu direct address to listeners, signaled the existence of a new attitude toward the recording apparatus. The refusal to be cowed by the apparatus became the basis of an entire postwar "alternative" recording posture, that was in time to inform and largely define the dominant postures of rock 'n' roll and late twentieth-century rock. Erving Goffman provides another context in which Hutchison's interjection might be viewed, and that may prove useful to understanding the practices that followed:

One overall objective of any team is to sustain the definition of the situation that its performance fosters. This will involve the over-communication of some facts and under-communication of others. Given the fragility and required expressive coherence of the reality which is dramatized by performance, there are usually facts which, if attention is drawn to them during the performance, would discredit, disrupt or make useless the impression that the performance fosters . . . a basic problem of many performances is information control; the audience must not acquire destructive information about the situation that is being defined for them.[9]

Goffman uses the metaphors of "actors," "performance," "front" and "staging" to characterize processes of self-representation in everyday life, but his remarks apply no less to "performance" in its more literal sense (that is, musical performance) and provide insights into particular public/private ambiguities that obtained in popular music recording. The processes and procedures of making the recording, the precise circumstances inside the "studio," and usually the location of the studio—all this composes "backstage" information; and, as Goffman suggests, information from backstage has the potential to critically undermine the conceits being woven on stage, for the audience. Information from backstage threatens to unmake the territories on stage.

In the 1920s this situation clearly obtained in popular music recording. As described in the previous chapter, as a relatively new apparatus in homes and public places, the behavioral codes surrounding the gramophone were new and still "unfixed." The "default" code for behavior on the record side of the apparatus was one of high decorum. Extraneous sounds and utterances had no place, nor did references to recording's own means and practices of production. Hutchison's extemporized statement is in the "backstage" realm. But it is more than the sonic equivalent of an accidental filmic gaffe such as "boom in shot." Hutchison deliberately "invites" listeners backstage, so to speak, and in so doing willfully disregards the privilege of the "front of house," the product gloss. He not only invites listeners backstage, he all but shares his bootleg liquor with them. The "front of house" construct, he implies, is little more than a pompous folly. "*Here* I am," Hutchison is saying, "backstage." If listeners wish to "make contact," backstage is where to find him. And in declaring his territory so clearly, Hutchison increases his own cachet. He shows himself to be up to the task of challenging the territorializing forces of the apparatus.

But Hutchison is nonetheless performing. He is producing a piece of recorded music for which he presumably had high commercial hopes. In many ways, in Hutchison might be seen an early exemplar of what was to become the tradition of the righteously "down-home authentic." The persona that Hutchison presents might in the end be every bit as much a performance as those given by the most straight-faced, tuxedo-wearing popular singer contemporary. But Hutchison's type of performance was of a new order, and drew directly on the behavioral practices drawn from the singer's everyday life. Hutchison does not in the end deconstruct the dichotomy of "front" and "backstage," but he draws them nearer to each other. Implicit in Hutchison is the idea that the elaborately staged bourgeois recording front is nothing but a vanity. What Hutchison brings to the front instead is an unprecedented admixture of the private self.[10] Over the following half century, recording would come to rely more and more on such inclusions of the actual, and performances that made no attempt to include at least a little of the everyday, the "genuine" or the eccentric would come to sound ever more staged and pompous.

But Hutchison himself in his own day remained largely marginal to the process; he retired from recording soon after "KC Blues" (to run a store in his native Kentucky). Perhaps the most fully realized, if more polished instance of this posture is to be found in the recordings of Jimmie Rodgers, who not only brings to recording a new kind of personal insouciance and strongly asserted selfhood, but also one of the earliest and most consistent uses of managed reverb in vernacular, nonclassical recording.

Jimmie Rodgers' recording career began on the same day as that of the Carter Family, on August 4, 1927, when both arrived at a Bristol, Tennessee, hotel room to audition for Ralph Peer, field recording pioneer and, at that time, Victor's leading artists and repertoire (A & R) man. Both acts went on to legendary successes, and each has since been accorded key originary roles in the emergence of country music as a genre. Rodgers exerted immense influence, both immediate and long-term on country music, and he remains an iconic figure in the discourses associated with the genre. His blending of blues, vaudeville, Tin Pan Alley and "old time" stylings helped set one of country music's broad agendas; his instrumentation, particularly the frequent deployment of Hawaiian guitar on his recordings helped set country music's textural/instrumental agenda; and his own persona, that of the amiable, charming "rounder," the working man/drifter and "friend of the little guy" helped fix the class coloration of country music. The brevity of his recording career (from 1927 to 1933, when he died of tuberculosis) also helped "concrete in" the trope of the tragic, untimely end to the short, brilliant career—which was to become almost a cliché of country and later rock music.

But of greater importance to this study is the extent to which Rodgers was able to project so much "personality" to his public. Certainly there were interviews in newspapers, occasional radio programs and some magazine articles about Rodgers while he was still living, but there was very little that resembled the publicity machinery associated with even a middle rank or minor star of later years. While publicity photographs, reproduced on sheet music covers and songbooks did much to convey the Rodgers persona, I believe most of the "information" about Rodgers was disseminated by the recordings themselves. And within the recordings the Rodgers posture was enacted as much by the skillfully controlled use of production devices, as by strictly musical and verbal contents.

"Blue Yodel No. 1 (T For Texas)," recorded at Rodgers' second recording session (November 1927) might be pinpointed as a landmark moment in the history of popular recording production practice. The recording begins with a simple three-note bass run on the acoustic guitar that settles into a "boom-ching" strumming pattern. This guitar playing would be at the most rudimentary end of the technical expertise spectrum for a popular release in the 1920s. The guitar sound, however, is particularly "large." Bass tonalities are richly present, as are the "steely" higher frequency overtones, but overall the small-bodied Martin guitar produces a stridently *mid*range sound. There is a clearly discernible reverberant quality to the guitar, and the playing volume is without noticeable fluctuations. Even before the vocal has begun, effects have been achieved. There is a spatiality here, the sort of virtual "depth" normally reserved only for "high" classical recording. There is an implicit space to be occupied, and the "voice"—the acoustic guitar—is not for a moment overwhelmed or intimidated. Instead it calmly and confidently "takes possession" of the sonic space. Indeed, the clarity and sonic "authority" of the guitar playing, basic though it is, anticipates qualities (especially the aggressively mid-range bias) that would much later come to be associated with electric guitar in the blues and rock 'n' roll era.[11]

Like the guitar sound, Rodgers' voice has a strongly reverberant "authority within the space." He makes playful asides between verses ("hey, hey," "lord, lord!" and "sing 'em boy!"), yodels with exuberant abandon (as though he is particularly enjoying the acoustics of the studio), employs a seemingly careless rubato, and makes no effort to suppress his southern accent, especially evident on words such as "water," "hollow" and "barrel."

The sum effect of these sonic codings is to present to the listener a remarkably complete sense of an actual personality. Unlike the persona of the rube act, by then an already old vaudeville and recording staple, the projected personality here is quotidian. In this and other Rodgers recordings, there is a strongly conveyed sonic "comfortableness"; the sense that much of and about the actual Jimmie Rodgers is being transmitted via the recording. The authenticity of this and other Rodgers records (and on hillbilly recordings in general) may have itself been a contrivance of sorts, but it was a contrivance that referred to and elevated the vernacular, the everyday. The process whereby these relatively uncontrolled, "unprofessional" behaviors became part of the finished recorded product, in direct contravention of the reigning sonic etiquettes was an innovation of considerable importance for popular music recording. Rodgers deterritorialized and reconfigured the recording space so to allow vernacular artists the sort of sonic privilege that had hitherto been reserved for the highest of highbrow performers.

In fact, Rodgers had literally strayed into high-art recording territory. The session at which "T for Texas" was recorded was held at Victor's flagship studio, the former Trinity Baptist Church in Camden, New Jersey. The building had originally been purchased and fitted out in the hope that its uniquely reverberant acoustics might help the company lure Leopold Stokowski to record for them. Rodgers demonstrated sonic mastery within that potentially daunting environment, and later replicated that acoustic control elsewhere; the powerful guitar and voice qualities described above recur throughout Rodgers' recorded oeuvre, regardless of where the recordings were made.

Prior to recording for Victor, Rodgers had long focused his attentions on recording per se and it is significant that Rodgers' southern "superstar" status followed almost entirely from his success as a *recording* artist; Rodgers had been a spectacularly unsuccessful and chronically impecunious entertainer before his recording career began.[12] His biographer Nolan Porterfield suggests that Rodgers' primary aim had always been to make it as a recording star. He had long made a habit of buying and closely analyzing phonograph records "by the ton," according to his widow, Carrie Rodgers.[13] He listened to records repeatedly

> to learn whatever he could. In the process he inadvertently came upon the crucial elements that distinguish recorded performances from live ones, and developed into a discerning judge of what may be termed "recording presence," . . . he was drawn almost instinctively to the vitality a performer might transmit on record, the clarity of his pronunciation, the organic relationship between voice and instrument.[14]

Rodgers, Hutchison and others, in their different ways enacted a powerfully demotic move, acquired a new kind of public voice, a new way of occupying virtual space: they were both setting up and taking control of sonic spaces in ways hitherto only associated with the most highbrow of classical artists, but with the added cachet of spontaneity and improvisational license. There was an implicit strongly anti–class privilege political tinge to this, one that has remained available to popular music recording ever since. It is perhaps of little surprise that some of the most overtly leftist political musicians of the time—Woody Guthrie, Goebbel Reeves, "Mac" McClintock and others—would draw directly on the styles of Rodgers, Hutchison and the Carter Family.[15]

But the sound semiotic of Rodgers' records remains essentially populist. The "everyday" accent, the use of material drawn from a broad base and played in a range of different styles, the reverberant acoustic "framing" of the sound on record—all bespoke a powerful populist message, that of the Everyman exalted, recalling Huey Long's famous populist slogan, "every man a king." Rodgers' persona was hardly regal, however. The sonic record in combination with the photographs and interviews that circulated at the time all went to suggest an amiable, resolutely informal "little guy," a charming rounder who is, for now at least, holding money and prepared to buy drinks all round, a drifter and roué experiencing a well-earned run of luck. At the same time, should his luck turn bad again, the character will take it in good part: not through a dogged, denying of pain and suffering, but rather through a courageous willingness to face and fully experience the pain and darkness, and ultimately sublimate it into "art"—a "blues" consciousness, perhaps.

One more point should be made about hillbilly, race and fringe market recording in the 1920s: by and large it was carried out in the shadow of recording industry "best practice," and was frequently regarded by technicians, A & R men and company executives as something of an embarrassment. For people who had recently near perfected electrical recording of large orchestras, dance bands, crooners and opera singers—the products of which were distributed via sophisticated global marketing structures—the appearance in the studio (and in catalogues) of "primitive," undisciplined, often untutored rural entertainers was often seen as running embarrassingly counter to company policy.[16] In fact, the same day that Rodgers recorded his four sides at the Camden Studio, one of the most famous Victor dance orchestras of the day, Fred Waring and His Pennsylvanians had been in the studio, recording what was to be a hit for them, "I Scream, You Scream, We All Scream for Ice Cream."[17] The highly paid, highly professional Waring orchestra wore tuxedos for their sessions, and Jimmie Rodgers must have represented a particularly maverick presence in contrast.

At the same time, however, the general disdain of the industry for this low-cost, "low-tech" corner of their enterprise allowed performers a unique freedom. For artists like Rodgers, individuals with sufficient personal confidence and "front" to follow a band like Waring's into the highest tech studio of the day and not be intimidated, the studio represented a kind of New World, an open, deterritorialized space. Part of what even modern listeners might hear in Rodgers' recording of three-quarters of a century ago is the exuberant assertion of self within that newly accessed space.

Significantly, at least one extremely popular recording artist from the Tin Pan Alley mainstream, contemporary with Rodgers, did on occasion employ reverberation. Gene Austin, although perhaps not so well known today as Rudy Vallee or Bing Crosby, was by far the most successful crooner of the 1920s. His 1927 recording of "My Blue Heaven" sold more than five million copies, making it the most successful recording of the 1920s and one of the biggest-selling sound recordings of all time.[18] Austin was a particular favorite of Rodgers, and was to become in time a close personal friend.[19] The points of similarity and difference between Austin's "My Blue Heaven" and Rodgers' Camden session are instructive.

"My Blue Heaven" begins with a reverberant, off-microphone cello and piano, gently playing the recitative. The lyrics—sung on-mic and recorded "dry"—describe the scene, using sentimental, romantic images and rhymes typical of 1920s Tin Pan Alley songwriting:

> Day is ending
> Birds are wending
> Back to the shelter of
> Each little nest they love.
>
> Night shades falling
> Love birds calling
> What makes the world go round?
> Nothing but love.
>
> . . . .

When whippoorwill calls and evening is nigh
I hurry to my blue heaven.
I turn to the right, a little white light
Will lead you to my blue heaven

A smiling face, a fireplace, a cozy room
A little nest that's nestled where the roses bloom
Just Molly and me, and baby makes three
We're happy in my blue heaven

The reverberant cello and piano are in contrast to the close-miked, open-throated voice of the singer. The establishment of the sonic near and far is wholly in step with the verbal scene-setting. The spatiality here is primarily pictorial.

The spatialities set up by Rodgers and Hutchison on the other hand are not "anchored" to the pictorial. Their "spaces" are not so much a sonic mise en scène, as simply an assertion of each one's own personhood, existential rather than pictorial. But with Austin's recording, too, a different recording tradition was, if not set in motion, then at least given wide currency. The deployment of echo and reverb in the sonic evocation of *occluded* space was to become a standard device in singing cowboy music (discussed in chapter 4) and in cinema sound effects. In time, crepuscular scenes, whether urban or rural, in which supernatural or worldly presences lurk unseen came to be significations strongly associated with echoic/reverberant sound recording. Here, however the effect is entirely benign; the distant, reverberant cello in contrast with the intimate voice conveys a sense of dimensionality characterized by a restful stillness. The domestic idyll so rendered may be criticized as being not particularly "verité" perhaps, but it is not without its own highly wrought charm.

The Austin recording represented industry "best practice." Its spaces are already territorialized. The "hollow," open-throated, early crooner voice tonalities (which soon after came to sound contrived, even parodic) and the use of "poetic" rhymes and archaisms ("When evening is nigh")—all serve to idealize the scene, and move the text away from the unself-conscious and everyday. Indeed, the production sought to improve on the real, in a way reminiscent of the nineteenth- and early twentieth-century genre painting tradition. The lyrics, the instrumentation, the recorded spatialities and other sonic codings here are all in accord with one another: they are suggestive of the singer's quietist contentment with his modest ambitions and the modest rewards they bring. Contradictions and conflicts submerge, fade in the enchanting half-light surrounding the bungalow. This recording is spatial, but its spaces are depoliticized, deproblematized. The space conjured up here is out of the way, a suburban niche, "a little nest that nestles where the roses bloom." The sole sovereignties "allowed" are all firmly in the private, familial realm. The recording pointedly refuses to allude to, to comment on larger, contested public zones. Austin purports to speak of the private, personal realm, the intimate "backstage" of workday life, but his means of portraying it are resolutely of the most highly staged, "front of house," performance traditions of the day.

Rodgers on the other hand "would rather drink muddy water, sleep in hollow log / than to be in Atlanta, treated like a dirty dog." Elsewhere he sings that "Portland, Maine, is just the same as sunny Tennessee / Any place I hang my hat is home sweet home to me"). As well as financial, material and sexual ambitions these recordings have broad territorial ambitions. And where Austin presents a stage persona, the Rodgers recordings gesture toward the richness and complexity of a "real," "live" presence, one that refused, or simply lacked the requisite professional polish to fully knuckle under to the disciplines of the studio. The records' rich sonic field contains whole complexes of nuance and "actuality"—the same microtraces that mainstream Tin Pan Alley recording deliberately sought to exclude. It should also be noted that Rodgers was apparently just as happy to perform material every bit as conventional as Austin's: songs of high sentimentality, novelty songs and so on. For every "rounder song" like "T for Texas," Rodgers had a number like "Mother, Queen of My Heart" (1932).

Victor's (and other companies') casting of southern vernacular performers as local exotics may well have been a major aid in developing the highly differentiated, deterritorializing performance practices that they did. Framed as others from the outset, performers such as Hutchison, Rodgers and the Carter Family were almost expected to be outlandishly different in some way. Perhaps this gave them a head start for innovatory practice over more mainstream, nonsouthern performers. In many ways, recordings by Rodgers, Hutchison and the Carter Family might not present to modern listeners as especially "old-fashioned," despite their old-timey leanings. The use of generic, often unconnected verse fragments from blues and old-time music gives many of their songs an almost haiku brevity, an open, freely associative nonspecificity more consistent with the literary codes of high art. Their refusal or inability to employ the "fruity," overcoded techniques of their popular singer contemporaries forced them to bring other techniques and devices into the studio. The Carter Family drew on their own domestic music-making practices; Rodgers brought to the studio space an early version of "good ol' boy" amiability;[20] if it was a shtick, it was one in which the front of house and backstage personae were in close accord. The close listener was automatically partly "conveyed" to some undercoded, only partly defined offstage zone. The recorded field had attained a new spatial ambiguity.

"Hear that Wind Howl": Robert Johnson and Intensive Studio Space

Robert Johnson has been the subject of at least four distinct waves of interest, beginning in his own lifetime, when word of his uncanny singing and guitar-playing abilities and charismatic presence spread among mostly African American followers of country blues in the Mississippi Delta region. His modestly selling ARC recordings of the 1930s expanded his word-of-mouth notoriety to draw in more widely spread buyers of "race" recordings, including some northern music fans (among them jazz promoter John Hammond). Another wave of interest followed the release of the Columbia LP record *King of the Delta Blues Singers* in 1961 (more than twenty years after the singer's death), which perhaps as much as any other single record stood as flagship of the entire 1960s blues revival in Europe, England and the United States. Yet another "blues wave" occurred through the 1990s, as back-catalogue and noncopyright items were widely reissued on both prestige and budget-priced CDs.

The success in the rock market of singer/guitarists such as Stevie Ray Vaughan has led to a large-scale global marketing of what might be called "blues paraphernalia": expensive replica electric and acoustic resonator guitars, amplifiers, various electronic devices and foot pedals, instruction videos and CDs, books and magazines devoted to the subject. In the United States, Dan Aykroyd's "House of Blues" chain of themed bars attempts to replicate the ambience of southern juke joints for white, middle-class patrons. Through this the Johnson cult has continued to grow, to the point that some fans and researchers have recently begun to question both the hype surrounding Delta blues in general and the long unquestioned privileging of Robert Johnson as the emblematic blues artist.[21]

It is true that both as recording artist and live performer, Robert Johnson was at best a fleeting presence in 1930s popular music. And it is true that the process of "canonization" and felicitation of individual performers in popular music (as elsewhere) has the effect of shifting focus away from movements and their broader social bases while at the same time setting up certain individuals as bearers of an ineffable, intrinsic "greatness." Whole fields of endeavor and expertise are thus forgotten or lost, and the careers of less-feted individuals go unremarked. Until the release of *King of the Delta Blues Singers,* Robert Johnson (and country blues in general) was one of these largely forgotten presences; if today the Johnson cult reinstates the same kind of individualist "unique artistic genius" discourse that left him in obscurity for so long, his recordings nonetheless demonstrate a controlled, deliberate and thoroughly innovatory use of certain production techniques[22] of particular relevance to this study.

It is difficult today to reconcile the evidence of a coolly self-aware, highly realized recording musician with the mythology of the darkly private, supernaturally gifted, fear-driven figure who had allegedly made an unholy compact with voodoo deities at a lonely Delta crossroads. It has long been part of the Johnson mythology, for instance, that at his first recording session, conducted in a hotel room in San Antonio, Texas, Johnson placed himself facing into a corner of the room—too shy, it was said, to face the engineers and other performers present.[23] Certainly, it is not difficult to imagine Johnson being intimidated by the surroundings: a hotel room in the segregated south was hostile territory, a "despotic" territory in Deleuze-Guattarian terms, one that under normal circumstances Johnson as a black man would not even be allowed to enter.

But guitarist Ry Cooder for one has cast doubt on this version of events:

> You know how they talk about how he was nervous and wouldn't face the room? I don't believe that. . . . I'll tell you what he was doing . . . find yourself a plaster corner without wallpaper or curtains sometime—all those hotel rooms were plaster. Go and sit facing the corner with your guitar tight up against the corner, play and see what it sounds like. What you get is something called "corner loading." It's an acoustic principle that eliminates most of the top and bottom end and amplifies the middle, the same thing that a metal or electric guitar does. . . . If you stick your face up into that corner and listen, you'll hear that sound. It ties the notes together and compresses the sound, too.[24]

Although it is quite impossible for us to know Johnson's precise reasons for facing into the corner of the room (although its happening is attested to by an eyewitness), Cooder's thesis has appeal. When the *King of the Delta Blues Singers* LP was first released in the early 1960s, there were no extant photographs of Johnson, and the mythos of the haunted individual stood unchallenged. Photographs have since surfaced, and one, at least, shows a snappily dressed, confident, apparently assertive, broadly smiling Johnson.[25]

Certainly the sonic evidence of the recordings themselves lends weight to Cooder's thesis. An acoustic guitar (or any acoustic instrument) played in a furnished domestic space will tend to produce a relatively "mellow" sound, as higher energy, higher frequency overtones are absorbed by soft furnishings. Played in a bathroom or a hallway however, the same instrument will produce a dramatically louder, more strident sound. A resonant room in fact becomes an extension of the instrument, a kind of larger, secondary resonating chamber (just as the Victor Camden studio did for Jimmie Rodgers' acoustic guitar).

As Cooder points out, corner loading engineers the guitar tonalities. "Mellow," "restful" qualities are sacrificed in favor of a tense, modified sound. In fact to a modern listener, Johnson's guitar frequently suggests the dynamic possibilities and chordal textures of an electric rather than acoustic guitar.[26] Corner loading can have a similarly galvanizing effect on the sound of the voice. This effect in turn then may have a powerful secondary effect on the music producer's experience of his own music. The singer/guitarist facing into the plastered or wood-paneled corner hears his own voice and instrument in a singularly direct, total way, as he becomes immersed in sounds that are of his own making. This gives rise to a literal self-awareness, a much enhanced kind of "self-audiencing." A cybernetically driven intensity becomes possible: the musician is immersed in the sounds that he himself is producing, and that immersion encourages a further Dionysian "abandonment" to the music, expressed as a greater intensity of performance—a more focused concentration, a greater sensitivity to nuance. A feedback loop is set up: the musician makes sounds, the sounds resonate off the walls, the musician hears that resonance, as well as the sounds coming directly from the instrument, and accordingly adjusts and intensifies his own manipulation of the sound-making apparatus, be it voice or instrument. He is now in control of an entire sonic environment. He plays the room.

The experience of music perhaps is at its most intense for both listener and musician when this oceanic sense of immersion is invoked, when the listener is simultaneously contained within a larger, extrapersonal sonic regime, and contains the music within him/herself, where the external music and the most private, personal affect are in accord. The listener/musician immersed in his own ocean of sound is simultaneously agent and object of the music. The listener is contained within the (nondespotic) territory of the music; simultaneously, the music intimately resides within the territory of the self. The satisfactions associated with the "oceanic mode" of musical apprehension might be seen as either a reaching back—a (temporary) recuperation of a long-lost imaginary—or as a reaching forward, a momentary breach of the quotidian sense of the small "self" irrevocably alienated from the larger world, a temporary participation in larger worlds. Both constructions are consistent with a notion of participation, the integration of the self into suprapersonal cybernetic networks.

Corner loading and the manipulation of acoustic amplification in general is an ancient and integral partner in music making. Indeed, it is sometimes suggested that music was invented when cave dwellers first discovered and used the sonorities of maintained pitch inside reverberant caverns.[27] Robert Johnson's deft use of acoustic resonance in corner load-ing was not in itself anything particularly new. But the application of acoustic engineering techniques to recording, especially to a popular music recording session conducted in such makeshift circumstances, in retrospect might be seen as a major landmark in the development of a specifically re-cording sound aesthetic.

It can be assumed that corner loading as Johnson used it was not a tech-nique most suitable for the sort of places where he typically performed: at juke joints, dances and house parties, where the performer literally and metaphorically "aimed" the music at the audience. Corner loading might be seen rather as a practice arising out of solitude, out of long hours of "woodshedding"—extended periods of intense concentration on sound and technique development. Whereas public performance is typically ex-troverted (at least in part), the refining work of sound development sug-gests an almost monkish withdrawal from the world. Up until the time of Robert Johnson's work for ARC, it might be said that popular music re-cording had in the main been more in the extroverted performance mode. Quite literally, the recording artist performed "at" the microphone (or acoustic horn). The record was just that: a sonic facsimile of a perfor-mance, a copy, a secondary, lesser manifestation of the prior event. The per-formance itself was the "real presence," and the recording was a mere trace, an echo of that.

It was suggested above that Jimmie Rodgers' "largeness" as a personality and as a sonic presence enabled him to occupy the existing recording space in a way that previously only high-art performers had dared. The largeness that Rodgers brought to the studio was partly technical (that is, specifically related to how he played and sang), partly culturally geographic (deriving from the literally wide-ranging place references in his lyrics), and partly concerned with personality and personal (the expansive rounder character portrayed again and again in Rodgers' recordings). These in the main were in the public, extroverted, extensive mode.

Robert Johnson on the other hand, while proving himself more than comfortable in this extroverted mode, achieved his most dramatic effects through intensive means. By singing directly into the corner of the room, Johnson enacts a temporary exponential enlarging of his own subjectivity. The room architecture itself is enlisted so as to become a temporary aspect of the self. The walls ring, resonate and echo. (But as with mythic Echo, the resonance continually infers, hints at its own possible autonomy.) The singer hears the resonance that is both self and other, and so amplified, works more deeply, more powerfully, more intensely into his perfor-mance. Rather than being simply "centrifugal," from the center outward, the process involves a complex cybernetic loop. The peripheral partici-pates in the activities of the center, and vice versa.

The recording microphone is carefully, intimately interposed between the singer and the architecture, at the "eye" of this sonic grid. The microphone is itself immersed in the sound (even, as a mechanical "audience" partly com-plicit in its production), but "impossibly" located within the intimate sonic regime. Rather than simply taking a sample of a typical performance, the re-cording apparatus is "inside" the moment in a way that an actual human lis-tener might otherwise never be. The musician, the physical environment and the microphone are compacted in a forceful sonic contract.

While we cannot ultimately know what Johnson's intentions in the hotel room in San Antonio were, it is clear that through corner loading as much as through instrumental technique, Johnson's voice and guitar gained "supercharged" qualities that enabled a hugely enhanced dynamic range. "Small" gestures and nuances, delicately picked licks and high notes, verbal asides and the "accidental" sounds, such as that of the bottleneck rattling against the strings—all became as equally present on the recording as the loudest, most declamatory chord or vocal sounds.

One feature of Johnson's recordings that stands out to a modern listener is how arranged the pieces are, but arranged in ways quite unlike anything else of the time. Johnson's guitar work itself has more in common with the most "angular" melodies and sudden, tightly voiced guitar chords typical of much-later electric guitar music than with the styles of the day. Driving bass riffs are suddenly interrupted by carefully picked high bottleneck licks; a tempo is set up and then is interrupted by a sudden shift to walking bass; or a succession of quick, "choppy" double time, two- or three-note chords are suddenly and unexpectedly inserted in a piece. This improvisatory free-dom is particularly evident on songs such as "Cross Road Blues," "If I Had Possession over Judgment Day" (1936/1961), "Preachin' Blues" (1936), "Walkin' Blues" (1936), "Ramblin' on My Mind" (1936), "Traveling River-side Blues" (1937/1961) and "Terraplane Blues" (1936)—in all of which Johnson's changes within the piece suggest a kind of "channel surfing" ef-fect, a kind of cut-and-paste accumulation of disparate feels and fragments. Johnson's execution of individual riffs and passages, his wild scalar rang-ing, his sudden shifts in amplitude and tempo, his refusal (in these songs at least) to keep a single feel for the duration of the song—all are carried out with immense assurance. For all the wild freedom the changes suggest, they never give the impression of being in any way accidental or out of the performer's control. On the contrary, the huge dynamic variety seems to arise as much from Johnson's confidence in his ability to modify and engi-neer his sound as it does from simple instrumental virtuosity.

Robert Palmer sees in Johnson the same sort of deliberateness as a recording artist as Porterfield reports of Jimmie Rodgers:

By the time Robert got to San Antonio, he'd been hard at work polishing his songs for months, perhaps in some cases for years, discarding and adding verses until he had tight, compact pieces just long enough to fit onto 78 records. . . . [His approach] was distinctly unlike the approach of Charley Patton, Son House, and the Muddy Waters of the Library of Congress recordings, who still considered themselves primarily live entertainers and whose songs tended to be fairly loose assemblages of traditional and original verses that could be stretched out, often to the detriment of their thematic continuity, according to how much people wanted to hear and how long they wanted to dance. Robert Johnson could perform that way too, of course, and often did, but by 1936 he thought of himself as something more than a juke joint entertainer. He was self consciously an artist.[28]

Johnson's special command of room acoustics surfaces repeatedly in different ways, to different purposes. In "Come on in My Kitchen" (briefly discussed in chapter 1) he achieves a kind of extreme aural close-up, with muttered asides, each progressively more sotto voce, and slide licks, each more delicate than the one before, punctuating the vocal lines. By the end of the sequence the listener's attention is intimately focused on the very small sounds of the bottleneck slide rattling against the strings.

> [*Guitar lick*]
> Baby can't you hear that wind howl? [*spoken*]
> [*Different slide lick, softer*]
> Oh, can't you hear that wind howl? [*spoken*]
> [*Repeat slide lick, followed by barely discernible rattling of bottleneck on string as last note is held.*]

Performers such as Bob Wills, Blind Willie McTell, Emmett Miller, Fats Waller and others had already adapted the "Mr. Interlocutor" persona from minstrelsy and vaudeville, and made a habit both live and on record of punctuating sung lines with "hollers," irreverent interjections, ironic answers to and commentaries on the song. But what Johnson does here is something quite different, and quite specific to recording. The softly voiced asides on "Come on in My Kitchen" (and "Traveling Riverside Blues"), and the guitar parts that answer them would almost certainly be lost in a live performance in a bar or juke joint. They were presumably done this way for the benefit of the recording. Their presence demonstrates immense confidence on the part of the singer in his ability to use and master the apparatus. During the break in "Come on in My Kitchen" the performance becomes so minimal and introverted that in the hands of a less accomplished performer, the song might have fallen apart at that point. But this does not happen. Rather than losing the audience, the singer effects a dramatic extending of the dynamic limits of the apparatus. Johnson successfully invites his listener to consciously zero in on his space, Johnson's space; he invites his audience to temporarily abandon actual space. Perhaps this is not so much a close-up as an aural zoom shot.

The short spoken break in "Come on in My Kitchen" resolves and completes the song's spatial constructions. Beyond the immediate territory of the singer's hearth is a terrifying and hostile world. By progressively dropping the amplitude and drawing the focus ever closer to himself, the singer indicates the numbing hugeness of the hostile outer world while simultaneously drawing in and strengthening the boundaries of the defendable inner safe zone: the spoken asides suggest that the only safe zone is not simply the kitchen any more, but the singer's own personal space. The singer presents his errant lover with the most ambitious possible spatial dialectic: a vast unfriendly world against the provisional safety of the singer's most intimate space. Yet the whole is of the singer's fabricating: the howling wind is after all his own slide guitar; the near and far of the song too are his work. The singer is a world-maker, a demiurge. He is both creator of the world and an actor within it.

The effect is in many ways the exact opposite of the realist recording ideal, which prescribes self-effacing recorded music at the service of the record buyer, its sonic spaces wholly subject to the territorial regimes of the domestic space, or whatever space in which the record might be played. The Johnson recordings not only set up their own spaces; they go on to toy with the construct and test the very limits of recorded spatiality by coaxing the listener into their particular sonic game, inviting full immersion in their sonic fields. Much later, in the 1940s and 1950s with the aid of magnetic tape technology and state-of-the-art West Coast recording studio expertise, breathy intimacy would become a staple in the recordings of Charles Brown, Julie London, Nat King Cole, Miles Davis, Patti Page, Mary Ford and others, and later still in the intimate-mode production regimes of singers such as Al Green and Barry White. And later still, stereo headphones, the Sony Walkman, hi-fi home stereos, large public sound systems, discos and so forth would all seek immersion responses from their listeners—the willing sense that the actual physical space the listener occupies is for the moment less real, less important, even less convincing than the virtual aural dimensionality within the recording.

Of course, Johnson uses the acoustic properties of the room for sound engineering purposes, as a device, but room ambience functions at deeper levels on his records. For all that mainstream recording sought the seamless, placeless, depthless signal, Johnson's recordings continually bring attention to their own internal relationships—spatial, musical and acoustic. They continually call into question the given, draw the listener to the physicalities of the place, the room itself. Through constantly changing amplitudes and through the use of corner loading, as with Jimmie Rodgers, we are frequently aware of the fact of architectural space on Johnson recordings. The sound reverberating from the room, from the walls is key to the recording. Rather than pure, ungrounded music, music "with no strings attached," the Johnson recordings present an emplaced music. The "pure" sounds of voice and guitar are in constant dialogue with their physical surroundings. In listening to these recordings the listener is obliged to deal with the fact of an entire musico-spatial complex.

Having set up this space, Johnson then uses it as a stage, a mise en scène. The effect on the one hand is of an uncomfortable Cartesian dichotomy: singer and room, voice and physical space. The voice and guitar "rattle around" within the sonic space, nervously, edgily. The space is at times like an ill-fitting suit of clothes. Yet the singer continually enlists the built environment as an acoustic accomplice; the result is a sophisticated sonic synergy, and Johnson's recording presence demonstrates a supreme, almost magisterial confidence.[29] The sense of simultaneous explosive exuberance and dark unease here anticipates the sort of recording ambience that in the wake of Elvis Presley was to become one of the highest aims of rock recording artists, but one rarely as effectively realized as it is here.

Johnson used these spatialities, apparently consciously and deliberately to achieve immediate musical artistic effects. But the unique spatialities of his recordings also give rise to other longitudinal effects, and these perhaps as much as the intrinsic musical properties of the recordings have been factors in the latter-day valorization of Johnson. Specifically, the recordings retain an almost uniquely documentary feel; the listener some sixty, seventy years later may feel a simultaneously disquieting and delicious sense of nearness to the original moment. The dramas surrounding the production of the record, the emotional grids out of which the music comes, the no doubt difficult relationships between Johnson and the recording engineers, the entire micropolitics of the time and place compose a vibrant semiotic complexity and true-life richness. The moment, rather than being closed or simply frozen in time, remains permanently active, permanently unresolved. It goes on. It escapes time.

The Robert Johnson story and mythologies attaching thereto have inspired a small army of enthusiasts, promoters, A & R people, researchers, musicologists, musicians, journalists, novelists and filmmakers to make pilgrimages to the Mississippi Delta region, originally in search of the man himself, starting with John Hammond, who had him marked for stardom. As it stands, very little is actually known about the circumstances surrounding his work in the studio. One fanciful re-creation of the myth, which nonetheless is fairly consistent with the corpus of Johnson anecdotes and apocrypha, occurs in the film *Crossroads* (directed by Walter Hill, 1986). The film establishes its spaces, acoustic and visual with a thoroughly well informed understanding of the kind of semiotic space that Johnson established in his recorded performances. It begins with a wide shot of a black man standing on a flat, open expanse. He is dressed in a suit and hat in the style of the 1930s, carrying a guitar case. Near him two dirt roads intersect. The next scene is of a field recording session in a hotel room. A white engineer ushers the man from the previous scene into the makeshift studio. The engineer is in the adjacent room with acetate cutting gear. He announces the singer as Robert Johnson. We see Johnson's back. He is holding a guitar, and a bottle of whisky is beside him. He starts playing, facing the wall. The distinctive opening riff is unmistakable as "Cross Road Blues," note for note, nuance for nuance. But the sound quality is too "good," the production values too modern for it to be the original recording.[30] The vocal begins: "I went to the crossroads, fell down on my knees." Next we get a close-up of the acetate cutting gear, in the adjoining hotel room. Next we cut to a modern, cheap cassette player. A cassette is playing. We can see by the cover art and hear that it is *King of the Delta Blues Singers*. It is the modern day. *Now* we recognize the recording playing on the soundtrack as the scratchy-sounding original.

The set direction for the hotel room in the film is reminiscent of the retro-styled drawing that graced the cover of the second Columbia Johnson LP. When the cover art for the second LP was produced, the Johnson legend was already old, and the artwork sought to suggest that legend. Hill invokes it again in *Crossroads,* and in both the album artwork and Hill's movie, certain of Johnson's spatial tropes are recognized. The record-making process is shown in the film, as a kind of cultural mining, or distillation. The opening shot is of a wide, geographic space (clearly the Mississippi Delta) but it stands as a cultural space as well, that of black, southern rural life of the 1930s: the juke joints, labor camps, cabins, woods. All lonely, haunted places. Next he is in a closed space, the hotel room, which is now doubling as psychic or psychological space, or a kind of alchemical crucible. The Johnson character is shown to be distilling, reducing the larger realms of social, geographic and personal experience down to the most potent concentration. The close-up of the needle cutting into the disc itself is the last concentration, the essence, and presents as the antithesis of the open, indistinct Delta fields. The film at this point is fascinated with the idea of the temporary studio as a kind of social and psychic workshop. The recording has sampled the life of the area, and some local magic has been retained, to be transmitted across time and space.

In the previous chapter it was suggested that popular music recording in its early days sought a zero-degree depth, sought to entirely flatten the space on the "other side," the record side of the apparatus, while privileging and sonically enhancing the listener's actual space, the playback zone. Here the filmmaker displays an almost complete inversion of that aim. The playback zone is a crowded contemporary suburban bedroom, the device a cheap cassette player. The expanded zone is the Delta itself. The territorializing flow is entirely from the wide expanse of the Delta, remote in time and space, onto the present urban. By the time the film was made in the 1980s, however, notions of the black south, and its magically territorializing powers were clichés of rock, blues and folk discourse. Although director Walter Hill works carefully to stage the Johnson legend, the construct is curiously uninformative, and the Johnson we see is almost entirely without personality. The most powerful presences in the opening scenes rather are geographic and architectural.

Hill was here endorsing an enduring and potent mythos, and one of special relevance to this study: the mythos of itinerancy. The singer is shown as a drifter in the rural south. The recording studio is a kind of mining mechanism, the record a kind of core sample. Or perhaps the studio is like a remote weather station, taking readings of the local conditions. The singer himself is little more than the bearer of an essence, a transmission vehicle for condensing aspects of the territory onto the sound recording. The singer's specialness comes neither from technical mastery, nor from an intensely conscious understanding of his craft and its technical processes. Rather, it derives from his own shamanic relationship with the territories through which he journeys, processes over which he is shown as having little control. When he presents himself to the apparatus, he brings references to the "out there," references that themselves refer to even further away (the "cross roads" that lead off to the four corners).

The social construction of the mythos of the itinerant[31] has a long and complex history. On the one hand, rootless itinerants may be regarded as anathema by more settled societies, as are the griots of northern Africa, the tinkers in Ireland, the gypsies in Central Europe. Lone travelers may be feared and shunned as sexual degenerates, as child abductors, as thieves, as bandits or as murderously deranged former warriors. At the very least, the unsocialized drifter is considered beyond the pale of polite society; he comes to the back door for a handout. On the other hand, there are itinerants, such as Mark Twain's Huck Finn character, at base too decent and moral for the hypocrisies of settled society. There is the religious seeker, such as John Bunyan's pilgrim, a lonely traveler journeying toward his own salvation. There are medieval pilgrims in Europe, mendicant monks in the

East. Other "noble itinerants" include Arthurian knights, Thoreauvian freethinkers, Franciscan nature worshipers. Then there are pioneers, frontiersmen, boundary riders, cowboys, refugees, migrants, who may under certain circumstances also be constructed as worthy itinerants. So too, "drifters" may be represented as being either the "hunted" or as seekers and free spirits—or as both.

Jimmie Rodgers is presented in the "seeker and free spirit" posture, mostly. A rambler, rounder and railroader, he ranges over wide territories, although mostly confined to the grid of steel rails that crisscrosses the United States, an escapee from the strictures of the family and monogamy. Other times he is a down-at-heel hobo, a gambler, sometimes a cowboy and sometimes a humble itinerant laborer. The Frank Hutchison of "KC Blues" is also an itinerant: a southerner who has found himself "in the Union Square hotel," and who is proceeding to "get right on good red liquor"—a self-determining free spirit. The Robert Johnson construct, both in Walter Hill's film and in many discourses of popular music is presented squarely in the category of the hunted. He is a kind of shaman without power, an almost passive bearer of a profound, immensely larger dysfunctionality that is at once geopolitical, and of the psyche (although, even in this individual aspect, the dysfunctionality relates more to a general "human condition" than specifically to Johnson, the person).

In terms of music recording, these constructions serve to set up an exchange between immense territories. On the one hand there are the regions, on the recording side of the apparatus ("through the looking glass"): the open spaces and small towns of the Mississippi Delta (or, in the case of Rodgers, the extensive regions of the southern United States); the large geographic regions to which the performers lay claim. These are counterbalanced by the regions "on the listener's side": the greater geographies inhabited by the listeners, the different territories, different countries in which the recording is distributed and heard. The recording apparatus is lodged in the middle as a pivotal (though according to the Hill formulation, not especially important) point of exchange between these immense complementary social and physical zones.

Ry Cooder, however, is especially concerned with the zones and energies constellating immediately around the apparatus. As an intensely focused musician himself, and a dedicated longtime student of recorded music, Cooder's primary interest is in the conscious and deliberate interventions, moves and tactics employed in making the record, as much as in the larger, less specific mythologies of place (although these are present in his own discourse elsewhere in the same interview). Cooder's view of Johnson as a consummately knowing music maker runs counter to the customary constructions of the Johnson character: "Listen to Johnson's singing and his forceful personality. This is a guy who was afraid of the audience? Hell, no! This is a 'chew them up and spit them out' kind of a guy."[32] Cooder's fantasy ascribes to Johnson a degree of agency in his own music that the other constructs, including the visuals in the film *Crossroads,* deny him. Rather than seeing Johnson as the unreflecting bearer of spirit of place, as the junior partner in a deal with the devil, as passive, depersonalized victim of southern racism and so on, Cooder's focus is on the person, in that place (the makeshift studio), at that moment, masterfully in control of his own performance.

I think he was sitting in the corner to achieve a certain sound he liked . . . he wants to hear wang! . . . [He] wants to hear that boosted mid-range . . . it's a great thing, because all of a sudden the whole projection of the instrument is changed radically.[33]

The intimate zone immediately surrounding Robert Johnson's person conforms to what Erving Goffman has called a "territory of the self."[34] Goffman describes a number of different types of such territories. Some he says are "fixed," and preserved by law (such as fields, houses and real estate); others are situational, their occupation temporary, made available in the form of goods while in use (park benches and restaurant tables). Then there are egocentric preserves that move around with the claimant, he being in the center.[35]

In Goffmanian terms, Robert Johnson's corner of the San Antonio hotel room falls primarily within the category of the "stall": "a well bounded space to which individuals can lay temporary claim, possession being on an all-or-none basis."[36] Examples include a comfortable chair, a table with a view, a telephone booth, a theater seat. "The point about stalls . . . is that they provide easily visible, defendable boundaries for a spatial claim."[37] Goffman distinguishes the stall from the first of his territories of the self, "personal space," saying a stall can be left temporarily, at least, while personal space cannot. And unlike personal space, a stall can be shared. Yet another of Goffman's territories of the self is "use space," the "territory immediately around or in front of an individual, his claim to which is respected because of apparent instrumental needs."[38] Examples are a workman swinging a pick, a gallery-goer regarding a picture on a wall, or persons holding a conversation over a distance.

Robert Johnson's territory in the hotel room then might involve all three of these categories, and in this case, the three are congruent: the stall corresponds closely to his personal space, as it does to his use space. The boundaries are defined by the two walls and his own body, the hard material boundaries, the visual boundaries and the sonic boundaries all being in accord. Considering that hotel rooms themselves are a kind of stall (though in this case in the possession of others, and therefore a kind of alien territory), Johnson's setting up of an intensely concentrated territory assumes special importance. The sonic outcome of all this, the recordings, retains powerful elements of these concentrations. Indeed, the microphone is an egregiously alien presence located at the epicenter of these overlaid personal territories. But the microphone is not an inert presence; rather it is a conduit to the world, the "out there." Whereas more common performance practice has performer and audience comfortably and unambiguously located on either side of an actual or imaginary proscenium arch, a front and a back stage, Johnson turns the formulation inside out. The audience is suddenly impossibly located in intimate proximity to the singer. But even the word "proximity," with its implication of linearity—"nearer to" or "further away from" something—fails to describe the fundamentally unfixed placement of the microphone within a reverberant and decentered zone. The microphone is taking samples from within a charged field of interactivity, in which direction, in which normal hierarchies of nearer and further, left and right, bigger or smaller, have been upset, rearranged or, for the duration of the music, done away with entirely. Rather than hearing from an audience member's "point of view," the microphone is picking up something nearer Johnson's own corner-loaded aural experience of himself. As much as it stands in for an imagined physical listener, an addressee, the mic is standing in for Johnson himself, transmitting an intensely private sensory experience. The resultant sound recording then is dizzyingly fluid, as much of the self as of the other and as much *to* the self as to the other.

Robert Johnson set up his own temporary territories using his physical self and his surroundings. Johnson's territories are fluid but powerfully evoked. Physical geographic reference points are nonspecific, and freed from physical fixity; the conjured space operates on the listener in ways that a literal, coherent represented space might not. But rather than seeing Johnson's project as an isolated work of genius, we might view it as an instance in a tradition of "centripetality"; that is, characterized by forces working towards the center (as opposed to operating from the center outward). A recording roughly contemporaneous with Johnson's, Billie Holiday's recording of "Swing, Brother, Swing," made with a subset of the Count Basie band at the Savoy Ballroom as a live radio broadcast in 1937, exemplifies this. This highly energized recording features an aggressive horn-section introduction and a steady, close-knit minor-key riffing behind the vocal. No solos are taken. The entire lyric here is an address to and about the band and the music.

This rhythm captivates me
Hot rhythm stimulates me

Can't help but swing it, boys
Swing it, brother, swing.

The lyrics are overtly about immersion in the very music of which they are a part. The singer is "captivated" by the music, yet she demands even more from the musicians, whom she addresses repeatedly (using the tag "boys" at the end of the first line, and the universal hipster argot address term "gate" at the end of the next line). As the song progresses Holiday begins naming names: "Come on and swing me, Jo!" (directed at drummer Jo Jones, who responds with a series of taps on the cowbell) and later, "Come on and swing me, Count!" (to bandleader Basie).

Holiday is registering the musicians' performance, simultaneously approving it while calling for even greater intensity. As well as being the prime participant, the front-line figurehead, the singer here is directing her attention (and thus the listener's) to the back line. She is "audiencing" the band—hearing, listening, and letting them know that she is listening. At the same time drummer Jo Jones can be heard in the background answering Holiday ("Yeah, yeah, yeah!") and urging on Holiday and the band. His utterances simultaneously answer Holiday and also call upon the musicians to maintain and increase the intensity of the moment.

This particular version of the song stands in marked contrast to Holiday's studio version. The live take is slower but with a more pronounced "raunchiness," a thicker sound in the lower registers, and a generally more pronounced overall bluesiness. At this time (the late 1930s) the Count Basie Band, and the various five- and six- piece combinations drawn from it under Basie's leadership were renowned for their ability to simultaneously harness two apparently contradictory tendencies: (1) the seamless, effortless-sounding though highly disciplined blending of horns and rhythm sections and (2) a high level of individual and collective improvisatory freedom, spontaneity and rhythmic drive.

The musical and vocal conversations going on in "Swing, Brother, Swing" then simultaneously set up, maintain and comment on a charged though entirely temporary, ephemeral grid of musical interactivity. Just as the singer is "captivated" and "stimulated," so too might dancers or passive listeners be enmeshed in the sonic web. In the live situation perhaps the band might be separated from audience by stage and proscenium arch, but on record no such spatial fixity obtains. Furthermore, the mock references to trance states in the lyrics, the intensively interlocked grids of call and response in the performance, the passionate commitment of the participants, counterbalanced by the ephemeral, temporary nature of the musical phenomenon recalls more than anything perhaps the intensity of ecstatic religious practice[39] (or of a drug high). Not only is there no visually grounded "here" and "there" or left and right, the invocation of magical and ecstatic transports further dissolves real-world spatialities and divisions—as indeed it does all hierarchies that rely on visual markers.

The Holiday-Basie recording of "Swing, Brother, Swing" might be placed generically within the vigorous, but (in the 1930s) still emerging tradition of small band jazz, "race" blues, hokum and swing recordings—all musics with a significant improvisational component. Although a hugely diverse grouping—ranging from the globally distributed recordings of Louis Armstrong, Duke Ellington and Fletcher Henderson groups to highly idiosyncratic recordings made for local blues-buying communities—certain recurring sonic-spatial qualities might be identified. As discussed in the previous chapter, Read and Welch saw "realist" recording practice—characterized by "flatness," depthlessness, the (apparent) absence of "distortions" (that is, easily discernible tonal or spatial modifications to the "pure" and "natural" sound of the instruments)—as unquestionably dominant in early electrical popular recording. And certainly that regime seems generally typical of high-production-value Tin Pan Alley recordings of the period.

In the world of small ensemble jazz-swing-blues-hokum recordings, however (which went virtually unnoticed and unremarked by Read and Welch), many instances are to be found that possess a distinctly spatial quality. "Jubilee Stomp," by Duke Ellington and His Orchestra, from 1928, for example, features a marked sense of aural depth. Here the rhythm section is relatively "dry," but successive soloists are by turns more, and then less, off-mic; that is, some are reverberant and "far off" sounding, others are not. This separate emplacement serves to mark out each voice from its predecessor and, combined with the shifts in timbre and improvisational style, helps to accord each with a distinct identity. There are no special textual markers, no "space fixers"; we (the participating listeners) are not specifically cued to imagine a western prairie, or a beach in Hawaii, or a dreamy domestic idyll. The music simply sounds as though it is occurring in or coming from an acoustically active physical space. There is no readily identifiable centralized lead voice here, and amplitudes vary from voice to voice regardless of whether that voice is more or less on-mic. (Indeed, the most prominent voice in the whole piece is the slapped bass break). The slightly reverberant, off-mic qualities of the soloists, rather than signifying relatively subordinate or peripheral importance, serve rather to set up and enlarge the musical field, creating a zone in which physical space and musical coordinates are in a sort of accord. The music is spatial and the space is musical. Von Schelling's famous maxim that architecture is frozen music is here inverted: *this* music is a kind of liquid, but nonhierarchized architecture.

The apparently hollow quality of this and records like it—of which there are many—might be considered as a kind of concavity. In contrast to the convexity of Read and Welch's "realist" recording aesthetic (the effect of "the orchestra and soloist being transported into the living room, the singer or soloist singing just for you")[40] the "concave" recording locates the music at a physical remove from the listener. Despite the extroverted boisterousness of Ellington's music, the concave sound quality serves to keep it contained, or othered, within that nonspecific space. Perhaps a conscious or unconscious racism or classism was at work on the part of record producers and engineers: musicians who were encountered by A & R men and studio technicians as socially other are sonically distanced in the recorded artifact. Or perhaps the sonic concavity arises from the exigencies of recording relatively nonhierarchized ensembles, in which the musical "focus" continually shifts from one improvising soloist to another. These soloists would be further aided by extremely fluid dynamics from the ensemble behind them. Rather than deriving a strict Tin Pan Alley–type microphone placement, which privileged a single lead voice over the accompaniment, engineers might simply have opted for centrally placed, catchall microphones, around which the musicians could more or less arrange themselves.

Perhaps too this sonic emplacement was, at least in part, Ellington's choice. The setting up of these sonic spaces—free from the rigid codings obtaining to later, spatially "authorized" western and Hawaiian recordings—allowed for certain powerfully expressive liberties. Indeed, listening closely to these recordings so many years on is for many listeners an inexhaustible experience. The sense of partaking intimately of a moment remote in both space and time that recordings afford is for many a considerably more powerful experience than, say, viewing moving film footage. Whereas the filmic image may provide the viewer with deep aesthetic satisfactions, and those occasional charged moments in which the real makes itself present—the effect Roland Barthes famously called "punctum" (the pointed, piercing, semiotically irreducible intrusion of the real into the otherwise controlled, fabricated visual field [or studium])[41]—the real in such sound recordings as Ellington's, Johnson's and Basie's is both pointed and dispersed over entire fields of interactivity, expressed both in the contingent, improvisational presence of each individual voice, and in the almost infinitely nuanced and complex spatial relationships between voices.

A principle that informed small swing band recording in particular, all of jazz music more generally, and, eventually, all recorded popular music is the quest for the one particular take in a session that is better than all others, the version that "takes off," that achieves transcendent synergy, that summons, as Zak says, a kind of "magic": "For records represent more than the expression of their creators' talents, ideas, emotions and influences; they also capture physical presence and action . . . at some point in the making of a successful record there is a magical transfer of aura from artists to artifact."[42]

As mass-market commodities, Ellington's "Jubilee Stomp" and Billie Holiday's "Swing, Brother, Swing" were presumably intended as "convex" artifacts to be vigorously but unproblematically present in the reception space. At the same time, however, the attention-grabbing virtuosity and spatial separateness of each successive voice in the former, the mutterings, in-group references and intensity of the feel in the latter serve to invite the listener to focus away from the playback space and toward the virtual coordinates of the musico-sonic space. There is a reward there for the listener who responds to the magically charged "concavity." And present here we might detect what was to become a key spatial device of early rock 'n' roll recording; the invitation, implicit or explicit to the listener to enter the space.

Robert Palmer links this kind of intraensemble "space" making to the "ring shouts" of the southern United States' ecstatic religious practice.[43] This idea of the inspired, unique, transcendent performance is in (partial) opposition to the ideas of musicianly professional standards: that the professional orchestra musician should play the written arrangement as precisely as possible, and that one skilled professional player could be substituted for another with no apparent alteration to the performance. In reality, much of what has been uncritically celebrated as "improvisatory" may not always have been,[44] and even within the strictures of the conventional sight-reading dance orchestras, collective and individual performances might vary greatly. Nonetheless, in the recording of jazz and swing groups of the 1920s and 1930s can be found an increasing sense of the special, unreproducable performance (the band may go on to produce many other "special moments," but each is seen as unique to itself). If such a moment is successfully captured on record then the unique is made potentially infinite; the recording can be replayed at will, forever. Music on records is often described in the present tense; for its listeners, it *is* (rather than *was*).

Although this sort of concave recording would not quite seem to be the dominant practice of its time, certainly it is common enough to be of note, and seems to be generally most present on the recordings of the pace-setting small band recordings of the time, including hillbilly stringbands, calypso, "Hawaiian" guitar combos and western swing groups. This emplacement tends not to be verbally anchored in the same way as some Hawaiian or cowboy music; nonetheless, a tune might be referenced by its title, as say is Sidney Bechet's "Chant in the Night" (1938). On this recording the reverberant, strident minor-key clarinet suggests a specifically urban soundscape, in which the nocturnal activities of others are heard but not seen. But more generally the space on these emplaced small group recordings is simply heard. A strong sense of containment is created; the sound is spatially othered, "confined" in a way that the more high-profile, white Tin Pan Alley groups, broadly speaking, tend not to be.[45] To play the flat-recorded Glenn Miller band or Bing Crosby on the parlor phonograph was to vicariously "admit" those people into the parlor. To play a Count Basie or Robert Johnson recording, on the other hand, was to temporarily enter into an "other" space, an unspecified elsewhere, for a limited time only (just as white New York nightclubbers in the 1930s and 1940s visited famous jazz clubs on 52nd Street for their after-hours carousing).

The kind of "atmos-spatial" recording described here, this acoustics of otherness, became ever more frequently employed through the early 1940s, and can be heard on the recordings of such acts as the Ink Spots, the Nat King Cole Trio and especially Louis Jordan and His Tympany Five (and many others). By the 1950s this type of nongeographic spatializing decisively informed recording activity at Sun and Chess Studios, and thereafter came near to being dominant recording practice. Milt Gabler, who produced many of the most successful sides for Count Basie and later Louis Jordan and the Tympany Five went on to use very similar production regimes—featuring clear, resonant bottom-end sound, with each section voice distinctly and separately "emplaced," and with the whole characterized by driving riff-based solos—with Bill Haley and the Comets. This particular production quality—voices singly and collectively hyperenergized, manifestly in dynamic interaction with each other and with their physical space—is most frequently simply described as "live."

The "concave" sonic qualities of small, improvisatory group recording and the assertive selfhood of Jimmie Rodgers, Frank Hutchison and Robert Johnson represented important deterritorializing moves against the strictures of the early electric period recording apparatus. These moves remained largely confined however to "fringe" recording areas. These (sometimes) meaningfully idiosyncratic practices that were, in time, to so define modern recording practice and ideals, were enabled and even encouraged by the perceived peripherality of the musics recorded, and of the markets for which those recordings were intended. The broad practices of "hillbilly," "race" and "ethnic" recording, and especially field recording, provided circumstances that allowed into the recording studio behaviors strictly expunged from more capital-intensive, high-end popular music recording.

Johnson, Rodgers, Holiday and Ellington were in the main, initially at least, from outside the mainstream popular music industry. Gene Austin, however, emerged from its dead center. The spatializing practices of the former were frequently contradictory, unresolved, open-ended, sometimes disturbed and disturbing. With Austin, Tin Pan Alley demonstrated that it had "cracked the code"; here was a comfortable, contained space, from which doubts and contradictions had been seemingly expunged. A "little white light" would lead the listener to his or her blue, sweetly seductive suburban idyll. The space of the record was friendly: birds sang in the trees, the scene was bathed in soft twilight, the reverberating cello suggested that even the hard surfaces, had a soft, well-appointed, well-furnished warmth to them. The singer was fully territorialized and loving it. Perhaps this construct was most appropriate to the boom times of the mid to late 1920s.

In the 1930s the Great Depression forced millions of men, women and children worldwide into actual itinerancy. While the largely uncircumscribed, deterritorialized spatializing of Rodgers and Johnson and others came out of this period, Tin Pan Alley also delivered a product that dealt with itinerancy—but one that drew more on the Gene Austin tradition of strictly literal, territorialized spatiality. Nonetheless, once established, singing cowboy music was to be key in the later emergence of fully spatialized popular music.

CHAPTER 4

"Blue Shadows on the Trail"
Space and Place in the Imagined West

➤◆◄

Cowboys and Hillbillies

The global craze for "western" or "cowboy" music of the 1920s through the 1940s saw the emergence of new spatial techniques in music recording. The various attempts to render in sound (highly coded) notions of "the west" had the effect of making available a number of new production practices and recording tropes, some of which gained wider currency and were to go on to become staples of recording practice. But the attempt to render certain "desirable" notions of landscape and region in popular music saw the repression of other representations of the regional, and the suppression and refiguring of other less heroic, even "shameful," spaces and places. This chapter will briefly examine constructions of the U.S. "south" and the "west" in popular culture, and the corresponding music industry categories of "country" and "western," and how "heroic" spatial overlays were employed to replace more awkward or embarrassing geographies. The precise means by which these heroic spaces were realized on record will then be looked at; to do this, however, it will be necessary to look first at corresponding realizations in movie soundtracks and even cinematography from around the same time.

In the movie *The Blues Brothers* (directed by John Landis, 1980) a woman in a honky-tonk bar explains to Jake and Elwood that "we got both types of music here—country *and* western." The line frequently wins a laugh, as an instance of unthinking redneck foolishness, although the distinction was one long made in the music industry by marketers and performers from both camps. Around and between these poles—country (or hillbilly) and western—operate a confusing number of performers and styles, both genuinely regional and pseudoregional. As well, there are to be found a number of genuinely regional shape-shifters who shuck off the trappings that signal their true origins, or are assigned an image that, however erroneous, signifies to a remote audience a more romantic origin. These include southern urbanites who look like vaudeville hillbillies, hillbillies who look like stage cowboys, hillbillies who look like slickers, genuine cowboys who look like stage cowboys, city slickers who look like stage hillbillies, slickers who look like cowboys, Australians and Canadians who look like slickers looking like cowboys. . . . [1]

Broadly speaking, "western" was a trade category that included two distinct subgroups. First, there was music actually of the southwest. This comprised overtly commercial but nonetheless inescapably regional music such as the big band swing-influenced music of Bob Wills and the Texas Playboys and the small band swing of Milton Brown and His Musical Brownies, as well as a host of lesser known honky-tonk and swing groups that featured "take-off" guitar/fiddle/piano solos in their playing. It also included the relatively small corpus of genuine cowboy songs, which had been gathered and published by folklorists since the previous century and records made by authentic cowboys such as Jules Verne Allen, Carl T. Sprague and Haywire Mac McClintock. But as well as the geographically authentic western styles, the trade category "western" also included music that pertained to the pop-mythic west: the music of so-called singing cowboys such as Gene Autry and Roy Rogers, of close harmonizing pop vocal groups like the Sons of the Pioneers, the Riders of the Purple Sage and of the legion of professional musicians who worked as radio, vaudeville and movie cowboys.

In fact, there is not a clear dividing line between the authentic and the ersatz "western." Plenty of musicians and composers in the pop cowboy school did in fact come from the rural southwest, although they were much less likely to have ever been true cowboys. At the same time lots of them came from the urban east, and could no doubt identify with Johnny Mercer's satire of the "old cow hand from the Rio Grande" who has never roped a steer, nor, indeed, seen a cow. The Sons of the Pioneers drew members from as far afield as Ohio, Canada and Texas. Many cowboy acts were based in California, where they could conveniently record transcriptions for radio broadcast, make records, play to large audiences and remain on hand for possible movie appearances. Further complicating the picture is that for southwestern musicians of all types—including pop, western swing, hillbilly, R & B and jazz—the major recording centers, and often the loci of their greatest popularity, were Los Angeles, San Diego and other new population centers on the West Coast. The Wills Band, for instance, from the early 1940s on was based in California, while still retaining and embellishing its western image.

The singing cowboys slotted into an already well established pop tradition. Since well before the beginnings of the phonograph industry, novels of the American West had enjoyed immense worldwide popularity. Since the publication of James Fenimore Cooper's early novels, the American West had been presented to the world as a sublime, pure, inherently restorative and ennobling expanse.[2] The tradition was continued in western "dime novels" of the early twentieth century. The western movies came in on a well-established popular, romantic tradition, and the cowboy singers followed the movies, and sartorially followed the style of the movie cowboy, whose styles were more than anything the product of studio wardrobe departments. The business of clothing and stage gear is of special relevance to this discussion and I would like to dwell on it for a moment.

Some of the conventions of the stage cowboy singer—especially the wearing of "western" garb—were first set down by Otto Gray, who led a band on a tour of radio stations and then the RKO vaudeville circuit from 1923 to 1928. But the biggest single impetus to the commercial singing cowboy shtick came from Jimmie Rodgers. As mentioned in chapter 2, Rodgers covered a number of different musical bases: blues, sacred music, parlor balladry, minstrel, hillbilly, barbershop smut songs, etc. He also wrote and sang a number of songs about Texas and the west that deftly blended the mythic with the lived, including "Land of my Boyhood Dreams" (1929/1933), which refers obliquely to his own terminal illness, or "Waiting For a Train" (1929) in which the singer, a railway hobo, gets thrown off a train out in the awe-inspiring landscapes of the American West. The singer, enraptured though he is by the boundless spatiality of his surroundings ("He put me off in Texas, a state I dearly love / The wide open spaces around me, the moon and the stars above") turns around to travel "back to Dixieland." Rodgers was photographed variously as a railroad-town swell (wearing a modern suit and straw boater); as a brakeman, in cap and overalls; and as a "cowboy," in cowboy hat, kerchief, leather chaps, boots and spurs, and wearing a gun in a holster. This last image of Rodgers was to prove hugely influential and spawned a great number of imitators.

In the wake of Rodgers, who died of tuberculosis in 1933, the dominant conceits and iconography of Tin Pan Alley cowboy were formulated most clearly and enduringly by the group The Sons of the Pioneers, whose highly successful career ran from the mid-1930s well into the 1950s.[3] The Sons' recordings utilized a number of different spatialities. They used the kind of aural "deep focus" that is evident on the Foy Willing recording discussed earlier, and textually, they were obsessed with landscape. The Bob Nolan–penned songs "Cool Water" (1941), "Hills of Old Wyoming" (1936), "There's a Roundup in the Sky" (1935) and "Tumbling Tumbleweeds" (1934), as well as many others, depict lonely cowboys manfully doing their job in an epic, often dangerous landscape of desert, mountain and prairie, wherein they must undergo initiatory experiences that will test and ultimately prove their manhood. They must deal with an uncompromising natural world, and threatening manifestations of the social world, which include cattle rustlers, hostile Indians, and the occasional sidewinding slicker who would cheat the naive westerner given half a chance. But it is all worth it, in return, the cowboy is afforded moments of mystical revelation not vouchsafed the city-dweller.

Western radio and movie serials further cemented the iconography of the pop west: immense buttes, mesas and mountains, deserts and thirst, poisoned waterholes, buzzards, skeletons, stagecoaches, ambushes, abandoned mineshafts, quicksand, buffalo, campfires, guitars, comical sidekicks, stampedes, boots, horses, saddles, few women, outlaws, rodeos. And graphic artists, photographers, moviemakers portrayed the cowboy as at once migratory, in the most heroic sense of the word, and musical, by depicting him as a guitar-strumming horseback rider. Thus were wedded the ideas of movement through space and the simultaneous playing of music, a fantasy that achieves its fullest realization with the Sony Walkman and the modern car stereo.

But the itinerancy suggested in the songs of Bob Nolan and others differs from that of the western movie or pulp novel cowboy. The latter concern themselves in the main with action and high adventure: gunfights, stampedes, fistfights, duels, ambushes, high-speed chases, bank robberies. They are concerned with a determinedly objective and, in the main, *social* world, a peopled world. The songs of pop cowboys on the other hand depict a lonely, reflective, introverted figure, occupying a landscape wherein dwells the deity, the landscape of the echo. The movies could render gunfights much better than they could mysticism.

Tin Pan Alley cowboy music, on the other hand, through the manipulation of production devices could "do" consciousness shifts, numinous experiences or the suggestion of profoundly moving visual/aesthetic experiences—such as, say, the mood engendered witnessing a sublime crepuscular landscape—more effectively than it could, say, a holdup. The singing cowboy is a Moses-like figure, undergoing solitary travails, and is rewarded with a privileged access to the Deity and His works. At the same time the figure is quite at odds with the actual migratory groups moving through the southwestern landscapes at that time: the dispossessed "Oakies" and "Arkies" heading west along the highways to California.[4]

The singing cowboy is also a wholly other figure to the barefoot, moonshine-drinking Appalachian hill person of popular imagination. It was largely from the latter—mainly rural musicians of the southeastern states—that "hillbilly music" had emerged as a new subclass of popular music about ten years before the emergence of the singing cowboy craze. The name carried pejorative connotations, and capitalized on the medicine show and vaudeville figure of the yokel: gauche, poor, and slightly stupid. When southeastern musicians of the "first wave" of commercial country music such as Frank Hutchison, Charlie Poole, Riley Puckett or the Carter Family had performed or posed for publicity photographs they had tended to present themselves in their best suits, clothing appropriate for public appearance, and that would not look especially out of place in any North American or European city. If they were to be "regional" at all in their dress, they would sometimes, like Bradley Kincaid or Bill Monroe, affect the jodhpurs, high boots and planter's Stetson of the successful southern plantation-owning gentry. But promoters and publicists, perhaps with the complicity of the performers themselves, "tweaked" the image of country and old-time performers to bring it into line with how people of the rural south tended to be perceived elsewhere in the United States—as hillbilly rubes and inbreds. Modern suits of the performers' choice were frequently replaced by old checked shirts, patched, ill-fitting overalls, workboots, battered hat. Commonly, at least one member of a band was made up with a blacked-out front tooth and given the "kitchen haircut."

In 1936 Howard Odum's *Southern Regions of the United States* described the southern United States as comprising two quite distinct regions. Both, he said, were "the south" but economic, social and geographic differences dictated that it would for most purposes be more accurate to regard them as two separate regions. These two "souths" were the southeast, consisting of Kentucky, Virginia, Tennessee, North and South Carolina, Georgia, Florida, Alabama, Mississippi, Louisiana and Arkansas; and the southwest, made up of Oklahoma, Texas, New Mexico and Arizona. Odum's project was to render a sociological description of the south free of the impressionistic definitions that had so muddied previous discussions of the region, in which "The South was race, or it was land, it was manners or it was kinship."[5] Ultimately Odum's work was criticized as seriously flawed by the same impressionism he had sought to escape.[6] However the "impression" that there were "two souths" was widespread. Wilbur Cash readily endorsed it in the introduction to his influential *The Mind of the South*.[7]

If southerners often regarded the south as a bicameral entity, so too did the fabricators of representations of the south for consumption elsewhere, particularly in North America, in Europe, and Australia. For these latter audiences, however, the dichotomy inherent in "southernness" was less likely to be based on a sound knowledge of southern geography and sociology than it was on "impressions" garnered from movies, novels, songs, comics, vaudeville and minstrel show acts. In these traditions of popular representation the southwest/southeast opposition provided a structuring dichotomy that separated the shamed from the heroic, the despised from the longed-for. For all that the southwest was imagined as grand, open, ennobling and mythic, the southeast was seen as shamed, degenerate and confined. The south as a culture had been defeated in the Civil War, whereas the famous defeats of the southwest, at Little Bighorn and the Alamo, were seen as heroic defeats that only served to strengthen the resolve of the nation builders. A tradition of representation of the south evolved that proposed a region every bit as mythic as the west, and in many ways its obverse.

A tradition of "southern gothic" stretches at least back to Edgar Allan Poe and Mark Twain. From Poe came the picture of the decayed, implicitly southern aristocracy, most notably in *The Fall of the House of Usher*. Twain portrayed the brutal "white trash" drunkard figure in Huck Finn's father, and the crazy recluse in Injun Joe. In the late nineteenth and early twentieth century, folk song collectors such as Cecil Sharp on field trips to the south encountered a kind of musical gothic, in the form of local "naturalized" versions of a number of folk songs of the British Isles—particularly those that told of sudden and seemingly unmotivated murder, such as "Oh, the Wind and Rain," "Banks of the Ohio," "Knoxville Girl" and "Down in the Willow Garden."[8]

In 1920, H. L. Mencken had published a satirical exposé of southern life and culture, "The Sahara of the Bozart," in which he claimed that as a result of the Civil War, the south had been "drained of all its best blood," and the land left "to the harsh mercies of the poor white trash" in whose veins flowed "the worst blood of Western Europe."[9] The image of the Deep South took a particular battering during the so-called Monkey Trial of 1925, in which the anti-Darwinian "creationist" tendencies in southern fundamentalism were exposed to worldwide ridicule.

Just as that new institution of the 1890s, the paperback best seller established an imaginary frontier west, so too did it give the nonsouthern United States and the rest of the world some of the most enduring stereotypes of southern life and southern history. Jack Temple Kirby[10] describes the evolution of southern gothic out of and as a counterpart to the Old South romances of Thomas Nelson Page and John Fox, Jr., on the one hand, and the "sharecropper social realism" novels of Ellen Glasgow, on the other. T. S. Stribling, William Faulkner and, most popularly, Erskine Caldwell (in *God's Little Acre* and *Tobacco Road*) portrayed a south characterized by poverty, violence, brutality and perversion. Movies furthered these representational motifs and added some new elements of "southern grotesque" in the exposé penal films *I Am a Fugitive from a Chain Gang* (directed by Mervyn Le Roy, 1932) and *Hell's Highway* (directed by Roland Brown, 1932).

In these works remote southern regions (remote to the industrialized northern and midwestern United States, and to the "civilized" world in general) were seen as kinds of enclosed spaces, impenetrable places isolated from the renewing and refreshing flows of broader sociality; fetid, septic places wherein madness and brutality might breed unhindered. The characters of southern gothic continue today to turn up in movies and documentaries, biography, pulp and middlebrow fiction, popular music and news programs.[11] Gothic combined in the popular imagination with the old figure of the unsophisticated rural yokel. This latter stereotype has always found plenty of affectionate expressions as well, particularly in America, but if affectionately or respectfully portrayed the figure will almost certainly turn out to be a westerner rather than a southerner.

And so in popular representations there evolved two quite separate American outlands. A series of oppositions might be constructed showing the perceived qualities of the southeast ranged against those of the west and southwest.

SOUTH EAST	WEST/SOUTH WEST
mountains or lowland swamps	prairie and deserts
wet	dry
fetid	clean
the coal mine	the range
farming	grazing
walking	horse riding
crushed by war	ennobled by wars
Deep (= below, subterranean) South, vertically remote	laterally remote
incestuous, inbred	dynastic, pioneering
feeble	strengthened by hard work
lazy, relaxed	industrious
ignorant southerner	laconic but knowing Westerner
certainty of inherited poverty	chance of huge profits
vices of moonshine drinking, miscegenation, domestic violence, incest	relatively wholesome vices of gunplay, cattle rustling and payday hell-raising
shameful race relations, lynchings, institutional racism	myth of contented Hispanics
the interfamily feud	the range war, Indian and Mexican wars
decadent, plantation-owning, anglophile "aristocracy," backward looking	progressive new wealth, cattle and oil barons
occult and crackpot fundamentalist Gothic	God-fearing Romantic

The negative stereotypes on the left—many of which may apply to the representation of cultures of poverty anywhere—tended, in the minds of some to constellate around the image of southeastern "hillbilly" musics, while "cowboy" musics sought to absorb the heroic qualities and figures of the southwestern stereotypes.

And so it was all too easy for southeastern "folk" musicians of the 1930s to "relocate" themselves as westerners (and consequently redefine themselves as heroes) by donning the clothing of the movie cowboy. This process removes the southern musician from location in the problematical actual south—the south of impossible economic and social contradictions, of disastrous race relations, of residual trauma dating from the Civil War, of ancient resentments and bitterness—and relocates him or her in a newer, cleaner, simpler, more hopeful region. But I do not mean to suggest that the southern musician was exchanging the real for the mythic. As Wilbur Cash argued in *The Mind of the South*, "the south" was itself a product of a "perception," its very contours, lifestyles and aspirations defined by a series of myths. The hillbilly musician was trading in a myth rife with shame and ignominy for one simply and simplistically heroic, one of confinement for one of boundless spatiality:

[In the mid-1930s] from New York to California individuals responded to the western myth and "cowboy" singers and groups sprang up in all sorts of unusual places. "Western" became a rival and often preferred term to "hillbilly," as a proper appellation for country music. It is easy to understand, of course, why "western" should be preferred to the seemingly disreputable backwoods term. "Western" specifically suggested a music that had been developed by cowboys out on the Texas Plain; more generally it suggested a context that was open, free and expansive. In short, the term fit the American self-concept.

. . . except for the fabric of usable symbols which surrounded him, the cowboy contributed nothing to American music. The "western" music which became fashionable in the mid-thirties came from other sources.[12]

Thus in the 1930s through the 1950s, in the wake of Jimmie Rodgers and Gene Autry, it became commonplace for country and "old time" musicians and stage performers to style themselves as "singing cowboys," as an alternative to the "rube" image. Country singers adopted names with a western flavor—Tex, Slim, Hank, Zeke, Chuck—had sequins and elaborate embroidery stitched onto their shirts, sported cowboy Stetsons and tooled-leather riding boots, and posed for publicity stills on horseback. Gradually public perceptions of "southern" and "western" musics blurred into one another, to the point that the gag in the Blues Brothers movie becomes possible.

But the southeast/southwest binaries subscribed to by Howard Odum and many others need further qualification, according to Bill C. Malone. In

Singing Cowboys and Musical Mountaineers,[13] Malone points out that numerous positive constructions of southernness were included in early commercial country music:

> Although the impulse toward self-burlesque and parody remained strong in country music . . . a countervailing desire to stress the dignity of mountain life also constantly asserted itself. A few performers in the first commercial decade, including Bascom Lamar Lunsford, Buell Kazee, the Carter Family, and Bradley Kincaid, appropriated positive images of mountain life rooted in a society of traditional values—images of morality, stability, and home-centeredness—and used them in their songs, styles and stage personae.[14]

Within the broad southern binary, Malone suggests another split that informed, consciously or otherwise, the image of early country musicians. The Carter Family, he says, "launched their professional career at a time when vague but rather romantic notions about mountain life prevailed."[15] Although there is no real evidence that they or Ralph Peer of Victor Records consciously attempted to exploit mountain imagery:

> Given the context of the 1920s when the lowland rural South suffered from a multitude of evils both real and imagined (sharecropping, pellagra, illiteracy, racial bigotry, moral degeneracy) it is tempting to equate the Carter style with the more pristine mountain image.[16]

The Carter Family recorded and performed on radio (including the powerful, widely broadcast Mexican border radio station XERA) a number of songs extolling the virtues and attractions of mountain life: "My Clinch Mountain Home" (1928), "Foggy Mountain Top" (1928), "My Old Cottage Home" (1930), "'Mid the Green Fields of Virginia" (1931).

Popular singer Bradley Kincaid built a career around the image of a mountain boy singing to an audience of city people, calling himself "the Kentucky Mountain Boy" and referring to his music as "mountain music."[17] The middle-class Kincaid was consciously informed by the academic folk song tradition of Sharp and Child. He saw "mountain music" as a product of a moral culture, and spoke disparagingly of "hillybilly songs." The mountain people from whom he obtained his songs were "a people in whose veins runs the purest strain of Anglo-Saxon blood."[18] The widely popular Kincaid appeared occasionally in the attire of English or bluegrass gentlemen horsemen: leather riding boots and jodhpurs, and at other times in cowboy garb:

> Kincaid tried to lend respectability to his music by associating it with an image of Appalachian mountain folk . . . the conception of an ethnically pure and morally virtuous people who value tradition. Archie Green maintains that Kincaid's contributions had lasting implications: "our very conception today that much American folksong is by definition undefiled, a precious elixir for national well-being, stems in part from Bradley Kincaid's achievement."[19]

Images of southernness then were deeply contradictory, split between the aristocratic and nobly pioneering and the utterly degenerate. The south was at once, for northerners, a near exotic place of aristocratic rusticity, and simultaneously a shameful degenerate other. As Douglas Green noted, talking of Gene Autry: "no youngster in the thirties and forties ever wanted to grow up to be a hillbilly, but thousands upon thousands wanted to be cowboys, and by treating the country song with dignity and respect Autry made it part of the shining good deeds and character of the cowboy."[20] It might be added that in the formulations of the respective myths, membership in the southern mountain gentry was something into which one was born, whereas the life of the cowboy, like that of the seaman, was something that was chosen, embraced; one might "run off to become a cowboy," just as one might run away to sea. The choice implied an embracing of largeness, a committing of the self to a life of travel and adventure in the great world. The ambience of life in the Appalachian hills on the other hand was of a claustral sense of enclosure. The mountains and woods, rather than leading into and out to the greater world, presented as a labyrinth. The folk riches perceived to be held hidden within—the Child ballads and such—were themselves archaic and baffling residues of a former greatness. Unlike the myths of the southern mountains, the myths of cowboyism were open, democratic, available.

Significantly, the western conceit exerted immense appeal in Canada, Australia and New Zealand. In Canada, Hank Snow, a Nova Scotian, dressed in cowboy rig and dubbed himself "the Yodeling Ranger." Another Canadian, Wilf Carter, released records in America under the name "Montana Slim," and enjoyed considerable popularity for many years. (Carter may also have been the first artist to use delay-type echo on record to suggest the Western canyon/butte/mesa landscape.) Bob Nolan himself hailed from Canada, moving to the United States in his teenage years.

In Australia, Tex Morton, "the Yodeling Boundary Rider," adopted the cowboy image and recorded a mixture of songs that spoke of or were otherwise associated with the American West—"Texas in the Spring" (1936), "The Oregon Trail" (1936), "Wyoming Willie" (1936), "The Prairie is a Lonesome Place at Night" (1936) and "Red River Valley" (1938)—and an initially smaller number of songs with an overtly Australian setting, such as "On the Gundagai Line" (1936) and "Beautiful Queensland" (1940, a reworking of the song "Beautiful Texas"). Morton quickly "indigenized" his material, however, and by the late 1930s his themes and tropes were overwhelmingly of the itinerant life in the Australian bush. On record his accent was recognizably Australian (with some American-sounding modifications).

On at least one occasion Morton posed for publicity shots in stage cowboy gear—western hat, tooled boots, lasso—with the somewhat bizarre addition of a boomerang. The implication inherent in this particular persona of Morton's (he had many: cowboy, stockman, ranger, swell, and later made an international name as a magician and mentalist) is that the western cowboy and the Australian "boundary rider" are near identical characters, that Australian bushmen are like Wild West cowboys. It is also implied that the boomerang was part of the Australian stockman's kit. The Australian stockman is thus linked at once to the romance of the American cowboy, and all that implies, and to the chthonicity of Australian aboriginal cultures. In one sense, this might be seen as a case of attempted ennoblement through manipulation of image on a par with that practiced by the "deep southern" hillbilly-cum-cowboy described above. At the same time, however, Morton achieves a remarkably comfortable synthesis between the almost wholly fabricated tropes of an exotic "cowboyism" and the specifics—places, names, work and travel practices—of itinerant life in Australia in the 1930s.[21]

In terms of recording engineering, Morton achieves an unusually strong and assured presence. His acoustic guitar playing is simple, but bass runs are strongly and confidently executed, and his vamped chords are crisply damped. His singing voice too is assured. Morton maintains stable amplitudes and confident delivery (in contrast to the diffidence so often found in early Australian popular music recording). Certain of Morton's early recordings also display a ringing spatial reverberancy. On "Crime Does Not Pay" (1938), the singer, putatively in his jail cell, tells of his misspent life. The voice and guitar are highly reverberant, imparting a strong sense of physical emplacement, indeed, of enclosure. In this song, as in others, Morton is at his most assertive during the yodel. Quite unlike that of other country singers, Morton's trilling, freely melismatic yodel displays a high degree of unself-conscious virtuosity. Here, as elsewhere, Morton establishes a strong presence before the apparatus, and his sonic mastery of space is at a remarkably high level.

New Zealand country singer Les Wilson went to great pains to achieve a "western" echo sound for his "Old Faithful and I."[22] Unsure exactly how to achieve the sort of deep echo they had been hearing on western recordings, Wilson and his engineer had lugged their heavy disc-cutting machine across a mountain range to the acoustically resonant New Haka Hall sixty miles away. Music historian Eric Watson describes how "they got the sound they wanted, after some judicious placement of the single mike, by having Les sing directly into the microphone until Les came to the yodels, for which he simply turned his back and sang at the walls."[23] This redirection caused the guitar and vocal volume to fluctuate wildly and somewhat bizarrely each time the song goes into a yodeled chorus. Wilson's efforts today might seem quaintly naive—or they could be seen as heroic. Certainly, he was moved to go to considerable lengths to render on record a faraway, mythic "western" space, although perhaps the landscape he ended up rendering suggested more the very real mountains of New Zealand that he had to traverse to make the recording.

By the early 1940s then the "cowboy west" was a well-established imaginary region, a backdrop available to any entertainer who might adopt the right name, wear the right outfit or sing the right lyrics. When the producers of Foy Willing and the Riders of the Purple Sage's version of "Blue Shadows on the Trail" located the central voice on-mic, with the other voices progressively further off-mic, they set up a sense of here and there, of center-stage and side of stage, of self and other, apparently confident that record buyers would supply the absent visual accompaniment; that is, they would correctly identify the scene as "western." In so doing they would invoke, consciously or not, a range of favorable connotations—personal, social, political, religious—associated with the construct of westernness. And just as the singing and instrumentation of groups such as the Riders of the Purple Sage, The Sons of The Pioneers and other "high period" singing cowboy acts display a seamlessly polished surface, so too is it all but semiotically closed. Negatives have been largely expunged; doubts, inconsistencies, contradictions, subversive or naysaying voices are kept at a fixed distance. The sonic scenery is as apparently controlled, fixed and framed as a romanticized, heroic, "western" landscape painting.

Ghost Riders: The Adult Western and the Uncanny West

Although the "cowboy west" in 1920s and 1930s popular culture was arranged around a conspicuously fabricated set of tropes and techniques, its sonic representations might nonetheless be broadly regarded as "realist"; in both music and film, aural spatialities generally equated with pictorial spatialities and together they sought to construct a "concrete" world. It may have been highly idealized, even by the standards of 1930s popular culture, and it may have sought to repress more than it showed, but it was a "picturable" world nonetheless. By the mid-1950s spatial effects were being employed on popular records to construct non- or antispaces, impossible and contradictory spaces. The mode here was often antirealist. It will be argued that a close synergy between (some) popular music production practice and (some) movie sound effect practice in the late 1940s provided a sonic "missing link" between these two broad modes, an intermediate "realist supernatural" mode. Specifically, it will be argued that in sonically representing the uncanny, the mystical or supernatural, moviemakers firmly assigned to echo and reverb new connotations of the mystically empowered "loner hero."

"Classic" cowboy movies of the 1930s and 1940s might be grouped into two broad strands: low-budget semimusical "programmers" featuring such stars as Roy Rogers, the Sons of the Pioneers, Gene Autry, Rex Allen, Foy Willing and Bob Wills and the Texas Playboys, and action-adventure westerns, often B-features, starring actors such as John Wayne, Errol Flynn, Randolph Scott and Gary Cooper. The late forties and early fifties saw the appearance of a third broad category of western movie, the so-called adult western. This included films such as *Pursued* (directed by Raoul Walsh, 1947), *High Noon* (directed by Fred Zinnemann, 1952), *Shane* (directed by George Stevens, 1953), *The Naked Spur* (directed by Anthony Mann, 1953) and *The Searchers* (directed by John Ford, 1956). This latter group of films was characterized by a tendency to focus narrative attention on the alienation of a loner central character, often with a dark past. Communities on the other hand were often typified by a mood of fear, compromise and moral decay. Outbursts of violence were generally shorter but more intense than in the prewar cowboy movies, and the violence generally bore a greater resemblance to real-world violence than did the chases, fistfights and shoot-outs of the older movies.

Soundtracks were often less busy than those of the earlier westerns, with less grand orchestral background music and less incidental fill. Protagonists were often accorded a much greater degree of "contemplative space" within the diegesis. The long sequences of Gary Cooper's lonely trekking from one place to another in *High Noon* as he tries vainly to drum up support for his coming showdown with the Miller boys is a prime example of this. Paradoxically, the relative aural starkness of these films—longer periods without background music—tended to throw sound and sound effects into more dramatic relief and certain effects achieved a new or heightened psychoactive importance in cueing shifts in mood and action. It is not my intention to construct a general catalogue of spatial sound effects in western movies; that is far too large a task to be undertaken here. But it is useful to note certain key moments in some widely distributed, much watched movies that made notable use of echo sound effects in particular, exemplifying and amplifying their signifying power, "charging up" the effects with added potency, while making them all the more current and available to popular music producers of the period. (This is not to necessarily accord primacy or originary status to movie sound effects over music recording practice but rather to demonstrate that certain effects were simply very much in currency during this period.)

In *Shane* a lone stranger comes to the aid of a family of farmer settlers who along with other farmers in the district are in dispute with a powerful cattle rancher. The rancher is using increasingly more violent inducements to drive the farmers off the land so that he can return to free-range cattle raising. Joey, the boy of the family quickly forms a deep admiration for Shane, who after an initial reticence displays his considerable skills as a gunman (in contrast to the boy's father). The mother too forms a strong though largely unstated bond with Shane, and even the father after an initial suspicion comes to respect Shane as a man of decency (although significant pauses and glances indicate his own unstated anxieties about Shane's unwitting usurpation of his wife and son's affections). The story is resolved when Shane kills the rancher's sadistic hired gunman in a shoot-out and then, against the anguished pleas from the son, rides away into the hills.

The echoic moment in *Shane* occurs at this point of the film, as Shane slowly rides away. Joey calls out to him: "Shane! Come Back! [echo: *Come back! Come Back!*] Mama wants you! [echo: *Wants you, wants you*]. I know she does." Although echo effects in movies frequently exceed the requirements of strict "realism," they are usually accorded some degree of diegetic motivation. In *Shane* the echo appears to be diegetically "caused" by the mountains in the distance (although such a relatively short delay between the voice and its echo would need a much nearer reverberant surface than that of the distant mountains).

Shane is set on a wide, slightly undulating plain, against a spectacular backdrop of immense, snow-covered mountains. Similar arrangements of plains and mountains recur in western movie iconography. While there are pragmatic reasons for this—the proximity of Monument Valley and the Sierra Nevadas to Hollywood ensured their frequent inclusion in movies of the genre—these landforms also perform deeper symbolic functions. In the case of *Shane,* the distant mountains might be seen as a kind of visual stand in for a number of coalescing forces, all more or less related to the law, civil or "natural." The territory of the narrative in *Shane* (and in western narratives in general) is a jurisprudentially liminal zone; it lies at the fuzzy edge of the reach of the civil law. The normal guarantees of property rights and civil order, the due processes of criminal prosecution and punishment are often only nominally in force (as exemplified by the western movie staple of the weak sheriff figure). Organized and effective civil power and governance is remote. It is stated more than once in *Shane* that "the Law is three days' ride away." The action takes place in a partly deterritorialized zone.

The spectacle of the mountains looming in the distance in *Shane* might be seen as a kind of symbolic rendering of "the Law"—simultaneously remote from the immediate action, but an immense, immutable and immovable presiding presence nonetheless. Given western narratives' obsessions with the constructing of masculine subjectivities and with issues of law and order, the immense natural monuments of the "western" landscape iconography might be seen to function as complex emblems of power. The ubiquitous, ancient, weathered buttes and mesas of the western movie could be seen as a kind of remnant, as atrophied replicas of the institutions of the paternal and/or patriarchal, both "the Law" and the laws of settled society "back east."[24] At the same time they bespeak a nearer "natural" or divine power, and invoke biblical traditions of sacred mountains as the sites of divine revelation, as indeed the very haunts of the deity. Thus, following this construct, the mountains might be seen as (among other things) enacting or presiding over a nervous, ambiguous moment of transition or contestation between divine law, civil law and anarchy.

The sonic marker of the mountain is the echo. In the real world, the phenomenon of echo in open spaces is caused when sound waves encounter a large obstacle and are reflected in such a way that they retain enough of their original characteristics to be heard as a delayed, reduced replica of the original sound. If these mountains in some way stand for "the Law," then the echo here might be the voice of that law: a (diminished) voice of the father, an "absent paternal." Joey forms a filial attachment to gunman Shane, disdaining his phallically impaired (that is, unarmed, nonviolent) father played by Van Heflin. His mother is also sexually attracted to Shane, although this is not overtly acknowledged by her.

But echo as encountered by the human listener is an uncanny phenomenon, as if the sound has been emitted by the mass that reflects it. An echoed human voice then sets up the anthropomorphic illusion that the mountainside (or whatever reflected the sound) has "spoken." As with the Greek myth of Echo, the effect is profoundly dichotomized. On the one hand the echo is clearly of the self that produced the original signal, operating as a powerful signifier of aloneness (indeed, of utter loneliness and desolation, of the Void). At the same time it signifies the animate other, the double, and its very existence hints at the chance of a participatory bridging of separations. Indeed, echo effects so powerfully evoke notions of simultaneous aloneness and of invisible presences as to forcefully background social collectivist associations (such as the presence or absence of civil law) in favor of "inner" and supernatural issues—religious, mystical or animist. The most Christianist reading would see the echo "emitting" from a mountain operating as a kind of voice of God.[25] Western movie echo might be seen as an enactment of the Protestant conscience: the solitary, nonconforming pilgrim, free from the mediatory interventions of a corrupt social world, provided he is sufficiently pure, may count on receiving divine guidance. The lone rider possesses a conveniently portable "mobile phone" to God. The Puritan deity speaks from inside the heart of the believer. Like echo, the deity's voice will sound remarkably like that of the believer.

The figure of Shane himself is important here. The character-type originated in the pulp mass-market cowboy and western novels that first appeared in the 1890s. The itinerant gunman character promptly found a home in the western movie, occupying those regions from which the law is always "three days' ride." By 1953 the Shane figure could still be represented as relatively virtuous (although troubled by his own rootlessness and by the knowledge that any involvement along the way was likely to end in bloodshed). Shane's territory is that region where the paternal is absent, weak or subject to contestation—the landscape of the echo. The "good gunman" easily carries the weight of heroic viewer identification. Despite the gunman's oft-repeated claim that his life is not all it's cracked up to be, that he would in fact like to settle down, have a family, raise a few cattle, such rarely happens in western narratives. He retains his territorial freedom. God approves. The gunman's life will "continue" after the movie as it was before: the life of a nonurban itinerant, divinely mandated to enact occasional explosive violence. He will ride slowly through epic landscapes, his horse's hooves thundering on the stones and echoing off the ever-present buttes and canyon walls. Such is the life of the screen gunman. Echo attends him as an index of his aloneness, as a signifier of that almost fatherless/lawless deterritorialized realm he inhabits and as a marker of his divinely granted privilege. At the same time, echo marks moments of transition: Shane's departure, and Joey's own moment of transition to adulthood.

High Sierra (directed by Raoul Walsh, 1941) provides a telling (and considerably earlier) deployment of echo and reverb effects. The action in the last part of the film draws inevitably to the location cited in the title, Mount Whitney, the highest mountain in the United States.[26] The forces of law and order close in on aging gangster Roy Earle (Humphrey Bogart), cornering him on the slopes at the base of the mountain. He abandons his car and clambers a way up the mountain, finally digging into a cleft in the rocks. The sheriff leading the pursuit calls out to him: "Hey you! You got no chance! Come on down!" There is a distinct echo added to each utterance. Roy's reply is even more echoic, with two echoes and reverb added to the original signal. The reverb serves to distance Roy's voice, to locate it off center, suggesting that the listener is sharing the sheriff's point of view, looking up the mountain toward Roy.

In the next scene it is evening on the mountain and a crowd of police, press and onlookers has gathered. A reporter talks into a microphone:

This seems the coldest place on earth tonight, cold and unreal. One is awe-stricken by the gruesomeness of this rendezvous with death—the morbidly curious onlookers standing by as if they watched to gain, the tall pine trees clustered around like a silent jury, the officers of the law waiting for the kill—all in the sight of the highest mountain peak in the United States.

The Roy Earle character as an ex-con is an outsider from the very beginning of the film, but at this point he is making a further transition away from the realm of the everyday, of the social, in a sense of the real, as the reporter's speech suggests. The echoic moment marks a movement into mythic space.

A little later there is another exchange between Roy and the sheriff, similarly echoic, in which Roy again refuses to surrender although it is clear that he has no hope of escape. After this last exchange Roy is alerted to the presence of his girlfriend, Marie, in the crowd when her dog runs up the mountain to Roy, seeking out his voice. Roy throws caution to the wind, stands up and calls to Marie (echoic) and is picked off by a sharpshooter. The gunshot does not actually echo, but the sound effect used is that of the ricocheting bullet (a hyperreal effect; the single shot kills Roy and thus would be unlikely to ricochet).

The Sierras figure prominently throughout the film, in a way not wholly unlike the mountains in *Shane*. At one point Roy gazes at the range as a gas station owner identifies Mount Whitney as the highest mountain in the country. Later Roy and his partners occupy holiday cabins virtually in the shadow of the mountains. They could be seen as a symbol of Roy's approaching showdown, or of the forces of law and order themselves (much nearer here than in *Shane*), or as symbol of Roy's lonely subjectivity, or a kind of Calvary. The echoic moment(s) are those of Roy's greatest isolation. As an outlaw run to ground and finally executed, and also as a folk hero in the making, in the tradition of Pretty Boy Floyd (Roy too is originally a farmboy) or John Dillinger, Roy himself is becoming a kind of monument, a legend. At this point Roy becomes virtually a creature of the air, a spirit. Marie tells the cynical reporter present at the shootout that Roy has "crashed out," which the reporter himself has just informed her is jail argot for breaking out. The overt level of meaning here is religious, that Roy has transcended this vale of tears, that he will be free in heaven. At another level, perhaps, it signals that the figure of Roy has entered the social imaginary, that his death has provided a kind of stability to the idea of Roy, in order that the legend may mutate freely, unhindered by any real-world actions of the corporeal Roy.

The echoic moment on the mountain then is a kind of dialogue between Roy and his echo—the disembodied voice of the mountain—the voice of God (the Father), calling Roy to heaven, or perhaps to immortality as a folk hero in the John Dillinger, Pretty Boy Floyd, Clyde Barrow mold. The sniper who picks him off does so by climbing higher up the mountain than Roy himself is, in fact "higher up than anyone has been before." It is only when Roy calls out to Marie below—a call back to corporeality—that the sniper gets a chance at the shot that kills Roy.

In both these films the echo is a product of the natural world—monumental landforms—and bespeaks the ordering presence of God, notwithstanding the absence or remoteness of human law. Even though Roy is finally cornered and killed by the very human forces of law and order, the fact that the final scene takes place "in the sight of the mountain" gives a sense of naturalness or mythic inevitability to the showdown. The human marshals are little more than agents in a process that transcends human sociality. The echo effects in *Shane* and *High Sierra* are employed to embellish pivotal moments in each narrative—numinous moments, moments of metaphysical transition, of gnosis. The figures at the center of both narratives are constructed as "sacred loners," as outlaw prophets. The echo used in these is not primarily a spatializing device; it functions not so much to construct a general sense of physical space and dimensionality (the visual scene-setting does this) as it does to construct a mystical space, an ambiguously inner and outer space, a fictive, subjective "zone," one not necessarily possessing physical parameters, but rather one that is fluid, notional, undefined, both "inside" and "above" actual physical space. The echo marks a momentary swelling of "mindspace," a momentary partial eclipsing of the simply material.

Both films rapidly switch points of view at their key moments, back and forth between the observers (Joey in *Shane,* Marie, the police and press in *High Sierra*) and the outlaw. The outlaw figures are rendered as both observers and as observed, as both self and as other. Almost without fail, echo and reverb are used when the outlaws are distanced or othered in point of view terms, but their respective "otherings" carry distinctly heroic, Christlike overtones: Shane's ascension into the mountains, Earle's Calvary-like mountain death.

Another "high visibility" deployment of western echo and reverb effects roughly contemporaneous with the above occurred in Vaughn Monroe's million-selling record of "Riders in the Sky" (1949) on Victor. Textually, the song is related to the earlier mystical Bob Nolan–styled cowboy songs of the 1930s, except here, rather than a gentle, meditative moment of heavenly revelation in the wilderness, the central character experiences a terrifying vision of hell. An old cowpoke alone in the wilderness on a dark and windy day stops to rest and witnesses the appearance of a herd of ghost cattle, their brands on fire, their hooves made of steel, their horns black and shiny, thundering through the cloudy sky. Moments later the terrified cowpoke sees the ghost riders following in (literally) hot pursuit, and he hears their mournful cry, the distantly reverberant, "yippie-eye-ay, yippie-eye-o." The riders draw closer and he sees their sweaty shirts, gaunt faces, and blurry eyes. Somehow the cowpoke knows the phantom horesmen (whose mounts snort fire) are doomed to pursue the ghost herd across the aerial range forever. In the final verse one of their number warns the cowpoke directly that unless he changes his ways, he too will suffer the same eternal punishment.

As well as drawing on the relatively recent singing cowboy traditions, the song's lyrics reach back to several medieval traditions: that of the vision of hell, the dream visitation of the damned (who have been granted divine permission to return in order to deliver a cautionary tale to the living) and the legends of the cavalcade of the dead, or Herlequin's Ride, which "Riders in the Sky" most closely resembles.[27] Of the latter, a Germanic peasant belief, Davidson says: "Whereas the otherworld vision is normally presented as taking place in spirit while the dreamer is ill, seeing Herlequin's ride is portrayed as a real experience which takes place while the singer is alone in a desolate place at night."[28] The earlier peasant pagan formulations of the myth of the wild ride generally lack the didacticism of the later Christian retellings: rather than bearing a message for the living, the dead simply appear, terrifyingly, to the witness. The trope was still vigorously extant in twentieth-century popular music, with a heavy overlay of didacticism: the reprobate who receives a warning, in the form of a vision, of the fate that awaits him should he continue in his godless pursuits, or a plea from a departed loved one to change his ways: for example, Jimmie Rodgers' "Mother, the Queen of my Heart" (1932) or Reverend A. W. Nix's "Black Diamond Express to Hell" (1928), the theme of which reappears in Chuck Berry's "Down Bound Train" (1955).

The mood of "Riders in the Sky" is, accordingly, one of high portent, in keeping with the motifs of ghostly visitation and spiritual edification. The rhythm guitar plays a flamenco-like rhythm, simultaneously referencing the mock-high seriousness and the drumming feet of the flamenco dancer. The rhythm here also mimics the thundering hooves of the ghost horses and cattle, and provides a feeling of relentless forward movement. (After the huge sales success of "Riders in the Sky" that particular feeling became a western staple, recurring in the theme music for the television shows *Bonanza, Have Gun Will Travel, Rawhide, Johnny Yuma,* and *Outlaws* among others.)

The voice of the singer is close-miked and dry, while the chorus is kept off-mic and richly reverberant, as are the muted horns (although the latter, referencing hunting horns perhaps, are less reverberant than the vocal chorus). The exaggerated differential between Monroe's very close singing and the distant chorus sets up a vastness, a wide-open spatiality, in keeping with the pictorial western setting. As well as simply locating the male singers "in the distance," the reverb on the chorus also perhaps brings to mind the acoustic regime of Christian church architecture (consistent with the sermonlike aspects of the song's lyrics). At the same time the effect powerfully (even if by contemporary standards, perhaps "cornily") reinforces the supernatural, disquieting impact the appearance of the ghost riders has on the observer.

Significantly, "Riders in the Sky" was one of the few million-copy sellers in the United States that year, and Sanjek[29] puts the song's success partly down to the easy manipulability of the (then) new magnetic tape. (The record also, according to Sanjek, "did more than anything to sell Americans on the 45 rpm concept.") It is perhaps also significant that so spatial and dramatic a recording should be a standout commercial success at precisely the time Americans were generally buying few recordings, but were enthusiastically turning to the visual spatial-dramatic pleasures offered by television.

But apart from the different "hardware" used in its construction and distribution, "Riders in the Sky" does not in textural terms greatly differ from Willing's "Blue Shadows on the Trail."[30] Both recordings feature an upfront, nonechoic lead vocal contrasted against a distant reverberant voice: the comforting steel guitar in "Blue Shadows on the Trail," and the disturbing male chorus in "Riders in the Sky." In both cases, the centrally located voice is louder in the mix than the removed voice(s). The echoicity of the steel guitar, as described above, connotes unseen presences: nightbirds, coyotes, perhaps a more mysterious spirit of place. In "Riders in the Sky" the echoic quality of the voices is a mark of both their putative physical distance from the singer and their noncorporeality, their ghostliness. Both songs set up a dialectic between here and there, self and other, center and margin, ego and id, embedded within a rendered virtual spatiality. The Willing record apparently uses real-space acoustics—the sound of the studio itself—to construct its distance, while the Monroe record uses tape delay to create its spatially other. The effect, a blend of the landscape pictorial and the uncanny, is similar in both. Elsewhere, at about this same time some fringe record makers (such as John Lee Hooker and producer Bernie Besman) were using reverb to denote magical or uncanny presences that were not strictly physically located within a realist aural mise en scène; the reverb was an intrinsic marker of the voices' magicality and potency rather than of their placement within a putative literal field (discussed in greater detail in chapter 7). In "Blue Shadows on the Trail" and "Riders in the Sky," however, the connotations of ghostliness and the denotation of "in the distance" are still not separable.

In terms of lyrical content, however, there are sharp differences between the two. The visually occluded other denoted in "Blue Shadows on the Trail," the various sounds of the twilight on the trail constitute warm, unthreatening, companionable presences. The aural scene is suffused with a sense of serenity and beauty. The "plaintive wail from the distance" is a source of pleasure for the singer, a trigger for a moment of rapture. But the other in "Riders in the Sky" is a terrifying, unholy force; rather than remaining at a stable and reassuring remove from the observer, the ghost riders approach from the distance, address the observer and then even hint at abduction ("cowboy, change your ways today or with us you will ride"). Singer Vaughn Monroe's steely on-mic baritone suggests an equally steely ego that will no doubt withstand terrors that emerge from liminal zones.[31] The last chorus from the ghost riders suggests a fading away into the distance, a diminution of the threat.

Yet subtle points of correspondence and identity between the observer and the unholy other set up troubling undercurrents. For the first three choruses, for example, the "yippie-eye-ay, yippie-eye-o" chant (perhaps the true hook of the song) is sung by the reverberant ghost riders only, but by the fourth chorus Monroe himself sings it; for all the righteously God-fearing terror at the surface of the song, there is also clearly manifest in the singing a sense of exhilaration, of pagan abandonment. The ghost riders have the best part of the song, and singer Monroe wants in on it. The unholy dead transmit to the singer a delirious energy.

Echo and reverb are used in movies from this same time to signal ghostly and unholy presences. In *The Body Snatcher* (directed by Robert Wise, 1947) Boris Karloff's character, Gray, is a grave robber, who digs up corpses late at night and delivers them to a local surgeon, MacFarlane, in his cab. On a number of occasions we (through the point of view of MacFarlane's assistant) hear Gray's cab echoing on the cobblestones as he goes about his nefarious business. Here the reverb has a real-world motivation: it is late at night and so sounds might be expected to carry, the streets are narrow, the surfaces are hard and highly sound-reflective and so on. But the reverberant sounds at the same time serve as an index of the assistant's feelings of fear and apprehension—like Vaughn Monroe he is fearfully awaiting the approach of the dead. Here the simple addition of reverb, every bit as much as the late-night setting, the gothic trappings and the music, establishes the eeriness of the scene.

Later in the story, when the local cemetery has been exhausted of fresh corpses, Gray fills an order by murdering a blind, young woman street singer. Afterward her voice can briefly be heard, highly reverberant, as MacFarlane and his assistant talk about her, in an effect akin to what Bruce Kawin[32] terms *mindscreen*—the singer is dead and could not produce a "real" diegetic sound, so the singing on the soundtrack must be what the onscreen characters are "hearing" in their memory. Later still, after Mac-Farlane has murdered Gray, he hears Gray calling to him as he drives the cab along a country road, at night, in a violent storm. The voice that calls MacFarlane is also highly reverberant—again another "mind-sound," although taken as real by the guilt-crazed MacFarlane. The echo and reverb mark a switch to a haunted, distracted interiority.

I Walked With a Zombie (directed by Jacques Tourneur, 1943) also makes use of the effect at highly charged moments. The heroine Betsy is awakened on her first night in her new employer's house by the sound of a woman crying. The sobbing sound is both echoic and reverberant. It is also quite loud, at first seeming to come from somewhere in the darkened room in which Betsy is sleeping. She goes searching for the source of the sound, which does not actually seem to get any closer; neither the volume nor the reverberant quality change as Betsy moves across the courtyard into the tower on the other side. The suggestion is that the sound is not external to Betsy at all, but is at least partly interior. Moving toward the tower Betsy encounters the zombie, her employer's mindless wife (who is not the source of the ghostly crying; Betsy never does trace the sound to its source, which we later find out was produced by a woman crying at the birth of a baby). Later on Betsy again wakes up and crosses the courtyard, and again sounds are highly reverberant. This time the main sound is that of dripping water. On both occasions Betsy has awakened from sleep; on both occasions she is alone and attempting to resolve an enigma, an enigma of place in this case. Such transition cues all strongly suggest that the "space" has changed at least partly into an internal, psychic space.

A similar dripping water motif had been earlier put to use by Tourneur in the horror film *Cat People* (1942). The story centers around the mysterious foreign woman Irena, who believes she bears an ancient Balkan curse: whenever her passions are sufficiently aroused she is subject to a demonic possession: she temporarily becomes a ravening panther. Irena fights against the curse; she refuses to consummate her marriage, certain that for her to do so would be to the fatal detriment of her husband. In the tradition of Dr Jekyll and other shape-shifting villains, Irena does her best to resist the curse, but once it takes hold she enthusiastically acts out.

A famously echoic moment occurs when Alice, a friend, visits an indoor swimming pool after spending the afternoon with Irena's husband. At this stage in the story the viewer, Irena and Alice are all in slightly different ways unsure of Irena's true status: is she or is she not in fact a murderous demon? Alice goes downstairs to the pool, and moments later Irena arrives and follows her down. What follows is represented from Alice's point of view: first she sees a kitten, which alarms her unduly. The echoic sound of dripping water can be heard at this point, unnaturally loud, and the pool itself is weirdly illuminated, in near darkness, with strange reflections playing over the walls. Next Alice hears the roar of a big cat and sees what looks like a panther shadow coming down the stairs. She flees to the pool in terror and watches as the shadow drifts around the walls and ceiling of the room, blending with the watery reflections. The roars of the beast become louder, more reverberant and seem to engulf her. She screams and the lights come on. Irena is standing by the light switch, smiling slyly. Up to this point all sounds in the sequence are extremely reverberant—the roaring, the dripping water, the splash as Alice dives into the water, and her screaming—but once the light is turned on, the sounds become dry, nonreverberant.

In both *Cat People* and *I Walked With a Zombie* the dripping water effect is diegetically justified to a point, although the relative loudness and reverberant quality of the sounds suggests spaces other than those actually depicted. The literal suggestion is of an enclosed, damp, subterranean space—a mine, a sewer, a cave, perhaps a cellar—activating in the viewer a claustrophobic revulsion. In both films, with their overt concerns with psychosis and psychiatry, it is not difficult to see the enclosed spaces as representative of the unconscious. When the sound becomes reverberant in both films it signals that even while the image is of diegetically real space, the world presented is just as much an inner one.

In both films the onset of echo and reverb corresponds to a moment of relative visual occlusion, and in so doing recalls the trade-offs and complementarities between seen spaces and heard spaces present in the myth of Echo and Narcissus and in the recordings of "My Blue Heaven" and "Blue Shadows on the Trail." When the lights dim, the aural space swells out, but once this happens the position of remote actants (ghosts, night sounds, cat people) can no longer with certainty be fixed. Even solid, quotidian presences in the echoic twilight thus become like spirits, at best enchanting mysterious presences (like the night sounds in "Blue Shadows on the Trail," or "My Blue Heaven") but at worst terrifying and malevolent shape-shifters. Furthermore, the shift into the crepuscular is also a shift into a simultaneously, ambiguously inner and outer zone. Lacking the concreteness and fixity of the material daylight world the echoic space assumes the characteristics of a dreamed space—acausal, unstable, nonlinear, nonrational. But dynamic, infinitely richer with possibility. It is significant that *Cat People* is at its most disquieting at its least cinematic, least visual moments. The horror effects are achieved by obscuring the visual and allowing the aural mise en scène to expand nightmarishly. Echoic space is used to create soft-sell (and relatively inexpensive) horror effects.

It is significant that the semiotic range and impact of these sound effects should have been so fully realized in movie laboratories, considering that sound production has generally been seen as one of filmmaking's poorer relations. Film's most engaging moments, according to the common wisdom, will be achieved by appealing to the eyes rather than the ears of the audience. But in (some) 1940s cinema we see potent filmic spatial effects wrought primarily with sound. The echoic and reverberant sound devices discussed here achieved their results in concert with the visual. Echo and reverb created secondary spatialities that were often at odds with the visual evidence—Joey's voice in *Shane* echoes "unnaturally," suggesting the presence of unseen walls, of boundaries that are only partly material (they cause sound reflection but do not register visually) composing a hidden structure at once material and of the psyche.

Just as music recording in the 1930s through the 1950s displayed growing territorial ambitions, seeking to expand its own weakest capability—the representation of visual space—so too filmmaking increasingly experimented with its own supposedly weakest tools, the sonic representation of space. By focusing activities in their respective (purportedly) least effective modes, film sound production and popular music recording both necessarily moved into less strictly realist styles of representation; in so doing they significantly added to the range of psychic meanings that sonic spatial representations might thereafter carry.

In the end, however, neither film nor music recording can be credited with fully originating the device of the "uncanny echo in the cowboy-western landscape." Echoes recur in pulp western fiction written well before the coming of talkies and before the beginnings of electrical recording. In the book *Riders of the Purple Sage,* by Zane Grey, for example, echoes and reverberant sounds feature importantly at moments of terror, extreme danger or violent action, or when the eerie loneliness of the western landscape is being emphasized. So too echoes feature at moments of quasi-mystical revelation:

Suddenly from the mouth of the canyon just beyond her rang out a clear, sharp report of a rifle. Echoes clapped. Then followed a piercingly high yell of anguish, quickly breaking. Again echoes clapped, in grim imitation. Dull revolver shots—hoarse yells—pound of hoofs—shrill neighs of horses—commingling of echoes—and again silence! Lassiter must be busily engaged, thought Jane, and no chill trembled over her, no blanching tightened her skin. Yes, the border was a bloody place. . . . (302)

Much of the action in *Riders of the Purple Sage* is centered around a mysterious lost canyon, in which the thunder from the frequent desert storms is massively amplified.

Black night enfolded the valley. Venters could not see his companion, and knew of [Bess's] presence only through the tightening hold of her hand on his arm. He felt the dogs huddle closer to him. Suddenly the dense, black vault overhead split asunder to a blue-white, dazzling streak of lightning. The whole valley lay vividly clear and luminously bright in his sight. Upreared, vast and magnificent, the stone bridge glimmered like some grand god of storm in the lightning's fire. Then all flashed black again—blacker than pitch—a thick, impenetrable coal-blackness. And there came a ripping, crashing report. Instantly an echo resounded with clapping crash. The initial report was nothing to the echo. It was a terrible, living, reverberating, detonating crash. The wall threw the sound across, and could have made no greater roar if it had slipped in avalanche. From cliff to cliff the echo went in crashing retort and banged in lessening power, and boomed in thinner volume, and clapped weaker and weaker till a final clap could not reach across the waiting cliff.
    In the pitchy darkness Venters led Bess, and, groping his way, by feel of hand found the entrance to her cave and lifted her up. On the instant a blinding flash of lightning illumined the cave and all about him. He saw Bess's face white now with dark, frightened eyes. He saw the dogs leap up, and he followed suit. The golden glare vanished; all was black; then came the splitting crack and the infernal din of echoes. . . .
    . . . Then the storm burst with a succession of ropes and streaks and shafts of lightning, playing continuously, filling the valley with a broken radiance; and the cracking shots followed each other swiftly till the echoes blended in one fearful, deafening crash.
    . . . The lightning played incessantly, streaking down through opaque darkness of rain. The roar of the wind, with its strange knell and the re-crashing echoes, mingled with the roar of the flooding rain, and all seemingly were deadened and drowned in a world of sound. (174–176)

Grey here is drawing directly on the eighteenth-century tradition of the romantic Sublime, the attitude to nature and art that celebrated the wildest natural phenomena and the most rugged landscapes—mountains, chasms, fjords, gothic forests, craggy outcrops, windswept cliffs, remote and barren natural places—as sites in which suitably sensitized viewers might allow themselves to be caught between terror and private aesthetic rapture, resulting in a near mystical experience. The idea of the Sublime in its (relatively) modern form was championed most notably by Edmund Burke in his *A Philosophical Enquiry into the Origin of Our Ideas of the Sublime and the Beautiful* (1757), and Burkean ideas informed the perceptions of the American west through the nineteenth and twentieth century. That the lowly cowboy should be the witness to the western Sublime may represent a democratization of the earlier formulation: the eighteenth-century Sublime was implicitly available only to the most refined and romantic sensibilities, not to unlettered members of the laboring classes.[33]

CHAPTER 5

"And as the Sun Sinks Slowly in the West..."

Sobbing Guitars, Distant Horizons and the Acoustics of Otherness

In 1912 the musical stage play *Bird of Paradise,* opened to great success at the Daly Theater in Broadway. The *New York Times* remarked that the play's Hawaiian setting "gave opportunity for scenes of much color and for the introduction of the weirdly sensuous music of the island people." The music was provided by an ensemble of guitar, acoustic steel guitar, ukulele and *ipu.*[1] The show went on to tour the United States, Canada, Australia[2] and Europe.[3] In 1932 RKO released a movie version,[4] which was remade in 1951 by Twentieth Century–Fox.[5] Some of the songs from the play, like "Mauna Kea," became pop Hawaiian standards.

The music program at the Hawaiian Pavilion proved to be one of the sensations of the 1915 Panama-Pacific International Exposition in San Francisco. Visitors to the pavilion (there were many; the expo on the whole attracted seventeen million people over its seven months) were introduced to a number of soon-to-be standards, including "Waikiki Mermaid," "On the Beach at Waikiki," "Tomi, Tomi" and "Song of the Islands." The music was supplied by the Royal Hawaiian Quartet (guitar, steel guitar and two ukuleles) and various guests. People left the pavilion, it was said, humming the new songs.[6]

In the wake of these two events—the *Bird of Paradise* stage show and the 1915 expo—"Hawaiian music" in various forms quickly became a major presence in the mainland United States and soon world popular music, and was to remain so for more than two decades. Recordings by mainland-based ethnic Hawaiian guitarists such as Joe Kekuku, King Benny Nawahi,

Sol Hoopii, Andy Iona and others were among the highest-selling items throughout the recording industry's boom period the 1920s. "Hawaiian acts," whether ethnic Hawaiians, or "rebranded" hillbilly, western or pop string bands became a staple of the vaudeville stage. "Hawaiian rooms" were set up in such establishments as the plush Lexington Hotel in New York, the Roosevelt Hotel in Chicago and the Mayfair Hotel in London,[7] and there was a Polynesian Room in the New Tokyo Hotel in Japan.[8] Hawaiian music and themed decor became a cabaret and nightclub staple, especially on the West Coast. Hawaiian music programs sponsored by the Matson Shipping Line were broadcast in North America and in the mid-1930s *Hawaii Calls* began broadcasting live from Honolulu, and was to continue into the 1970s.[9]

Hawaiian music repertoires included Hawaiian language songs (many written in the nineteenth century, often using melodies from hymns) and more recently penned *hapa haole* (or "half-white") songs, which used combinations of English and Hawaiian language. Others, such as "On the Beach at Waikiki," were entirely in English but were written in Hawaii and had "Hawaiian" themes. Mainland Tin Pan Alley songwriters also produced numerous songs that attempted to exploit the Hawaiian craze. Many of these, such as "Doo Wacka Doo," "Yacka Hula Hicky Dula" (performed by Al Jolson) or "Oh, How She Could Yacki Hacki Wicki Woo" crudely parodied Hawaiian language, while others, such as "I Can Hear the Ukuleles Calling Me" simply attempted to musically and lexically reference notions of "Hawaiianness."[10]

The Hawaiian-style slide or steel guitar, present in virtually all of the vaudeville shows, the stage plays, and ubiquitous on Hawaiian recordings was perhaps the single most defining sonic feature of the Hawaiian craze. In the late 1920s steel guitars began appearing on recordings that did not allude textually to Hawaii—most notably on recordings by Jimmie Rodgers and other hillbilly acts such as Cliff Carlisle and Darby and Tarlton. A number of mainland vaudevillians of the 1920s, such as guitar virtuoso Roy Smeck spectacularly mastered Hawaiian-style guitar, and various guitar players around the world began using "Hawaiian" stage names, and sometimes performing in costume. In 1931 Richard Tauber recorded "Ein Paradies am Meerestrand" (A paradise by the sea) with Hawaiian guitar backing, and in 1937 Bing Crosby, backed by Lani McIntyre and His Hawaiians, had a worldwide hit with his version of "Sweet Leilani." Hawaiian guitar was also greatly subscribed to by amateur players. Hawaiian music schools—such as the Oahu Publishing Company of Cleveland, Ohio, from whose franchises some 200,000 students are said to have graduated[11]—opened in the United States and worldwide. In Australia, for example, through the worst years of the Great Depression, Hawaiian schools in Sydney and Melbourne ran full classes all day, every day, and staged mass performances in town halls.[12] Students were offered lessons in Hawaiian guitar, "regular" guitar and ukulele. Teacher/performers not infrequently adopted faux-Hawaiian stage names.

As a mélange of musical features married to what were in the main rather crudely drawn geographic, cultural and racial conceits, "Hawaiian" as it was trafficked in Western popular music might be included with various other subcategories of early twentieth-century popular music: "cowboy," "Irish," Latin, blackface and so on. Such geographic, racial and occupational conceits had been fundamental to nineteenth- and early twentieth-century popular music practice. Music hall and vaudeville performers appeared almost without fail, in costume, as "racial" types (Irish, Jew, Italian, Gypsy, Negro, Hawaiian) or as character/occupational types (sailor, cowboy, toff, washerwoman, barrowmen, navvy, serving girl, soldier, hillbilly). Characterizations included both "locals" and "exotics": gypsies, Native Americans, Latins, Africans, Polynesians, Cossacks. Rhythmic, melodic and harmonic motifs, purporting (accurately or otherwise) to be of exotic origin colored and broadened the sonic palettes of Tin Pan Alley popular music in successive waves and crazes throughout the late nineteenth- and early twentieth-centuries. Pictorial tropes accompanied the effects, most notably "themed" stage settings and nightclub decor, and elaborate landscape graphics on sheet music covers. As with the mass-mediated cowboy west, the "Pacific-exotic" was also a strong presence in mass-market fiction, both in magazine short stories and in cheap novels.

The category "Hawaiian music" was always an unstable entity, and from at least the 1920s produced almost continual authenticity debates among its participants. In his definitive work on the subject, George Kanahele points out that musical cultures of the islands have always displayed a "phenomenal" rate and degree of acculturation and assimilation,[13] making identification of "Hawaiian" as a musical category difficult. Nonetheless, Kanahele offers a periodicized schema of the emergence of Hawaiian music. The dominant form at the arrival of Captain Cook in 1778 *mele*, or chant, was actively suppressed in the nineteenth century, and the tradition, although it continued, did not figure prominently in the emergence of what became known both in Hawaii and elsewhere as twentieth-century "Hawaiian music."[14] Kanahele's periods thus are broadly defined according to the arrival of various major non-Hawaiian musical trends and influences. The first period, from 1820 to 1872, is characterized by the arrival of hymns introduced by missionaries, and secular tunes from an array of European, American and Asian sources ranging from Mexican,

Italian, German instrumental and vocal ensembles, to Burmese singers. The period from the early 1870s to 1900 sees the guitar become the instrument of the "common folk," while the European waltz becomes the form of choice for the Royal Hawaiian Band and the various royal music clubs. The music at this stage is firmly based in hymn-harmony. In the period 1900–1915 "ragtime seep[s] into Hawaiian music and engulf[s] it," and composer/musicians such as Sonny Cunha begin writing songs with English words, so launching the *hapa haole* style. In the next period, 1915–1930, "jazzed-up Tin Pan Alley versions of *hapa haole* music spreads to mainland America."[15] The period 1930–1960 in Kanahele's schema sees the export of *hapa haole* to the world, the appearance of big band *hapa haole*[16] Hawaiian music being used increasingly on film soundtracks, and the spread of Hawaiian-styled revues. Hawaiian guitarists become recording and touring sensations on the U.S. mainland.

For many listeners, the sliding steel guitar (its characteristic sound so often described as "haunting") came to stand for "Hawaiian music" in general, and for many non-Hawaiians thereafter the term would mean music containing, whatever else, a steel guitar. Conversely, steel guitar, whether used in a "Hawaiian" piece or not would tend to connote, to some degree, a notion of "Hawaiianness" and things exotic. It is in this interzone of loose, shifting connotation, dubious authenticity, mixed metaphor and hazy, often naive association that some of the more potent spatial acoustic "tactics" were to appear.

"Hawaiian guitar" and "steel guitar" are inexact terms, with multiple meanings. "Steel guitar" may refer to both a method of playing—in which the guitar is placed flat on the player's lap (or on a stand) and the strings fretted with a sliding piece of steel held in the left hand—or it may refer to a certain type of guitar, most notably the National and Dobro resonator guitars manufactured in the 1920s through the 1940s by the Dopera brothers, specifically, but not exclusively for Hawaiian-styled playing. At the higher end of the National and Dobro instruments' price range were the gleaming "all steel" guitars and mandolins, which featured one or three resonators, and were etched with graphic motifs (most typically palm trees). Later the term "steel guitar" came to refer to other lap or table-styled electric guitars made by Gibson, Rickenbacker, Fender and many others, and eventually as well the contemporary pedal steel guitars (which, like the earlier all-steel Nationals, also typically featured gleaming expanses of chrome and steel).

The steel sliding bar used in Hawaiian guitar is moved freely up and down the neck and any string can be played at a limitless number of points. The characteristic sound of Hawaiian guitar therefore is the glissando, the fluid, analogic movement of pitch, as opposed to the "digital," "on the fret" mode of the conventional guitar. Without care and skill on the part of the steel guitar player, intonation will easily drift slightly above or below "correct pitch." The setup of the Hawaiian guitar encourages the player to shift and color the pitch by means of vibrato and various other microtonal movements.[17] (The novice player of the Hawaiian steel guitar can achieve a satisfactory musical result, with a distinctive sound relatively quickly, and steel guitar and the ukulele were staples of the "Learn a tune in 14 days! Be the life of the party!" type of mail-order trade.)

Steel guitar music of the 1920s was characterized by a high degree of formality and musical exactitude, perhaps as a counterbalance to the inherent "slipperiness" of the steel guitar. Modern listeners to Hawaiian music of the twenties (whether made on the mainland, or in Hawaii) will not generally encounter the wild informality and raw "vernacularity" that characterizes much recorded hillbilly, old-timey, country blues and "hokum" music of the time. The Hawaiian groups more often feature extraordinarily precise harmonies, and sing with the elaborately "correct," almost British-sounding pronunciation typically used by crooners of the day.[18] Although much early pop Hawaiian music used staccato guitar and vocal effects and sometimes driving, syncopated rhythms, it is not difficult to imagine how different and how weirdly "other" the gently picked slide guitar and ukulele pieces, and the delicately voiced harmonies—which often included a high falsetto—must have sounded in comparison to the hyperenergized ragtime songs, fox-trots and Sousa marches of the decade prior. But this "otherness" came mostly from within the perimeter of established melodic and harmonic practices of popular music.

In the 1930s Charles Edward King, composer, businessman and leader of the Royal Hawaiian Band attacked the radio program *Hawaii Calls* (along with its sponsor, the Hawaii Tourist Bureau) for "murdering" Hawaiian music, by "pepping it up":

You cannot improve the melodious and gripping songs of our islands by the new-style treatment. Don't try it! . . . [O]rientalizing or even Dardenella-izing our island songs is a sheer waste of time.[19]

King asserted that Hawaiian music should be in the Hawaiian language, should be "about" Hawaii, and its melodic quality should be *nahenahe* (literally "sweet"), rather than "jazzed-up."[20] Although King's was a Hawaiian voice, attempting to protect what he perceived as authentic Hawaiian elements in the music, the sort of "sweet" and melodious music he advocated was by then firmly partnered with narrative and imagistic tropes that were themselves consistent with an exoticizing, "Orientalizing" construction of

Hawaii and its culture. Edward Said famously formulated "Orientalism" as the complex of maneuvers by which Western art cultures of the eighteenth and nineteenth centuries constructed the East—in conscious or unconscious sympathy with the project of Western imperialism—as a mysterious, exotic, sensual other.[21] A number of writers have begun to examine the operations of the Orientalizing imagination in Western music. Born and Hesmond-halgh[22] cite Ralph P. Locke's discussion of Saint-Saëns' opera *Samson et Da-lila*, for example, in which he identifies a prototypical "Orientalist" narrative:

Young, tolerant, brave possibly naïve white-European tenor-hero intrudes at risk of disloyalty to his own people and colonial ethic, into mysterious, dark-skinned colo-nized territory represented by alluring dancing girls and deeply affectionate sensi-tive lyric soprano, incurring wrath of brutal intransigent tribal chieftain (bass or bass-baritone) and blindly obedient chorus of male savages.[23]

Born and Hesmondhalgh go on to broadly characterize musical Orien-talism as invoking a gendered binary, in which the "other" is figured as a highly sexual, desirable and desiring female, who represents both tempta-tion and threat to a morally and intellectually superior collective "Self."[24] While some studies have found nineteenth-century Orientalist opera, such as Borodin's *Prince Igor* to have been unequivocally in the service of an ag-gressive nationalism, seeking to provide a racialist endorsement of expan-sionist projects,[25] others have found (occasional) elements of an implicit critique of Western culture. Locke finds for example that in *Samson et Da-lila* Saint-Saëns casts the Hebrews (stand-ins for the self, the West, male) as less enticing, less vital and less animated than the other, Delilah's, tribe of Philistines. An "erotic and exotic languorous hedonism," embodied in the represented other became one of the key conventions of emerging nineteenth-century musical Orientalism.[26]

The two events that so furthered the Hawaiian music craze on the U.S. mainland and across the rest of the world were both shaped around Orien-talist and imperialist thought. The plot of *Bird of Paradise,* for example is synopsized by Kanahele:

An American visiting Hawai'i in the 1860s falls in love with Luana, a native princess ordained to be the bride of Pele. He takes her away to a secluded spot. When the volcano erupts, the Hawaiians decide to throw Luana in as sacrifice. She is saved and sends the American away.[27]

Clearly, *Bird of Paradise,* with its positing of a sensual, passionate other, whose seductive lure the Western protagonist must resist, offers at least a rough fit with the Orientalist template. At the same time the stage show, based on the play *In Hawaii,* written by longtime island resident, Grace A. Fendler, was rather more than simply a naive projection of Western concerns and anxieties onto a sketchily and all too conveniently rendered "other." Luana's sending away of the American at the end, for example, might be seen as a move to preserve the integrity of the island culture. The Broadway play also went to considerable pains to present an authentic range of Hawaiian music, including chant and *ipu*. Likewise the high-budget 1932 RKO movie of the play, filmed in Oahu and using more than one hundred location setups, employed Hawaiian consultants, including Charles E. King. The film featured, as well as the *hapa haole* music of Johnny Noble and Sol Hoopii, traditional chants and hulas, and music played on ancient instruments such as the *pahu* and *'uli'uli*.[28]

The Panama-Pacific International Exposition in 1915 was staged to celebrate the completion of the Panama Canal. It was thus a celebration of U.S. engineering, and indirectly perhaps of modern capitalism. And the housing in the one precinct of the numerous elaborate pavilions, representing various foreign countries and the different states and territories of the nation offered a symbolic enactment of the hitherto remote suddenly rendered near. Tourists from eastern states could more easily visit Hawaii, and representations of an imagined, heavily mediated Hawaii began to circulate widely in the mainland sign economy.

"Languorousness" figured increasingly in commercial Hawaiian music in the 1930s and 1940s (despite King's alarm at its "jazzing-up"), and it certainly remained a key motif of the *Hawaii Calls* radio program. Broadcast weekly from Honolulu, and heard around the world from 1935 until its cessation in 1975, the program promoted an image of Hawaii as earthly paradise—one that listeners were encouraged to physically visit, as well as imagine. Staged "under the old banyan tree in the courtyard of the Moana Hotel," the "liveness" and seductive authenticity of the setting was much stressed. Indeed, some mainland listeners to the original broadcasts apparently imagined the oscillations in the shortwave signal to be the sound of waves lapping on Waikiki. When the signal was improved the producers received complaints from listeners, and thereafter a microphone was placed near the water to pick up the real ocean waves. "Before long", says Kanahele "the roar of the surf had become the trademark of 'Hawaii Calls'"[29]

The program, notwithstanding King's later denunciation, had originally been founded as a response to the sort of "jazzed-up" Hawaiian music considered by its founder, Webley E. Edwards, to be inauthentic. But by that time, the mid-1930s, mainland-based Hawaiian players such as Sol Hoopii, King Benny Nawahi, Andy Iona and many others were more involved with the "jazzed-up" style. Theirs were small guitar combos who performed, along with older, slower Hawaiian waltzes and *hapa haole* songs, contemporary show tunes and newer, "hot-styled" jazz and dance tunes, with sometimes breathtaking dexterity. Indeed, in some ways their nearest musical relations were contemporaries like jazz/blues guitarists Eddie Lang and Lonnie Johnson, early western swing bands, or even the Quintet of the Hot Club of France.

Mainland-based Hawaiian performers found themselves in a curious situation, playing their contemporary, often "placeless" music against elaborately exoticist backdrops. We might picture Sol Hoopii, surrounded by fake palm trees and island scenery, performing "Lady Be Good" in a Los Angeles Chinese cabaret; or Sol K. Bright and his "Hollywaiians" singing Harry Lauder's "A Wee Doch-an-doris" (in a Scottish accent) with Hawaiian guitar and ukulele accompaniment. Such egregiously mixed metaphors must surely have confounded to some degree the Orientalist/exoticist impulses that had in part created them.

Richard Middleton has examined how another exoticist and racist staging conceit of the day—the infamous jungle settings and African-themed floor shows at the Cotton Club in Harlem where Duke Ellington and his so-called "Jungle Band" performed in the late 1920s—was cannily reappropriated and "spatially" recast so as to "license" dramatic musical innovations.[30] Music works by structurally and semiotically manipulating difference, says Middleton and the inclusion or appropriation of various "others"—exotic and "primitive" sounds, structures, harmonies, textures—was thus necessary for the maintenance and continued energizing of eighteenth- and nineteenth-century Western music. At the same time (referencing Hegel) music in the nineteenth century was seen to function by "directly representing consciousness to itself." In the Nietzschean context, this means the project in part becomes the recuperation of the "Dionysian spirit" as a corrective to the sterile academicism of Western culture. But as Western music is both captured within and is itself an enactment of systems of dominance, the "other" so necessary for its continued renovation poses a threat to the authority of the bourgeois self. The contradiction is managed, says Middleton, by twin strategies of assimilation and projection that, however divergent their tactics, seek to reduce the threat by incorporating it into a stable hierarchy: "This may be configured either through binary distinctions, dividing centre from periphery, or through co-option of the peripheries into the center's sphere of influence."[31] But hierarchic closure is not so easy to maintain, says Middleton, who draws a line from the apparent stability achieved in *The Magic Flute*—in which the "low other" represented by the comic figure Papageno after a long and complex musico-narrative process is seemingly assimilated—to George Gershwin's *Porgy and Bess*. Despite the musical complexity of the latter, Middleton finds that a monologic authorial control obtains, which ultimately renders its "low-life" as merely picturesque and patronizes its low other.[32]

Middleton goes on to consider Duke Ellington's period at the Cotton Club in Harlem, from 1927 to 1932. At first sight, the Cotton Club, with its "jungle" decor and elaborately costumed dancers offered an ersatz and racist exoticism for the diversion of middle-class white slummers. Yet Ellington, intensely serious about his music (and keenly conscious of racist stereotyping; he was to dismiss *Porgy and Bess* for its "lamp-black Negroisms")[33] was able to work with and appropriate crude notions of the "jungle," "jungle music" and the "primitive" in developing hugely important textural innovations. These were enacted both in sounds and styles of individual players (such as Bubber Miley's "gut-bucket" trumpet and Joe Nanton's growling trombone, both so aggressively other to reigning notions of "purity" of tone and musicianly decorum) and in the collective blending, sequencing and counterpointing of sounds and successive solos, which posited a community spun almost magically from the confluence of such impossibly idiosyncratic, individualized voices. The "jungle to Harlem" narrative, says Middleton, "[relocates] the jungle into a modern here and now—a narrative then which rather than assimilating completely to Darwinian models of social and racial progress worked to inscribe them in a project organized around the laying out of a quite 'new territory.'"[34]

The received pictorial "space" of the cabaret then, despite its crudely wrought primitivist tropes becomes a precursor of the new territories of musical texture and recording depth and dimensionality, a template for the new "unlit" imaginary zones shared by both listeners and players. At the same time another, not unrelated development out of the jungle theme, with its connotations of chaotic Darwinian struggle, and of thrilling and unexpected happenings, of danger and delight copresent was the emergence of the trope of the urban soundscape. There is no great distance between, say, "Jungle Nights in Harlem" (1930) and such smoothly raucous recordings as "Take the A Train" and "Harlem Air Shaft" (both 1940). But again, as much as the idea of a soundscape might seem to hark back to nineteenth-century pictorialism, Ellington's sonic cities become conceits for exploring unlikely collisions, surprise dialogues and discoveries. The city is the big band, the big band a city.

The small combo work of Hawaiian guitarists was similarly staged—literally in the case of film and live performance, figuratively in radio broadcasts and on record—against a backdrop of received pictorial, exoticized, spatiogeographic tropes that had previously been used to first locate and then assimilate the Hawaiian "low other." But Ellington's and other jazz bands of the time introduced aggressive, "confronting" sounds and rhythms to audiences, forcing them either to reconsider and broaden *their* ideas of musicality or not to participate at all. And with those musical choices came wider cultural affiliations. For white clubbers in the 1920s, a visit to the Cotton Club was also an endorsement (perhaps merely symbolic) of "Jazz Age" values; an endorsement of the bodily freedoms associated with new dances, an endorsement of new expressive and sexual freedoms for women in particular, and a repudiation of Prohibition values. To affiliate with hot jazz of the twenties was to affiliate, to some extent, with a transgressive and possibly radical cultural position.

On the other hand "Hawaiian" music, emerging largely from the interstices of established Western popular music practice, was markedly not associated with any particular moral panic. Nonetheless, "Hawaiian" of the time sometimes achieves its own sly derangements of standards and expectations. When "Jim and Bob the Genial Hawaiians" play the western-themed "Song of the Range," for example, "weird otherness" is amply present, but it does not so much challenge as sneak up on the listener. After a few choruses of delicately picked, mildly syncopated playing, the lead steel guitar suddenly starts embellishing the melody, tunefully and with great precision, using large, ambitious, intervallic leaps, and an exaggerated, effortless rubato. Within an instant the tune has become dizzyingly, crazily ornate, but the improvised runs and ornaments remain scrupulously and effortlessly "correct." The one or two "blue notes" in the improvisation offer the merest nod in the direction of the "jazz other." The tune, which somehow remains always recognizable during even the most ornate improvisation, has been used seemingly to "smuggle in" a wholly surprising, almost hallucinatory construction, remaining at all times on its best behavior. We may have *thought* we had the song's number, but the players politely prove us hopelessly wrong. Thus the apparently territorialized subaltern remakes territory.

Significantly both these movements—Duke Ellington's "jungle" remade as modernist city soundscapes, and Hawaiian pictorialism remade into "utopia" (in the sense of an impossible, nonexistent territory) occur in the years immediately after the coming of electrical "orthophonic" sound recording, with its greatly increased capacities for capturing acoustic nuance. Both Ellington and the mainland Hawaiian players, each beginning with a received pictorial Orientalism quickly and deftly "lift" the idea of space in the abstract, with all its attendant liberties and licenses, and remake it to suit their purposes. Such maneuvers potentially achieve more than simply inverting and subverting a repressive conceit so as to remake performance modes; the possibility opens up of transporting the spatial liberties *from* the domain of the live stage, with its strict physical limitations to the spatially boundless, "ungrounded" acoustic domain of the sound recording. As Middleton says, "While music can never belong to us (as myths of authenticity would wish) belonging *to* a music (making ourselves at home within its territory) is distinctly possible." The semiotically muddy but nonetheless potent emplacements of "hot Hawaiian" guitar music rendered it ripe for future territorializing. These ingredients—improvisatory freedom and fluidity, the positing of a potentially limitless, "oceanic" spatiality, largely shorn of its imperialistic and Orientalist connotations—would continue to resurface and recombine throughout twentieth-century music recording, and especially informed the development of the electric guitar in recording.

Which is not to say the picturesque, languorous territories promoted by the *Hawaii calls* style wholly conforms to the Orientalizing template either. This was an image that (some) Hawaiians at least remained partly in control of; unlike the Orientalizing constructs of the nineteenth century (some) real Hawaiians (and the real, geographic Hawaii) were major participants in and promoters of these fantasies. Although how happy and compliant that participation was is open to question: Elizabeth Buck, for example, describes how Hawaiian music became both a commodity in itself (sold worldwide via mainly U.S. companies) and also a key part of a larger commodification process (that of "selling" Hawaii, mainly to U.S. vacationers). While elements of Hawaiian culture were appropriated and trivialized in the constructing of "tourist-friendly" motifs, racial ideologies excluded Hawaiians from middle- and upper-echelon occupations. Limited, strictly defined roles existed for them in the tourist industry as service providers and entertainers, which saw them cast as "happy go lucky beach boys, friendly bus drivers, smiling *lei* sellers, funny entertainers, or beautiful women performing an exotic and somewhat erotic form of dance."[35] But whatever else may be said about the confusing and contradictory categories of "Hawaiian," *hapa haole* and steel guitar music from the 1920s through the 1940s, the "Hawaiian" semiotic whole—with its attendant suites of set-piece images, implied and actual sceneries, its colonial stereotypes, and the presence of actual Hawaiians and elements of Hawaiian culture—had a huge impact on the evolution of recorded popular music's spatial imagination. So pervasive and (within limits) so persuasive were Hawaiian music's spatial conceits that few player/participants at the time were not in some way influenced by them and to some extent complicit in their maintenance.

If the unambiguously austere iconography of the "cowboy" west was aimed primarily at masculine audiences (and especially prepubescent boys), then the spatial iconography of the Hawaiian Islands, with its emphasis on indulgence, sensuality and fecundity was energetically promoted by commercial tourist interests to appeal to mainland married couples, and especially honeymooners. Pop western was about masculine trials and travails, about striving and *becoming* a man, in the acceptable, self-willed, individualistic western capitalist mode. Pop Hawaiian seductively offered a chance of undoing, unwinding, letting go, ebbing. "Hawaii" became both a practical opportunity (if one had the wherewithal) and a symbolic template (even if one did not) for the mainland industrial worker's annual, or maybe once-in-a-lifetime vacation. The drifting glissandos of the steel guitars, the lightly voiced male and female harmonies, the soft rhythmic strumming of the ukulele and *tiple*, the swaying of hula dancers—all suggested the antithesis of the rigors, demarcations and repressions of day-to-day life in industrial society, a watery dissolution of the quotidian. In the imaginary Polynesia, boundaries dissolve and bodies are freed of encumbrance.

A quick, informal survey of *hapa haole* song titles and lyrics reveals continually recurring words, themes and notions: voices whisper of "sweet Hawaiian kisses," of tranquil lagoons and sunsets, of tides gently flooding and ebbing, of moonlit seascapes and deep blue twilights; words suggestive of liminal mental states recur: love, night, paradise, magic, drifting, enchantment, dream, sway, faraway, heaven, heavenly and lullaby. The primary mode is the hypnagogic state, the intermediate zone between full consciousness and deep sleep, in which the rational "daytime" mind-set and the surrealistic succession of dream images briefly coexist. Hypnagogic states are typically experienced for a brief period as one drifts off to (deeper) sleep, or immediately after waking, before full consciousness takes hold. Defenses are down. Anything could happen. Anything might be imagined. Musically this is enacted most pointedly in the glissandos typical of Hawaiian steel guitar music. The sliding nonfixity of pitch, the sixth chords that drop by a semitone and then drift lazily back up to "true," the high sliding ring of false harmonics might all be analogous to a melting of boundaries, to a willing giving up of the self to dreamy sensuality.

But *hapa haole* Hawaiian music has rarely been seen as especially oppositional or as presenting any sort of serious confrontation with the repressive moral regimes of Western industrial life. Nor have Western devotees of *hapa haole* Hawaiian been notably associated with any special degree of sexual libertinage or Dionysian excess. Indeed, by the time rock 'n' roll and rock music emerged, Hawaiian music represented to many the epitome of suburban, petit bourgeois monogamous "squareness." But given the mix of tropes present in *hapa haole* this unthreateningness is perhaps not surprising: the imagined Hawaii is a place one visits, briefly, and then leaves, for good. The Hawaiian interlude may represent a return to childlike polymorphous libidinality, but it is temporary, dimly remembered and vaguely enacted. Perhaps the best known of all Hawaiian tunes is "Aloha Oe," and the sad farewell to Hawaii—enacted in the tourist-focused rituals of throwing the *lei* into the water as the cruise ship departs and the cliché of the "sun sinking slowly in the west"—is every bit as integral to the Hawaiian package as is the dreamy eroticism. "Hawaiianism" may be more concerned with the ultimate renunciation of the idea of "escape" than with the casting off of inhibition.[36] Hawaiian acts in Australian clubs often made mildly risqué sport of the title, but the song "Memories of a Lovely Lei" nonetheless quite neatly sums up one of the core experiences of the Hawaiianist imagination.

The Oscar-winning film *From Here to Eternity* (directed by Fred Zinnemann, 1953), although manufactured outside the period being discussed, nonetheless well encapsulates certain of these "Hawaiianist" constructs. Set in the lead up to the bombing of Pearl Harbor in 1941, the two central characters (played by Burt Lancaster and Deborah Kerr) are involved in an adulterous relationship (she is his commanding officer's wife), while the Montgomery Clift character conducts a liaison with a "hostess" from a nearby club (Donna Reed). Whenever they leave the army base to carouse in town the male characters change from their well-pressed uniforms into lurid (notwithstanding the fact that the film is in black and white) Hawaiian print shirts. One particularly famous scene, from which numerous promotional stills were taken, is of Lancaster and Kerr lying on the sand in the twilight, embracing, semiclad, as waves wash over them, invoking the familiar Hawaiianist tropes of ejaculatory fluidity and the dissolution of bodily boundaries. The Japanese bombing marks the call back to duty for all; the sexual interlude is unambiguously over. In the final scene the two women (Kerr and Reed) are on an ocean liner as it sets sail for the United States. They throw their leis into the sea, marking their own individual renunciations.

The renunciation of (an imagined) soft, sensual physicality in favor of the industrial work ethic recalls certain aspects of the Echo and Narcissus myth, insofar as the act of renunciation by Narcissus—his failure to recognize the other—leaves Echo lamenting, unseen forever. Not surprisingly the word "echo" occurs not infrequently in *hapa haole* song lyrics, as does the figure of the native girl left heartbroken in the little grass shack. "Sobbing" reverberant Hawaiian guitars lament the departure of the visitor, call vainly for his or her return.

The enactment of these tropes in production practice becomes most markedly manifest in *hapa haole* music of the 1940s, and coincides with the postwar rise of mass tourism. Before the war a trip to the islands may have been a once-in-a-lifetime experience for middle-class Americans, but in the postwar period the tropical vacation became increasingly affordable for blue-collar workers and their families. It is perhaps no accident that it is in this period that Hawaiian spatializing is at its most literal and pictorial.

Felix Mendelssohn and His Hawaiian Serenaders were a popular British Hawaiian act and certain of their recordings of the 1940s enact a variety of spatializing techniques. Their version of the tune "Bali Ha'i"[37] (from the Rodgers and Hammerstein stage show of 1949, *South Pacific*) begins with an eerie off-mic, upper-register recitative played on the electric steel guitar, a phrase repeated three times, answered each time by a little figure played on marimbas. The band joins in and as the song progresses the steel guitarist plays in a variety of registers and with widely varying amplitudes. Lower-register octave harmonies, midregister, and finally in "harmonics"—the much-used steel guitar practice of halving the string interval with the fingers or palm of the hand and plucking the string so that a "floating" or "singing" high harmonic note is sounded, rather than the full fundamental. The effect is used to invoke a sense of ungrounded ethereality, of "bodilessness." When combined with reverb the effect is of a *double remove:* the sound is "laterally" removed by the reverb and then "lifted" off the ground into the ethereal realm. Another way of seeing this might be to say that the harmonic provides a celestial other to the grounded, reverberant (already othered) voice. The others themselves have others. The echoes are multiplying. The centrally located self is left bemused, confused, or perhaps charmed, as what was thought to be a dead, alienated natural world displays in fact a multifarious animatedness.

But the echoic steel guitar of the recitative (which grows steadily stronger as the song progresses) is also a kind of siren song—a mortal peril that must be resisted. Bali Ha'i is a quasi-forbidden island (off-limits to rank-and-file servicemen) but it "calls" from across the water. The familiar hard-headed, pragmatic "Hawaiianist" renunciation once again becomes an urgent necessity if calamity is to be avoided.

Other much-used devices employed in late 1940s Hawaiian music include the contrasting of the dry, on-mic, "whispery" crooned vocal with the off-mic steel guitar. The voice is near, the guitar distant. This recalls the production regime extant in much singing cowboy music from the same time (as discussed in chapter 4), just as it does the spatial dynamic of Gene Austin's much earlier recording of "My Blue Heaven" (discussed in chapter 3). In Austin's suburban idyll, in Bob Nolan's mythic west and in *hapa haole's* Hawaii, the visual is frequently partly occluded, suffused with a hypnagogic blue twilight (and nearly always dusk rather than dawn; it is always getting darker, never lighter). With the fading of the visual, the sonic space swells out; the crepuscule is alive with presences, but they float, unfixed, beyond the controlling gaze of the self. Whereas the reverberant sonic presences in *Cat People* and "Riders in the Sky" were unholy and/or demonic, *these* presences are invariably friendly. The submerged threat, the sirenlike call can be easily resisted. One has booked a return ticket. The worker's vacation is of strictly fixed duration (vacationers may detest the return to work, but does one ever ring in to extend the vacation, however perfect it may have been?).

It is ironic that *hapa haole* should have become so rigid, stable and prescriptive a signifier of looseness and dissolution, considering the boldness and inventiveness of so many of the early wave of performers. The virtuoso players of the 1920s and 1930s frequently exploited the instrument's strangeness, and this exploiting frequently had a strongly spatial aspect. In part the spatializing was caused by the acoustic machinery of the guitar itself. Regardless of how close one is positioned to the source, the sound from a resonator guitar seems always to emanate from a prior chamber; the music comes out of the guitar already sounding reverberant. This "bottled-up" quality is more or less present in all instruments that make use of an amplifying chamber (that is, most stringed instruments) but is especially pronounced on guitars that use metal resonator cones. Sol Hoopii in particular utilized specific qualities of the steel guitar—its human voicelike timbre, its "wobbly" vibrato that directly indexed the minor muscular tremors of the player's left hand, the sweeping analogic fretlessness that parallels the voice's ability to move freely in pitch and the reverberant priorness of the sound—to create uniquely spatial effects. As well as the lamenting "crying emanating from the next room" sound that was to become such a staple, Hoopii and others used the instrument in novelty pieces to create a complete sonic environment. Hoopii's "Train Song" for example, is a virtual aural travelogue: the guitar mimics the sound of train whistles, bells, the "choofing" of the train leaving the station, the sounds of hens, cows and donkeys as the train crosses the countryside—all this interspersed in and around the melody line, which is derived from the gospel hymn "Life's Railroad to Heaven."

This mimetic style of playing was not restricted to the steel guitar. Instances of it are not uncommon in music of the southern United States: for example, in Eddie Lang and Lonnie Johnson's "Bullfrog Moan" (1929, played on steel-string Spanish guitar), Sonny Terry's "Fox Chase" (1934, on harmonica), Bob Wills's "Way Out There" (1936, drums simulate the sound of a train on the tracks), Jimmie Rodgers's train-whistle yodel and Deford Bailey's harmonica soundscapes. While the farmyard "soundscape" piece recurs in early (pre-electric) sound recording and farmyard animal sound effects are a staple of central European string bands.[38] In the hands of the Hawaiian and steel guitar players, however, the device becomes much more than simply a novel addition to a stage act. With the coming of electric amplification, and the new expressive possibilities it introduced, steel guitar was ready to realize a new type of obbligato, one that made use of implicitly spatial effects.

By the late 1930s steel guitarists in orchestras and smaller combinations (and sometimes solo players) were commonly using electric steel guitars, played through small onstage amplifiers, typically of three to five watts' power output. Electric steel guitarists in (some) swing bands began to overdrive their amplifiers causing their guitar sounds to move further away from the "organic" acoustic guitar sound into a new realm of electrically modified sound. Most famously, Bob Dunn the steel player with Milton Brown and his Musical Brownies, played fast, jazz- and blues-inflected runs using a thick distorted electric tone that recalled in some ways the aggressive sounds of brass instruments (notably the trombone, Dunn's original instrument).

During this period the electric steel guitar, particularly in jazz and jazz-influenced music was used more than occasionally to produce sounds that bore little resemblance to the (still dominant) acoustic guitar styles of such players as Eddie Lang, Freddie Green, Albert Casey and Django Rhinehart. One influential piece was "Floyd's Guitar Blues," recorded by the big band Andy Kirk and His Clouds of Joy, in 1939 (apparently as a spontaneous end-of-session time filler).[39] The tune, a slow blues, begins with the horns playing a loud, "blaring" turnaround, which is repeated at softer volume. The lead is then taken by the electric steel guitar, played by Floyd Smith, through four choruses, with the horns coming in again for a big finish on the final turnaround, a replica of the intro.

While the piano in "Floyd's Guitar Blues" sounds like a piano and the bass is unmistakably a bass, the guitar, with its piercing electric tonalities and its volume swells (presumably effected by working the volume control to counteract the natural volume decay) bears little sonic resemblance to the acoustic steel guitar. Through the five choruses the guitarist plays in turn sliding midrange chords, piercing high single string passages, chordal horn-like riffs and some barely audible "low down," single string passages. Smith here catalogues a number of playing styles normally associated with other instruments—horns, blues guitar, clarinet—yet uses newer, magnetic pickup/valve amplifier tonalities. The strictly "organic-acoustic" relationship between the instrument and the sound it produces has been jettisoned: the instrument does not have *a* sound now, as such, but rather many, and all are markedly and unashamedly fabricated, the product of playing strategies employed so as to invoke responses wholly dependent upon the electronic configurations of the guitar and amplifier. The acoustic steel guitar, with its languid glissandos was already free of fixity of intonation, and therefore potentially ripe for adaptation to more disruptive musical practices. Here however (as in the playing of Bob Dunn), the instrument has been dramatically cut loose from its acoustic timbral moorings. The guitar sound and its dynamic deployments on "Floyd's Guitar Blues" stand in marked contrast to other recorded electric guitar sounds of the period. Floyd Smith's guitar sound here is unmistakably electric—with its trebly, overdriven high notes, its relatively long sustain/slow decay (characteristic of overdriven magnetic pickups), its thick valve-distorted chords and especially the piercing, metallic quality to the louder parts of the solos—all stand in marked contrast to guitar sounds commonly produced at that time. Indeed, Smith's sonic manipulations here resemble more than anything those of the electric blues and country players of the 1950s and 1960s.[40]

The timbral distancing of electric steel guitar from its acoustic "roots" provides an approximate counterpart to the spatial distancing evident on such recordings as "Blue Shadows on the Trail" (described in chapter 4). In the latter, distancing is evident in a split between the body of the musician and the musical sounds produced; the main sound will emit from an amplifier, rather than from the physical instrument held in the musician's hands. The amplifier itself may or may not be immediately beside the musician, and regardless of how close it remains, the sound produced will necessarily be othered in a wholly different, more radical way. Although R. Murray Schafer uses his term "schizophonia" in relation to the dislocations and re-spatializations attendant upon phonograph recording and reproduction (see chapter 1), another more subtle but highly significant schizophonic alienation occurs around the live deployment of the electric guitar. The removal of the sound production apparatus from the (literal) embrace of the musician, must surely have suggested to both musicians and record producers that any degree of spatial drift was possible: if the amplifier could be placed a foot away from the player, why not six or ten feet?[41] Thus it is perhaps not surprising that the sort of off-mic spatializing techniques exemplified in Felix Mendelssohn's 1940s recordings, or in "Blue Shadows on the Trail" should involve electric steel guitars.

Another technique used by Floyd Smith is "swell": the manipulation of the volume control to counteract the natural decay of the note. By the 1940s, this effect—exclusive to electrically amplified guitar—was being regularly used by steel players, most commonly by means of a volume pedal. Steel players also around this time began manipulating the guitar's tone control to produce an early version of the wah-wah effect. Floyd Smith may well have used this effect (the heightened tonal shifts on "Floyd's Guitar Blues" may be the result of judicious rolling-off of the tone control) but here the effect, if in fact used at all, is deployed between choruses: the guitarist resets the tone before playing the new chorus. By the late 1940s the effect was increasingly used to tone-shift sliding chords, to alter the sound of the note *while it was being voiced,* in a rough analogy to the way the human mouth and throat might be used to alter sounds produced by the voice.

These wah-wah effects combined serendipitously with the valve distortion produced by early amplifiers. The amplifiers used by steel players in the 1930s and 1940s were by modern standards very small—typically three to five watts, rarely more than eight—and players working in noisy dance halls and juke joints were often forced to overdrive amplifiers in order to be heard.[42] Even at lower recording-session volumes, these small amplifiers produced much thicker "grungier" chords than did later amplifiers, and the steel guitar sounds produced by early western swing and country players such as Bob Dunn, Herb Remington, Noel Boggs and Jerry Byrd bear little similarity to the cleaner pedal steel sounds of 1950s and 1960s country music.

It is perhaps no surprise then that on the landmark late 1940s recordings made by Hank Williams, the steel guitar obbligato should be such a defining feature. "Obbligato" refers to a type of accompaniment, a second voice: literally, "obligatory," a necessary, indispensable component of the music. In popular musics the term is often used to describe improvised instrumental playing "behind" the main vocal: for example, Lester Young's freewheeling tenor sax accompaniments to Billie Holiday's singing. The obbligato provides a kind of off-camera voice, a running commentary on the foregrounded vocal. Its relation to the first voice is roughly analogous to the relation in cinema of music to image and dialogue: not always consciously heard, but functioning to signpost the main action. In terms of this present study, obbligato might be characterized as intrinsically Echoic (that is, pertaining to the Echo myth); it provides a disembodied other voice, regardless of whether or not it possesses reverberant qualities.

In western swing recording, Bob Dunn, steel player with southwestern group the Hi Flyers and later with Milton Brown and his Musical Brownies played lines and solos described by Palmer as "startlingly futuristic."[43] Dunn's melodic lines were clearly derived from jazz improvisation—fast, inventive work employing the same sort of jazz scales and phrases used by horn players—but at the same time Dunn's guitar sound was unlike anything else. Playing an acoustic lap-style guitar with a pickup fitted, Dunn's overdriven sound bore little resemblance to other recorded guitar sounds of the day. Steel players in Bob Wills's band, most notably Noel Boggs and Herb Remington, also played jazz-inspired accompaniments; although their respective sounds did not especially recall Dunn's thick "dirty" tone, their electric solid-body instruments were capable of producing a wide range of sounds, none of which particularly resembled the sound of the acoustic guitar. Through the late 1940s Wills's steel players increasingly wove intricate obbligato melodic lines and chord progressions around the lead vocal.

This emerging new relationship between electric guitar and the voice is sharply exemplified in the recorded work of Hank Williams. Williams's steel players, Jerry Byrd and Don Helms, both make much use of the effects mentioned above—train whistle wah-wah, sobbing tremolo—to reference "offstage" places, to provide a voice from "outside the studio," from beyond or outside the singer's personal space. This sort of obbligato might also be linked to an older country blues tradition wherein (usually slide) guitar lines are interpolated into and around vocal lines, in a kind of call-and-response format.

The Echo myth suggests some important attributes of echoic sound effects: echo as feminine, echo as voice (and implicitly, mind) without body, echo as repressed functions, and echo as a kind of sentient (but in that she can only repeat the syllables of others, nongenerative) spirit of place. Even though Echo in a sense "knows more" than Narcissus, she is incapable of initiating speech. She does, however, perceive and understand, and she worships Narcissus quite autonomously. She exists separately to Narcissus. The guitar obbligato is not merely a sonic counterpart to the mirror image. Narcissus's reflection cannot love him back.

Williams's recording of "My Sweet Love Ain't Around" (1947/1948) well exemplifies these effects. The recording begins with a four-bar introduction in which the fiddle is strongly foregrounded. Then Williams begins singing. "Listen to——," he sings, holding the last syllable while the steel guitar plays a rubato "train whistle"–type semitone slide up to the sixth chord (the sixth being a characteristic sound of late 1940s honky-tonk steel guitar). The guitarist (Jerry Byrd) then quickly drops the steel back a semitone and briskly recovers the note, lending a strongly bluesy inflection to the obbligato. Williams, who has held the last syllable of "to" through all this, continues, "——the rain a-fallin!" The guitar then plays a "rain-like" arpeggio. "Can't you hear that lonesome sound?" he sings, which is immediately answered by a wah-slide up to the third, and is in turn followed by a falling slide. And so the first verse continues, as Williams reveals that his heart is breaking (answered by another lamenting steel riff) because his "sweet love ain't around."

The first solo is then taken by the fiddle. The (nonsteel) electric guitar plays the obbligato on the next verse. Then the steel takes a solo, a series of opened-out, discontinuous bluesy chords and runs, played with enough rubato to redirect the listener's attention (momentarily) to the second line—the "sock" rhythm guitar and bass. The steel maintains this slyly diffident, "low down" aspect through the solo.[44] But now, rather than simply referencing falling rain, or lonesome whistles, the steel guitar riffs reference affects—although whether they belong to the singer or the world or both (or neither, for that matter) is not entirely clear. The steel here and elsewhere in Williams's work enters into dialogue with the singer, remaining ambiguously inner and outer, providing a complex and subtly nuanced other voice, one that sometimes seems to empathize with and underscore the vocal, and at other times to mock the singer. It both draws attention to itself and simultaneously focuses the listener's attention on the singer. The steel guitar on Williams's records functions with a markedly broader affective and musical range than any other accompanying instrument. On the one hand, the steel can provide freely fluid, timbrally muted, jazzy, "abstract" chord progressions that strongly counterpoint Williams's strict, almost harshly vernacular-accented vocal line. At other moments the steel, using its human voicelike qualities, is much more complicit with the singer's plight, empathizing with and restating his various woes. In moving freely between these poles, the nonacoustically anchored electric steel guitar on Hank Williams's recordings acts as an almost autonomous other.

Williams begins his famous "I'm So Lonesome I Could Cry" (1949) with another auditory imperative: "Hear that lonesome whippoorwill, he sounds too blue to fly." Although there is a strong suggestion that the outer world and Williams's inner state are closely linked, it is not the case that the external world serves solely as a narcissistic projection of the singer's emotional states. There is also a kind of deep focus operating here: the outer world, the middle distance are vocal, but nonverbal participators in the moment of the song. "Place," in the largest sense of the word, is acknowledged. Place answers. In the strictly Narcissistic construct, the singer finds only reflections of the self "out there." The Echoic construct involves on the other hand an encounter with the genuinely other, an other who is integrally involved in the drama of the moment, who participates intimately with the self. It speaks, it laments. It knows the speaker. In turn it is recognized, but never quite reclaimed.

But we have seen that the steel guitar's location, like Echo's, is indeterminate, and its role as secondary voice is never wholly stable. We may not find a body at the place we think the sound is coming from; or perhaps the sound is coming from a place that is specifically not visually accessible, from out of the blue shadows or from the next room—beyond the controlling reach of the gaze. And the voice itself might be single notes or chords, it might match the melody, or set up a dialectic or seemingly "go its own way."

Given that slide and bottleneck guitar were trademark Mississippi blues styles, it is tempting to posit that Jerry Byrd's steel might also allude to a southern United States "near other"—alienated, repressed but not voiceless black presence. Byrd (and many other of the hillbilly steel players of the time) favored a thick chordal style of playing—a densely multivoiced obbligato—that further suggests a social collectivity. Both Tony Russell[45] and Nick Tosches[46] have suggested that despite the seemingly unbridgeable social and political gulfs, the complicated webs of taboos and resentments between southern whites and blacks, there has often existed in southern musics a covert mingling, a profound and often respectful interaction between African American and European, of a type that was rarely possible in daily life, and rarely acknowledged verbally. Indeed the characteristic bluesy chordings used by steel players, favoring the microtonal zones immediately below the third and fifth notes of the scale in particular, might well have referenced to their contemporary listeners the playing of black southern blues and gospel guitarists. The steel guitar in effect "sang the blues" behind the singer.

The tensions and interplay between the voice and the steel on the Williams recordings might be seen then as setting up a number of possible spaces from the material world heard "out there"—trains, rainfall, birds. Yet this space may turn out to be a solipsistic construct, by which the entire outer world serves as an expression of inner melancholy: the world as being really just the displaced self or at best a kind of stage prop.

Yet at the same time this represented world might be a covert stand-in for the genuinely other both in terms of gender and race. Formalistically too it is other: it counterpoints the harsh materiality of the self with a freely abstract immateriality, which may be a ghostly imaginary zone or a set of coolly cerebral puzzles, or oblique statements, or even dadaist non sequiturs. Race, gender, space, landscape, architecture, the purely ideational— the representational integrity of each remains intact, despite semiotic blurring. In the hands of Williams and the Drifting Cowboys, a richly spatial, social and psychic synchrony is depicted.

Hank Williams's work, both the songs as material performed by others and his own recordings, represent a landmark moment in the emergence of postwar popular song. Building on the prewar country and hillbilly traditions of voice deployment and lexical choice, Williams used the vernacular, everyday voice and "down-home" pronunciation (such as the "g" dropped from "ing" sounds) and other idiomatic phrases (such as "Get that chip *off of your* shoulder" in "I Just Don't Like this Kind of Living," 1949/1950) to explore particular negative, antiheroic mental states: unhappiness in love, the sense of being forever doomed to failure, defeat, a chilling sense of melancholy and despair. The moments of jubilation in Williams's songs are more likely than not associated with reckless drinking, and will usually be followed by a cold, remorseful hangover. Williams's recordings set up a hugely expanded psychic stage that greatly helped to enable the vernacular expressive experimentation of songwriters in the 1950s and 1960s, ultimately leading to the lyrical freedoms enjoyed by the singer-songwriter schools, and by rock songwriters in general.

It is doubly significant then that Williams's recordings should be so strictly nonreverberant. They stand in marked contrast to the 1940s Hawaiian-style recordings described above, just as they do to the echoic sonic effects increasingly employed in western-themed music of the time. Williams's Nashville-recorded sides are without exception sonically "dry," mostly depthless (the steel solo in "My Sweet Love Ain't Around," with its minute gaps between guitar phrases that ever so briefly direct the listener's attention to the backgrounded rhythm section, is quite unusual). They consistently eschew the reverb-constructed mise en scène that these other landscape and mindscape-referring styles were increasingly using at the time.

In one respect, this dry, relatively effects-free production regime might be seen as a major component in Williams's "naturalness effect": like the deadpan, anti–Tin Pan Alley singing of the prewar Carter Family, the suggestion here is that the matters sung of are simply too important, too loaded with affect and unresolved hurt to be rendered in cheap effects. The production regime here implicitly privileges and even sacralizes the feelings and sensitivities of the singer, who at the same time is pointedly identified as coming from the rural southern underclass. The dry immediacy of the Williams recordings might be seen then as a powerfully democratic tactic. The singer's emotions, more than simply coloring existing reality, actually construct and map out a world that is at once empirical and psychic, both out there and internal. His recorded performances are markedly without the front-of-stage vocal and production devices that, while they may help engage audiences at one level, covertly reassure them that the performance is really only a contrivance, a series of effects that ultimately do more to conceal than reveal the *actual* real-life feelings of the performer behind a largely depersonalized code of stage affect.

The production also privileges the listener. Williams's sacralized sufferings, which remain nonetheless commonplace emotions—unhappiness in love, feelings of remorse, self-doubt, fear of death, and recurring bouts of crushing, all-pervasive melancholy—are rendered without stagy distancing devices and thus invite a closer, only minimally mediated participation from listeners. Indeed, it might be said that his recordings refigured the relationship between listener and recording, ushering in a potentially much closer participatory nexus between performance and listener, one that perhaps was predated only by certain prewar country blues and gospel recordings.

In the wake of Williams, country singers (and later southern soul singers) sought more than ever to mine their personal affect, and represent it in song in a similarly unvarnished manner. Singer/songwriters like George Jones wrote songs in the 1950s that, like Williams's most intensely melancholic moments, constructed a world out of bleak affect: "Seasons of My Heart" (1954), "Cup of Loneliness" (1955) and "Color of the Blues" (1957) all amplify the despair of the speaker to the point that any contrary perception of the actual is wholly eclipsed. Whereas Jimmie Rodgers filtered his lived experience through the persona (real enough, no doubt) of the roué and the rounder, whose hedonistic behaviors and knowing humor were sufficient to see him through even the worst trials, the Williams and Jones personae are quite without such protections. The hurtling, abandoned, suicidal slide to self-destruction in Williams's music (as indeed in his life) makes a kind of sense: he encounters the world in such a deeply fearful way, his perceptions so raw, so forever open to hurt that the only alternatives are Dionysian abandon and death. This formulation, so much a part of the Williams/Frizzell/Jones myth, and afterward one of the defining myths of rock 'n' roll and rock, derives directly from the romantic movement of the eighteenth century. But in the Hank Williams school the myth is there to be experienced, lived by anyone who might punch in the right number on the right juke box.

Carl Perkins was fond of stating in interviews later in his life that rockabilly music owed its greatest debt to Hank Williams; yet at the same time rockabilly could not come into being so long as Williams was around. Certainly, the Williams recordings, the latest of which are just a couple of years before the earliest rockabilly, are in some ways like and at the same time completely not like rockabilly and rock 'n' roll. He eschewed reverberant spatializing; his voice, the band and his world are neither here nor there. His world is rendered with precision, but in words and in music rather than in an acoustically reverberant *there* and a dry *here*. Ultimately, all is here, even the there.

CHAPTER 6

"How Near, How Far?"
Inner Voices, Weird Space and the Ghostly West

The instrumental "Peg o' My Heart," by Jerry Murad and the Harmonicats was one of the biggest recording successes of 1947, selling well over a million copies in the United States. Recorded at Bill Putnam's Universal Studio in Chicago and released on his independent Vitacoustics label the song is generally regarded as the recording that made the use of the "echo chamber"—artificial reverberation—more or less acceptable as an overt recording gimmick.[1] Bruce Swedien, an engineer at Universal and highly successful engineer in his own right recently described it: "That record, you see, was the first time that anyone used reverb artistically. . . . Up 'til then, people used reverb only to re-create the sound of the studio; they tried to use it in a natural manner. Bill [Putnam] changed that."[2]

The recording opens with a simple figure played on a reverberant electric guitar, single string–style, followed by the main melody played on a chromatic harmonica. The sound is dry and on-mic until the last few bars of the first verse, when the reverb markedly swells around the harmonica. The "dry"-to-"roomy" pattern is repeated in the second verse, while the third sees another harmonica, richer in timbre and highly reverberant, take the lead, followed for the final verse by a drier, thinner-sounding harmonica. In combination with the "ambling" tempo and slightly behind-the-beat feel, the effect has much of the landscape/pictorialist about it. Perhaps we are meant to picture a lonely, wistful subject ambling down a deserted nighttime street.[3]

At the same time the reverb imparts a strong sense of "manufacturedness" to the sound, especially to the "beefed-up" chromatic harmonica sound on the third verse. Although the effects used in "Peg o' My Heart" (and subsequent echo-reverb–affected and multitracked pop songs) construct spaces predominantly in the landscape/pictorial modes, the quest for ever more novel, arresting effects ("gimmicks" in the trade parlance of the time) saw the range of devices, and their significations broaden considerably over a short period of time. Double (or multiple) trackings of the same voice, with reverb selectively added to one track, the use of highly reverberant male choruses, reverb that came and went during the course of the recording—such effects remained underwritten by verbal guarantors, but the worlds they so realistically constructed themselves became increasingly futuristic, uncanny, supernatural or, sometimes, entirely "inner" worlds.

Although it has become a truism of rock historiography that the use of slapback echo and reverb were pioneered at Sun and Chess in the early 1950s, in fact from 1947 until the coming of rock 'n' roll seven years later pop recordings by artists such as Patti Page, Les Paul, Rosemary Clooney, Vaughn Monroe and others (occasionally) made pronounced use of spatializing devices, including echo/reverb effects. A surprising number of these are among the pop best sellers of the period. Furthermore, the use of spatial techniques both tested conventions and played out some of the deeper paradoxes surrounding "presence" and performance in sound recording. Although women singers and instrumentalists were to remain a decidedly minority presence in early rock 'n' roll, it was on the recordings of the big female stars of the pre–rock 'n' roll period that some of these effects are most pointedly exemplified.

One such star was Patti Page, whose version of "Tennessee Waltz" sold over two million copies, making it, according to Russell Sanjek "the biggest popular hit in twenty years."[4] Like her earlier hit "Confess," "Tennessee Waltz" made a feature of Page's double-tracked voice. The closely harmonizing voices are both dry and on-mic (while the trumpet introduction and break midsong are both reverberant). The earlier "Confess" (1948) features the two "separate" voices in a call and response relationship, in which the call is "dry" and the response, which simply echoes key phrases from the lyrics, is slightly reverberant. The electric guitar figure that opens the song goes from reverberant to dry over its two bars. As Lacasse has noted, the apparent intention of the record makers was to render the answering Page voice as representing the singer's nagging conscience.[5] Page's "The Voice Inside" (1955) makes it even more explicit: "Can't you hear that voice inside you, mister won't you listen?" she asks, and immediately we hear a reverberant, female voice singing a high, wordless melismatic phrase—reminiscent of the various "love calls," such as Jeanette MacDonald and Nelson Eddy's 1932 version of "Indian Love Call," or Adelaide Hall's "Creole Love Call" with Duke Ellington (1927). The intertextual reach may go back much further, however, than these early pop recordings.

The prohibitions as to what can be said, and when, the limited agency of the secondary voice and its inability to initiate speech, the secondary voice's aching need to be heard, and the implicit reproach in what it might have to say—all recall aspects of the myth of Echo and Narcissus.

Songs based on the conceit of a female singer's "overheard" soliloquy are not uncommon in the pop output of this period, and such records are frequently constructed around a production binary of extreme dryness and dense reverb. Rosemary Clooney's "Hey There" (1954), for example, begins with a recitative: "Lately, when I'm in my room all by myself / In the solitary gloom I call to myself." The song proper is the singer "quoting" her own inner voice: "Hey there, you with the stars in your eyes." The inner voice goes on to counsel her on the futility of her unrequited love for another. The second time the verse is sung, however, the counseling inner voice is highly reverberant, and each line is answered by a dry, on-mic spoken line. Now the speech takes the form of a real dialogue:

INNER VOICE: Hey there, you with the stars in your eyes [*sung, reverberant*]
SINGER: Are you talking to me? [*spoken, dry*]
INNER VOICE: Love never made a fool of you [*sung, reverberant*]
SINGER: Not until now [*spoken, dry*]
INNER VOICE: You used to be too wise [*sung, reverberant*]
SINGER: Yes, I was once [*spoken, dry*].

And so on, until both voices sing the final line in reverberant harmony: "Is it all going in one ear and out the other?" Again, there is the suggestion of reproach, the weary assumption that the message from the "inner voice" will go unheeded.

"Sultry" female singers such as Patti Page, Rosemary Clooney, June Christy, Julie London and Peggy Lee were among the strongest presences of Tin Pan Alley pop music in the period from the end of the war to the coming of rock 'n' roll.[6] Typically blond, usually photographed or filmed in sparkling evening gowns, they embodied the idea of the "glamorous," and offered a sonic counterpart to images of contemporary movie stars such as Rita Hayworth and Marilyn Monroe. On record, their voices were often breathily forward in the mix, according the listener a vicarious "closeness." As Sean Cubitt points out:

Like the close-up screen image of a favorite star, the . . . voice of the popular singer, especially when amplified, promises . . . a physical intimacy. But in the case of recorded songs that presence is illusory. The voice is the site of a paradoxically simultaneous promise and denial of intimacy. . . . Like a close-up, an amplified and recorded voice marks an absence.[7]

The recording machinery "gets close" to the singer, and the listener vicariously experiences that closeness. Like the movie star, the "glamorous" pop singer offers her physical self—elaborately dressed, coiffed, made-up, with facial expressions carefully controlled—to the listener. The singer herself is a kind of "finished product." Not surprisingly, a recurring trope in trade and fan literature, publicity screeds, biographies and biopics about female pop stars is the pairing of the large-voiced, closely present, glamorous and "available" female singing star and the controlling Svengali-like "genius" offstage producer. Patti Page, for instance was associated with charismatic producer/A & R man Mitch Miller, Patsy Cline with Owen Bradley.[8] In this construction, the singer is depicted as having largely relinquished agency, which has been assumed by the Svengali producer/manager character. Her performances become an expression of and testimony to *his* genius. Nick Tosches[9] traces the "musical wizard" motif back to the Greek myth of Orpheus, but a nearer correlate can be found in the nineteenth century's fascination with the idea of the mesmerist: Charles Dickens's *Mystery of Edwin Drood* and George du Maurier's *Trilby* both feature sinister male musical masters who control their unwillingly compliant female subjects by means of "mesmerism," "animal magnetism" or "mind control."[10]

Minus the demonic intent and nineteenth-century pseudoscience (and with the addition of an apparently good-humored, modern domesticity), a not dissimilar male-wizard-and-compliant-female-subject trope was frequently invoked in relation to one of the most commercially successful musical partnerships of the pre–rock 'n' roll period: that of guitarist/producer Les Paul and singer Mary Ford. Paul's early guitar instrumentals such as "Lover," "Brazil" and "Nola" (from the late 1940s)—and later recordings featuring the voice (and rhythm guitar) of Mary Ford (most notably "How High the Moon"), with their dazzling use of multitracking, echo-delay and high instrumental "brightness"—are among the most technologically adventurous, "streamlined" commercial sound products of the time. The sales success of the Paul-Ford recordings did much to free the recorded music product from the need for it to be a true, pure analogue of a prior real-world sonic-musical event. At the same time, as historical curios, the Paul-Ford recordings offer some of the most pointed expressions of the repressions and hidden tensions associated with the female body, female presences and with "masculinist" technologies obtaining in the postwar period.

A generation of rock guitarists knew the name "Les Paul" simply as that embossed on the end of their Gibson solid-body electric guitar, the preferred guitar of many white rock guitar players. In many ways easier to play than its main solid-body rivals, Fender's Stratocaster and Telecaster, the Les Paul guitar's humbucking pickups gave a rich, thick and predictable distortion when overdriven, and a warm, dense sound at lower volume. By the mid 1970s it had become a kind of Model T of electric guitars, dependable and ubiquitous, prompting *Guitar Player* magazine to interview Paul at length in 1977.[11] Interviews in hi-fi magazines followed as the full extent of Paul's importance to postwar popular music and recording became apparent to a younger generation of musicians, fans and researchers. A biography appeared in 1993,[12] and in 1999 Steve Waksman devoted a long chapter of his *Instruments of Desire* to Paul's work, attending to both its musicosonic qualities, to Paul's achievements as an engineer, as well as to aspects of the gender constructions surrounding the public marketing of Les Paul and his partner Mary Ford.[13]

Musically, Paul's eclectic background uniquely positioned him to respond to the tidal pull from both the most mainstream popular music: that of Bing Crosby or the Andrews Sisters, on the one hand; and jazz, blues and down-home musics, on the other. Hailing from Wisconsin, as a young guitarist/piano player in the 1930s, Paul recorded hillbilly and novelty sides, jammed with jazz legends Roy Eldridge, Art Tatum, Louis Armstrong and Charlie Christian, and recorded race records with blues singer Georgia White. During the war he recorded with Nat King Cole, and led the Armed Forces Radio Service (AFRS) house band, backing up Bing Crosby, Dinah Shore, the Andrews Sisters, as well as many others.

In 1946 he built a studio in his garage in Hollywood and, using two Cadillac flywheels as recording lathes, proceeded to record and back up many of the same people he had worked with in the AFRS. After supplying the distinctive guitar part to Bing Crosby's hit "It's Been a Long, Long Time" (1946), Paul went on to record a number of minor hits under his own name, including "Lover" (1948), "Brazil" (1948) and "Nola" (1950), all of which, though recorded on disc (rather than magnetic tape) featured ground-breaking use of multiple tracking. Until "Lover," Paul was quoted as saying, "I'd never been able to combine all my inventions and recording techniques into one bag of tricks—to use delay, echo, reverb, phasing, flanging, sped-up sounds, muted picking."[14]

When Paul began recording with magnetic tape in 1949[15] these old "disc multiple" techniques were all more easily achieved. Mag-tape recording also brought a new degree of clarity and brilliance to recording.[16] The million-selling "How High the Moon" (1950/1951), Paul's first "mag-tape hit" made a feature of multitracking and of echo and reverb devices, applied to Paul's guitars and now to the voice of his vocalist wife Mary Ford. "How High the Moon" is recorded in brisk two-four time, driven by vamped, multitracked rhythm guitar chords, with an overlay of (mainly) two-note-chord lead electric guitar riffs. The slapback echo applied to the guitars exaggerates every minor incidental string noise. Every little tap of the plectrum on the strings rebounds *in tempo*—an important effect that has been called "synchro-sonic feeling"[17]—adding a sense of drive and urgency to the music. Mary Ford's singing is heard as a breathy, lightly uttered, on-mic crooning, doubled (or trebled) to resemble the sort of close-harmony swing singing made famous by groups such as the Boswell Sisters and the Andrews Sisters (Paul had toured extensively with the latter prior to his association with Ford). The echo and delay on the multitracked voices also greatly heightens incidental sounds, in particular the breezy sibilants.

Paul was apparently skeptical of simple radial spatialities; for all their three-dimensional ploys and plays, his production spatialities tend to resist the sort of unpacking that earlier spatialized recordings allow. Stereo-phonic recording, with its strongly lateral left-right spatialities, swept the recording industry a few years after Paul's early tape experiments (and significantly, after his great success with "How High the Moon"). But Paul claims to have remained unimpressed with stereo: "I don't want to sit there and hear a train go by," he told interviewers.[18] Paul in the main chose not to pursue the sort of horizontal, center-periphery spatialities that were so evident in (some) western and Hawaiian pop music recordings of the time—the monaural spatializing practices that prepared the way for stereo. He seems to have conceived of his recorded music on a *vertical*, rather than a horizontal axis.

In the *Guitar Player* interview,[19] Paul described his approach to early, pre-tape "multitracking": a track was recorded and played back; during the play-back a new musical line was played (or sung, or both), and the combined playback with the new accompaniment was recorded on a separate machine. This composite track was played back again and yet another line added and so on. "But weren't you degrading each of the early tracks with each track that you added?" a later interviewer asks. Paul's answer is illuminating:

'Course you degrade. But the degrading depends on what you're degrading. You're at the Hilton Hotel and you don't know what you're sittin' on down underneath the hotel, do ya? Okay, on my recording we don't know what's down underneath. . . .
. . . Like a drum is in the background, he's just stirring around, he's unimportant . . . but you get that bass, you gotta have him right up front, and you better have him just right. That lead guitar better shine, and he better be brand new. That vocal better be so clear that the four part harmony may be off in echo and it may be half a block away. So your perspective has to be in mind.[20]

The strategy here is spatial, though not in the sense that a place—a gridded-out, geographic landscape—is being represented (as, say, with "Blue Shad-ows on the Trail"). Rather, Paul seeks to enlarge his recording field by exca-vating, by creating a hollowed-out vertical space. In eschewing horizontal space here, Paul takes a step down the same path that Johnson had trod; he constructs a space, but without the legitimizing, naming presence of "place." Indeed, although his recordings are rigidly, methodically and consciously constructed, the end result recalls the contingent, provisional improvisatory spaces of some jazz recordings (described in chapters 3 and 5).

Paul also overturned the accepted procedures concerning vocal presence and microphone placement. Accepted production practice at the time was to locate singers—even the most on-mic crooners—at roughly arm's length from the microphone. For Paul however, close-miking meant "lipstick on the mike."[21] The extreme close-up meant that singers had to sing at much lower amplitudes to avoid overloading the microphone, and so Mary Ford's voice suggests a relaxed, breathy intimacy. The listener and the singer are "placed" now in intimate proximity. Whereas the arm's-length mic placement located the listener in comradely proximity to the voice, close miking bespoke a familial or sexual closeness. At the same time the apparent lack of physical effort from the singer suggests a certain offhandedness, something of the quality of "cool," a knowing withholding of excessive affect. The production suggests smoldering rather than explosive affect.

Close miking also largely excluded actual room ambience. The amplitude of the voice is proportionately much greater than that of the incidental reverberations, room noises and such, and so the overall recording level can be turned down, producing a strong vocal sound with negligible ambient room noise. Yet the incidental pops and whispers, the ringing guitar sounds, the brushes "stirring around" on the snare, the slapback echo on the Paul recordings combined to suggest a sonic environment nonetheless, although not one that yielded so readily to *pictorial* imagining. Rather than using sound to suggest a visual landscape, Paul fabricated a kind of sonic equivalent of "sparkle."

With reliable synthetic echo, reverb and close miking, Paul made records that were no longer dependent on the real spatiality of the studio. The sound signals that emanated from the gramophone were no longer simple analogues of real physical events that had taken place in a studio, but rather were the many-layered product of the total recording apparatus—which included voices, real space and the physical machinery with all its new possibilities. So "synthetic" was Paul's approach to recording that some artists were reluctant to work in his Hollywood garage, so little did it resemble the recording studios they were familiar with.[22] But many of Paul's techniques eventually became industry standard.

"How High the Moon" was a hit simultaneously in the pop and R & B (the postwar name for what had previously been called "race" music) charts. Paul's comments quoted above employ metaphors of verticality. He imagined his music on a vertical axis, certainly, but it was markedly unlike most of the electric guitar–based R & B that emerged during the same period (discussed in subsequent chapters). "How High the Moon" seems all above ground. The briskness of the tempo, the relaxed musical precision combined with the sense of cool vocal intimacy, the favoring of higher frequency pops and rings, the relative absence of earth-bound, "grungy" lower frequencies and the lyric themes of altitude (moons, heavens and faintly heard tunes)—all combine to give Paul's production a breezy, high and dry, professionally "glossy" ambience. In blues and country music, echo and reverb effects at this time and later were increasingly used to suggest shadowy, subterranean, marginal presences. Paul's work largely paved the way for this to happen, but he partook of virtually none of it himself. Self-consciously hip though he may have been, his project was pop, and his recorded soundspace was as pristine and freshly painted as the living room of the postwar Californian dream home.

Magnetic-tape multitracking of the voice in Paul's hands sometimes had a distinctly antispatial, antiechoic aspect. With sound-on-sound and delay echo, each voice ("voice" meaning distinct musical entity, be it drums, guitar, horn or a human voice) could be independently "emplaced," rather than the whole ensemble having to be subject to the one acoustic regime. In "How High the Moon," Mary Ford's voice is both multitracked using successive takes in harmony with one another *and* doubled by means of a tape echo set at very short delay. But rather than having the echoic second voice replayed at diminished amplitude (thereby suggesting a distant presence), the echo matches the amplitude of the original. Rather than an Echoic other then, the effect is of a second singer singing in unison. When the echo sings a harmony to the main melody line, rather than a "self plus other" configuration, the listener hears equally weighted voices, singing twins (or triplets). Each of the multiple voices is the same person, a little separated from the others. The effect suggests a single subjectivity replicated to compose a community—not unlike three women in military uniform perhaps, or members of a gang. It is perhaps no accident that the device was produced at that particular moment in the early postwar period, following the mass mobilizations of the war. In the United States at precisely that time groups ranging from the most highly marginalized (outlaw bikers and ethnic street gangs, for instance) to those hailing from the center of the mainstream were enthusiastically adopting the wearing of uniforms, affirming the replicability of their identity.

But while Paul and Ford multiplied singing and instrumental voices in the studio, on stage (and in photographs) they retained the appearance of singular, central "out front" musicians; she the singer/rhythm guitarist, he the lead guitarist. Before the overt use of echo doubling gained acceptance via R & B and rock 'n' roll recordings, the use in the studio of delay, reverb and doubling were frequently regarded as a kind of cheating, as an unacceptable artifice whose use dishonestly enhanced possibly mediocre musicianship. Even in the late 1950s, Read and Welch were writing with unmasked suspicion of "purposeful distortions to the recorded groove"[23] used by Les Paul in his so-called New Sound. Paul turned this mild taboo to his own advantage, using the technical gadgetry as a stage gimmick.

Making the multiple recordings . . . and doing the echo delay and sped up sounds, it rapidly dawned on me that people would want to hear a sound like the records when we performed live. You walk out there with just one voice and one guitar, and you've got a problem. If they yell out "How High The Moon" you've got to give them something as close as possible. So I came up with the bright idea of taking Mary's sister and hiding her offstage in a john or up in an attic—wherever— with a long microphone. Whatever Mary did onstage, she did offstage. If Mary sniffled, she sniffled. It just stopped everyone dead. People couldn't believe it or figure it out.
 . . . One night I hear the mayor of Buffalo sitting in the front row tell his wife, "Oh it's simple. It's radar."
 . . . they began to think that they heard more than one guitar. They began to think they heard all kinds of things. They put in things that weren't there.[24]

Clearly, for Paul and Ford the recording studio, rather than the bandstand, was by this time the central location for their artistic work, the live stage almost a secondary, less perfect site for the creation of music. Paul eventually built a remote tape control unit (the "Paulverizer") for use on stage. With it he could selectively multiply voices—guitar, vocal, or other sound effects. Despite the use of the "Paulverizer," Mary Ford's sister was kept in the act for years and, astonishingly, none could figure out how the doubling was done until a man brought his daughter backstage one night who asked Paul where the other lady was. "It took a little kid who didn't have a complicated mind," he said. "Everybody saw machines, turntables, radar—everything but the simplest thing."[25]

 The multiplying of the voices is an uncanny effect, a kind of double exposure. While it may be seen in retrospect as merely a rather facile trick, at the time it marked the appearance of a textural effect in popular music recording that was, in time, to enable the production of pop recordings of a new emotional depth and a greatly increased dramatic range. In later chapters I shall argue that the spreading use of echo and reverb in popular music recordings allowed and encouraged new ways for listeners to engage with popular music records. Certain recordings became vehicles for and enactments of highly personal, private meanings, setting up imaginary private spaces, even as they retained their public, collectivist aspects (dance music, tavern music). While the pop Les Paul may not be the best exemplar of this new aesthetic introversion, his use of largely aspatial doubling and his facility for sonic illusion begins to hint at new, almost magical possibilities in sound recording. We may at this point begin to investigate the device from a psychological point of view. James Hillman, for example, speaks of the clinical significance of multiplying identities:

multiplication of persons may be used as a therapeutic tool in order to bring home the realization that 'the ego complex is not the only complex in the psyche.' By actively imagining the psyche into multiple persons, we prevent the ego from identifying with each and every figure in a dream or fantasy, each and every impulse and voice. For ego is not the whole psyche, only one member of a commune.[26]

The spotlighted circle in the center of the concert hall stage might be seen as a representation of the realm of ego, of consciousness. The disembodied voice offstage suggests a counterpart, an other that may remain unknown, unconscious forever, or it may suggest a presence waiting in the wings, waiting to make an embodied appearance, or waiting to be correctly identified, if only as the "other lady."

At the same time, the other voice is locked in synchrony with the front voice. It may at most sing a harmony to the first voice, but more often sings unison. The second voice is, however, more than a simple echo, a lesser simulacrum of the primary voice. Invisible it may be, but aurally it shares the spotlight. The unseen sonic presences that follow Alice (at a distance) into the enclosed subterranean swimming pool in the movie *Cat People* (chapter 4) threaten to destroy and replace Alice's ego self; self and other cannot share the same space. In the Paul construction on the other hand the self and other "magically" seem to occupy the same space, one seen, one invisible. Rather than being a murderous intruder, the other here is a replica, a clone of the self. The closeness of self to other here threatens to dismantle the "atomic" model of nuclear self and orbiting other; the nuclear unit itself remains irreducibly multiple.

This sort of "equal partner" sonic doubling—perhaps first used on Patti Page recordings such as "With My Eyes Wide Open I'm Dreaming"—was again employed much later in a recording by Al Green, "Jesus is Waiting" (1974), and its use there might be seen as one particular logical extension of the Paul-Ford tape doubling. On the Green recording the other voice is fully autonomous, entering into a kind of pseudodialogue with itself, answering, adding to, amplifying, much more akin to a true counterpoint than the close shadowing of the Paul-Ford recordings. As the two voices weave around each other, singing harmony, then unison, then call and response, it becomes impossible to tell which voice is the "real" one (the track recorded live with the band) and which one the later overdub. The authenticity of the live voice is earlier proved when Green sings directions to the studio band

("I wish the band would just bring it way down low!") to which they respond by dropping the volume, building up again later for a big finish and fade out. With the Ford-Paul overdub by comparison, the split is incomplete: Mary Ford's other remains attached, like a shadow or a Siamese twin.

The multiple voices of Mary Ford are in a kind of lockstep with one another and as such display very limited agency; there are no "breakout" moments, such as were heard in much vocal rhythm and blues of the time and rock 'n' roll shortly after. And in another way, the totality of Ford's presence is firmly pitched as secondary, subservient to Paul's, despite her forwardness in the mix. Indeed, Paul, "the wizard of Waukesha," was represented as being strongly in control, while Ford was correspondingly seen as being controlled. Steve Waksman has shown how this relationship was played out, tongue in cheek, in an episode of their radio show *At Home*. In a reworking of the story of the sorcerer's apprentice, Mary "borrows" Les's "Paulverizer," takes it to the basement and makes unauthorized use of it, producing sonic multiples of herself. The device begins smoking from overuse, until Paul finally reclaims it, sternly admonishing Ford.[27] The forefronting of Ford's voice(s) on record, a counterpart to the filmic close-up, on the one hand renders her, as Cubitt points out, as "large," as potentially a figure of power, but this power is entirely mitigated by the all-controlling presence of Paul. As Waksman points out, Paul's central function as producer-inventor-musician was strongly exploited by record company publicists, and the spectacle of Paul as genius-inventor was also central to the Paul-Ford stage show. In this context, the forefronting of Ford on record might be seen not as a sign of empowerment but the reverse: she plays a kind of Echo to Paul's Narcissus. She cannot initiate speech, and the utterances she does make are a replay of his, or somehow otherwise under his control. Her musical accomplishments thus end up being in a sense his. The presence of Mary Ford on record is that of a kind of sonic "trophy wife," ensconced in an imagined postwar dream home. Just as her multiplied voices are in lockstep harmony with one another, the entity "Mary Ford," on record is presented, ultimately, as little more than an instrument of Paul's creative will, another cleverly wrought music-producing device at his disposal. (Indeed, Paul's choice of "Ford" as stage name for the former Colleen Summers hints at her status as a kind of machine.)

In a recent discussion of Gary Lewis and the Playboys' 1960s pop song, "This Diamond Ring," David Brackett has invoked Mikhail Bakhtin's notion of the monologic and the dialogic.[28] In a dialogic text,

consciousness . . . is always found in intense relationship with another consciousness. . . . Every experience, every thought of a character is internally dialogic, filled with struggle, or is . . . open to inspiration from outside itself.[29]

"Monologism" conversely "denies the existence outside of itself of another consciousness with equal rights and equal responsibilities. . . . Monologue is deaf to the other's response."[30] Brackett uses the idea of the dialogic and monologic to understand how "sealed" pop songs like "This Diamond Ring" and open, more participatory recordings such as Wilson Pickett's "In the Midnight Hour" might set up relationships with their audiences.

The two terms might equally be applied to the internal structures of the recording itself. Ford's musical voice, speaking only when spoken to, remains, in what might be yet another sense of the term, *Echoic*—secondary, lacking in agency—in relation to Paul's. Whatever powerful emotions Echo might feel, her verbal capabilities are strictly limited to what Narcissus chooses to say. Thus, despite an apparent conjugal dialogism in the Paul-Ford oeuvre, it could be said that in reality only one voice speaks.

Informants report that just such a relationship was played out in Ford and Paul's real life together. "She was insecure, like all she needed was someone to provide some steadfastness in her life. . . . She was appreciative of anyone who would step up to the plate and take charge," an associate told Mary Shaugnessey, Paul's biographer.[31] Others report on Ford's considerable instrumental skills. Western bandleader Cliffie Stone said, "She was a delicate talent with an amazing ear . . . she sang quietly, succinctly and always in tune . . . she was a terrific rhythm player."[32] Certainly, the way Ford was seen by associates and the way she was represented accords with her position on what might be seen as a popularly understood "art to pop continuum." At the "art" end of the scale we would find performers with a high degree of apparent autonomy and creative agency, while the nearer we get to the pop end, the more we find accurate (sometimes freakishly accurate) singers and instrumentalists, able to replicate high production value performances on demand. At this end, we are mostly in the passive voice: performers are produced, are acted upon. It is easy to see how Mary Ford's vocal and instrumental skills, her apparent lack of confidence, her compliance, would dovetail with Paul's obsessive drive. Technically, the painstaking multitracking of a single voice to create close harmony passages requires exactly the sort of easy precision (and malleability) that singers like Patti Page, Rosemary Clooney and Mary Ford possessed.[33]

Shaugnessey tells of a stage routine in which Ford would literally echo Paul's dazzling guitar licks, passage by passage, until finally Paul would jokingly unplug her guitar.[34] As Steve Waksman points out:

Through such measures, Paul worked to ensure that instrumental virtuosity remained his domain, even as he showcased Ford's musical skills, and managed to do so with levity. The power imbalance characteristic of Paul's maneuvers pervaded the couple's careers, and effectively reinforced their image as a couple who reinforced the boundaries of gender propriety during a period when those boundaries were being defended with renewed force.[35]

Yet for all that, the modern listener might detect beneath these superficially playful displays small traces of the tensions and "struggle" more generally absent from the tightly controlled recordings. Many listeners today hear in the couple's biggest-selling hit, the hard-swinging "How High the Moon" a freshness and energy lacking in so many of their other recordings. We learn from Shaugnessey that in fact one of the most forceful presences on the recording, the driving "hot club" style rhythm guitar, was provided by Mary Ford, a fact with which Paul remains apparently uncomfortable.[36] On this recording, all voices seem to be racing to keep up with the driving rhythm, and only just making it. The result is exhilarating; a rare "wild card" element in the Les Paul–Mary Ford oeuvre, and perhaps one of its few genuinely dialogic moments. [37]

But for all his controlling of voices, Paul did ultimately effect a powerfully anti-Echoic move. The old orthodoxies of "realism" and "authenticity" represented sound recording itself as fundamentally Echoic, in that the recording was meant to offer an absolutely authentic, "noncounterfeit" playback of prior sound events. While it is questionable if music recording was *ever* as simply deterministic as that, the sheer inescapable, unapologetic "manufacturedness" of the New Sound and the publicity surrounding its production did much to recast the idea of the recording apparatus, as being at least partly autonomous, as productive in itself, in a kind of dialogue with its human users.

Inspired and "licensed" by the commercial success of hits such as "Peg o' My Heart" and by the Les Paul and Mary Ford recordings, a number of other record makers in the few years before the global breakout of rock 'n' roll made more than occasional use of echo and reverb effects, and again, some of the most commercially successful recordings of that period used the devices in highly distinctive ways. While none of these quite show the radical reconfiguring of echo, reverb and "space" that early rock 'n' roll records effected, nonetheless an expanding vocabulary of effects, increasingly weird, though still fundamentally pictorial can be traced.

Speedy West was a leading Los Angeles–based session steel guitarist, who during the pre–rock 'n' roll period recorded a popular series of duets with Telecaster-playing Jimmy Bryant. The largely spontaneous, studio-improvised recordings were showpiece guitar instrumentals, sparsely backed by a crisp rhythm section, with the occasional addition of piano, and given a characteristic bright, clear West Coast production sound. The playing of both guitarists evidenced great dexterity but retained a relaxed, unforced, freely improvised feel—in marked contrast to the highly wrought and not infrequently bland productions of their Capitol stablemate Les Paul. Pedal steel player West was (and still is) famous for his dynamic chord work and "impossible" tone-bending effects, used to great effect on a number of West Coast pop and country recordings, including hits by Tennessee Ernie Ford. The Bryant-West collaborations are described by David Toop as an "alternative view of futurism,"[38] while Rich Kienzle describes them and their music as being "products of the Bold New World of Postwar L.A. . . . where cutting edge innovations in everything from fast food, freeways, aviation—and amplified guitars—were routine."[39] Popular music listeners have long since become familiar with an extraordinarily wide range of possible electric guitar sounds, but in the early 1950s West's and Bryant's electric guitar instrumentals must indeed have represented a wildly adventurous departure, radically unlike their immediate predecessors (including even their commercial rival Les Paul).

"West of Samoa" (1954) is in some ways a typical Hawaiianist recording: a languid guitar lick played against a descending minor key bass line introduces the song, while a variety of echoic bird calls, croaks, taps and cries ring all around. West plays a bass lick on the steel, using the swell pedal to extend each note. The first verse features a not atypical Hawaiian-styled steel guitar riff—major key, "upbeat"—while the electric guitar plays ukulele-styled rhythm. The following verse returns to the ominous bass string riff, this time with even denser jungle noises in the background, with added slithering, croaking and tapping sounds. During the jungle verses, all voices are echoic, though to differing degrees, while all is relatively dry during Hawaiian. The alternating "wet" and "dry," minor and major verses, with and then without sound effects, serve to cast the listener in and out of a mysteriously exotic, more than a little threatening soundscape. In the Hawaiianist verses, all is reassuring, familiar; in the jungle verses, all is sonically othered, all is spatially separate from the ego, regardless of whether it is nearby or distant. The ego itself here has no instrumental stand-in during the jungle verses; there is no voice at the center where the listener is implicitly located. Kienzle describes the "West of Samoa" session:

At a late night 1954 session, they had one tune to finish. . . . Fighting the effects of sick headache, [West's] taste and ingenuity were unimpaired. "I was runnin' to the bathroom after every take and throwin' up," he recalled. "I said, 'Ken, turn the tape back on; I want to overdub some sound effects.' I had no idea what I was gonna do." Maybe the headache helped West dig into the far reaches of his throbbing mind, for he created exotic sounds in ways even a Martin Denny couldn't conceive. By scraping and plucking the strings of his Bigsby [steel guitar], he created a thoroughly realistic set of tropical birds.[40]

Although listeners may have pictured a jungle landscape, Kienzle's remarks suggest that for West at least (and subtextually for listeners perhaps) the space was every bit as much a dark mindspace as it was empirical. And the jungle itself intrinsically defies the pictorial; the dense undergrowth hides more than it reveals. We are, in this sense at least, back in the familiar territory of the echo, with its partial occlusion of the visual. Here, however, rather than adding a comforting twilight softness to the world, the occlusion conceals both wonders and terrors, as nightmarish creatures struggle ferociously for existence, near but unseen.

As producers became generally bolder with their use of reverb, yet another effect appeared, in which voices came in and out of reverb, both between verses, but also within passages. The same voice (human or instrument) would alternate between dry and roomy. Tommy Duncan's Capitol recording of Jimmie Rodgers's "Gambling Polka Dot Blues" (1949) extended the reverberant passages to include not just the trademark yodel but whole sections of the chorus as well. Whenever the singer begins to lament his bad luck, or sing in falsetto, or mumble and cry to himself, the reverb comes in. Although the song is generally anchored by the dry, centered vocal, that the same voice is then distanced creates something like a spatial ambiguity, but stops short of dismantling the realist spatiality entirely.

Tennessee Ernie Ford's "Mule Train," also recorded in 1949 (and like many of the tracks discussed so far in this chapter, originally released on Capitol Records) begins also with a reverberant call of "Mule Train!" that becomes even more reverberant as the long final vowel turns into an upwardly inflected whoop. A reverberant steel guitar lick (played by Speedy West) comes in, followed by whiplike sound effects. The sung verse then is relatively dry, but each time the singer calls "Mule train!" the reverb returns. The effect here is to render the dry upfront vocal as a kind of intimate voice-over to the overtly pictorial rendering of the mule train, and its rough-hewn teamster.

The effect was used as late as 1956 on Howlin' Wolf's Chess recording of "Smokestack Lightnin.'" Here the famous Wolf falsetto moan is given an extra boost of reverb. Given Howlin' Wolf's imposing physical presence—well in excess of six feet tall and extraordinarily athletic on stage well into his sixties—and his frequent invocation of voodoo and supernaturalist tropes, it is not difficult to read the reverb here as an intended reference to the supernatural. The singer is able to roam at will through the recorded field, to be here or there as and when he chooses. Chess used the same device to create moments of spatial ambiguity on Little Walter recordings as well, again suggesting a kind of dominion over space—although, significantly, until the appearance of rock 'n' roll the effect was used mostly on instruments rather than the human voice, and when used on the voice was generally restricted to yodeling or other "floating," nonverbal falsetto passages.

In the slow blues "When the Lights Go Out" (1954) Jimmy Witherspoon admiringly describes his girlfriend: "I love to look at my baby's face, I love to feel that silk and lace, and when she kiss she never makes me shout." All this is recorded dry, on-mic, but the punch line that ends the verse—"Great God almighty, when the lights go out!"—is deeply embedded in reverb; the lights go out and the aural space swells. The next verse is again dry, as the singer returns to visually describing his baby: "I love to see her walking down the street, she always dresses so nice and neat"—and again the reverberant punchline corresponds to the visual occlusion.

Julie London's million-selling hit of 1955 "Cry Me a River" featured a minimal accompaniment (guitar by Barney Kessell, bass by Ray Leatherwood). A notable production hook present on the recording was the lush reverb enshrouding both the vocal and the electric guitar. The song ends with London repeating the line, "I cried a river over you," as the volume progressively drops and the reverb progressively increases. The singer seems to be moving away from the listener, disappearing into a fog or a twilight.[41]

Johnny Guitar Watson's instrumental "Space Guitar" (1954) also makes use of a radically fluctuating reverb. The comments made above about how radically new and different Speedy West's playing must surely have sounded to audiences of the 1950s would be doubly true of Johnny Watson's music, and this track in particular. Speaking specifically of Les Paul, West and Bryant, Hank Garland, Bo Diddley, Bill Doggett and Johnny Guitar Watson, Toop says:

> an obsession with weirdness, threat and rebellion merged with instrumentals that represented marginalized American communities. . . . Their music was an alternative view of futurism, either a regionalized expansion of sound technology and recording techniques, or at its most extreme, a dystopian leer facing off against the utopian charm school smile of Welk and Conniff. . . . No guitarists were ever more daring.[42]

Although Les Paul might reasonably be excluded from the above company (many of his most successful recordings were very much of the easy-listening "charm school" style), Toop's remarks neatly capture the sense of aggression and adventurousness in this early 1950s West Coast music.

Recorded in Los Angeles for the R & B label Federal, "Space Guitar" features fast and frantic guitar playing interspersed variously with brief, nervously subdued "jazzy" chord passages, sax breaks, a quote from the *Dragnet* theme, double-time riffs and dead stops. The guitarist intersperses the fast and aggressive trebly single-string blues licks with rapid, jagged slides along the entire length of the guitar neck, producing voicelike cadences. Listening to the manic riffs, bent notes and overdriven chords, we can easily picture the wild and extravagant body movements needed to produce such sounds, a regime of body use the direct opposite of that of the 1950s Les Paul/Barney Kessell–styled jazz guitarist: sitting hunched over the guitar, the treble controls wound back, face dispassionate, the lefthand movements displaying a professional but noncommittal dexterity, the whole performance an exercise in the withheld. "Space Guitar" on the other hand invites its listeners to imagine the stabbing, flailing movements of which the recorded sounds provide a direct index.

Watson moves rapidly and impatiently from idea to idea and the production space fluctuates just as wildly. A fast, dry, stop-time riff opens the song, followed by a deeply reverberant first four bars, then a dry four, another reverberant four, a reverberant theme quote, another verse with a whole new mixture of nervous-sounding themes and ideas. Then a sax comes in that also alternates between dry and deeply reverberant. Significantly, the track was recorded before the launch of Sputnik 1, and well before the United States' more notable successes in the space race. In the early 1950s, rather than being imagined primarily as a zone ripe for heroic colonizing—the territorialized space of screen productions such as *Outer Limits, Star Trek*, or *2001: a Space Odyssey*, or pop instrumentals like *Telstar* (1962)—"space" was as much a source of terror, from which nuclear weapons or grotesque, hostile invaders might come, worldly or otherwise. It was the terror-space of such early 1950s films as *Killers from Space* and *War of the Worlds*.

Watson's "Space Guitar" keeps all its options open, however, and its space(s), moods and effects compose an intense yet playful montage—one that thwarts any attempt at constructing a coherent or unitary spatiality. But, like the examples already cited, the spatial effects in "Space Guitar" are essentially serial; the reverb switches on and off, and each segment of itself more or less "makes sense." "Space Guitar" remains essentially outside the sort of parallel, nonrealist and polyspatial production regimes that characterized much early rock 'n' roll. By rapidly switching from "near" to "in the distance" the guitar plays the part of both the self *and* the invading other, but never quite manages to simultaneously suggest both.

Red Ingle was another Capitol artist, a longtime pro musician with major-league big band experience whose "Tim-Tayshun," a hillbilly-esque parody of the standard "Temptation" became a surprise hit of 1947. There followed a series of increasingly deranged send-up recordings, including "(I Love You) For Seventy Mental Reasons" (1947), "Pagan Ninny's Keep 'Er Goin' Stomp" (1947), "Cigareets, Whusky and Wild Wild Women"

(1947/1948), "Cigardust," a parody of Stardust (1947/1948); and "Moe Zart's Turkey Trot" (1947/1948). As Red Ingle and the Natural Seven, the group toured widely. As with their recordings, a feature of their zany stage act, which featured numerous costume changes and elaborate musical high jinks,[43] was their demonstrably high degree of musical skill.

Ingle's recording of August 1948, "Serutan Yob" was a hillbilly-ized parody of Nat King Cole's recent hit, "Nature Boy" (1947), a strange song, for its time, of nature mysticism, written by protohippie Eden Ahbez.[44] The title of Ingle's parody is both a near anagram of the actual title, and a reference to an extensively advertised laxative, Serutan. The song begins with a reverberant, pained human howling, followed by a threnodic whistling and a strummed ukulele, all reverberant. The song proper then begins in the familiar Natural Seven style of brisk tempo music behind a broadly hillbilly-esque deadpan vocal: "there was a boy, a plum enchanted boy who wandered furr." Slang terms recur throughout.

[Due to an American Federation of Musicians ban] union members Ingle and [arranger/musician] Washburne couldn't participate on the session, but singer Karen Tedder could. Washburne decided to produce the record in layers. First Tedder cut her vocals and timed interruptions onto an acetate, accompanied by union-exempt members of the Pasadena Uke Club. When Tedder was done, popular Los Angeles radio personality Jim Hawthorne laid down two overdubs. For the first he . . . played a Duo-Lyka, a novelty instrument with a bass-like sound. For the second he essentially went into a free form rap, adding [a] break from his trademark musical device, the hogantwanger . . . [which consisted of] graduated hacksaw blades mounted on wood.[45]

The sound of the hogantwanger is rendered all the more strange by the application of dense reverb. There follow more sound effects and vocal overdubs, in which the singer quarrels with Hawthorne, competing for musical space, eventually cutting him off completely, before the whole song collapses in argument, finishing with a metallic breaking sound. A play of dialogism that offers an alternative to Les Paul's later rampant monologism.[46]

Recorded well before all the other tracks discussed in this chapter, and six months before even "Riders in the Sky," "Serutan Yob" could well be mistaken for a sonic satire from a much later time, and it is noteworthy that so spatially playful and deconstructive a recording should predate infinitely more straight-faced spatial recordings. It may be significant that some of the more serious spatializing "western" recordings such as Vaughn Monroe's "Riders in the Sky" and Foy Willing and the Riders of the Purple Sage's "Stampede" (1949, for the movie *Trigger Jr.,* directed by William Witney, 1950) both feature the kind of dramatic, high-adventure narrative associated with cinema and television westerns, while Ingle's recordings, and "Serutan Yob" in particular owe more to the zanier end of radio broadcasting practice.

Slim Whitman's hit recordings of the early 1950s are firmly in the pictorial western spatial mode, yet Whitman's recording of "Indian Love Call" (1952) constructs a baffling, almost hallucinatory spatiality, in which the rigidity of the singing and instrumentation is counterposed against double and triple echoes, "breakout" yodels and steel guitar harmonics, to the point that the "space" becomes a wholly delirious zone. This deliriousness remains unacknowledged in the verbal text of the song, however: on the surface, it is as earnest and po-faced as any pre–rock 'n' roll of the period. "Indian Love Call" was a well-known pop tune when Whitman recorded it: it had been the feature number of the 1924 stage show *Rose-Marie,* which was filmed to great commercial success in 1932 with Jeanette MacDonald and Nelson Eddy in the leads. Invoking the familiar "masculine-Narcissus-calling-into-the-wilderness-responded-to-by-a-hidden-female-Echo" construct, the song sets up the standard horizontal here/there, self/other, masculine/feminine dichotomies. The roles should be clear: the song is organized around the motif of call and response, with the call from the self coming first, answered by the hidden Echoic other.

The first sound, before even any words are sung, is Whitman's yodel; the voice of the self, presumably. Yet this first yodel is already slightly echoic, in the familiar Tennessee Ernie Ford–Tommy Duncan style already described. The "answering yodel" that follows is even more so. The first sung line, "When I'm calling you," however, is quite dry, but the drawn-out yodel that tags onto the end of the first line (slightly overlapping the held "you," indicating that it is the result of multitracking) is richly reverberant. The narrating Whitman is "close by" speaking confidentially to the listener while his own prerecorded voice echoes elsewhere (perhaps on an imagined screen), "answered" by his own echoic voice and/or the steel guitar that sometimes seems to stand in for his voice, sometimes answers it, in the Hank Williams–Jerry Byrd style described in chapter 5.

The steel guitar itself is reverberant, and the player makes frequent use of high harmonics, which act as a kind of counterpart to the yodel, a steel guitar falsetto, a floating, disembodied, "aerial" voice. One would expect that the spatialities here *should* be clear and coherent, yet the overlapping pairings of self and other, voice and falsetto, dryness and reverberance, nearness and distance serve rather to create a kind of sonic hall of mirrors. The echoes themselves produce more echoes; the others spawn even more others. Figures are multiplying out of control, and some of them are taking to the air. There are whole squadrons of them.[47] There are horizontally removed others and there are vertically removed others, and they are swapping places with each other and with the self. The surreal effects of the sonic doubling and treblings in "Indian Love Call" are further heightened by the repressively strict tempo of the rhythm acoustic guitar, and by Whitman's almost freakishly accurate intonation, particularly in the falsetto range.[48] There is not a trace of the knowing, conspiratorial wink at the audience here. Neither the voice nor any aspect of the musical arrangement acknowledge even for a moment the swelling, ambient craziness. An almost parade-ground seriousness is in force.

The items discussed in this chapter (with the exception of "How High the Moon," recorded while Les Paul was temporarily relocated in New York, and "Smokestack Lightnin'," recorded in Chicago) were all recorded in Los Angeles. All tracks make a feature of the fact of spatiality. Produced in the city from which the U.S. film industry operated, it is not surprising that these pop products should have made such a show of sonically fabricating space, and that those spaces should be so glossily rendered. And perhaps that is what most defines the sort of West Coast echo and reverb surveyed in this chapter; it invariably sets up and operates within a virtual proscenium arch. The dazzlingly constructed West Coast pop spaces afforded listeners little in the way of participatory response other than as passive audience—an entertained, charmed and intrigued audience, perhaps, but one never for a moment allowed to forget its place as receiver of product. West Coast pop music rarely invited its listeners to "inhabit" its virtual spaces, to become cocreators of its inner worlds in the way that southern rockabilly or Chicago blues (sometimes) did.

CHAPTER 7

"Off the Wall"

Blues Recording at Sun and Chess Studios, 1947–1954

⊨◇⊨

[We] noticed, you know . . . these, these singles would sell every week-end, every week. We noticed that the electric sound, the echo, all those kind of gimmicks catching on, something new . . . then we started looking for new and different things, you know, that's what, you know, we, we saw that the original and the fresh stuff, the fresh sound was what sold records. So we, we developed a sensibility to look for that and help develop it on our own with, with echo, with our studio.—Phil Chess.[1]

During the period roughly from the end of World War II up to the global breakout of rock 'n' roll music in the early to mid-1950s, many of the most important new developments in popular music recording occurred away from the big media industry centers of Los Angeles and New York, in the smaller independent studios trading primarily in the race and country markets. The epoch-making importance of "indies" such as King, Starday, Atlantic, Aristocrat/Chess/Checker, Excello, Savoy, Aladdin, Modern, RPM, Sun and others has been extensively examined, and need not be recounted here.[2] The sonic/spatial innovations wrought at Sun and Chess, however, are of particular interest, and the often halting, trial-and-error developments made at those two studios eventually provided radical reconfigurations of the widening, deepening sonic spatialities that were entering the mainstream in West Coast studios and elsewhere.

The recording activity at Sun and Chess has often been characterized (retrospectively) by the integral role played by producer/managers Sam Phillips and Leonard Chess, and the close and complex relationships between those men and the musicians they recorded. Phonograph recording had always required the agencies of a particular kind of go-between, a person who could both understand to at least some degree something of what the performer was attempting to achieve in the studio and at the same time oversee the purely managerial and entrepreneurial functions involved.[3] The term "producer," however did not come into common usage in music recording much before 1957.[4] Prior to that, the terms most frequently used were "arranger," "supervisor," "engineer" or most commonly "artists and repertoire (A & R) man." For the purposes of this study, "producer" is used loosely to include both functions pertaining to the operating of the recording apparatus and the directing and supervising of the session.

Whether the term was in currency or not, the producer had always been of prime importance in music recording. A "performance" presupposes a listener. In the recording medium, the listener—the record buyer, the live listener—is not normally present, and this absence might threaten to undermine the entire performance. It is not difficult to imagine how challenging the sterile, coldly functional ambience of the recording studio might be to a seasoned performer—or to a neophyte, for that matter. Lacking the support and encouragement of a studio audience, the recording artist might rely all the more on whatever "listening presence" the studio may provide, even if that presence is a single engineer in a control booth. Performance "demands" a witness, a destination of some sort. Performers and their listeners construct feedback loops. This feedback may take the form of more energetic dancing by an audience (who themselves may be in a sense performing for or to the musicians), or it may be manifest in shouts of encouragement to the musicians. It may amount to little more than a polite silence, a contented nod from a concertgoer, a coin thrown in a busker's cup, or merely the *sense* a performer may have that at least someone in the crowd is listening.

In the absence of a physically present audience a conductor or bandleader may "audience" the playing of the orchestra members, and his (usually) devoted attention to their playing may coax superior performances from them. In smaller ensembles, the musicians themselves may act as each other's audience (as in Billie Holiday's version of "Swing, Brother, Swing" discussed in chapter 3). With trios, duos and individual performers it becomes more problematic. Generally speaking, the smaller the performing unit, the more critical the presence of an external audience will become. The exigencies of the recording studio—the need for both a controlled, *private* sonic environment, and simultaneously for "audience"—led to the appearance of quite literally "self-conscious" recording artists, such as Robert Johnson and Jimmie Rodgers.

The lucrative business of recording "race," hillbilly, Cajun and other musics of the impoverished American south in the 1920s and 1930s required entrepreneurs with at least a modicum of musical and personal sensitivity. If nothing else, the successful producer had to have an ear for what the potential record buyers would want to hear; otherwise, he would have little guidance in making decisions as to which artists to record of the many who presented themselves at the temporary studios rigged up during southern field trips. These empathic tendencies sometimes coexisted with the most exploitative practices, but the fact remains that the serious producer was obliged to make some attempt to understand his temporary milieu.[5]

And then the producer had to preside over a potentially antagonistic situation: the artists finding themselves in unfamiliar surroundings, with only the company of the (usually) culturally alien producer. In the late 1920s Englishman Art Satherley was responsible for recording race artists for Paramount, a leading producer of race and hillbilly records. His attitude may not have been atypical: "I didn't just say 'Sing this and go out and have a drink somewhere,' I spent my time in that studio getting them ready for the people of the world . . . when I spoke to those Negroes, I would talk to them. I would tell them what we had to expect."[6] Producers of race and hillbilly music like Satherley, Ralph Peer, H. C. Speir and Frank Walker might be seen as more or less venal ethnographers, profit-driven cultural anthropologists. They were adept practitioners of the field trip. There were potentially valuable cultural resources to be obtained — which, like natural resources, would require special skills and knowledges to extract. The producer/engineer was the cultural go-between linking regional undercultures with often global distribution networks.

In the days before Les Paul and Sam Phillips, when race and country music records were most often hastily made "snapshots" of a performance that had been worked up and road-tested away from the recording studio (with the notable exceptions discussed in earlier chapters) the producer's job was basically in the Gaisberg mold, "to take a sound photograph." By 1950 producers such as the Chess brothers in Chicago, Bernie Besman in Detroit or Sam Phillips in Memphis were searching not so much for generic raw material as for a "quality." Among the various products they were peddling (which included such older styles as gospel singing, sermons and recitations, old-timey hillbilly) was a new strand of raucous, small combos, often based around amplified guitars. The purchasers of *this* product were frequently blacks and whites who had moved to big manufacturing cities from the country during and after the war. Their roots, language and memories were rural, even if their lives were now irrevocably urban. The producer operating in this milieu needed all the qualities of his prewar counterpart, and considerably more: he was "pitching" product to more complex social positionings, a more sophisticated, urbanized audience. If the earlier producer was a kind of cultural prospector and trader, the latter was a craftsman in his own right.

Sam Phillips in particular might be seen as one of the first of the modern, interventionist producers who, like Legge in the field of classical music, would play a much greater part in artistic decision-making. Just as Phillips was to spend months rehearsing with the young and naive Elvis Presley before cutting any records, so too would later producers such as Phil Spector, Berry Gordy, Jerry Wexler, Jim Stewart and George Martin rehearse, coach, and not infrequently personally manage their artists. Their work was more akin to alchemy than prospecting; for them and their artists the studio space itself was the crucible.

Sam Phillips opened his small recording business, the Memphis Recording Service, in January 1950. The company specialized initially in vanity pressings and radio transcriptions, and provided a mobile recording service for Rotary dinners, birthday parties, bar mitzvahs and the like. Phillips also recorded local blues and R & B artists, and sold or leased masters to established independent labels such as Chess in Chicago or Modern in Los Angeles (operated by the Bihari brothers).

A number of these then obscure recordings and the artists who made them went on to achieve canonical status in postwar blues and rock 'n' roll music. Ike Turner, B. B. King and Howlin' Wolf all made early recordings with Phillips in Memphis. Ike Turner and the Delta Rhythm Kings' record "Rocket 88" (1951), B. B. King's "She's Dynamite" (1950) and Howlin' Wolf's "Moaning at Midnight" (1950/1951), like so many tracks made at the Memphis Recording Service featured loud, often anarchic-seeming rhythm sections, riffing rather than soloing horns and, loud, distorted, prominently featured electric guitars.

In 1952 Phillips established Sun Records, following separate disputes with the Bihari and Chess brothers. He continued to record local blues and R & B acts and release them on his own label through the next couple of years. In 1954 he began to work with some white acts including Harmonica Frank, Hardrock Gunter and Elvis Presley. Following the runaway success of the latter in late 1954, Phillips concentrated on developing and exploiting the new hybrid "rockabilly" and his black acts moved on or retired from the business. Phillips went on to record hits by Carl Perkins, Roy Orbison, Jerry Lee Lewis, Johnny Cash and Charlie Rich. Throughout this second period—the predominantly white rock 'n' roll phase of Sun Records—Phillips's product featured the slapback echo sound that was so widely imitated and which quickly came to be regarded as a quintessential trademark of the "rock 'n' roll sound."

Through all this success, however, the company failed to achieve the scale it might have. Other independents such as Atlantic, Chess, Specialty, Imperial and later Motown went on to become sizable corporations but Sun remained a shoestring operation. All its major artists sooner or later moved on to greater success with other companies; while many of them continued to express respect and affection for Phillips, frequent mention was made of Phillips's cautious, financially timid business style.[7] Through the 1960s Sun scaled down operations, with Phillips finally selling the back catalogue to Shelby Singleton in 1968.

The black blues and R & B that Phillips recorded prior to the Sun Records–Presley and post-Presley rockabilly phase reveal many of the still nascent tactics that Phillips would later refine. Right from the beginning, Phillips revealed himself to be not over concerned with established industry production values, valuing individual and idiosyncratic expressive power over technical niceties. The wordless humming that opens the celebrated recording of Howlin' Wolf's "Moaning at Midnight," for instance, which Phillips holds up as one of his own peak achievements, seems to be clearly overloading the microphones.[8] Carl Perkins describes working with Phillips:

you just forgot about making a record and tried to show him. . . . I'd walk out on a limb, I'd try things I knew I couldn't do, and I'd get in a corner trying to do it and then have to work my way out of it. I'd say "Mr Phillips, that's terrible." He said, "That's original." I said, "But it's just a big original mistake." And he said, "That's what Sun Records is. That's what we are."[9]

Much of Phillips early recording work is full of such "mistakes": sloppy horns, distorted electric guitars, tempo irregularities, slightly out of tune instruments and off-mic shouts. Phillips had had experience sound engineering respectable, popular music: in the 1940s he had recorded big bands, including the Dorseys and Glenn Miller, at the Skyway Lounge in Memphis's Peabody Hotel for a local radio station, and eventually for nightly national broadcast on the CBS network. He became frustrated by the restrictions on individual expression within the big band format: "you just don't have that instinctive intuitional thing, and these dudes—I can remember well—they might have played the damned song 4000 times, and they were *still* turning the pages."[10] Although Phillips's studio and his studio practices have long been fetish items of rock historiography, not everyone was so impressed when they were current. Johnny Cash recalls that the Memphis disc jockey "Sleepy Eyed John" would preface Sun singles on his radio show with remarks such as "Here's another Sam Phillips sixty-cycle hum record."[11]

By 1953 Phillips was finding that his most promising black acts, following a general southern migratory trend, were drifting away to bigger cities and better established R & B record labels in Los Angeles and Chicago. He began recording some white acts, including Elvis Presley. Following the latter's tearaway local success, he concentrated on recording white "rockabilly" acts. The activities at Memphis recording Service/Sun might be broadly divided into two periods: an earlier predominantly black R & B period and a later mainly white rock 'n' roll period. The R & B period recordings were tailored for sale mainly to black adult record buyers, while the later period recordings were aimed at the new international white teen market. The effects used and the sonic spatialities created in the two modes largely reflect these differences, although certain key tropes carry over the two. In particular, at Sun Studios notions of guitar and voice placement were developed and refined to a point where the unique spatialities of the later period became possible.

Chapters 5 and 6 traced the evolution of the electric guitar—specifically the Hawaiian or steel guitar—which saw it being increasingly "located" remote from the singer, acoustically away from the anchored, "spotlighted" central area of attention. In this offstage position the steel acts as a kind of commentator on the main vocal line. As improvised obbligato, the steel guitar voice is in a sense much freer than the primary sung melody, and in the hands of western swing or honky-tonk players like Don Helms in Hank Williams's band, the steel achieves an expressive richness that regular guitar is hard-pressed to equal. In the recordings made at Phillips's studio we see nonsteel electric guitar in the process of taking over again from steel, gaining a primacy in popular music that it has retained to the present.

Heavily distorted electric guitar sounds were a feature of Sun recordings. Elsewhere electric guitar sounds were generally getting cleaner than ever before as guitar pickup and amplifier technology advanced. As amplifiers became more powerful it became easier for guitarists to achieve clean, ringing sounds, as amplifiers could be run at high volume while remaining in the low-output, nondistorting range of the amplifier and pickup. Les Paul's guitar sound is a good example: the guitar produces a wide-spectrum sound with clear trebles, a warm midrange, and clean bass tones. The tape-echo effects that Paul used further heightened the clean, "glossiness" of the sound. At about the same time that "How High the Moon" was charting all over the world, Phillips was recording blues guitarists playing through overdriven amplifiers, outdoing even the steel players of the early electric period for distortion. The sound of Willie Johnson's guitar on the Howlin' Wolf records is a typical example.[12]

Joe Hill Louis's "When I'm Gone / Treat Me Mean and Evil" (1952) features the familiar on and off-mic "radial" motifs discussed earlier. The voice is dry, the electric guitar deeply reverberant. Unlike western or Hawaiian recorded spaces, however, the echoic guitar here does not conjure up reassuring images of pasture, prairie or tropical idyll. The spaces suggested by the Hollywood cowboy spatial mode are both geographic (that is, "real") and mythical. Underlying the singing cowboy's songs and encoded in the recording practices is the assumption that the speaker—the cowboy—has privileged access to those spaces, that he has a kind of natural right of occupancy. His bond with the land and the sky is divinely sanctioned, transcending "mere" legal ownership. When Foy Willing sings "Blue Shadows on the Trail," the imaginal space stretches away to the prairie horizon. The fantasy contained an implicit justification and vindication of specifically white, English-speaking European economic and demographic expansion. It is hard to imagine that Joe Hill Louis's records evoked this kind of spatial fantasy in their original listening audience. The cowboy fantasy finds perhaps its nearest real-world expression, ironically, in suburban home ownership—the backyard as the exclusive natural domain of the homeowner. The bigger the backyard, the nearer the district is to the countryside, the closer it approximates the natural expanses of the cowboy song.

Such a relationship to land and the possibilities of holding any sort of land title were much less within the reach of a black Memphian of the early 1950s.[13] It is unlikely that the "here" and "there" of the Louis record referred metaphorically or otherwise to tracts of real estate the singer or his local audience of the time might one day own. Indeed, the nonpictorially anchored sonic spaces of "When I'm Gone" might more readily summon a sense of haunted, uncanny space, of graveyards at midnight, of lonely, dark spaces, of dangerous presences. In one sense, this is precisely the imagined domain of the itinerant country blues singer: junkyards, crossroads, back streets at night, swamps and dark hollers, the implicitly acknowledged territory of country blues since W. C. Handy had written of his first encounter with a country blues slide player (in the middle of the night while waiting for a late train at a lonely Mississippi Delta station in 1903).[14]

The "spookiness" of the recording is enacted partly in the guitar *sound:* in its loud, highly distorted timbre, and in unusual, angular melodic lines that rather than resolving on the "expected" tonic note, repeatedly terminate on a low fifth, seemingly signaling a move into the turnaround (that never seems to happen). The usual chord change landmarks are present, but normal expectations are thwarted. A different, less usual order seems to govern the proceedings.

The deep reverb powerfully compounds the eeriness. A temporally near antecedent in such use of reverb can be found in some of the horror and suspense movies of the time. In films such as *The Body Snatcher, I Walked With a Zombie,* and *Cat People* as well as *He Walked by Night* (directed by Alfred Werker, 1948) and *The Third Man* (directed by Carol Reed, 1949), reverb is used to signal quite specific conditions: deserted streets at night, or gloomy subterranean environments wherein lurks a mortal threat. Reverb is very much the characteristic of the built environment, but more than that it signifies the *nighttime* built environment, the precinct that has been abandoned by its "authorized," daytime occupants. It is the everyday location imbued with menace. In the movies, this "reverb moment" typically sees depicted a solitary character threatened by an unseen presence; the character seems to be alone, but a menacing other lurks in the shadows. Reverb indicates a kind of pregnant off-center space, neither fully occupied nor truly empty. It typically suggests the imminent appearance of the threatening presence.

Horror movie reverb also marks the eclipsing of the social. It occurs at night, when people are "meant to be" safely at home with family, or in the tavern with companions. The hero or heroine in such moments has abandoned or been abandoned by the social, the collective. These moments and the events that transpire in them are not therefore experienced by or authenticated by a social consensus, and commonly the hero or heroine is later met with skepticism when s/he tries to speak of them in the daytime social world. There is an ever-present suggestion both within the diegesis and beyond it that the streetscape, the danger, the darkness itself even is an inner one, that it is all hallucination. The stuff of the night street is as much of the psyche as it is of the material world.

We do not know whether or not Phillips and Louis were thinking any of this when they made "When I'm Gone," and I am not aware of any mention of this admittedly obscure recording in any of the published interviews with Phillips. It is, however, not unreasonable to assume that Phillips, Louis and the buyers of their records would have been familiar with these well-established horror (and western) movie sound design conventions. The films cited above were all widely distributed, and the devices described are to be found in many like films. The significations arising from reverberant sounds can be assumed to be part of a shared language, as much now as it was then. For Phillips then, here was an available, easily produced vocabulary of signifiers that readily suggested both real and interior spaces. Whatever the conscious intentions of the producers, the use of these devices is creatively consistent with their uses elsewhere, offering a novel reconfiguring of the basic elements. The reverb on the Louis record might be seen to evoke simultaneously the nightmare mise en scène of the B-grade horror movie and the "lived" spaces of southern blacks, the secondary urban and rural spaces of a highly segregated society: railway yards, bus stations, back streets, lonely crossroads, sharecroppers' cabins; the dark end of the lonely street. Places fleetingly occupied, seen by the migrant, the transient.

The horror movie reverb might also hint at the social experience of southern blacks, of being menaced and terrorized, the sense that one might be subject to terrible violence without warning. This menace might be the almost casual violence of white gangs, the Klan or the police, or it might refer to institutional violence: offhand daily refusals of service in restaurants, banning from public restrooms, the denial of medical treatment and so on—the full range of impoverishments of everyday life brought about by deeply ingrained segregation. Such structurally grounded terrors are perhaps suggested by the architecture of the horror film, by the impersonal but malevolent architecture and streetscapes of the horror/suspense film, an evilly sentient built environment, of which reverberant sound is the key aural marker.

The spaces represented might be unholy in another sense. The western frontier landscape, characterized by the echo is the domain of God the Father, but the reverberant space is the haunt of pagan deities, forces that may just as easily and capriciously give help to a supplicant as destroy him, trickster figures interpreted by Christians as satanic. But these figures are potentially empowering as well. The persona that speaks from the reverberant space possesses a special charisma, has been touched by a god, may have special powers over members of the opposite sex, or may be able to cast spells. Muddy Waters in boast songs such as "Mannish Boy" (1955), "I'm Your Hoochie Coochie Man" (1954) and "I've Got My Mojo Working" (1957) stated—and soon after parodied—the image of the "hoodoo man." So too did Howlin' Wolf, John Lee Hooker, Bo Diddley and Screamin' Jay Hawkins. On record, the "dark-priestly" bearing that these performers affect is heavily dependent on their use of reverb: they speak from a haunted place that they have been given permission by the resident deity to occupy.

The sound semiotic of Louis's record is complicated, however, by the selectivity of the reverb, by its application to the guitar rather than the voice. To understand the relationship between the voice and guitar on this record it is necessary to consider briefly the relationship between instrument and vocals in blues and country music of the time. Joe Hill Louis performed as a one-man band, and his rudimentary electric guitar, harp, high-hat sound harked back to older country blues, and a different, though related tradition of guitar/voice interplay. In the examples of electric guitar / voice interplay discussed in chapter 5, the guitar and vocal were produced by different players in a group. In the country blues tradition, the singer more often *was* the guitarist, both functions carried out by the one person. This is not to say that the guitar's running-commentary-on-the-vocal effect was any the less, but it was a little different. Whereas Jerry Byrd's steel guitar obbligato is quite other to Hank Williams's voice, and so fitted to bespeak the socially other, the country blues person in himself was already othered, even within his own milieu; his primary presence was always of the socially marginal, the transient, the scarcely or incompletely socialized. In the hands of a country blues singer/guitarist, the guitar did not operate simply as the voice of the other secondary to and counterpointed against the ego self. It was also a performance of virtuoso skill sometimes bordering on the magical. The singer's whole presence was "other." His instrumental skill, as in the case of Robert Johnson, was taken as evidence of his solid contractual arrangements with the dark forces.

The musical instrument is a machine, or a prosthesis. It performs what was originally a bodily function, the controlled voicing of specific sound frequencies, in some way "better" than the body itself could. Dexterity with the guitar (or any machine) represents a literal disembodying of function, a transference of power from the limbs and musculature to a device (to, literally, an instrument). The will in a sense has been abstracted from its residence in the physical body. Rather than impoverishing the body, however, this operation enriches and animates inert matter with human "will." Twentieth-century cultures have been much taken with figures of transient men who possess a virtuosic skill with a particular device—and a portable device at that. In the movies it may be the gunfighter for hire, or the pool-playing Minnesota Fats figure. In music it may be the jazz instrumentalists—primarily horn players—like Charlie Parker, Art Pepper, or Dizzy Gillespie. The combination of almost freakish dexterity with the device, unrestricted mobility and the performance of some sort of socially useful or necessary function has provided a widely appealing twentieth-century construct. Titles such as *Man with a Movie Camera* and *Young Man with a Horn* sum it up, although perhaps the most succinct statement of the ideal comes from the 1950s TV program *Have Gun Will Travel* (which, significantly, was lifted for album titles by both Duane Eddy and Bo Diddley in the early 1960s as "Have Guitar, Will Travel" and by Eddy Noack in the honky-tonk recording "Have Blues, Will Travel." In music, the figure has an ancient ancestry. From the enchantments wrought by Orpheus in Greek mythology, the medieval troubadours of France, the harpists and fiddlers of Celtic legend, the griots of West Africa, and the gypsies of Central Europe—all combine mobility, marginality, musical skill, the performance of important social functions and the reputed possession of supernatural powers.

As it had with the steel guitar in the thirties, electrification of the instrument represented a distancing of the sound from the body. In a sense it also indicated an abstracting of subjectivity from the body, as though the instrument itself had adopted a persona. The steel guitar players had already used the instrument to give voice to an imagined physical or social environment. But something slightly different occurs with the singer/guitarists; some aspect of the singer's "consciousness" is projected into the instrument. The instrument is not primarily the voice of that which is other to the singer, but rather is a kind of ventriloquist's dummy. Or perhaps it could be likened to the golem of Jewish legend—the being conjured up by magically adept rabbis out of clay, spit and semen. "When I'm Gone (Treat Me Mean and Evil)" captures the guitar sound in the process of its removal from the singer. It functions as a kind of essence, a distillation of the singer's subjectivity (but still firmly under the singer's control).

The distant guitar speaks of a more dispersed but perhaps a more integrated subjectivity. "My voice is here but my guitar sound is (or seems to be) over there" means I have a power that extends across space. This is my voice, but it is also not my voice, or it is different from my voice, it speaks not with words but is voicelike, follows some of the pitch contours of speech, but has its own characteristic pitch contours as well. This kind of action-at-a-distance renders my location in space problematic, difficult to pin down; I am here and truly here, just as I am over there, and truly over there. These paradoxes suggest both a relinquishing of titled real estate and a simultaneous more diffuse, ephemeral occupying of space. The up-front voice and distant guitar sound hints at shamanistic powers over space and matter, or perhaps the "teleporting" of sci-fi literature, or the telekinesis of New Age lore (effected on record by Louis through the agency of Leo Fender's then strangely futuristic invention, the Telecaster guitar).

Muddy Waters recordings at Chicago's Aristocrat/Chess Studios from 1947 through the 1950s demonstrate textural and production developments that parallel and build on those being employed elsewhere (notably at Sam Phillips's Memphis studios and at Bernie Besman's Detroit studio, both of which regularly leased masters to Chess). At the same time certain spatial strategies employed at Chess on early Waters recordings in particular display unique reconfigurings of the performer/listener spatial contract—some of which were to be crucial to the emergence of rock 'n' roll a few years later.

Robert Palmer talks of how Chess developed what was to become their trademark production aesthetic on Waters's early recordings:

Muddy Waters' recording career at Chess is one of the earliest examples of a producer, engineer, and musician working together to create an electric-guitar sound . . . that consciously creates the illusion of a juke-joint guitar cranked up to ten but is actually recorded at lower volume, with effects created through judicious manipulation of room acoustics and recording technology.
. . .The Chess repertory of idiosyncratic recording techniques grew to include using the studio's tile bathroom as a resonating chamber for guitar amps, mixing the sound of a directly miked amplifier with room ambience, and recording both guitar and lead vocal 'hot,'—so close to distortion on the VU meter that the very loudest notes push the needle just a shade into the red. The records created in this way jumped out at you. They were scary enough as songs, with their tales of hoodoo hexes and gypsy fortune-tellers. Everything about the production amplified and focused that scariness. . .[15]

Broadly speaking, prior to 1952 the spatial production tactics employed on Aristocrat/Chess blues recordings, like those used by Besman and Phillips, center primarily on the use (or pointed absence) of reverb. Specifically, tape echo and delay begins to appear on R & B recordings intermittently in 1952 and later (presumably as local responses to Les Paul and Mary Ford's commercially successful use of tape delay on "How High the Moon"). This key development will be examined in the following chapter. Earlier recordings show a steadily increasing use of reverb, on guitars initially, and later on voices.

Muddy Waters's first local hit, "I Can't Be Satisfied," backed with "I Feel Like Going Home" (1947 or 1948)[16] shows virtually no use of reverb—voice and guitar are distinctly dry—yet both voice and guitar evidence the "hot," extreme on-mic quality Palmer describes. Waters's guitar sound displays almost no residues of hollow-bodied acousticity; the sound is wholly "electric," and the timbre of the low guitar notes seem to shift from one riff to the next. The timbre of certain of the longer held notes also modulates, as decaying notes become slightly more trebly. As with the Robert Johnson recordings of ten years before, the slight, incidental secondary sounds can be heard. In Waters's case we hear the rattling of the slide against undamped adjacent strings, which further adds to the phase and tone–shift sound-alike effects. The sound objects here—Waters's voice, the slide guitar and upright bass—fully and grandly "occupy" the sonic space; they "jump out at you." Even Waters found himself unsettled by his own record's ability (for the time largely unprecedented) to breach the sound field's virtual proscenium arch:

I'd be driving my truck, and wherever I'd see a neon beer sign, I'd stop, go in, look at the jukebox and see is my record on there. I might buy me a beer, play the record and then leave. Don't tell nobody nothing. Before long, every blues joint there was, that record was on the jukebox. And if you come in and sat there a while, if anybody was in there, they gonna punch it. Pretty soon, I'd hear it walking along the street. I'd hear it *driving* along the street. About June or July that record was getting *really* hot. I would be driving home from playing, two or three o'clock in the morning, and I had a convertible, with the top back 'cause it was warm. I could hear people all upstairs playing that record. It would be rolling up there, man. I heard it all over. One time I heard it coming from way upstairs somewhere, and it scared me. I thought I had died.[17]

Following the strong success of "I Can't Be Satisfied" in the R & B market, Chess recorded a number of sides with Waters, similarly spare, often in a distinctly down-home country blues style (wholly opposite to the reigning jump or cooler Charles Brown/Nat Cole R & B and jazz styles). On the 1951 recording "All Night Long" reverb has been added to each single musical voice:[18] electric guitar (again, low, "brooding" single notes), harp and vocal. In previous chapters I described how reverb was used to locate voices remote from an imagined "center stage." Yet here, the reverb in combination with the characteristic hot miking of voice and guitar has a different effect: the richly timbred voice and steely electric guitar remain intimately close by the listener. The voice in particular, rather than being placed in the distance is imbued with a new, magical authority.

That particular vocal sound, simultaneously reverberant and on-mic, became a Waters staple. Recordings such as "I'm Your Hoochie-Coochie Man," "Still a Fool" (1950), "Mannish Boy" and others further capitalized on the same strategy. These songs characteristically begin with Waters calling on the listener using "preacherly" imprecations, such as the intoned "Ooooh well, ooh well, I said everything gonna be all right this morning." Indeed, Waters (who briefly considered a career as a preacher) here comes close to re-creating the reverberant qualities of the medieval cathedral described in chapter 2. Waters's threnodic recitatives suggest a priestly orator "warming up," testing the acoustics of a huge vaulted cathedral, sliding his voice up to find the "sympathetic" note of the space and, having found it, imbuing that space with vocal energy, enlisting the mass and solidity of the sacred building in the service of the divinely authorized voice.

Although never a virtuosic guitarist, Waters was able to produce some of his strongest sonic effects playing a few apparently simple low notes on his electric slide guitar. In fact, the subtle, shimmering tone shifts, the rich timbre of the low strings and the incidental rattling and ringing of adjacent strings combined to produce a recognizable and highly distinctive Muddy Waters guitar sound. The comments above about Waters's deployment of the voice might equally apply to his low string guitar sound, which characteristically featured attention-grabbing octave jumps, terminating in a rocketing slide up to the tonic note. Other times Waters would play rapid "stabbing" slide notes on the bottom string through the V–IV–I turnaround of a twelve-bar song. Indeed, clichéd terms like "low down blues" and "deep blues" have a literal truth in Waters's case.[19] The low string work might be seen as a particular activation of things "down there"—the genital region of the body, the underground, the underworld.

The drama of Waters's early recordings is heightened by musical dynamics: sudden, unexpected gaps open up in the sonic fields, brief near silences in which only room ambience and faint tape hiss can be heard, followed by "chunky" ensemble riffs. Shellac 78s had abrasives incorporated in the material that helped to shape the metal stylus, but that also produced a continuous rumbling sound. With the introduction of magnetic-tape recording and the switch to vinylite in record manufacture, it became possible to produce near silence on record. Waters and Leonard Chess made skilled use of this extended sonic palette to create an even greater sense of moment. Given the sound recording and broadcast aversion to "dead air" (of avoiding as far as possible any hiatus in the flow of sound), Waters's spacey production sound and the frequent near silences bespeak and convey a sense of great assuredness. This performer is manifestly not sacrificing his dignity, not making any attempt to grovel to or importune his audience. But the simultaneous nearness, the sense of recording presence prevents him from sounding aloof. He truly behaves on record like a high priest of Palmer's "Church of the Sonic Guitar."

On these early Muddy Waters recordings can be perceived some of the fundamental changes in recording aesthetics (and possible listening practices) that came to define much of the rock 'n' roll and rock music that was to follow. With Muddy Waters, the act of listening to the record changes. Chapter 3 dealt with idiosyncratic musicians such as Frank Hutchison and Robert Johnson, and how the latter in particular brought a new self-awareness, an inwardness to recording. Waters and Chess took this further. The ultramodern production values, in concert with Waters's particular performance strategies and skills afforded listeners new, additional ways of engaging with the recording. Rather than sitting back and having the manifestly pro performer "pitch" to him, the listener was invited to participate in a seemingly private moment. The technology by this time was able to supply the space—no longer a distant, thin-sounding, boxy enclosure "inside" the phonograph. Neither was it the elaborately constructed sonic mise en scène of West Coast sound production, the sound stage that remains the exclusive province of pro entertainers (which may beguile and thrill its listeners, but just as surely keeps them firmly in their place).

The Chess sound-producing apparatus delivers listeners right into the shared imaginal space of the recording. The "visual" attention is inward, toward a center.[20] The references in these songs are frequently highly specific. Just as John Lee Hooker in his "Boogie Chillen" (1948) referred by name to Henry's Swing Club (a Detroit bar frequented by Hooker), Waters refers to locations specific to his own life, with little apparent concern for whether his listeners will "get" the reference: Stovall's Plantation is mentioned, his home town of Rolling Fork, and so on. Waters also speaks of the strictly local and quotidian in a highly charged way, as in "Rolling Stone" (1950) when he sings, first in declarative mode but then in a confidential murmur,

I went to [*pause*] my baby's house [*pause*] and I sat down on her step [*pause*].
She said "Come on in now Muddy [*pause*], you know my husband just now left [*pause*].
Sure 'nough he just now left."

The encounter is charged with a narrative import and the rendering of sequential events borders on the cinematic, or the literary.

The effortless inclusion of such personal references in music that was produced for local and, it was hoped, national markets shows the extent of this new type of inwardness in recorded music. It would be difficult to imagine Frank Sinatra or Nat King Cole singing about their respective New Jersey or Chicago homes with the same degree of autobiographical specificity. For all the intimacy these latter singers effected on record, their trajectory was essentially outward: they performed "in character," nearly always behind the persona of the professional entertainer, speaking the mostly classless and placeless language of the professionally written popular song, a language of and directed to young urban adults that could be as easily understood in Melbourne and Edinburgh as it was in New York and Los Angeles.

Waters's music spoke most immediately to a specific group—southern blacks recently resident in Chicago—and made few concessions to larger audiences. Nonetheless Waters's (and Hooker's) music found and continued to find much larger, widely dispersed audiences. Such too is perhaps a function of its centripetal trajectories: if we give it the attention it demands we will be rewarded, if we follow the imaginal pathway through the glass into the studio, join the singer in his inner spaces we will be taken much further. Cole and Sinatra offered their female listeners an urbane, erotic presence. To teenagers necking in an automobile, singers like Cole or Sinatra on the car radio might have been heard as speaking *to* the female and speaking *for* the male; their presence was at the disposal of their listeners. Even given that these two were probably the most introspective, introverted pop male presences of the time, they scarcely approach Waters and Hooker for inwardness and self-involvement. Waters offers a whole physical and social geography, but his recorded music does not present as especially egocentric or self-absorbed. He is like the shaman who has made contact with unseen forces. He knows the portals, the secret conduits to other places. The recording apparatus itself is one.

CHAPTER 8

"Train I Ride . . ."
Rock 'n' Roll Echo

The recording practices pioneered at Chess and Sun Studios, and the "Chess sound" and the "Sun sound" have long been staple topics of blues and rock historiography, and the subjects of much outright myth-making. Each place has become a kind of "sacred site" of rock music, and the performers and producers have been accorded legendary status in rock writing and fandom. Both studios are often seen as representing down-market but heroic and ultimately victorious opposition to the bland niceties of mainstream postwar popular music. While this way of characterizing Sun and Chess (and the other down-home indies of the time) retains considerable validity, it would be wrong to assume that the sound recording practices developed in each place occurred in a stylistic vacuum. The reverb that both studios began using in the early 1950s had already been well established as a Tin Pan Alley recording device. Similarly, there is no evidence that either studio began using their legendary echo/delay *before* Les Paul's high-profile and spectacular commercial success with "How High the Moon." The deployment of echo/delay at Sun and Chess seems also to have followed the lead set by the West Coast commercial mainstream. Yet the devices when used at these studios had radical rhythmic and timbral outcomes. Furthermore, both studios had established traditions of recording complex, eccentric, highly idiosyncratic performers, performers who were willing to "be themselves" on record, rather than adopt the smooth glossy persona of the professional entertainer. Perhaps as much as anything, Sun and Chess were able each in their own ways to use the available spatializing devices to create not just a more dazzling aural "stage set," but an unanchored space, a nonpictorial, deterritorialized space that was as much the province of listeners as performers.

In the wake of "How High the Moon," overt echo and doubling effects, produced by the judicious manipulation of magnetic tape began to make appearances in blues, country and R & B recording. John Lee Hooker's "Walkin' the Boogie" (1952)[1] features a weirdly doubled lead vocal, perhaps produced by running the tape past an additional playback head, and/or by overdubbing a near-unison second vocal line. Sam Phillips applied a slap-back effect to the guitar on Dr. Ross's "Boogie Disease" (1954) and tape delay was presumably used on the drums and harp in Little Walter's 1952 R & B hit, "Juke." While this sort of delay and doubling inevitably had some degree of spatial impact, its primary effects were rhythmic and timbral. It modified sounds in sometimes strange ways without necessarily locating the action within an imaginable space.

Corresponding with the advent of rock 'n' roll, Chess and Sun began to use these rhythmic delay effects in combination with a range of other spa-tializing strategies, most notably reverb. The sum effect of this was to undermine the center-periphery pictorialism previously associated with re-verb, while still making use of its connotative potentials—in particular the heroic ego qualities of the empowered voice and the marginalized, outsider cachet of the reverberant voice. At Sun this newer spatializing found its most pointed expression in recordings by Elvis Presley, Carl Perkins and Jerry Lee Lewis, while at Chess the effects were used initially on recordings by Bo Diddley, Chuck Berry and Little Walter.

Echo/delay seems to have been first used on a Chess recording in 1952, and appears on the hit instrumental "Juke." Robert Palmer writes:

In May 1952 Little Walter recorded a rocking instrumental at the end of a Muddy Waters session, with Muddy and Jimmy [Rogers] on guitars and Elgin Evans on drums. . . . Leonard Chess decided to issue it under Walter's name and to title it "Juke." . . . Walter reverted to the jump-oriented style that made his reputation in and around Helena; most of the phrases he played were saxophone phrases. His harp was amplified, and the electricity and his masterful manipulation of both the instrument and the microphone brought out a richness of tone and a subtlety of inflection that hadn't been evident in his acoustic playing on earlier records. And beginning with the second verse of the record Elgin Evans broke into a light trip-let figure on his ride cymbal that set a pattern for much subsequent Chicago blues drumming and seems to have prefigured one of the most characteristic rhythms of early rock 'n' roll.[2]

Palmer identifies this recording as "[synopsizing] the immediate past while pointing unerringly toward the future."[3] By late 1952 "Juke" was the number-one R & B record in the United States, and it remained in the top ten for sixteen weeks,[4] making it the most successful Delta/Chicago–de-rived blues recording of the time (and far more commercially successful than any of Waters's recordings of the period).

What Palmer does not remark on is the presence of a variable slapback echo on the recording, and the extent to which this "synthetic" element serves to give the recording its distinctive character. Indeed, the recording displays textures, spatialities and dynamics that shift continually from verse to verse. The first verse begins with Walter's distorted harp leading in repeated ascending riffs, with "answering" ninth chords on the electric guitar. Both the harp riff and the guitar chords are suggestive of current R & B saxophone ensemble riffs; simple and strongly rhythmic, the "response" side of a "call and response" construct. The drumming is conventional swing/shuffle drumming, quite loud in the mix, played mainly on a closed hi-hat. Lower in the mix is the other electric guitar, which plays a quiet but steady riff around the I–flat III–III–V notes of the scale. The whole is relatively dry. For the second verse Walter switches to a simpler riff that "worries" the tonic note in the midrange, producing a wailing, driving effect, again reminiscent of R & B sax riffing. The drumming becomes more complicated, with the addition of the triplet figure. The selective addition of reverb to the harp, the particularly simple but forceful riffing and a slight increase in volume—all combine in the second verse to give the harp more space, a greater centrality. The guitars continue much as they did in the previous verse. In the third verse the harp goes into a long, reverberant wail over two bars while the guitar switches to a walking bass pattern. This puts the drums in a clearer space, and now (to *this* listener at least), it sounds as though the drum triplets are being produced by tape delay—the addition of subsequent synthetic beats to each original. By the fourth verse the harp is using some vibrato, which slightly replicates the "pulsing" effect of the drum triplets. By the fifth verse, the stop verse, the drum triplets seem to be now quite clearly produced by tape echo, displaying the characteristic "synchro-sonic" machinelike strictness. By the sixth verse it becomes clear that delay has also been added to the harp, when a long note is played, followed by a clipped single note, after which we can clearly hear the echoes (which are at the same rate as the ride triplets).

As has been noted, tape echo has a way of emphasizing high, sibilant tonalities, and by this point in the song, clicks, pops and hisses seem to be erupting everywhere, as though the entire sonic environment and each element within it has begun to vibrate of its own accord. (We might think of individual members of an ecstatic religious sect slipping into possession states as the service progresses—moving both individually and in concert.) In the last verse, verse eight, the drums and guitar initially drop in volume, as the harp plays a "low down" riff. Now we can hear another echoic clicking, possibly quiet rimshots from the drums, or perhaps slap bass, although until now no bass has been evident. The whole band comes up in volume for the final four bars.

It could be safely assumed that Phillips was familiar with "Juke."[5] He was certainly highly aware of the Chess operation in Chicago, as he had been leasing masters to the company since 1950. While it is not the intention here to pinpoint the precise moment of origin of rock 'n' roll and rock 'n' roll spatialities, this particular recording does seem to predate Sun Studio's use of slapback echo, and (unlike Les Paul's echo/delay) the echo in "Juke" begins to suggests the fluid, wildly energized "open" spatialities of later rock 'n' roll and rockabilly.[6]

Although the commercial and artistic success of "Juke" is generally attributed to the skill and shrewdness of Leonard Chess, we must wonder about the role played by Bill Putnam in the emergence of the "Chess sound." From 1948 until 1956, virtually all Chess, Checker and Aristocrat recordings were made at Putnam's Universal Studio. Putnam was certainly the engineer on "Juke" and on presumably most if not all the Chess sessions at Universal. It is fascinating to consider the connection Putnam provides between two of the most significant recordings in the history of postwar spatial effects, both of them harmonica instrumentals: the Harmonicats' "Peg o' My Heart" from 1947 and Little Walter's "Juke."[7]

Later Little Walter instrumental tunes such as "Thunderbird" and "Flying Saucer" re-created the echo delay effects of "Juke," employing repeats to snare and ride and/or hi-hat beats. Also present is heavy reverb and delay on the harp itself. The addition of extra beats in triplet time creates an effect of "crowding," as though the original signal is being pushed and jostled from behind. It brings a sense of urgency, impatience and restlessness to the recording. The voices are "jittery," but the jitters are rhythmic, they "fit together" constructively. The reverbed, echoic, distorted, amplified harp sound combined with Walter's characteristic simple (but often extremely tricky to execute) melodic statements, combine to create a sense of ominous presence not dissimilar to that found on John Lee Hooker recordings of the time or the Joe Hill Louis song discussed in the previous chapter. But Little Walter's instrumental textures and spatialities might be seen to create a kind of sound snapshot of a specifically urban sonic environment. On tunes such as "Sad Hours" (1952), "Blue Lights" (1954), "A Quarter to Twelve" (1954) and others, the reverberant harp recalls as much the sound of a distant siren, foghorn or car horn as it does a tenor saxophone.[8]

Sam Phillips began to use a fully realized slapback echo in 1953 or 1954. Whereas Les Paul had produced his echo/delay using a "boxcar" effect (that is, by fitting a number of moveable playback heads to a tape player),[9]

Phillips achieved his slapback echo by bouncing the signal between two separate Ampex recorders.[10] Using multiple heads and variable speeds, Paul was easily able to vary the number of echoes. Phillips, however, was largely restricted to a single slapback. The effect can be clearly heard on the Dr. Ross recording "Boogie Disease." Although Chess Studios may have predated Sun in first using slapback echo/delay on an R & B record, the effect achieved on "Boogie Disease" was quite different to that on "Juke." Colin Escott describes the circumstances:

The blues releases on Sun tapered off during 1954. There were two singles (and reels and reels of unissued cuts) from the eccentric Dr Ross, who epitomized all that Phillips loved about the blues. His approach was rhythmic, propulsive and countrified. . . . By 1953 Phillips had perfected his use of slapback echo and used it to give a depth and resonance to the primitive drive of Ross's music; yet even a superficial comparison of that music with the R & B hits of 1953 and 1954 show how anachronistic Ross had become.[11]

"Boogie Disease" was released in November 1954, after the first Presley Sun releases (although Escott's implication above is that it was recorded earlier). "Boogie Disease" marks what is possibly Phillips's first use of fully developed slapback echo (although, significantly, it is used only on Ross's electric guitar, and is not evident on vocal or drums).

The record begins with repeated high electric guitar chords, played on the beat, with simple downstrokes. The slapback is evident from the outset and—unusually—nearly as loud as the original note, and timed to effect a doubling of the tempo, a kind of "boogification." Drums are in evidence, lower in volume, apparently well off-mic, playing a ragged time on hi-hat, with occasional snare fills answering the vocal in the gaps between the sung phrases. Although off-mic, the drums are otherwise dry (unlike the drum sound on "Juke"). The raggedness of the drumming on "Boogie Disease" is in many ways typical of Phillips's recordings. A not dissimilar sound and style of playing can be heard on many earlier blues recordings, such as those by Howlin' Wolf, Jackie Brenston and Joe Hill Louis, right through to the eccentric rockabilly and country recordings of Jerry Lee Lewis, Carl Perkins, Warren Smith and others. Unlike the precise, finely measured drumming of Fred Below and Elgin Evans at Chess, the Sun drummers frequently seem to fluctuate in tempo, and inject random loud hissing clashes and snare drum rolls. The drums characteristically display a push-pull relationship with the singer and other instruments—sometimes outracing them, other times holding back behind the beat. Other voices similarly seem to make their own decisions as to tempo and feel, and the listener frequently is left with the impression that strict unity of sound and feel was not a high priority on Sun recordings. Whereas the effect of the

Chess recordings of Muddy Waters and Little Walter is one of drive, of finely wrought, highly energized but disciplined feels, the characteristic Sun mood is of jubilant near anarchy.

Such is the case on "Boogie Disease." The vocal is very dry, on-mic, also like many early Sun blues. The guitar goes into a first position A-chord John Lee Hooker/Floyd Murphy–styled boogie figure, rendered more rhythmically complex by the loud single echo. Again to contrast this and other Sun blues with Chess blues records, there seems to be little attempt here to create a consistent, believable spatiality. The difference between the close vocal and the distant drums seems too great to imagine that Phillips sought to deliberately render a spatiality here, unlike the Chess recordings. On the latter, the careful balancing of reverb on voices places all participants within a logical, coherent space. With "Boogie Disease," it is as though the very idea of spatiality is being contemptuously exploded. To again invoke a cinematic comparison, where Chess carefully constructs a mise en scène, Phillips here turns his mise en scène inside out, by constructing an impossible, M. C. Escher–like space.

Like "Juke," "Boogie Disease" is suggestive of quivering spasm states, yet the tremors are restricted to the electric guitar only. The slapback guitar might be seen as enacting, or corresponding to, a joyful waywardness in the singer's extremities, his body parts manifesting an uncontrollable animatedness, a kind of palsy—Saint Vitus' dance, perhaps, or indeed the boogie disease itself.

It has long been a cliché of rock historiography to celebrate Elvis Presley's early Sun sides over his later RCA work, and any examination of early period Presley runs the risk of becoming little more than a search for a mythological "golden age" origin. Nonetheless, the early period Presley recordings clearly demonstrate recording textures and spatialities at a key moment of transition. And although Presley's worldwide megastar status was achieved mainly on the strength of his later RCA recordings, studies such as Peter Guralnick's biography[12] confirm that Presley's Sun-period work galvanized teenage audiences locally and throughout the south in a way largely unprecedented in popular music history, providing a forerunner to the responses Presley would soon engender nationally and internationally.[13]

Presley's earliest studio work remains crucial to any understanding of his larger corpus and his place in popular music. Unlike many R & B and country performers who found their way onto record well into their musical careers, Presley markedly did not have "track form" from bars, honkytonks and dance halls. He, Moore and Black *first* found their voice in the Sun Studio. Although session players were brought in to supplement the three-piece band for the RCA recording sessions, this same basic "Sun sound" combo (with the addition of D. J. Fontana on drums) performed on the *Ed Sullivan Show,* as well as on the Milton Berle and Dorsey Brothers television programs, and became a hugely famous sensation performing with this stripped-down, minimal combo. He started out and learned his craft as a recording studio act; the famous stage presence came later.

Presley's first release on Sun, "That's All Right" with "Blue Moon of Kentucky" on the flip side (1954), evidences new and radically different spatial and textural features—epochal departures for popular music recording at large, and radical even in relation to Phillips's already quirky work at Sun. The first few Sun recordings have no drums at all. Some of the slack is taken up by Presley's strummed acoustic guitar playing—a key component in the sound (and one frequently overlooked in discussions of the Sun rockabilly sound). Bill Black's double bass features frequent slap-bass technique, imparting a "clicky" rhythm component to the sound, and Moore's electric guitar playing typically features steady downstroke guitar chords that approximate drum fills. So rather than diminishing the rhythmic impact, the absence of drums on these early Sun sides paradoxically helps create a zone that is spatially (and temporally) wide-open. Sidemen Moore and Black were not fully seasoned professional musicians at this stage: Moore was only twenty-one years old, and Black, although considered to possess "natural" showmanship skills was regarded still as being a rather less than fully professional bass player. But the deterritorializing tactics evident on the Sun recordings demonstrate much of what was paradigmatically different about them and much of the early rock 'n' roll that followed.

"That's All Right" represents a blending of musical elements, postures and practices. Although a blues song, Presley performs "That's All Right" with none of the usual framing devices drawn from the minstrel and medicine show traditions that white country singers habitually employed when they sang blues: hokum interjections, the use of elaborately "black" accents and slang, the specific mention of signifiers of black southern life ("Beale Street," "high browns," and so forth) or the other coding devices that indicated to the listener that the singer was not wholly and unself-consciously identifying with the song, but rather playing a part, "singing like a Negro." Presley's rendition of "That's All Right" pointedly uses no such distancing devices. The song is powerfully voiced, but the performance overall is characterized by a sense of comfortable understatement.

The B side, "Blue Moon of Kentucky," features what was soon to become a defining production characteristic of rock 'n' roll music: the reverberant, echoic lead vocal.[14] Prior to this moment, spatial records were structured with few exceptions (John Lee Hooker's Detroit sides notable among them) on a dry center stage (self) versus reverberant margin (other) axis. As described in previous chapters, lead (singing) voices were almost without exception recorded dry. Reverb was sometimes used on yodels, falsettos or other special effects, or on secondary, "other" or notionally "distanced" voices. Reverb and echo were used to underscore the break between the *narrating* voice and the *narrated* voice, as in Tennessee Ernie Ford's "Mule Train."[15]

In retrospect, a progression in the use of echo/delay in recording production can be discerned. At first the effect is used in the main to create unambiguous spatialities, clearly and unmistakably "authorized" by the song's narrative. The echoic voice remains in the distance, on the periphery of the imaginal sonic field. Through the late 1940s the echoic voice moves ever closer to center stage, but until "Blue Moon of Kentucky," the anchoring narrative voice remains in the dry center. After "Blue Moon of Kentucky" the rock 'n' roll lead vocal would more often than not be rendered deeply reverberant.

"Blue Moon of Kentucky" begins with the quasi-boogified words "blue moon" repeated three times over the opening four bars, the singer barely hinting that the song at hand being so sacrilegiously boogified is actually Bill Monroe's canonical country song. Presley presents the remainder of the opening verse as a kind of recitative, the vocal line descending over the chord changes, while he mutters an offhanded précis of the song: "Blue moon keep on shinin' bright, you gonna bring me back my baby tonight, blue moon, keep-a shinin' bright." Here Presley uses the breathy baritone "chest voice" for which he became so famous (and which has been the stock sound of Presley impersonators ever since). The repeats of the "oo" sound in "blue" and "moon" combined with the echo delay give the voice a shaky, panting, "animalistic" quality; perhaps Presley is clowning, performing a baboon impression for his companions in the studio. Presley has performed a kind of leveling act here: on the one hand he sings Arthur Crudup's blues "straight," using no special distancing devices, producing a blues-inflected reading with no trace of parody—unself-consciously and unreservedly locating *himself* (and not a gross parody of an imagined "blackness") within the "blues space." Yet he takes liberties with "Blue Moon of Kentucky." That Presley's voice should be treated with echo—simultaneously signifying authority, heroic anti-authoritarianism and the distant (or subterranean) other—is entirely appropriate.

Bluegrass music was itself being put forward as a kind of purer, semi-sacralized form of hillbilly music. Simian and jungle references were staples of racist discourse, and potent symbols of "degeneracy" in the south and elsewhere. By applying his broad parody to the country song rather than the blues, Presley simultaneously mocks and aestheticizes the notion of the "degenerate other," displaying a reckless good-humouredness. A blues song and a country song, he says: here they are, both "degenerate," (despite the pretensions of the latter), but both available. On this first single the singer (as well as backup musicians and producer) are already indicating huge, seemingly unlimited zones yet to be occupied, genres and categories waiting to be exploded.

The vocal slapback is particularly noticeable on the first couple of words Presley utters: *"I said* blue moon of Kentucky. . . ." The echo is clearly discernible, although so far behind the beat as to thwart a simple "Juke"-styled "synchro-sonic" rhythmic enhancement. Rather, the slapback serves here to double the singer's presence, as though to indicate he is being shadowed by another voice. As with the doubling on Mary Ford's vocal, the paradigm is of replication, but the outcome on the Presley recording is radically different. The paradigm underlying the Paul-Ford collaborations is fundamentally militaristic, the impossibly close-harmony doubling of Ford's vocals suggesting a kind of aural formation flying or parade-ground maneuver. The tape effects metaphorically mirror the coming together and making homogeneous of the many, symbolized by the wearing of a uniform. Rather than the harmonious meshing together of tuned but fundamentally different elements—different pitches and timbres—this is a massing of identical elements, a kind of clone army. The participants, for all their West Coast cool, are subject to rigid external disciplines.

Presley's iconoclastic, "uppity" treatment of "Blue Moon of Kentucky," on the other hand, suggests a rebellious or deterritorialized presence. The answer echo, dragging just a little behind the beat, hints strongly at a disruptive presence; there's a troublemaker on the threshold. Or perhaps the ghostly other voice is a vehicle, an unformed presence into which the youthful listener may introject his or her own identity. At the same time the aftershock effect hints at the same spastic bodily instability foreshadowed in "Boogie Disease."

Presley's next release on Sun was a version of Wynonie Harris's R & B hit, "Good Rockin' Tonight" (1954) The song starts with a high, drawn-out "WEEELLLLLL, I heard the news, there's good rockin' tonight." The "well" recalls the hook in Junior Parker's "Feelin' Good," recorded by Sun the previous year, and a similar muezzinlike "call to the faithful" in Carl Perkins's "Gone Gone Gone," which was recorded the following year. In "Good Rockin' Tonight" the "well" is reverberant (although not treated with noticeable echo/delay), unlike the call in the Parker recording. It serves as a direct invitation, both seeking the listener's attention and announcing the speaker's intention to talk, a kind of "taking the floor" device. It invites the listener into the space. Like the reverbed voices of

Muddy Waters, John Lee Hooker and even Nat King Cole, the emplacement is suggestive of a shamanlike mastery of place. But Presley effects a double movement here, blending differing subcultural practices while omitting the sort of framing devices that had been normally used to authorize the transgression. He unapologetically suggests public uses of the body that in the public perception of the time at least, were restricted to black subcultures, the R & B dance scene, and certain Pentecostalist religious groups. Here Presley assumes that the listener wants to know about the "good rockin' tonight." The "good rockin'" is part of the quotidian, it does not require the conceit of a stage show, a minstrel act, a religious service, or a Negro-like "jazzing" act.

The spaces in John Lee Hooker's, Little Walter's and Muddy Waters's records were in a sense fully occupied by the singers. The singer's presence—his thoughts and affect—fill the space. His magicianlike mastery over the guitar or harp, his delineating of the near and far enact a spatial authority (one largely denied them in real life). Like a boxer who holds dominion over the charged square of the ring, these singers may have represented a potential or vicarious empowerment to their fans; as with the boxer, however, the contract is largely centrifugal—the power radiates outward from the space. The dynamic on the Presley record certainly retains aspects of this vicarious exercise of power, but there also is a centripetal action at work; the listener is explicitly invited to participate. The verbal invitation to participate, to "shake, rattle and roll" was a feature of much pre–rock 'n' roll R & B. Here, however, reverb and echo are being used to "create" a simultaneously public, open yet still "encysted," subcultural space, *out of* which the singer is calling, *into* which the listener is invited.

Early in 1955 Presley recorded "Baby, Let's Play House." Phillips adds both echo and reverb to Presley's voice here, fully realizing the production tactics already experimented with. The recording opens with Presley singing "Whoa baby, baby, baby-baby-baby," running the words together in an almost meaningless though highly rhythmic series of syllables, ending the line with a falsetto hiccup, the effects picked out and heightened by the echo delay. The guitar and slap bass play a few simple but driving, strongly percussive notes underneath. The parody of the "degenerate other" which was evidenced on "Blue Moon of Kentucky" is here taken all the way. The central voice remains deeply embedded in reverb right through the song. Instead of Tin Pan Alley's dry, anchored narrating voice at center stage, we get only Presley's hyperenergized, deterritorializing presence: the other has invaded and occupied the home turf. And, the song indicates, this is no bad thing. Nearly half a century later, Presley's echoic grunting and panting, and the deftly handled drama of the accompaniment still (to this listener) sound extreme. One can only wonder at how this record must have struck audiences and recording and broadcasting industry professionals in the 1950s, counterpointed against such "charm school" male singers as Perry Como, Nat King Cole and Dean Martin.

Presley's last release on Sun was the single "Mystery Train" (1955). "Mystery Train" (with "I Forgot To Remember To Forget" on the flip side) eventually became Presley's first no. 1 country hit; while it did not have the later global influence of his hit pop singles for RCA, it represented a significant development for him, both in terms of his sound and as a career landmark.[16] Over time the record has come to have ever greater significance. Greil Marcus used the title for his important book,[17] as did Jim Jarmusch for his movie of 1989, which features both the Junior Parker and Presley versions of the song.[18] Paul Simon's "Graceland" (1986) alludes to "Mystery Train," indirectly in the title of the song and in the guitar figure accompanying the hook line "I'm going to Graceland," which suggests Scotty Moore's distinctive riff from the Elvis Presley version.

The song is of interest to this study for its distinctive textural and spatial configurations. But arguably, what others have responded to, at least partly, is the way the use of textures and spatial dynamics so powerfully reinforce the lyrical, textual trajectories of the song, and the way that the (historicized) song encapsulates so well for us now the changes to music and culture that were taking place at that moment. By the time of "Mystery Train" Scotty Moore was using an inboard tape echo device, installed in an amplifier custom-built by Ray Butts.[19] Although Escott implies the echo on the track is provided by Phillips, the *delay*-type echo is primarily on the guitar, and the guitar in many ways leads and defines this track. The first sound heard is the guitar figure, a hammer-on on the fifth string, down to an open bass string. The sound is reverberant, as though the source is far-off. And spatial depth—an attempted depiction of landscape—is integral to the song. We hear the guitar playing a far-off reverberant repeated figure, with echo repeats on the guitar producing an added machinic quality. The bass is slapped, producing a series of rhythmic clicks, while the nonalternating bass fundamental note is heard underneath, on the beat. After a few bars Presley's rhythm acoustic guitar becomes evident, playing a seventh chord, which signals the change to the IV chord. The first line is sung over the IV chord (in the style of the "New Minglewood / Rollin' and Tumblin'" blues variant) rather than the more usual I chord.

The first words—"Train I ride, sixteen coaches long"—"back announce" the electric guitar and bass figures mimicking the sound of a train in the distance. The song is thus placed within that large body of songs—hillbilly, country, R & B, jazz and popular—that deal with trains. Songs about railway people, engineers, hobos, brakemen, or songs that chronicle train wrecks or celebrate particular rail lines. Songs in which voices or instruments mimic the minor third sound of train whistles approaching and passing by or that make use of rhythm to simulate the mechanical sound of the steam locomotive; songs that begin with a shouted "All aboard!" Songs about ghostly trains, trains to hell, gospel trains to heaven, trains that take all day to pass by, trains that take away the singer's beloved, or (less often) bring her back. Eerie night trains that symbolize freedom to jailed singers, last trains to anywhere, trains heard in the distance, trains that may take the jubilant singer away and then trains that promise to take the beaten world-weary singer back home. Trains from which the singer is existentially excluded and trains that call individuals together into religious, social or political collectivities. Lonesome trains, blue trains, honky-tonk trains, trains of love . . . and so on.

These songs may focus on the locomotive, the boxcar or other items of rolling stock, or they may deal with the *institution* of the railway—as communication medium, as transport, or as facilitator of some other end. The railway may be used to suggest the workings of other implacable or inexorable forces, social, metaphysical, biological or psychological. The train is one of the preeminent symbols of popular music, and its many referents include change, dynamism, structure and destruction, routine, order, social class and political change, industrialism and ruralism. A common thread in much of this is the suggestion of power, of unstoppability, of forces that far outmatch the individual. The mystique of the train makes for a kind of industrial (as opposed to natural) sublime—in which aesthetic pleasure is inextricably mixed with or generated by feelings of awe, powerlessness or even terror.

"Mystery Train" is firmly located in these popular song traditions. Frequently in this class of railroad song, wind instruments—harmonica or sax or falsetto vocals—are used to suggest "moaning" train whistles, while drums are used to mimic the rhythmic sounds of the locomotive. On Junior Parker's earlier "Mystery Train" the "train rhythm" is suggested by the interplay between the complex repeating guitar figure and the snare drum, played with brushes. Its pace is relatively steady compared to the faster Presley version. On the latter, which has no drums, the guitar and bass set up the train rhythm largely through use of echoic "aftershock" devices— tape echo on Moore's guitar and Black's slap bass. This multiplication of voices mimics the railroad's sequencing of percussive events: the causal chains of actions and reactions, the sum effect of locomotion pulling against inert loads, the jerking into movement of the latter, the relaying of the movement down the line of carriages, and so on.[20] The whole complex of events—collisions, explosions, hammerings, frictions, the "impossible" actions of a coal-burning furnace on wheels, the boiling of water, the escape of hot gases—and the entire sonic ensemble created is hinted at in the guitar and bass parts.

The first verse identifies the subject of the song as not simply *any* train, but the train the singer rides. Integral though the electric guitar and bass are, the singer is the "boss" here. He is riding the train—not simply observing it—and he is calling the changes. His voice is reverberant/echoic (but not greatly so) and the dynamic level is sufficiently high to allow the singer to be slightly off-mic. The reverberant voice and bass, the delay on the guitar—all serve to place the music in the distance, to create an effect of relentless approach, reinforced in the second verse, "Train train, coming round the bend," and the third verse, "coming down the line." It is coming, toward us. The singing voice appears to be both *on* the train and *with* us hearing its approach. The next sung verse (after the partial verse over which the guitar solos) is a repeat of the second. Thus three of the four (complete) verses announce the coming of the train, the train that brings the singer's "baby."

A high level of confidence is in evidence here. Given that Presley is performing in, for the time, a new and virtually unique style, and the band are using techniques and textures that had either never before been used on record, or never used in that particular configuration, the assuredness becomes ever more remarkable. Given Scotty Moore's notorious lack of confidence in his skills as a musician at the time, his especially strong guitar playing here is noteworthy. His use of echo creates a wholly distinctive rhythmic feel and a rich, warm timbre that continues to fascinate guitarists, even given the much greater timbral and technical sophistication of modern electric playing. Added to this is the fact that *this* recording was not simply another of the many southern independent studio or field recordings for the race or hillbilly market. By this time Presley had been a year at Sun; his performances in the south were being met with scenes of hysteria and not infrequent riots, and he was the subject of a general adulation never before encountered in country music. There was a national buzz in the music industry about this extraordinary phenomenon from the south, and the deal was in process to clinch the purchase of Presley's contract from Sun. Every Presley Sun record had charted high on country and R & B charts, despite the very poor distribution of the undercapitalized Sun Records. This particular moment then in the studio was not, in this sense at least, quite like the Peer, Satherley and Walker southern field recordings of the prewar years. The performers there could access the peculiar freedom that comes from the knowledge that they were relatively small-time and not part of the main game. The Presley Sun recordings were subject to a great deal of attention, much of it hostile.

It is significant that the trio finished their stay at Sun Records with a train song, and the trope of the railway train used right then and there had special added connotations. Lewis Mumford identifies the steam engine and the railroad as hallmarks of what he calls "the paleotechnic phase" of industrialism—the period in Britain and industrial western Europe dating from around 1750 to the early twentieth century, culminating in the mass destruction of the Great War. It is the age of the mechanic and toolmaker, and its endpoints are triumphs of mechanical work such as Babbage's calculating engine and the Brooklyn Bridge. It is followed by the neotechnic phase, which is typified by electricity and electronics (communications technologies, notable among them film and the phonograph) as well as transport revolutions, exemplified by airplanes and the motor car. For Mumford the motor car is to the neotechnical phase what the railroad was to the paleotechnic.[21] Bearing Mumford's categories in mind, we may question the belated celebration of the locomotive in American music, and indeed wonder at the use of *neo*technic means—the phonograph—to celebrate what was essentially *paleo*technic machinery. As for the celebration of the steam locomotive, it should be noted that this is a feature particularly of southern, "down-home" music, and in it we might find echoes of anxieties concerning the belated industrialization of the south, long-awaited, simultaneously anticipated and feared cultural and social transformations accompanying the change from poor agrarian economy to industrial urban, a longtime preeminent concern of writers on the south.[22]

The figure of the train might be seen as emblematic of industrialization, and attendant social changes. The railroad is nearly always depicted in U.S. popular music as being of the south, representing an implied meeting point between different cultural trajectories: the down-home and the metropolitan. The train is the conduit, the medium linking domains. The train as symbol is thus beginning to resemble the phonograph. The normally opposite impulses to nostalgia and modernity are momentarily at one. Both the late coming of industrialism to the south, and the relatively early penetration of communications technology in southern life are embodied in the phenomenon of the train song. The train being simultaneously heavy engineering *and* communications link makes it both the object commented upon and the means of comment. The machinery enables the comment about itself. In the case of Presley at Sun Studios, we remember that Presley was in a sense invented at Sun. Every statement Presley makes about his "mystery train" he could have made, metaphorically, about the studio itself.

In *Lost Highway*,[23] Guralnick examines the lives of (mostly) southern musicians and producers. As Greil Marcus[24] points out, the rural to urban trajectory in the lives of virtually everyone Guralnick writes about in that book is what ultimately destroys them. The "Lost Highway" is the road taken by the musicians—black and white—who take their music from its sources in small, rural, religious, communities to the machineries and markets of mass culture. The music, and the values that sustain it, "honesty, sincerity, refusal of ambiguity, loyalty between performer and audience, stoicism, endurance and dignity" compose an "antithesis of pop trash, sensationalism, irony, persona, frivolousness, or outrage."[25] So Marcus typifies Guralnick's position. He himself sees it differently:

I like minority culture, outsider culture that refuses to compromise with the mainstream—but there is no greater aesthetic thrill than to see the minority culture aggressively and triumphantly transform itself into mass culture, suddenly affecting the lives of millions of people who were not ready for it, and then to see that minority culture face a test it itself was not prepared for, to see if it can stand up against the bargain mainstream culture is always prepared to make. And that is what happened when twenty-five years ago a host of minority cultures—blues and country, bands of escaped tenant farmers, white and black—came together and stealing what they wanted from the mainstream, from Swing era jazz and bland white pop, from big city noise and suburban materialism, reformed as rock 'n' roll.[26]

Marcus goes on to talk about the foment taking place in Memphis in the mid-1950s, which was "finally feeling the pull of the postwar boom, and unsettled by the migration of thousands of Deep South farmworkers, like Elvis's parents . . . the town was less a home for folk culture than for a bohemia: a secret culture within the commercial culture every Memphian took for granted."[27] He goes on to describe the cabal-like culture that surrounded Sam Phillips's Sun studio: soon to be known as "the chicken-shack with Cadillacs out back," a place of "private languages and coded gestures, of talismans and disguises, pink and black, a secret public—it was a milieu in which unknown tongues were spoken and unmade things were made to happen."[28]

The "train coming round the bend" might simultaneously refer then to the technological apparatus and distribution machinery, the larger fact of industrialization, the aspirations of the southern working class, and particularly southern working-class youth, Presley's (and Moore's and Black's) personal optimism and Sam Phillips's optimism as to the prospects of Sun Records (which also was finally on the brink of major economic and artistic success). The singer being both on the train and watching it approach mirrors the slippery locating of all in relation to the phonograph: Are we inside the space? Are we the singer or are we being sung? The singer himself is only ambiguously inside the space; as he too is a listener, he too stands outside the larger processes. The acoustic reverb and echo regimes at the same time signal the abandonment of the center-periphery model: the outsider is now located at what used to be "stage center." But so is the listener, for that matter, and the singer himself is partially with the listener apprehending the performance. The fields have been momentarily deterritorialized, but not flattened out. great potential energies and explosive differentials are poised, balanced in impossible creative tension.

By the time "Mystery Train" was recorded, all the major elements of the "Sun sound" were in place. The last and arguably the most crucial innovations were to locate the singing voice "inside" echo and reverb, and at the same time dispense with the realist, pictorialist, landscape traditions of echoic/reverberant sound in favor of expressionist, nonliteral zones. At the same time, however, Phillips and Presley were able to harness many of the potent significations of echo and reverb that were already extant. In previous chapters reverb and echo were seen to be used in movies and on recordings as signifiers of the uncanny, of shifting consciousness, of ghostly presences, of subjective fear and awe, and of magical, shamanlike occupying of place and the exerting of power over objects. In cowboy songs and western films we saw that echo was a signifier of heroic aloneness, of privileged contact with the deity, of the eclipse or extreme attenuating of the reach of patriarchal power. The echo is the sound of pristine, "uncultured" environment, the new land, the forest, the jungle, but also it is the sound of the underground, the mine, the vault, the church. Mythologically, it is a counter to the visual obsessions of Narcissus; it is a sonically embodied physical world. It is place talking back, it is the inert animated, the sentient nonhuman calling to the human. It is also the multiplying of subjectivities, the replication of the type, the collectivity based on dress, gender, age or appearance—the subculture.

It is not difficult to see all of these copresent in "Mystery Train" and in much of the Sun rock 'n' roll and rockabilly that followed. At Sun these culturally available signifiers were synthesized for uniquely new purposes, but usually without single overarching or unitary organizing themes; Sun spatialities almost never attempted to set up a single privileged point of view. Phillips's innovations in the engineering/technical arena fell fortuitously into step with his own particular approach to the interpersonal dynamics within the studio and his personal vision of southern working-class music. He worked more closely and intensively with performers than virtually anyone in popular music production before him; where his predecessors from Ralph Peer on had regarded southern demotic musics as trash (albeit profitable trash) Phillips gave respect to southern music and music makers.

Virtually every commentator on Phillips notes his well-honed interpersonal abilities, his talent for gently but insistently encouraging performers and "bringing them out" in the studio. Phillips told Guralnick of his feelings of sympathy for southern blacks:

My mission was to bring out of a person what was in him, to recognize that individual's unique quality and then to find the key to unlock it. . . .

But I saw—and I don't remember when, but I saw as a child—I thought to myself: suppose I had been born *black*. Suppose that I would have been born a little down the economic ladder. So I think I felt from the beginning the total inequity of man's inhumanity to his brother. . . . It took on the aspect with me that one day some day I would act on my feelings, I would show them an individual, one-to-one basis.[29]

Coming from a rural background himself—he had picked cotton as a child—he had a close understanding of the feelings of low self-worth, abjection and embarrassment that stemmed from an impoverished upbringing, black or white, in the backward rural south.

Talking about egos—these people unfortunately did not *have* an ego. They had a desire—but at the same time to deal with a person that had dreamed, and dreamed and dreamed, looked, heard, felt, to deal with them under conditions where they were so afraid of being denied again. . . . It took an 'umble spirit, I don't care whether it was me or someone else. Because I knew this—to curse these people or just give the air of "Man, I'm better than you," I'm wasting my time trying to record these people, to get out of them what's truly in them.[30]

Talking of Presley, Phillips told Robert Palmer:

He tried not to show it, but he felt so inferior. He reminded me of a black person that way; his insecurity was so markedly like that of a black person.[31]

Guralnick and Palmer both talk of Phillips's intense focus in the studio, his ability to closely concentrate on the recording artist. He designed Sun Studios so that he looked through the control room window at the artist's eye level.

I believe so much in the psychological. . . . Number one is that caring figure. . . . I think at the time of our [his and Presley's] relationship there was a true trust. It was almost like a father-son or big brother–little brother relationship.[32]

Phillips's relationships with the artists at Sun, and their relationships with each other are frequently described in such familial tropes. Given that the "cabalistic," minority culture activities at Sun were so suddenly and dramatically transformed into majority, global cultures, it is worth considering how the family politics of Sun corresponded to the larger politics of Memphis and the south in the early 1950s and how these in turn were echoed in larger formations worldwide. The acoustic spaces of the Sun recordings might be seen as both enacting these local and larger politics and simultaneously providing a momentary liberatory alternative, the prototypical "temporary autonomous zone."

In a discussion of Hank Williams's work, Leppert and Lipsitz describe the postwar American social landscape:

After the Second World War, Americans married earlier and in greater numbers and had more children than had been true in the past. This extraordinary increase in marriages and births brought with it an unprecedented focus on the family by both private capital and the state. The nuclear family emerged as the primary social unit, a unit whose true home was the suburban shopping mall . . . and everything from the Cold War to the growth of suburbs to increases in private debt and consumer spending drew justification from uncritical celebrations of the nuclear family and heterosexual romance.[33]

But, say Leppert and Lipsitz, the Great Depression had witnessed massive dislocations to families. In particular a large number—one and a half million—had been left virtually fatherless[34] and many remaining family members had drifted into extended family arrangements, living with relatives. Furthermore, Leppert and Lipsitz record, the 1930s had produced large numbers of vagrant children. Taking a lead from Mintz and Kellogg[35] they argue that as women and children sought entry to the workforce, and more fathers walked off, the previous authority of the male breadwinner was subject to pointed challenge. These trends were accelerated by mobilizations of the Second World War, as a further six million women entered the workforce, and sixteen million people left home to join the armed forces. Under these conditions, "old ties of family and community broke down, and Americans experimented with new gender and family roles."[36]

In the postwar period, attempts were thus made to "re-Oedipalize" society, to reinstitute a dominant heroic image of Oedipal masculinity: a masculinity that has broken with the feminine, in that it has broken away from *dependent* mother love to assertive, independent, father-emulating mother love. It is a period in which "cultural voices ranging from the masculinist rhetoric of Mickey Spillane novels and John Wayne films to the conformist and paternalistic pressures of outer-directed corporate culture to the hedonistic appeals of *Playboy* magazine, all encouraged men to widen the distance between themselves and women."[37] For Leppert and Lipsitz, Hank Williams is a figure who in his music and in his personal life resists Oedipalization and the dominant mood of romantic optimism, seeking to remain in dialogue with the strong-willed women in his life. They admit that this refusal might be seen as consistent with Barbara Ehrenreich's description of the flight from responsibility and family, which was a key factor in the sexualizing and engendering of male consumer desire in the 1950s.[38]

While it is not necessary here to deal with the larger sociological questions, nor to decide exactly how and to what extent Williams resisted Oedipalization,[39] Leppert and Lipsitz's larger point about the attempted Oedipalization of postwar Western society may be used to further understand the intimate spatial dynamics operating on Sun rock 'n' roll and rockabilly recordings. Certainly Presley conforms to the anti-Oedipal type: his biographers describe his strong bond with his mother Gladys Presley and the much weaker presence in the household of father Vernon.[40] Presley would ring his mother daily, and observers speak of an almost private language between the two. Vernon, on the other hand, is spoken of as unambitious, ineffectual, and to a certain extent excluded by the close bond that existed between Elvis and Gladys.

Certainly the "weak father" is a recurring motif in certain key 1950s movies. In *Rebel Without a Cause* (directed by Nicholas Ray, 1955) James Dean is openly impatient with his equivocating father (Jim Backus), and the fatherless Sal Mineo character attaches himself to Dean, apparently more comfortable with the older brother figure that Dean presents. Patriarchal interventions prove either ineffectual (such as those attempted by Dean's father) or murderous (as when Mineo is killed by the police late in the film). Similarly in *Shane* (discussed in chapter 4), the father Van Heflin is "phallically impaired"—he cannot shoot—and the young Joey fixates on the rootless gunfighter Shane, who is seemingly more sympatico than is his own father. Shane, however, is not really an alternative father so much as an older brother/uncle/friend figure, and Joey consciously or otherwise steers Shane toward his mother, who desires him, in a last-ditch attempt to prevent him riding away.

In chapter 4 it was stated that the realm occupied by the Shane figure, the place from which he has come and to which he returns is the "landscape of the echo": a zone in which social and patriarchal law is attenuated, remote, in partial eclipse, in which the mountains, buttes and mesas stand like ancient, atrophied monuments to and of patriarchal power. But rather than proposing an *anti*patriarchal domain, the western constructs what might be called an *a*patriarchal zone. The western landscape is one in which males do indeed distance themselves from the feminine (as described by Ehrenreich and Leppert and Lipsitz) and renew themselves in solitary, mosaic or Christ-like trials. But the masculinity they recuperate is not strictly speaking patriarchal; these men are not fathers. Like Shane, they ride away from the beckoning family. Like John Wayne's Ethan in *The Searchers*, they continue to search, even after the quest is apparently resolved. They are not anti-Oedipal, but neither are they Oedipal; they do not accept the responsibilities of "mature" masculinity. The echoic zone to which they return is a kind of impossible space, a fantasy of that particular narrative form. The drifter cannot go back east, nor can he settle down. But in the movies, if not in real life, he can ride off, into the hills, into the sunset—somewhere outside the law, outside society and beyond the family.

But it would be wrong to assert that the 1950s witnessed a "crisis in the patriarchy" on the strength of a few movies and the existence of rockabilly music. Indeed, Kellogg and Mintz and May[41] see the period as a kind of golden age of the family in the Western world. Perhaps, as in other "golden ages" countercurrents and alternative discourses run near the surface. Indeed, it remains a moot point within current cultural studies as to just what extent the youth culture (which both predated and attended the birth of rock 'n' roll, and which continues to reproduce itself around popular music) was and is in fact emancipatory. In some ways we might see in the new spatiality of Sun and Chess records (and others) an imaginary space opening up—just as "teenager-hood" in the West appeared in the 1950s, as an intermediate zone between childhood and adulthood. It may have had its utopian elements (early rock 'n' roll certainly did, evidenced in desegregated dances in the south, for example) but at base it was simply *other* to stable, Oedipalized, optimistic, suburban existence, ultimately neither fully confronting nor ignoring it. The spatiality of rock 'n' roll suggests that the temporary community of the dance hall, milk bar and juke joint can be accessed virtually at any time; all that is needed is a record player and some rock 'n' roll records. The imperative of "growing up" is simply deferred, rather than overturned.

Barbara Ehrenreich[42] talks of the 1950s discourse of the "nonconformist," as an intrinsically apolitical way of talking about maleness, about male "growth" and the possibility of escape from oppressive discourse. In the 1950s the idea of the nonconformist was widely put as an alternative to the idea of the corporate man, the company man, the affluent, married-with-children, suburban (but fundamentally, often secretly, desperately alienated) white male. The nonconformist clung resolutely to his individuality, knew his own mind, and was prepared to swim against the social current. As Ehrenreich points out, the notion of the nonconformist was transpolitical or apolitical, in that it managed to be simultaneously not inconsistent with the stance of the rightist, the libertarian, the leftist, the anarchist, the "Playboy" stereotype male, the "beatnik," the intellectual or the he-man. And like the itinerant gunfighter of the western movies, who rode off into the landscape, into an imaginary realm, so too the nonconformist most frequently practiced his non-conformity "in his mind"—in his imagination. He could clock in at the factory or eat his lunch in the company canteen, take his vacation like everyone else, but in his mind at least, he was different; he did not believe. When the time came, he would have his own bachelor pad, smoke a little pot, have affairs, he would listen to Miles Davis records, perhaps grow a beard. . . .

Talk to Sam for any length of time and you will hear countless homiletics to the dangers of conformity ("I could have become a conformist and gone the quote unquote *beaten path,* and if that had happened I would have been a very unhappy man"), the glories of individuality. . . . [43]

[I]f it could be worked . . . to where just a few like Elvis could break out, then I would preach, I would become an evangelist if I were alive saying, for God's sake, don't let's become conformists—*please.* Just do your thing your own way . . . don't let the companies get this going real good and buy up all the rights of the individual some or the other. . . . All us damn cats and people that appreciate not the fifties necessarily but that freedom are going to forget about the feel. We gonna be in jail and not even know it."[44]

It is not difficult to see Phillips, as he himself does, as an older brother/mentor to Presley, Perkins, Lewis and Cash. He is not really "father"; he is only ten or so years older than Presley, and he is neither ineffectual nor a (would be) bearer of the law. He shows the way to another impossible zone, another imaginal/imaginary space, the echoic zone of the Sun Studios, or more correctly, the echoic zone of the recorded "space," which itself is a conduit, a way station to international stardom—a zone that is and is not real life, an existence like that of the movie gunfighter, shamanistic, but alienated from "real life." The Mystery Train—the communications conduit—also finds a rhyme in the figure of Phillips the facilitator, the means, the go-between, the vehicle, the magician who, unlike Shane, does not ride off into the hills. (Not immediately anyway; he does later, but after the Sun stars, Presley, Perkins, Cash, Rich, Howlin' Wolf, B. B. King, and Ike Turner have all departed.)

After Presley moved to RCA Sam Phillips worked closely with Carl Perkins, a collaboration that soon yielded Sun Records first million-selling record, "Blue Suede Shoes" (1955). Indeed,

Carl Perkins remembers when Sam Phillips showed up unexpectedly for Perkins' first appearance at Dallas's Big D Jamboree. "I was just about to go on the stage when he said, 'Wait a minute, cat'—he always called me 'cat'—he had this box under his arm, and he took out a pair of blue suede shoes that he'd had made . . . man, they was good looking shoes, and when the lights hit the things, that house went wild. And Sam flew from Memphis to Dallas to put them things on my feet.

Sam, he got a kick out of things like that. You got to remember that Elvis, Cash, none of us had anything. We were very poor, came from poor people, and it was Sam . . . bought me the first clothes I ever had to wear on stage . . . he really had a knack, he just seemed to know."[45]

For many fans (like the Japanese boy in Jarmusch's *Mystery Train*), Carl Perkins crystallizes Sun Records' most pointed achievements. He is simultaneously more "stone hillbilly," and more country "bluesy" than Presley. He wrote his own songs, and he played lead guitar, putting him in a league with blues and R & B performers like Muddy Waters, T. Bone Walker, Robert Johnson, John Lee Hooker and Chuck Berry. Like Chuck Berry he wrote cannily knowing songs about changing youth consumption and recreation patterns, to which his music both showed the way and provided an accompaniment, a mantra or an affirmation. And like rockabilly itself, Perkins's moment in the spotlight was brief. Many of the participatory spatial elements present experimentally in Presley's Sun recordings were brought to full maturity on Perkins's records.

Perkins's first release at Sun came out the same day as "Mystery Train," Presley's last (yet another transition marked by that song). Perkins's release was a honky-tonk country A-side, "Let the Jukebox Keep Playing," backed with the rockabilly "Gone, Gone, Gone," which is of specific relevance to this inquiry. The song begins with a call-to-the-faithful "WEEEELLLLLL," reverberantly "emplaced," as though Perkins is at the end of a long tunnel, or inside a hall or cavernous built structure. The first words reveal the song to be an utterance by a male, presumably talking to another male or a group, boasting about his girlfriend:

> Well, that must be my gal, yours don't look like that
> Yeah, that must be my gal, yours don't look like that
> I know my baby she's so round and fat.
> Well, well ['we're' or possibly 'I'm'] gone, gone, gone
> Gone, gone, gone
> (We're) gone, gone, gone
> Well I'm gone, gone, gone
> Yeah I'm Gone,
> Gone on down that line.

Much that distinguishes early rock 'n' roll and rockabilly is contained in this song. Perkins begins by "calling to the faithful," the faithful being "cats," people inclined to get "gone," literally prepared to be elsewhere, to be in some way *other*. Perkins's Sun oeuvre contains many such imprecations and addresses to the audience. Or to both himself and the audience, such as when he announces an instrumental break: "Get it, cat! Let's go now!" or "Hang on, children, let's rock!" (both in "Honey Don't," 1955) or "Rave on, children I'm with you, rave on, cats!" ("Dixie Fried," 1956); in "All Mama's Children" (1955) he calls "Rock now, let's go!" and "*Now,* rock! Go!" Indeed, there are few Perkins up-tempo songs that do not use this sort of imperative immediately before the instrumental break (or elsewhere). The words are voiced with intensity and urgency, like a team coach. Perkins's voice is high and strained when he makes these calls, as though these are the most important words in the song.

Perkins probably evolved the style in the rowdy honky-tonks he played prior to his recording career.[46] One can picture the (inter)action: Perkins calls out "Rave on!" to the crowd, then puts his head down to concentrate on his solo. The dancers on the floor respond to the invitation, throwing themselves into their dancing with greater abandon; perhaps the band members similarly "get into it." Everybody moves a little deeper into their own subjectivity; the pursuit is collective, but it is a collectivity of people who are seeking, exploring a heightened self-involvement. This oscillation between the collective and the inner, between the social and the personal is a hallmark of early rock 'n' roll, and the reverberant quality of the sound is consistent with this; the reverberant space simultaneously connoting the solitariness of the mythic cowboy or the lonely person walking a deserted street late at night while suggesting also the enclosed *collective* space of the dancehall or juke joint.

"Gone Gone Gone" starts with the reverberant voice of the singer, unaccompanied until the middle of the first line, stressing the individualism of the enterprise. Perkins might be calling to the faithful, but the initial aim is to draw their attention to himself (the preacher?) alone. Not even the limited collectivity of the band is represented at this stage. (We might think of Muddy Waters's "Oh well, Oh well" at the beginning of "Mannish Boy"). But the reverberant housing of the voice here suggests a "faroffness," as though Perkins is in a tunnel or some kind of underground space, and this notion of underground space suffuses virtually all Sun echoic and reverberant recording. In her perceptive and suggestive work on the underground, Rosalind Williams[47] in her study of physical and metaphoric undergrounds, demonstrates how subterranean spaces—mines, caves, excavations, sewers, tombs—have collected rich social significations over time. In antiquity, Williams says, undergrounds were despised, abject (though sometimes sacred) places, becoming by early modernity sites of sublime fascination. The Baconian quest for knowledge, and the entire modern enterprise of truth-seeking, is described as a work of excavation, and by the time of Victor Hugo's *Les Miserables* the study of history and society too are seen as either concerning or resembling journeys into the underground. Williams quotes the character Valjean in *Les Miserables:*

The historian of morals and ideas has a mission no less austere than that of the historian of events. The latter has the surface of civilization, the struggles of the crowns, the births of princes, the marriages of kings, the battles, the assemblies, the great public men, the revolutions in the sunlight, all the exterior; the other historian has the interior, the foundation, the people who work, who suffer, and who wait, overburdened woman, agonizing childhood, the secret wars of man against man, the obscure ferocities, the prejudices, the established iniquities, the subterranean reactions of the law, the secret evolution of souls, the vague shudderings of the multitudes, the starvation, the barefoot, the bare-armed, the disinherited, the orphans, the unfortunate, the infamous, all the specters that wander in darkness. . . . Is it the underworld of civilization because it is deeper and gloomier than the upper? Do we really know the mountain when we do not know the cavern?[48]

Williams continues:

For the past century and a half, historians have responded to Hugo's challenge, digging beneath surface manifestations to unearth submerged groups (homosexuals, criminals, women), submerged evidence (dreams, sexual customs, mental constructs) and submerged forces (economic, technological, ecological).[49]

She goes on to talk about the centrality of the subterranean metaphor to both Marx, in his ideas of economic substructure and the working class, and Freud, with his notion of the unconscious, concluding:

Both Marx and Freud depend so much upon subterranean imagery that it is now virtually impossible to read a text about the underworld without filtering it through a Marxist or Freudian interpretation—without reading the buried world as the unconscious, the working class or both.[50]

With reverberant sound being the principal aural hallmark of the underground, and bearing in mind Phillips's statements above, we must question to what extent, either consciously or unconsciously, Phillips (and Leonard Chess) flagged their products as being "from the social underground" through the use of reverb and echo.[51] It is perhaps no accident that the earliest (many would say most intense) expressions of rockabilly and rock 'n' roll music chose the sound characteristics of the underground as a defining textural feature. Indeed, Hugo's Valjean could almost be Sam Phillips talking about *his* project to tap the emotional expressive potentials of poor southerners, and to put the results forward on the national (and international) stage. It is eminently possible that the echoic emplacements Phillips used signified for him, and for the record buyers, however vaguely or unconsciously, the "underground" origins of the music and the musicians.

As "Gone, Gone, Gone" continues, the lyrics establish collectivities at every turn. The initial line is as though spoken to a friend, a peer, possibly at a dance, as the boys eye the girls. The next verse of the song concerns the dance at which "everyone's jumpin'" and the chorus is a meditation on, or a mantra to the state of being "gone, gone, gone." There is an escape, a release being proposed here, and it happens at or around the dance, but is more than simply dancing. The drum sound on "Gone, Gone, Gone" recalls the triplet figure on Little Walter's "Juke," and in combination with the slapback on Perkins's vocal constructs a similarly hyperanimated ambience.

Perkins's impoverished background—his family were sharecroppers, at one time forced to live in a converted one-room storehouse—is frequently acknowledged in his music, in which is evidenced recurring themes of diffidence, self-doubt and pessimism. These create a stark counterpoint to the wildly hedonistic mood of the music. "I was so impressed with the pain and feeling in his country singing," Phillips told Escott.[52] In "Matchbox" (1957) Perkins sings the old, profoundly defeatist couplet with conviction: "I'm an old poor boy, a long way from home / Yes, I'll never be happy, everything I do is wrong." In "Movie Magg" (1955), the singer asks his girl out for a date to the movies, warning that they must travel on horseback. "All Mama's Children" could be his manifesto. Like "Gone, Gone, Gone," it begins with only Perkins's voice singing the drawn-out first word, the band coming in as the tempo picks up.

> There . . . was an old woman that lived in a shoe
> Had so many children she didn't know what to do
> They were doing all right till she took 'em to town
> The kids saw them pickin' them up and puttin' them down.
>
> Now all your children want to rock, mama, all your children wants to roll
> They want to roll, want to rock, gonna flop till they pop,
>   all your children want to rock
>
> Rock now! [*instrumental*].
>
> Well, we're not trying to live too fast,
> But we might as well try to live in class
> We better move out 'fore the rent comes due
> Or we wanna live in a blue suede shoe.
>
> All your children want to rock *etc.*
>
> Now rock! Go! [*instrumental*].
>
> Well every night when it's quiet and still
> You can hear it echo through the hill
> Through a blue suede shoe on a mountain top
> All of mama's childrens are doing the bop.
>
> All them children want to rock *etc.*
>
> Rock! Go! Aaaaiiiieeee, let's rock! Ahhh bop, children!
>   [*over instrumental verse*]
>
> All your children want to rock *etc.*

"All Mama's Children" is a novelty song, a deliberately lightweight, "fractured" rendering of the nursery story of the old woman in the shoe, but Perkins's recurring concerns—the depredations of poverty, the burning desire to "break out"—are present nonetheless. In Perkins's telling poverty is endurable *until* the children go to town and witness "them" (presumably townsfolk) "pickin' them up and putting them down." Thereafter the children want to rock. There is no economic or political solution offered to the fact of poverty, but rather a kind of ecstatic escape, an intense moment of existential freedom. There is a point of identification here, between the impoverished children and Perkins himself (and his two brothers, who played bass and rhythm guitar). Music and dance provide a remedy to the hardships of poverty. But they are not "trying to live too fast"; Perkins is not proposing a wildly excessive, or revolutionary lifestyle, but rather simply expressing the desire, and implying that they have a right "to live in class." Later in the song the "children" in the narrative become identified with the "children" Perkins is addressing, his audience, when he says "Ahhh bop, children!" The "children" in Perkins's teenage audience are in fact the children in the song who have been led out of some impoverished, benighted state, and whose rocking can now be heard echoing through the hills. Perkins's audience was not composed only of sons and daughters of Tennessee sharecroppers; indeed, it included the young John Lennon and George Harrison in Liverpool, England. In speaking, albeit jokingly of an "awakening" to rock 'n' roll, Perkins conflates the poverty of the southern rural underclasses with the affectivities of emerging-world youth culture, and it is with Perkins that the notion of the "poor boy" becomes an archetype of rock 'n' roll.

The most notable earlier successes at Sun, Presley and Perkins, present paradoxes: the chronically self-doubting Carl Perkins somehow managed to record music radically and explosively unlike anything recorded before, and to deliver it with every appearance of unshakable confidence. Similarly, the painfully shy Elvis Presley produced epoch-making music, to the apparent surprise of all who knew him—teachers, school friends, relatives. These paradoxes signal larger transitions in practices occurring in recording: practices that were happening at large, but that were brought into sharpest focus at Sun, and that were pointedly reflected in textural/spatial qualities of the product. The quotes from Phillips and Perkins above, and the descriptions of Phillips's work modes in Guralnick, Escott and elsewhere indicate the intense focus that Phillips brought to record production. The relationship between Phillips and the musicians recording becomes much more than a simple encounter between technician/entrepreneur and creative personnel. Phillips coaxes, cajoles, encourages his artists, giving them to believe that he *understands* them, that he is on their side. They in turn sometimes become jealous of one another, feel that Phillips is giving his prime attention to another artist.[53] Phillips declared his goal to be "to open up an area of freedom within the artist himself, to help him express what he believed his message to be."[54] Phillips had his own program, agenda: simply to make a success of his business, to prove that he had been right to go it alone.

The Sun studio might be seen as a kind of "workshop of the soul," with Phillips as guru, analyst or therapist, priest, confessor, sponsor, mentor, and the sonic space *inside* the studio as a zone wherein the musician himself is transformed. The work of creating the artifact, the record, is simultaneously a soul work, and the aesthetically successful recording is not simply documentary evidence of the transformation having taken place; rather, it *is* the transformation. Phillips is of course hardly the first producer in popular music to have a close rapport with recording musicians, nor are Presley, Wolf, or Perkins the first musicians to bring a great intensity to the recording studio. But at Sun these qualities are consciously valued, and the magical moment of the transformation deliberately sought.

In time it became a commonplace of rock recording for an artist to attempt to plumb the depths of his or her subjectivity in order to activate buried affect, much the way a method actor might prepare for a role. The producer looks on from the side, monitoring, advising, pushing, approving or disapproving. And anyone who has ever spent any time in a studio will attest to the strangely private, inward feel to such places, where one is cut off from the signals of the passage of time, the changing light as the day progresses, and the attendant changes to sound ambience. There are no ringing telephones, no surprise visitors, no Mormons knocking on the door, none of the many small interruptions that may punctuate the normal day. Indeed, the experience of spending time in a sound studio resembles the spiritual "retreat," a temporary renunciation of daily concerns in favor of soul searching, prayer and contemplation. The pop recording studio under Sam Phillips's stewardship becomes like a monk's cell, or a therapist's consulting room. Like the ascetic's cell, the studio is without pictures on the walls, lacks comfortable furniture, offers no outlook save the dim picture of the engineer through the window.

To prolong the analogy, the ascetic/spiritual seeker quests after mystical revelation, union with the infinite, self-knowledge and salvation. At the same time he/she may, like the person in therapy, be primarily seeking a cure to a pathology, an end to his or her pain, catharsis, a chance to speak his mind, to unburden without reservation, to discover the precise cause and morphology of a neurosis. The "characterlessness" of the cell and the sound studio might both be seen as enactments of self-denial. In the case of the studio, there is no particularly pressing acoustical engineering reason for the interior to be so thoroughly drab. Perhaps the mortifying of the visual sense inside the studio is compensation for the privileging of vision outside.

So Presley in the Sun Studio is looking within, much as a method actor such as James Dean (much admired by Presley) might do. As was said of Robert Johnson in chapter 3, the singer's most intensely private moment becomes his most public; the most "inner connected" moment in the session becomes *the* take. The Sun sound then might also be an acknowledgment of how the recording studio and the fabrication of musical commodities were changing. The roomy, reverberant, echoic sound qualities suggest the cell, the church, or the unconscious itself, and the subsequent vinyl record faintly suggests Moses' stone tablets, or Joseph Smith's metal tablets, a material souvenir of an encounter with the Absolute.

Presley's version of "Milkcow Blues Boogie" (1954/1955), tacitly acknowledges this. The song begins as a slow, lowdown blues, but Presley stops singing after a few bars and says, "Hold it fellers. That don't *move* me. Let's get *real, real gone* for a change." He starts again with the characteristic "WEEELLL, I woke up this morning and I looked out the door," and now the song is in fast, high rockabilly mode. Presley's interjection is clearly not spontaneous; the inflections and delivery are learned lines rather than an unplanned halt to the proceedings, and Moore and Black are just as obviously well rehearsed in the "new" way of doing the song. The interruption, however, serves a number of deliberate purposes: it signals that old blues stylings are being reformulated here, and makes the point that the singer is calling the shots—what "feels right" to the singer *is* right, aesthetically, musically and commercially. The staged interruption purports to be the precise moment of revelation, fortuitously captured on record. The whole piece was perhaps intended as a comment, after the fact, on the group's wildly revisionist version of "Blue Moon of Kentucky," released just six months before. The whole sequence amounts to a none-too-subtle affirmation of the values of spontaneity, personal insight, revelation and pure energy over arrangements, routine, orthodoxy and professional detachment.[55]

But the revelation is neither cerebral nor spiritual. Presley's desire is to get "real gone," to occupy some physically ecstatic elsewhere, to take leave of his reason in favor of pure kinesis. On Perkins's records, this Pentecostalist impulse is even more marked, evidenced by his indecorous behavior, his increasing mania as a song progresses, his glossolalia-like use of nonsense sounds, his wide-ranging vocal dynamics, from whispers to screams, from mumbled low notes to strangled high sounds, and his preacherly encouragement to his constituency, the "children."

The contingent, minimally structured, maximally energized music from Sun Studio, with its push-pull drumming, its (by the standards of the time) harsh, unruly electric guitar sounds, its thumping pianos and slap basses, its explosively pained voices and its overall mood of riotousness, repeatedly made the invitation to listeners or fellow musicians (most frequently no distinction is made) to "come on over," to join the "whole lotta shakin'," to get *real* gone, to rock. The space of Sun Records is a participatory space and the many (by the standards of the day) small or large imperfections and breaches of professionalism conform perfectly to what Charles Keil has called "participatory discrepancies": the small breaches and spaces in the music that invite listeners to participate. ("Music," Keil says, "to be personally involving and socially valuable, must be 'out of time' and 'out of tune.'")[56] The spaces and echoic effects rendered heroic and simultaneously *anti*heroic all its participants; they were outsiders yet anyone could join. It was of the southern poor, but anyone could identify; it was the sound of the remote underground but it was right here. Whereas the West Coast pop producers unfailingly sought to signpost their spaces, to keep everyone—musicians and audiences—in their designated place, Sun Records jubilantly created huge, open, unfixed spaces that were capable of wholly redefining the actual spaces in which the recordings were played.

The first wave echo-delay recordings at Chess on the other hand, served more to enhance the charisma and presence of the actants. "Juke" or Muddy Waters's early small-band work create animated spaces, but the overall feeling of exquisite *precision*, particularly in the timing, does not invite participation in the same way that the Sun products do. The groove on the Chess blues recordings is not easily duplicated: the Muddy Waters bands, Little Walter and the Aces, Jimmy Rogers and others, for all their groundbreaking musical expertise, their powerfully expressive playing and often breathtaking timbral experiments, ultimately presented closed ranks to the listener. Little Walter might have cut sides with names like "Teenage Beat" and "Roller Coaster" but this was a gang that not just *anyone* could join.[57]

On recordings by Chuck Berry and Elias McDaniel/Bo Diddley, however, Chess produced moments of Sun-styled inclusiveness. On the latter's "Bo Diddley" (1955), "Pretty Thing" (1955), "Who Do you Love" (1956) and "Down Home Special" (1956) the triplet echoes that had been used so effectively on Little Walter's recordings were used to create a very different effect. The disciplined, never-a-stray-note aesthetic that so typified the Little Walter/Muddy Waters/Jimmy Rogers sides was quite overturned on Diddley's recordings. His were often one-chord, percussion-driven sides in which the lead guitar played simple one- and double-note figures, with choppy, driving rhythm guitar chords mixed deeply in with maracas, drums, bass and harp. Lead vocals were reverberant and/or echoic. Whereas on Walter's "Juke" the echo effect is clearly discernible—the echo can be heard when it is first applied to the drums, and later to the harp, a "figure" well-defined against the "ground" of the accompaniment—on the Diddley recordings the multiple doublings resist such clear dissection. Rather than hearing one element vibrating wildly against a stable background, in Diddley's recordings *everything* seems to vibrate, and as with Presley's Sun recordings, the echoic aftershocks provide powerful charges to the offbeat. And as with Les Paul and Mary Ford's "How High the Moon" and Slim Whitman's early 1950s sides, echo applied here to two or more elements creates a subjective effect whereby the number of discrete musical entities seems to multiply exponentially. Echoic and reverberant music under certain circumstances has a way of producing virtual voices—just as the architecture of Saint Albans reputedly provided the fourth voice for Fairfax's mass (see chapter 2) or Les Paul's audiences imagined extra guitars: "They began to think they heard all kinds of things. They put in things that weren't there."[58]

Despite considerable analysis and speculation by guitar players and writers, the "Diddley sound" remains difficult to unpack, and the guitar sound in particular has been only rarely replicated. Always distinctive, Diddley's guitar sound ranges widely from track to track, and many of his most notable sides do *not* feature the famous "hambone" (or "shave and a haircut, two bits") rhythm. Tracks like the deeply echoic "Down Home Special" feature both reverb and rhythmic echo/delay on voice, guitar, drums and train whistles. The long recitative is a single-chord groove, and the polyrhythms produced through both musical and engineering moves create an unrelenting locomotive effect, quite unlike anything produced up to that point. The song "Bo Diddley" uses tremolo to complicate the rhythm, "Pretty Thing" (apparently) uses both tremolo *and* a single echo (on the guitar), while "Who Do You Love" uses echo on the very distinctive rhythm guitar. With two separate devices, producing rhythmic "aftersounds," the range of sonic complexities increases hugely: the echo and tremolo might be set roughly in sync (as I believe they frequently are on Diddley recordings) or judiciously just out of sync. Indeed, Diddley told Charles Keil that the "Bo Diddley beat" was produced by having the tremolo set slightly out of time: "I call it offset. It ain't directly right on."[59]

Diddley's recordings feature many such participatory discrepancies, broader and more open than the often dauntingly precise Waters and Walter recordings, but all the more inclusive for that. Like the Sun records discussed above, the Diddley sides present a kind of decentered aural celebration, a loose but nonetheless intensely rhythmic sound collective, to which the listener might find seemingly limitless points of entry and, once "inside," countless sympathetic resonances. The one-chord grooves and reverberant chantlike singing lines produce a degree of drive that had no precedent in popular music recording. The denseness of the sound textures and the "tough" nonorganic timbres of the guitars are balanced by the manifest good humor of the vocals, creating a dark yet explosively liberatory sound field, a virtual world in which the possibilities for eccentric but simultaneously collective self-expression are seemingly limitless. The production sound on Bo Diddley's recordings remained largely a polar extreme; it showed some of the possibilities that tape echo and reverb afforded.

Ultimately, Bo Diddley records gave rise mainly to more Bo Diddley records, and not much else; there was little sign of a broader school of "Diddley-inflected sonic practice." Funk music would eventually make much of one-chord grooves, but in the mid- to late 1950s, apart from a handful of copycat feels from Buddy Holly and others, the "Diddley sound" would remain a genre with essentially a single practitioner, Diddley himself.

"Heartbreak Hotel," Elvis Presley's global breakout hit of 1956, might be seen as RCA's serendipitously unsuccessful attempt to replicate the Sun sound. Although the RCA engineers at the Nashville session were apparently unable to reproduce the Sun slapback echo,[60] the recording they ended up with that day was nonetheless powerful evidence of the extent to which Sam Phillips, Leonard Chess, Bernie Besman, Les Paul, Ken Nelson and others had set up the *possibility* of sonic "autonomous zones," of provisional "free states," in which, figuratively, anything might happen.

"Heartbreak Hotel" was recorded at Presley's first session with RCA (following the transfer of Presley's contract from Sun). The atmosphere in the studio on the day was very different from what Presley, Moore and Black had grown used to at Sun; instead of Sam Phillips's down-home friendliness, the mood at Nashville was cold, professional, industrial, and (for Scotty Moore at least)[61] intimidating. While settling in, the session leader Chet Atkins chatted with a nervous Moore about echo effects and the unique qualities of Echosonic amplifiers (custom-built amplifiers with on-board echo effects used by both Moore and Atkins at this time).[62] When the RCA engineers finally decided they were unable to create a Sun-like slapback, they opted instead for a heavy reverb sound. Using the hallway outside the studio as an echo chamber, they fed the reverberant signal back into the studio itself. The performers could hear the reverb as they played. (At Sun the slapback was added outside the studio, in the control room, unheard by the performers.) Of the trio, Presley alone was undaunted by the setting.[63]

The song itself had been inspired by a report of a teenage suicide, who had left a note declaring simply "I walk a lonely street."[64] Mae Axton's lyric tells of a hotel at the end of "Lonely Street," where the "bellhop's tears keep flowin'" and the "desk clerk's dressed in black," and a place where "broken hearted lovers cry there in the gloom." Although for many industry insiders the lyrics bordered on the absurd, and the huge, vaulted-chamber reverb sounded weird and unseemly (Sam Phillips called it "a morbid mess"),[65] Presley himself appeared to have complete faith in it, and his recorded performance shows no trace of doubt or hesitancy. His reverberant voice richly and unequivocally occupies the recording's virtual space, its baroque, horror film–like dead-end hotel located in the noirish

"Lonely Street." Instead of a Sun-styled open, flimsy (notional) juke joint that anyone might enter, "Heartbreak Hotel" was a gothic structure, and Presley a weirdly inflated presiding presence within it.

The reverberant production of the voice drew directly on the Muddy Waters, John Lee Hooker, Lightnin' Hopkins blues tradition, on the West Coast Capitol sound, and on the "close-up" pop sounds of Patti Page and Rosemary Clooney. But Presley's exaggerated use of what is sometimes called his "chest voice"—achieved by singing in the baritone range, with the head tilted slightly downward, the voice seemingly resonating in the singer's chest—works in concert with the reverb to suggest that the vaulted chamber is physically contained somehow within the singer's body. The singer is a participant within the represented world, but at the same time the represented world is "housed" within the singer. The refrain, "you feel so lonely baby, you feel so lonely, you feel so lonely, you could die," is close in both lexis and spirit to Hank Williams's "I'm So Lonesome I Could Cry." Williams's exterior world was so much a projection of the singer's pained subjectivity that its very exteriority was cast into doubt; the gloomy landscape he describes is equally (perhaps primarily) a landscape of the psyche.

But Williams constructs his world through strictly verbal and musical devices, pointedly eschewing any production trickery. Presley, six years later, uses reverb to elaborately *stage* his attempt at a not dissimilar effect. And unlike the consummately adult bearing of his vocal forebears (Waters, Hooker, Hopkins and Williams) Presley's performance here was unashamed in its inflation of adolescent angst. And the message to teen listeners worldwide was explicit in its delineation of a strangely inclusive space: "although it's always crowded," sang Presley, "you still can find some room." The zone was at once solitary and collectivist. "Heartbreak Hotel" presented as a kind of bastard offspring of Edgar Allan Poe and the blues, raised on a diet of "trash" EC Comics such as *Tales From the Crypt* and *Vault of Horror*.

The recording, not surprisingly, marked the beginnings of Presley's transformation into an object of near religious adoration: he is simultaneously assuming the world-creating power of a gnostic demiurge and the charisma of a dying young god, both the maker of territory, and, as a potential suicide, its destroyer. Whether seen as fatuous and absurd or as boldly transcendent, the record was a demonstration of the extent to which sonic spatialities had been, for the moment at least, deterritorialized. "Heartbreak Hotel" showed that in theory all bets were off and the market just might reward even the most unlikely musico-spatial experiment.

Following the success of "Heartbreak Hotel" the recording industry responded (independents more rapidly than the majors) with an enthusiastic quest for Presley look- and soundalikes. Deliberately or otherwise, record producers sought to reproduce the spatial effects and, in turn, aspects of the spatial politics that had been formulated at Chess, Sun and now RCA. Capitol producer Ken Nelson recorded Gene Vincent's "Be Bop a Lula" (in Nashville rather than Los Angeles) in which the echo-drenched vocals, guitars and background howls owed much to both "Heartbreak Hotel" and such Sun recordings as "Baby, Let's Play House." The singer's panting, hiccupping, barely intelligible vocals on both "Be Bop a Lula" and its flipside, "Woman Love," suggested a demented, drooling state of excitation. Vincent's follow-up single, "Race with the Devil" (1956) might be read as a "shook-up kid's" response to "Riders in the Sky" and all the other gloomy cautionary tales involving visions of the eternal fate that awaited sinners. The song begins on a stop-time vocal: "I've led an evil life, so they say, but I'll outrun the Devil on Judgment day." The singer's hot rod, he hopes, will "move [him] down the line," and thereby evade eternal damnation. Vincent gains an early lead by roaring out of sight, leaving the Devil standing at the lights. The Devil makes a comeback, however: "I was going pretty fast, looking behind, here comes the Devil doin' ninety-nine." It is not clear by the end of the song whether the singer has escaped or not, but he has certainly given the Devil a run for his money.

Like Vaughn Monroe's "Riders in the Sky," the vocals are saturated with echo and reverb,[66] but here it is the singer and his hot rod—rather than the supernatural others—who possess the supercharged spatial mastery. Indeed, Vincent in one sense *is* the other. With greasy, tousled hair, pockmarked face and characteristic sneer, and dressed in jeans and cloth cap, Vincent richly (and apparently happily) conformed to a then current stereotype of the juvenile delinquent, one of the great folk demons of the 1950s. His otherness is of an order that puts him almost in peer competition with the Prince of Demons himself. As both "star" of the narrative and one particular kind of menacing other, he can be anywhere he chooses to be within the sonic zone; so fluid and unfettered is he that all outside constraints, including moral law, are temporarily powerless over him.

Through 1956 and 1957, "big" reverb and delay effects became the pop music industry standard, heard on rock 'n' roll, rockabilly, country, blues and vocal groups recordings, and also on many jazz and pre–rock 'n' roll styled mainstream popular recordings. Many of the large number of rock 'n' roll records that called on listeners to rock, roll, reel, flip, shake, romp, stomp, flop, hop, sag, drag, fly, fall, bop, boogie, quiver, shiver, jitter, wiggle, rattle, rave on or "vibe-er-ate"[67] used Les Paul or Leonard Chess–styled diminishing echoes set in time to the beat in order to suggest the required body movements.

Significantly, however, the sort of obvious echo and reverb that so characterized Chess, Sun and Capitol recordings were markedly absent from the work of two of the biggest rock 'n' roll stars of the mid-1950s: Fats Domino and Little Richard, both of whom recorded their rock 'n' roll hits at Cosimo Matassa's J & M Recording Studio in New Orleans, with largely the same backing personnel. Cramped and often stiflingly hot, the Rampart Street studio produced some of the most distinctive music of the period. Solid drum sounds, driving, but easily meshed horn sections and powerful (yet often warm and strangely relaxed) vocal sounds were all characteristics of the J & M output. Years later owner operator Cosimo Matassa told Jeff Hannusch,

These guys [Fats Domino, Tommy Ridgely, Archibald and others] were doing these songs at their gigs and that's the sound I was trying to get. We didn't have any gimmicks—no overdubbing, no reverb—nothing. If Lee Allen had to blow a sax solo, he'd have to move up to the mike, or someone would literally have to pick up the microphone and move it in front of him."

J & M did eventually issue records with distinct echo and delay—such as Lee Allen's tenor instrumental, "Walking with Mr Lee" (1958). It is difficult to generalize about the J & M rock 'n' roll recordings, so unlike are Fats Domino and Little Richard. Whereas we might find in the open textures and slightly behind-the-beat feels of Domino's sides a friendly inclusivity, Little Richard's early rock 'n' roll sides present a youthfully aggressive, sexualized, explosively disruptive recording presence. The Pentecostalist-inspired vocal pyrotechnics, the hard-edged horn sections and the recurring lyrical concerns—hardcore partying, sex, dancing, and generally "ripping it up"—achieved a deterritorializing result that was in close collaboration with Diddley, Presley and Perkins. Indeed the *spectacle* of Little Richard probably did as much as the recorded sound to promote early rock 'n' roll's "hyperkineticity" globally.

Little Richard seemingly had no need for synchro-sonic slapbacks and cavernous reverb in order to set up his particular virtual "church of rock 'n' roll." It is worth noting too that Little Richard's "Tutti Frutti" (his first rock 'n' roll hit) was recorded in October 1955—more than a year after Presley's "Blue Moon of Kentucky," but still a few months before Perkins's "Blue Suede Shoes," and Presley's "Heartbreak Hotel." Bill Haley and the Comets' "Rock around the Clock," although recorded a year before, had only become a number-one hit three months earlier. So "Tutti Frutti" appears in the early, most deterritorialized phase of the rock 'n' roll breakout, the sometimes deliriously experimental period during which the most eccentrically local, least institutionally controlled musics were just reaching their global audiences. In 1955, the emerging new production methods and sounds had yet to harden into trade orthodoxies; Cosimo Matassa apparently felt no commercial or aesthetic need to rig up echo and reverb, relying instead on a distinctively "live" sound derived from nuances of musicianly feel and the raw sound of the Rampart Street studio.

CHAPTER 9

"Train Kept a Rollin'"
Popular Music's New Territories

The two or three years after 1955 are often seen as the "high period" of rock 'n' roll. During this period bemused but nervous music industry professionals, often at a loss to perceive the musical or aesthetic values in the new, highly profitable form, but desperate to find another Presley, threw open their doors to virtually anyone claiming some ability to rock, or bearing any sort of visual likeness to Elvis Presley. Many have since seen this as the most thoroughly antidespotic, open, democratically empowered moment in popular music up until then, perhaps ever. The ethos of the passionately unlettered artist, whose personal triumph represents as much the triumph of his or her class, racial, geographic subculture (which in turn marks a symbolic victory for *all* undercultures) remains fundamental to the rock mythos. Rock 'n' roll's founding spatiocultural principle—that voices from the periphery or beyond be brought collectively into the new charged, diffuse and inclusive space—also remains notionally in place. The figures of rhythm and blues and early rock 'n' roll who so deterritorialized recording—Muddy Waters, Little Walter, Elvis Presley, Chuck Berry, Carl Perkins, Bo Diddley, Little Richard, Gene Vincent—were each in his way unlikely outsiders, culturally, geographically and commercially; their and others' successes firmly established the twin beliefs that rock 'n' roll and rock would remain "outsider friendly," and that it would be forever open to novel, experimental and risk-taking production practices.

The new spatial license earned at Chess, Sun and elsewhere in the pre–rock 'n' roll period was a defining feature of high-period rock 'n' roll. Chuck Berry, for example, concocted a spatial mastery every bit as fantastic as Gene Vincent's in "You Can't Catch Me" (1956) in which the singer's automobile, a "flight Deville," is equipped with "hideaway wings," enabling it to evade the highway patrol on the New Jersey Turnpike by taking to the air. In the last verse the singer and his girlfriend are taking a long, leisurely joyflight in the car, enjoying the full moon above, listening to rock 'n' roll radio. Lost in their reverie, they run low on gas. The fact is noted before the situation can become critical, and they make an unhurried return to the ground. The new recording zones are independent of the laws of physics, too, if they choose to be. In the Hawaiianesque tradition the need to return to everyday life was a non-negotiable imperative; here it is done at the lovers' leisure, and once their car is gassed up, they will no doubt take to the air again.

Other early rock 'n' roll songs also seemed to offer a direct answer to the spatial prohibitions of earlier reverb-using musics. The conventions of *hapa haole* Hawaiian demanded that the sonically conjured-up exotic paradise, however much it is enjoyed, must in the end be firmly renounced. Sun's Warren Smith in "Ubangi Stomp" (1956) after traveling Italy, Spain and Memphis, arrives in Africa, where he discovers the natives "doin' an odd lookin' skip." Invited by the chief to join in the "heap big jam session," the singer starts beating a tom-tom ("that crazy thing sent shivers to my feet"). He jubilantly "rock[s] all night and part of the day, [has] a rockin' good time with the chief's daughter May." When the ship's captain tells him it is time to go, Smith refuses. "That's all right," he says, "you go on ahead, I want to Ubangi stomp 'til I roll over dead." He is having so much fun that even the clear prospect of his own destruction is of little account.

In "Flying Saucer Rock 'n' roll" (1957) Sun stablemate Billy Lee Riley similarly disrupts the familiar leave-and-return arc of pre–rock 'n' roll popular music narrative. The song is ushered in with a twice-repeated riff, weirdly (for the time) deranged by the vigorous application of the Bigsby tremolo arm, which sets the scene for the otherworldly happenings to follow. Here the aliens, "little green men" from Mars come *to* the singer (rather than the other way around) but, like the Ubangi, they demonstrate fabulously advanced talents when it comes to rocking ("the little green men they were real hep cats"). The singer, to the literally *screamed* approval of other band members, comes out of hiding and joins the aliens, and is taught "how to do the bop," apparently without suffering any ill effects.

In "Summertime Blues" (1958) Eddie Cochran uses the empowering qualities of reverb to enhance the sound of his voice and of his multi-tracked guitar power chords, and then goes on to satirize the effect. At the end of each verse the singer's plans and hopes are thwarted by a heavily re-verberant (but more than slightly ridiculous) voice of male authority: his father denying him use of the car "'cause you didn't work a lick," his boss demanding "you gotta work late," and ultimately his congressman telling him, "I'd like to help you, son, but you're too young to vote." In each the reverberant male voice contains enough residual authority at least to upset the singer's plans, but the deliberate overemphasis of the bass baritone range holds the voice and the authority behind it up to ridicule. *These* voices reverberate in empty, moribund space.

Link Wray's guitar instrumental "Rumble" (1958) offers a nonverbal evocation of juvenile delinquent tropes. Using low string riffs, power chords and a distorted echoic sound, the song suggests dark urban spaces, in which the subject is simultaneously menaced and the source of menace (recalling in its mood, if not in its musical features, Johnny Guitar Watson's "Space Guitar" of 1954 or Joe Hill Louis's "Treat Me Mean and Evil"). Duane Eddy's instrumental hit "Peter Gunn" (1960) follows a similar noir theme, the echoic low string riffs specifically suggesting the "tough guy" male presence—here the private eye. Ennio Morricone's soundtrack work on 1960s Sergio Leone westerns makes frequent use of similarly hugely reverberant, low string electric guitar (supertwangy, with treble turned up high) to accompany images of Lee Van Cleef, Clint Eastwood and other narrow-eyed drifting gunmen, good, bad or ugly, emerging ominously from the desert.[1] Surf instrumentals of the early 1960s also employ a modified "cowboy" echo to suggest, not mountains exactly, but rather mountainous waves, the figure of the single surfer replacing the lonely cowboy.

Following its successes with Gene Vincent, Capitol made rock 'n' roll sides with Wanda Jackson. Recorded with distinctive Sun-styled echo and reverb and aggressively twangy guitar sounds, the Jackson rockabilly tracks marked out a specifically female teenage space, with Jackson herself as the powerfully explosive presence within it. Jackson's rock 'n' roll recordings such as "Hot Dog! That Made Him Mad" (1956), "Fujiyama Mama" (1957), and "Let's Have a Party" (1958) represented radically new and assertive ways of staging the female voice (and body) on record, breaking dramatically with such jazz and pop female traditions as the masochistic diva and the sultry cabaret femme fatale. Jackson's richly accented vocal delivery suggested (however incorrectly) a tough, "trailer-trash" bad girl persona in an "atomically" activated sonic environment.

Patsy Cline's breakthrough hit of 1957, "Walking After Midnight" demonstrated an authority over reverberant space that drew on both the country and blues traditions of walking bass, sparse instrumentation, "loping" feel; and on the West Coast pop recording tradition of the carefully staged reverberant voice, the sense of presence heightened by the inclusion of sighs and near sobs. Cline's singing of "Walking After Midnight" was notable in that it bespoke a specifically female possession of and dominion over nighttime space. The feel of the recording recalls the reverberant "walking home through deserted streets late at night" series of jukebox hits of the late 1940s and early 1950s (such as "Blues Stay Away From Me," "Sad Hours," "Blues After Hours," "Long Gone" and "Whistlin' and Walkin'")[2] and the lyrics explicitly locate the singer in the echoic zone of partial visual occlusion. Here, as in the early cowboy western twilight, the sounds and sights of the late night are a source of comfort to the solitary ambler.

Like Wanda Jackson's, Cline's music was not simply a female singer's version of what the men were doing, but rather represented new ways of forming and locating female presence within virtual sonic space. As with earlier sonic spaces, the performing subject was an actor within the constructed space; simultaneously, that space itself was a "concretization" of the singer's subjectivity. Cline sang a version of "The Wayward Wind" (a hit for Tex Ritter), with lyrics revised so that the singer's beloved, rather than self, is the mythical rambler ("the next of kin to the wayward wind"), leaving the singer as the one lamenting the restless other. But Cline's vocal presence within the production space is so large and authoritative that, as with Hank Williams's landscapes of pain, the mise en scène here only barely contains her unhappy subjectivity. Cline's stately singing of space, the wind, the sound of the "outward bound" hints powerfully that, while the surface story of the song paints those phenomena as his domain, they are in reality the spatial coordinates of her own expanded subjectivity. (*He* hardly figures at all as a separate entity, representing instead, perhaps, simply a projection of her own unacknowledged desire.) When Cline sings the rising melodic line on the phrase "yearns to wander," dynamically pulling back on the attenuated "wander," it is hard not to conclude that she is singing about herself.

Of rock 'n' roll's early "breakout" period, 1955 and 1956, David Sanjek writes:

So accelerated and abandoned was the energy unleashed by popular music culture at this time that the very society frequently seemed as revved-up and hyperactive as the overwrought rhythms and hysterical vocals of the performers on the radio. And while portions of the country vehemently resisted the legal promptings towards integration . . . a vast majority of the nation eagerly assimilated an acoustic equivalent . . . in the routine amalgamation of disparate music forms—blues, country, rhythm and blues, jazz and pop—in rock 'n' roll.[3]

Sanjek points to the tendency of rock historiography to characterize 1950s musical culture, and rockabilly in particular as one of "the wild *boys* at play [emphasis mine], a brief moment when the grey-flannelled consciousness of American masculinity bordered on mania." He says, however, that Nick Tosches, Bill C. Malone, John Morthland and Charlie Gillett remain too uncritical of rockabilly's male-centeredness. Charlie Gillett writes that rockabilly "suggested a young white man celebrating freedom, ready to do anything, go anywhere pausing long enough for apologies and recriminations, but then hustling on towards the new."[4] In fact, says Sanjek, "[t]he preponderance of white male rock historians themselves pause all too briefly and apologize all too little for the gender-biased narratives they propose." He goes on to speak of some of the women and girl rockabilly singers who "[wanted to] assimilate some of [Elvis's] authority and cultural power and assert that they too were ready, ready, ready to rock and roll, rip it up,"[5] but were prevented from doing so. Rockabilly, says Sanjek, for all the opportunities and empowerments it may have offered, largely failed in regard to women. Furthermore, these exclusions continue even in the contemporary back catalogue and specialist reissue cultures:

No CDs and in most cases not even out of print LPs are available by Bonnie-Lou, Jo-Ann Campbell, Jean Chapel, Joe and Rose Lee Maphis, Lauri Lee Perkins, Lucille Starr and Bob Regan. They therefore remain marginalized without possibility of recourse.[6]

Sanjek's closing remark that "sound itself can create a new space and posit a new order when those who hear it allow the music to help them to negotiate the contradictions of their lives" brings us back to the notion of "space" as a literal and metaphoric representation of both social control and possibility, as an enactment of both the "despotic" and liberatory potentials of the moment.

In chapter 6's discussion of pre–rock 'n' roll pop singers, it was seen that the new postwar (but pre-rock 'n' roll) recording spatialities were highly contradictory zones for female musicians. On the one hand the close-miked amplification of the female voice, with all its breathy nuances, and the emplacement of that voice within an acoustic space threatened to offer a corresponding amplification of the singer's entire subjectivity. Yet her putative physical position—both as acoustically imagined within three-dimensional recording space, and as socially and geographically rendered in lyrics—tended to remain fixed. A closer look at those pre–rock 'n' roll recording spatialities reveals that they were rarely the deterritorialized frontiers for women that they were, sometimes, for men. While the singing cowboys of the 1930s and 1940s, for example, were presented as having dominion over physical space and the power to move about it at will, female singers more often sang of remaining introspectively anchored while others made journeys away. Jo Stafford in "You Belong to Me" (1952), for instance, wistfully encourages her beloved in his travels to exotic places: "see the pyramids along the Nile, see the sunrise from a tropic isle," and to "fly the ocean in a silver plane, see the jungle when it's wet with rain." There seems to be no hint that she herself would or could make a similar journey.

The song—a major hit for Stafford—stands in marked contrast to other (usually much less commercially successful) songs in which the woman singer herself does the traveling. Or almost does. Ella Mae Morse in the introduction to "House of Blue Lights" (1946) is invited by Don Raye to go "spinnin' at the track." She at first declines. "What's that, homie?" she says. "If you think I'm going dancing on a dime, your clock is ticking on the wrong time." Raye responds, "You call the plays, I'll dig the ways." Morse retorts that she has to "dig life with father," to which Raye in turn responds, "You crack the whip, I'll make the trip." At which the song, "one of the roughest, sexiest hymns to the night that had ever been heard," according to Nick Tosches,[7] begins. Morse, constrained and immobile at the beginning is willing to move once a suitable offer has been made.

The number itself might be located squarely in a tradition of songs such as Raye's "Down the Road a Piece," Louis Jordan's "Saturday Night Fish Fry," Amos Milburn's "Chicken Shack," or "Sax Shack Boogie," or Jimmie Lunceford's reading of "My Blue Heaven"—songs about hidden, secret "holes in the wall," juke joints, tea-pads or other utopian places of hedonistic license, open only to in-the-know hipsters. Interestingly, the song type both prefigures and coexists with the sort of notional autonomous aural spaces rendered on Chess and Sun records, and on rock 'n' roll records in general. Here Morse is unquestionably hip to it, and ready to go. Insofar as Morse's record was a rhythm and blues hit, but did not register significantly in the pop charts, this exploratory enterprise remained underground.

Other women recording artists from around this time and earlier performed even more uncompromising "territorial plays." Singer guitarist Memphis Minnie, for example, a strong recording presence in every sense, sang a number of songs of itinerancy and spatial dominion: telling of rugged traveling in "In My Girlish Days" ("I hit the highway, got me a truck, 1917, when the world was tough"), or a more stately spectatorship in "Looking the World Over" ("I'm looking the world over, I'm enjoying good things"). Sister Rosetta Tharpe, a powerful singer and guitarist, sang not infrequently of space and spaces in the gospel context—"Up Above My Head," "The Lonesome Road," "I Looked Down the Line (And I Wondered)," "This Train"—in which geographic journeys are primarily metaphors for the life journey and its travails, and physical space is charged with numinosity.

Charlene Arthur, a talented singer who recorded, with no significant commercial success for Bullet, Imperial and RCA in the late 1940s and 1950s, also began her career with an unabashed territorial confidence. In her self-penned "I've Got the Boogie Blues" (1949), she sings, "I boogied in

Dallas, Fort Worth too, I boogied so much I wore a hole in my shoe." The broad geographic reach of her boogying is matched by her control of intensive spaces: "when I went boogyin', I boogied on the floor, when I got through I wanted to boogie some more." The territorial confidence here is a direct antecedent to Patsy Cline's late-night rambling, or Wanda Jackson's cataclysmic perambulations ("I've been to Nagasaki, Hiroshima too"). Arthur claimed later to be a direct antecedent to those performers.

Wanda Jackson, Brenda Lee and Patsy Cline: all in some way, patterned their styles after me. I was a trendsetter. I was a blues singer and I wanted to sing something different. . . . I was the first woman in country music to wear a slack suit on stage. I was the first to break out of that Kitty Wells stereotype and boogie woogie. I was shakin' that thing on stage long before Elvis ever thought about it.[8]

Although Arthur's recordings are mostly without elaborate echo and reverb effects, the full-bodied "largeness" of her voice, especially evidenced on the brash, confident breakout moments lends considerable weight to her claim. Despite the strength, confidence and professionalism evident in her singing, she was far from being a biddable studio singer, clashing with powerful session leader Chet Atkins.

He and I would get up in arms. He always had songs he wanted me to record that I didn't wanta record, and I had ones I'd written that he wouldn't let me record. . . . I admire Chet Atkins's talents but I didn't like his guitar style. . . . I just felt he didn't have the right substance for my vocal style, but he was top dog and there was nothin' I could do. . . . I remember the last time we recorded together; me and him had it out good and proper. I was cryin' so bad.[9]

One recording of Arthur's, "The Good and the Bad" (1954) does make a feature of reverb and Echoic doubling, displaying a distinct break with practice elsewhere. The song, credited to Arthur and husband Jack, is in the squarely on-the-beat, fiddle and steel guitar country style. Alternately spoken and sung verses and choruses compose a kind of dialogue with the inner self, in the style of Patti Page's "Confess," or Rosemary Clooney's "Hey There." But whereas both of those songs endorse letting go of fanciful thinking and becoming resigned to a sad reality, "The Good and the Bad," comes out resoundingly in favor of risky, unashamed self-assertion. Arthur begins, singing,

> All my life I've been a dreamer and sort of a little schemer,
> Until I saw the boy across the street
> I wanted to kiss him

But then her reverberant spoken voice says

> But I knew that wasn't quite ladylike

She continues singing, leading into the chorus:

> Then something inside me started to repeat:
> "Go get your man, love him while you can
> Tell the world that you don't want to be sad"

These last two lines, accompanied by thumping piano triplets, are sung in a raucous bluesy style. The reverberant spoken voice immediately responds:

> But gosh, he might be married, and then what would I do?

And the chorus concludes with a wrap-up from the bluesy singing voice

> Well, that's the good with the bad

Presumably the "good" is the reverberant voice counseling caution, while the rough honky-tonk persona is the bad. The reverb voice here conforms to what, by 1954, was a well-established cinematic code: the reverb applied to the quietly voiced utterance to denote an interior monologue, as though the mind itself was an acoustic chamber in which thoughts (especially the promptings of the conscience) resonate.

In the second verse a way around the impasse is proposed. The singer will ask her brother to inquire discreetly "if there's another in his life or if he is alone." To this last, the reverberant voice of caution responds: "'Cause you know I'm afraid to," adding the afterthought: "And that ain't ladylike either." After another bluesy chorus, the spoken, hitherto timid voice abruptly becomes more determined. "I think I'll just go on over there," she says, "and tell that boy exactly how I feel. I think that would be the right thing to do." The barroom girl voice then concludes: "Well, that's the good with the bad." The diffident good girl—"the dreamer, sort of a little schemer"—had been the bad all along. Unashamed declaration of desire (presumably after the brother has confirmed the boy's availability) really had been the "right thing" all along. But rather than a simple triumph of one voice over another, there has been a synthesis of the two: the hitherto reticent voice, once convinced that sisterly propriety can be maintained, freely chooses forthright action over scheming.

Other recordings from around that time also set up the recording space as a kind of gladiatorial stadium in which women's voices—singing, speaking, dry and reverberant—contend with men or other women. Jean Shepard and Ferlin Husky's "A Dear John Letter," for example, a big pop-country hit in 1953, begins with Shepard singing the text of her letter to her erstwhile beloved, a soldier serving overseas, telling him that "tonight I'll wed another, dear John." Husky then, in a speaking voice reminiscent of Hank Williams's

Luke the Drifter pieces, tells of his joy at receiving the letter, and his relief that the "fighting was all over, and the battle had been won." But then he opens the letter and reads. Shepard again sings the text. Her voice, as in the first chorus, is dry and on-mic. She then immediately sings another chorus, but this time her voice is deeply reverberant and down in the mix, while Husky, struggling to control his emotion, reads the rest of the letter out loud. It asks him to return her picture—her husband wants it. Then the bombshell: the groom-to-be is the soldier's own brother. Throughout this Shepard's voice sings the chorus, off in the imagined distance. The reverb and mixing-down of the voice "move" the unfaithful Shepard far away from the intimate center, sonically and morally dominated by Husky.

The (dry) speaking voice in "A Dear John Letter" possesses all the narrative authority in the song, while the reverberant speaking voice in Charline Arthur's "The Good and the Bad" is much more ambiguously placed, and is ultimately disavowed. The simple fact of speaking rather than singing the vocal (the spoken bridge had long been a trademark of Ink Spots' records) would not appear to of itself carry any great charge, affirmative or negative; rather, it simply opens up a "private" space within the song. In these instances the use (or absence) of reverb anchors the voices as either "othered" or "samed."

This regime is overturned in Big Maybelle's "Gabbin' Blues" a rhythm and blues hit for her in 1953. Here the contest is between an apparently younger, speaking voice—recorded dry and on-mic—and Big Maybelle's huge singing voice, recorded reverberantly, and strong in the mix. As with "A Dear John Letter" the speaking voice addresses us directly, confidentially: "Here come ol' evil chick, always tellin' everybody she comes from Chicago. She got Mississippi written all over." Like the spoken introduction to the much later "Leader of the Pack," by the Shangri Las (1964) the utterance also places the listener as a temporary member of the little virtual assemblage being confided to. Big Maybelle—presumably overheard as she nears the little acoustic collective—squarely confronts her disrespectful rival:

> "You better stop tryin' to run my business—" [*sung*]
> "Haha. Look who's got business!" [*spoken*]
> "—Or I'll have to do what I hate to do." [*sung*]
> "Go ahead and do it. Ain't nobody scared of you!" [*spoken*]

Big Maybelle is not threatening to do physical violence, it turns out, but rather to speak the truth about her youthful antagonist. "I'll talk about you low down and dirty," she sings, and "Everything I say'll be true." Maybelle's power comes from superior knowledge, and her superior expressive abilities. She continues:

"You know I know I know—" [*sung*]
"You don't know nothing about nobody!" [*spoken*]
"—I even know the day you were born." [*sung*]

And so on. "Hey, watch out!" she sings finally. To no response—Big Maybelle has won the contest: The "lippy" youngster has been driven off, or silenced. In this case, the reverb sonically magnifies the authority already present in the rich timbre and magisterial pacing of Big Maybelle's voice. Rather than "move" her to the side of the stage, the reverb helps overwrite the space as being Maybelle's domain.

The "inner struggle" recordings of Rosemary Clooney and Patti Page, and the moral contestation in "A Dear John Letter" all reach decidedly conservative conclusions. Big Maybelle's dismissing of her rival is a powerful display of feminine strength; as performance of a senior voice silencing a younger, however, this too could be seen, in the context of the early 1950s, as a partly conservative outcome. Charline Arthur's adventurous inner voice wins out resoundingly over the voice of ladylike caution, but it is perhaps noteworthy that Arthur, in contrast to Shepard and Big Maybelle, enjoyed very little professional success.[10]

Wanda Jackson, despite her ingenue image, was a well-seasoned, though still young performer on the country–honky-tonk circuit by the time she eventually cut her rock 'n' roll sides (she was twenty when she recorded "Fujiyama Mama"). Generally, however, few artists with a pre–rock 'n' roll pedigree successfully made the transition to rock 'n' roll. Joe Turner, Laverne Baker, Bill Haley and Ruth Brown's commercial successes were restricted to the earliest phase of rock 'n' roll. Thereafter, rock 'n' roll as a recorded medium mostly excluded "old school" pro entertainers, favoring instead performers who, like Presley, "became themselves" in the studio. As discussed in the previous chapter, the record was not simply a representation of the transformation, but in a sense was its enactment. High-period rock 'n' roll was characterized by hitherto unlikely outsiders, who, like Presley, became themselves in the crucible of the studio. Yet the fact remains that until the coming of Wanda Jackson, virtually no female singers participated in the delirious freedoms of early rock 'n' roll! in the way Presley, Little Richard, Chuck Berry, Gene Vincent and numerous other male rockabillies and rock 'n' rollers did. If studios like Sun and Chess were so resoundingly able to give voice to racial or social outsiders, why were neither of them able to do so with women?

Chess records had never been a place for self-doubters. The aggressive, foul-mouthed Leonard Chess bore little similarity to the fraternal Sam Phillips, and recording sessions at Chess were famously characterized by rough repartee. The people who *did* survive and prosper at Chess—Muddy Waters, Chuck Berry, Howlin' Wolf, Willie Dixon, Sonny Boy Williamson, Bo Diddley, Little Walter—were self-possessed men of charisma or hair-trigger aggressiveness, habitually armed veterans of the tough local night-club scene and southern touring circuits. It is hardly surprising that few women rock 'n' rollers came out of this environment.

Sam Phillips, for all that he was able to see through the restrictive ortho-doxies of the recording industry of the time, seems not to have been moved to offer his transformative abilities to women performers. The Sun reverb on the recordings of Barbara Pittman, for example, often ends up having a con-servative outcome. While the uninhibited "I Need a Man" (1956) is firmly in the Sun rockabilly style, the production on "The Voice of a Fool" (1956, unis-sued) curiously, paradoxically works in combination with the lyrics to under-mine the authority of the singing voice. After a reverberant, doo-wop–styled piano intro, Pittman sings, melodramatically, "Hear the voice [*pause*] of a fool [*pause*] such as I pleading with you." The next verse begins, "I was wrong [*pause*] all along." The mood of abject apology continues into the next verse: "I thought I was smart, I made all the rules." Finally she declares once again, "Hear this fool, speaking again." Now, having presumably put aside her foolishness, she resolves, "I will obey instead of command." The construction offers an uncomfortable inversion of the "calls to the faithful" on Presley, Perkins and Lewis recordings. Rather than unleashing an out-wardly transforming force, the "amplificatory" power of the recording ma-chinery is here used to comprehensively undermine the self.

It would be wrong to make too much of this single example, which re-mained unissued at the time. Nonetheless, with his male artists, Phillips was able, sometimes, to mobilize an entire politics of self-doubt, first rec-ognizing and then working through the performers' internalized, personal-ized structures of poverty, class and race, triumphantly transforming feel-ings of shame, doubt and embarrassment into explosive license, entirely bypassing the hitherto dominant recording-industry notions of profes-sional gloss. Like a number of performers at Sun who, despite worthy re-cordings, failed to achieve a big pop hit, Pittman later felt that Phillips had not promoted her records as energetically or with as much focus as he might have.[11] At the same time, it could be said that despite being an ener-getic presence, Pittman's lower-pitched, sometimes muddy-sounding voice lacked the "twangy," cutting properties of Wanda Jackson's, whose voice meshed so distinctively with Joe Maphis's trebly electric guitar sounds, and with the crisp Capitol rhythm section sound.

In his discussion of Charline Arthur and other female rockabilly sing-ers who, through repressive practices or plain bad luck failed to find the audiences they deserved, David Sanjek remarks, "The disappearance of a vast number of recordings from public circulation reminds one that there is an acoustic component to the 'tree falling in the woods' conundrum of Philosophy 101: if a recording is made but no one can hear it, the performer effectively has been silenced."[12]

Insofar as Charline Arthur probably did help pave the way for Patsy Cline and Wanda Jackson, and thus, indirectly, the entire wave of women pop, soul and country singers of the 1960s, her and others' achievements are perhaps not so easily written off. Nonetheless the general exclusion of women from the ranks of early wave rock 'n' roll recording stars[13] highlights the existence of a zone that remains, in the short term at least, resolutely closed to the jubilantly liberatory potentials of the new sound configurations. But while early rock 'n' roll's deterritorializing power did not markedly extend to women musicians, it could be said to have allowed for future maneuvers that did. Just as rock 'n' roll's spatial empowerments did not "take" right away, by the late 1950s recording in places as far away as Oceania, Britain and Europe, the Caribbean, Indonesia had all been changed, and in many ways enabled by what had been done in American rock 'n' roll a few years before.

That first-wave hardcore rock 'n' roll lost impetus in the later 1950s is a rock-history truism. Landmark events signaling the shift included Little Richard Penniman's renunciation of rock 'n' roll while on tour in Australia in 1957, Chuck Berry's jailing on Mann Act charges; the plane crash deaths of Buddy Holly, Richie Valens and the Big Bopper; the car crash death of Eddie Cochran; Elvis Presley's induction into the army; the scandal surrounding Jerry Lee Lewis's bigamous marriage to his own underage cousin and so on. Virtually all of Sam Phillips's discoveries drifted away from Sun in the late 1950s. Some, like Jerry Lee Lewis, turned increasingly to country music in which themes of claustrophobia, enclosure, remorse, alcoholic despair, madness and guilt supplanted the celebratory spatial explosiveness of the rock 'n' roll / rockabilly period. Many others left the recording industry altogether, some to be (briefly) rediscovered in revivals of rockabilly and "classic rock 'n' roll" in the 1970s through the 1990s.

In production terms the late 1950s fading of first-wave rock 'n' roll was marked by the greater use of string sections, choral accompaniments and the like, and an overall toning down in recording and performing intensity. By the late 1950s and early 1960s a new wave of photogenic, image-managed "teen idols" largely replaced the first wave Sun and Chess–styled "deterritorializers." The emergence of stereophonic sound recordings as industry standard roughly coincided with the end of the first wave of rock 'n' roll and rockabilly music, and the period of 1958–1959 might be seen as a period of reterritorialization, in which many of the more unruly and utopian possibilities of early rock 'n' roll were systematically shut down (or willingly renounced by rapidly burning out performers).

Martin Denny's 1958 hit "Quiet Village" signaled a forceful return of Edenic pictorialist spatialities, although Denny, like the rock 'n' rollers, refused the Hawaiianist demand for renunciation; the new exotica was a place the listener embraced as a way of (notionally at least) rejecting corporate conformity, foreshadowing the "dropping out" so integral to the discourses of the 1960s counterculture. In a sense the very fact of early stereophonic sound, with its strict left-right axes, its triangulations that figuratively (and for earnest hi-fi enthusiasts, *literally*) located the listener at a precise point in relation to the apparatus, reinstated the virtual proscenium arch and seated the listener at some notional "sweet spot" in an imagined concert hall. Stereo simultaneously afforded a more convincing spatialized participatory contract between performance and listener while forcefully emphasizing to listeners that the space was ordered, and reminding them that the experience, however intoxicating, must necessarily last for the few minutes' duration of the recording and no longer.

Although cast into a commercial twilight, some of the first-wave rock 'n' rollers continued as music industry *presences* at least. Producing singles, largely for the jukebox trade (in mono) their modi operandi were largely unaffected by the spread of stereophonic recording. Through the late 1950s and early 1960s, although increasingly marginalized, Link Wray, Dick Dale, Chuck Berry, Bo Diddley and others continued to make strategic use of spatializing devices. Although the commercial success of blues-based R & B diminished through the 1950s, Chess continued to record small bands with the distinctive sense of emplacement that had so characterized the Muddy Waters, Howlin' Wolf and Little Walter recordings. Elsewhere Jimmy Reed and John Lee Hooker at VeeJay recorded similarly distinctive small-band blues with a Chess-like sense of spatial presence, as did Slim Harpo (and numerous others) at Jay Miller's Louisiana studio. This same body of performers and the small-band production aesthetics they enacted would soon crucially inform the British 1960s beat bands as well as the small-combo "jukebox jazz" of the electric guitar and Hammond organ–led combos recorded on such labels as Bluenote in the 1960s.

Despite the fading of hardcore rock 'n' roll as a mass-market radio presence, by the early 1960s demand for electric guitars and echo-making devices was such that Fender produced an amp with an inboard spring reverb device, the "Twin Reverb." Reverb and tremolo effects soon became de rigueur in guitar bands. In a sense the coming of the Twin Reverb marked (or at least coincided with) a broad shift to "do it yourself" music making. Commercial rock 'n' roll of the 1950s, despite the rapidly growing importance of electric guitar, had been largely dominated by horn sections, and by tenor saxes in particular—difficult instruments to master. The spread of the more easily mastered electric guitar and guitar-based bands (which increasingly dispensed with horns entirely) enacted a broad deterritorializing move. Teenage garage bands equipped with solid body guitars (real Fenders or cheap knock-offs), as often as not using the portable spatializing power of the Twin Reverb (or one of the many tape-echo units that became available during the early 1960s such as the WEM Copicat, the Echoplex, the Binson Echorec or the Selmer Truevoice 300), attempted in their own "creatively inept" way to reproduce the sound, space and feel of the hardcore rock 'n' roll and R & B canons (witness the Beatles' attempts to cover Carl Perkins and Chuck Berry or the Rolling Stones' approximations of the Chess sound.) In so doing they were invoking the rich semiotic traditions that wove through southern and West Coast popular music recording back to the early days of electric recording; or those that derived from the complex connotative tropes employed in movie sound practice; or those that were fed by ancient practices of building, architecture and the creation of sonically enhanced authority; or even those more ancient mythical and narrative traditions that negotiated the unstable nexi between image and sound, the here and the there, self and other.

The fundamental difference, however, was that by the 1960s sonic spatiality was a *portable* and inherently contradictory thing: garage bands might "build" unlikely, impossible or purely expressionist virtual architectures (or, alternatively, pointedly dispense with any reverb devices). The flick of the switch invoked the entire tradition and at the same time sonically imputed a temporary, "encysted" zone. Sonic spatiality, now well excised from strictly realist or unitary significations was available to be used in concert with other musical and lyric effects as a catalyst or potentiator, and as a disrupter of despotic spatialities. Yet the older, literal uses of spatiality remained equally available: an Australian Leagues Club Hawaiian act playing a beer and prawn night for middle-aged patrons in the 1960s or 1970s, for example, might just as readily have used reverb or tape delay to aid in the recreation of the old, strictly realist, Hawaiianesque renunciatory landscape.

Throughout the 1960s, spatial effects would be used to cross-refer between separate recording and performing domains: the recording studio musicians and producers used devices to invoke the great outside, while live performers used echo and reverb to invoke the residual connotative power of the entire twentieth-century *recording* tradition. In the latter invocations, however, the intrusion of imperfection necessarily provided an impetus for further spatial experimentation. The message, in the end, was not that one needed to revisit and inhabit the spaces and spatialities wrought at Chess and Sun Studios (although the Rolling Stones literally did visit and record at Chess Studios early in their career), but rather the empowering knowledge that spatiality was on call, to be used as was seen fit. Music amateurs and professionals in the United Kingdom, in Africa, in Japan, in Australia and Oceania, in Jamaica and elsewhere now knew that space—realist or expressionist, literal or metaphoric—might be created and made to signify by anyone willing to try.

Conclusion
"Race with the Devil"

⊢◇⊣

The spatial configurations of the "rock 'n' roll moment" (roughly 1954–1958) might be seen as a synthesis of a number of preexisting practices by which actual and fabricated spaces were represented in popular music recording. These practices might be gathered together into a series of more or less discrete types. Early recording practice with its narrow frequency ranges and minimal sensitivity to incidental room sound was obliged in the main to set up space through *verbal* description and through the use of iconic sound effects: the hooting of the steamer whistle in "Departure of the Troopship," for instance, or the lowing of cows on "Morning on the Farm." With the coming of electrical recording and playback in the 1920s, recordings were able to fabricate something more closely resembling the properties of actual acoustic space, and therefore became capable of creating a sense of spatial depth—an aural near and far. Reigning notions of class and etiquette, and the various protocols surrounding high and low art, dictated a split whereby music identified with the high-art classical Western tradition was accorded a "romantic" spatiality (often simply a sense of rich, reverberant roominess) while low, mass-market recordings were not. The listener humbly entered into the notional space of the classical recording, while the popular recording entered into the listener's space and put itself, as it were, at the listener's disposal.

A notable exception to the general aspatiality of popular music recording, however, appeared with Gene Austin's musical rendering of domestic bliss, the many–million selling "My Blue Heaven." The key spatial elements here—a soft twilight, comforting, reverberant sounds from the putative middle distance to soothe and enchant the narrator; the inference that this delightful moment has been won only at the end of a hard day's work—

quickly became the markers of what might be called picturesque spatiality. This kind of rigidly constructed aural spatiality was apparently an acceptable presence in the polite parlor, in the same way that a framed print of a landscape painting might have been.

Significantly, these picturesque sonic spatialities were often associated with a partial occlusion of the visual sense—as in the peaceful "twilight on the trail" of singing cowboy music or the moonlight littoral scenes of Hawaiian music. These early sonic spatialities posited a connectedness, or a specific reciprocity between the self and the hidden, distant others, that recalled the participatory mythic formulations of Narcissus and Echo. There were companionable others "out there" somewhere, kept at a (fixed?) remove from the notional center. Listeners were invited to identify with the aural perspective of the ego-centric singer.

Southern field trip recording of "race" and "hillbilly" artists in the late 1920s saw the emergence of important counterpractices to both the "dry," anonymous aspatiality of mainstream popular recording and to the emerging landscape picturesque spatial tradition. Jimmie Rodgers in particular asserted a powerfully idiosyncratic recording presence that significantly used reverberation and room ambience in a way that hitherto had been reserved almost exclusively for "high" classical music recording. Later Robert Johnson, Count Basie, Billie Holiday (and many others) set up zones of intense sonic interactivity. These recordings presented not so much as competently manufactured product, but rather as privileged samplings from *inside* unique sonic events. The spatialities set up here might be generally classed as *existential spaces*. The agents in these recordings significantly eschewed both the industrial, professional anonymity of the mainstream popular musician and the cultural baggage–laden demeanor of the "stars" of classical music recording. The "specialness" of the recording was an outcome not of the inherent greatness of the producers and musicians, nor simply an issue of high production values. It was, rather, the result of a subtle negotiating of music and place, an almost indescribably complex fluid interactivity among voices, between voices and their physical surrounds and between the whole and the recording apparatus.

Sound production practice in the 1940s saw the employment of an increasingly mobile "unseen other" to create sinister and uncanny spaces, particularly in horror film and crime melodrama. Echo and reverb combined with verbal text (in the case of music) or with words and images (in the case of film) to posit threatening, terrifying, often supernaturally powerful others. Footsteps echoing in fog-shrouded, cobblestoned streets, for instance, readily imparted a sense of mortal threat in movies, while some artists such as John Lee Hooker and Joe Hill Louis set up zones with both an ego center *and* an itinerant unseen other (the latter often embodied in the reverberant guitar playing). Hank Williams, markedly *not* using reverb, set up a not dissimilar voice/self versus guitar/other nexus; as with the work of Louis and Hooker, the sum effect was to create an intensely expressionist zone in which the psychic inner and empirical outer were ultimately indistinguishable. "Riders in the Sky" used echo and reverb to tell a relatively straightforward ghost story (in which the highly mobile ghosts seem to have all the excitement), while movies such as *Shane* and *High Sierra* used the rendering of sonic space (by means of exaggerated echoes and reverberations) in combination with broad daylight (rather than a sinister half light) to denote mystical and other transformations. These practices, while remaining broadly consistent with the fundamental hierarchies of the sonic picturesque, saw the progressive growing in power, stature and, significantly, mobility of the hitherto unseen companionable other.

Other producers, in seeking to set up "straight-faced" picturesque spatialities, created (apparently inadvertently) hyperreal spaces, as in the case of Slim Whitman's early hits. Other West Coast musicians, such as Red Ingle used exaggerated sound spaces for explicitly surreal, satirical effects, while Les Paul and Speedy West, armed with timbrally antinaturalistic solid body guitars, used spatialities as a futurist tool, evoking a kind of sonic equivalent of jet planes, drive-ins, freeways, and the technologically enabled postwar Californian dream home lifestyle. Each of these practices, in different ways, represented another undermining or outright subversion of picturesque sound space.

By the early 1950s spatial practice in music recording, seen over the broad range, was multifarious and contradictory. There was no longer a single accepted standard, but rather a discontinuous series of semiotic possibilities. These came together in rock 'n' roll.

Independent studios Sun and Chess were each well placed to produce new ways of being in the studio, new ways of arranging and locating sound objects on record and new ways that listeners might apprehend and participate in and with those sounds. The cities of Memphis and Chicago (home to Sun and Chess respectively) were prime coordinates of the axis of migrations from south to north. Emigré and itinerant populations of both cities, drawing unprecedented high wages, provided reliable sectional markets for Chess and Sun.

After experimenting with various types of music, Sam Phillips and the Chess brothers separately settled with styles that represented unique meldings of the down-home and the hypermodern. Whereas much of the country and R & B music produced on the West Coast was overshadowed by or stylistically subsumed into the machineries and protocols of the major studios and Tin Pan Alley global distribution networks, Sun and Chess were able to refine their products selling primarily to their local sectional markets.

The musical products of these minority cultures—urban and southern blacks, young southern people, both black and white—were uniquely placed for "breakout" potential. The U.S. recording industry's long-running practice of "mining" the south for musical talent kept the publishing centers of New York and Los Angeles and the liminal enterprises such as Sun and Chess in contact; the New York–based trade press, for instance, regularly reported doings at Sun and Chess and other independents. The studios were far enough out of the mainstream to develop eccentric practices but still close enough to effectively "upload" the product when the time came.

There existed well-established devices by which earlier sectional musical cultures had broken out globally: hillbilly had reinvented itself as "cowboy," while "low-down" race had found worldwide distribution as sophisticated jazz and swing. The performers in these fields, unlike, say, in some other sectional ethnic markets (such as the Polish or Yiddish fields), spoke English, albeit often strongly accented. But these very accents (unlike, say, Central European or Mediterranean-inflected English) had already acquired a strong cultural cachet, via western movies and other representation.

Similarly, the music that emerged from Sun and Chess finely balanced participatory discrepancies—"rough edges"—with modernist production practices. The spatialities of Sun and Chess product may well have been the serendipitous result of flawed attempts to reproduce the gloss of Les Paul and Ken Nelson. But trial and error taught both Chess and Phillips that to be successful in their respective local markets, their music needed to possess a high level of inclusiveness and accessibility. The "discrepancies" were more than simple ineptitude: when the right balance was achieved, individual musical identities within the mix were sufficiently combinatory (professional, polished) to operate collectively and synergistically while determinedly retaining eccentric, idiosyncratic individual identities. The end result simultaneously championed collectivist values *and* individual expression, present not despite each other but because of each other.

Combined with the "existential" recording tradition and with the deliberate addition of sonic markers of spatiality—particularly echo and reverb—these studios produced recordings that at a figurative level quite did away with the active performer–passive audience split. Now all were participants within the zone. And unlike, say, Les Paul's dazzling, highly structured recorded artifacts, *these* did not stipulate to listeners exactly how they should respond. Neither did they, like *hapa haole* Hawaiian, structure into the artifact the very termination of the experience; they invited listeners into their spaces, but once inside the rest was up to the listener.

Regarded in terms of emerging spatial practice, Elvis Presley's recordings at Sun (and less so, at RCA) do indeed represent epochal shifts. By assuming the sonic-spatial attributes of the (approaching) reverberant other, *and* the anchored self, Presley's recordings finally and decisively broke with the pictorialism of prior spatial practice, while still retaining its affective, expressionist powers. The notion of deterritorializing here becomes all but literal. On the representational plane something akin to a revolutionary usurpation of power had occurred.

But real political revolutions are based on programs, on plans, on systems. The all-encompassing inclusiveness of early rock 'n' roll was based in large part on its forsaking of consistent meaning and order: the participant could ally him- or herself with the heroic reverberant voice, or with the voice of the feared and despised other (the two of which were virtually indistinguishable now anyway). He or she might imagine and occupy the space as though it were an exhilaratingly terrifying horror movie mise en scène, or a dreamy, unconscious space or a noirish cityscape, or simultaneously all three. The listener could be inside the spatial zone of the recording, just as that spatial zone might be contained within the listener, both as a psychic zone and an intrabody zone. The listener might participate in a wholly somatic way, losing consciousness of the ego-self in a screaming, physical frenzy, or quietly merge trancelike into its hypnotic sonic networks. Or swap identities with the performers. Or maybe sit this one out entirely and just let the music go on. Classic rock 'n' roll was a form that allowed easy access and easy exits. "Any old way you choose it . . . any old way you use it," sang Chuck Berry ("Rock 'n' roll Music,"1957).

By the end of Gene Vincent's "Race with the Devil," the narrator seems on the verge of doubting his earlier confident assertion that he will "outrun the Devil on judgment day." The Devil has matched his every effort: "I thought I was smart, the race was run / [but] here comes the Devil doin' a hundred and one." He implores his vehicle, "Move hot rod, move me!" We can extrapolate from this: the singer will evade the Devil only as long as he maintains his mobility. The race itself may be exhilarating, but at some point further down the line, when the singer tires, or when the hot rod—the apparatus—fails, there *will* be an accounting. A hot rod race is necessarily short, noisy, dangerous and intense. (Indeed, an endless hot rod race would be as much a torment as the endless ride endured by the ghost riders in the sky.) The machinery of reterritorialization—here represented by the Devil—cannot be shaken off forever. Rock 'n' roll's Dionysian zones were manufactured with consummate Apollonian skill and judgment. But the two follow very different arcs: the Dionysian is necessarily brief and intense (like a hot rod race), while Apollonian perfection requires persistent effort over time (more like a long, hard journey). The rock 'n' roll Dionysian was bound to exhaust itself while the reterritorializing machineries of the music industry would grind relentlessly on.

So was rock 'n' roll ultimately then, like Hawaiian, another renunciatory space, a short-lived impossible zone, a frenzied interlude that would inevitably self-limit? Perhaps not. Hawaiian, singing cowboy and other earlier spatial recording practices located their spaces generally within strict narrative frameworks: either the songs themselves told a narrative, or else they were located within larger, implicit contextual narratives. Admittedly, rock 'n' roll songs frequently acknowledged the demands of the quotidian (indeed, Eddie Cochran, Chuck Berry, Carl Perkins and others made a feature of slyly, ironically listing the specific textures and onerous demands of everyday life) but rock 'n' roll's spatialities were in the end neither wholly *of* the everyday, nor entirely other to it. They were "utopian" in the most literal sense of the word: they were about "no-place." The antecedents of rock 'n' roll were largely musics of the poor, the unpropertied and the itinerant. The spaces of these earlier recorded musics were not titled real estate so much as fleetingly occupied, briefly deterritorialized affective zones. With the coming of rock 'n' roll, the emerging constituency of a global youth culture employed these sonic spatial traditions to create, provisionally stake out and remake its own imaginal and fleetingly occupied spaces: street corners, milk bars, bus stations, dance halls, schoolyards, playing fields, vacant lots, car interiors, back streets, fun parlors and so on.

Chuck Berry's anthemic "School Day" (1956) precisely and painstakingly recounts the tedium of the high school day, in a strictly linear, virtually hour-by-hour narrative. But when the second person "you" hurries to the juke joint at the end of the school day, the temporal narrative is suspended:

> Drop the coin right into the slot
> You got to hear something that's really hot
> With the one you love you're makin' romance
> All day long you've been wantin' to dance
> Feelin' the music from head to toe,
> Round and round and round you go

He, or "you," or all of us have entered "the zone" in which the narrative flow has been arrested. There follows a guitar solo after which the verse is repeated—more going "round and round and round." "Hail, hail rock 'n' roll," Berry sings next, "deliver me from days of old!" Deliver me from *time*, in other words. "School Day" is a narrative that cunningly takes its listeners to a place from which the narrative itself cannot be terminated, from which, as Berry sang in a later song, there is "no particular place to go." The rock 'n' roll record itself subverts the relentless exigencies of linear progression by creating an infinite, transcendent *now* that may be accessed by placing oneself (in the right company) within earshot of any jukebox stacked with the right records.

Although rock 'n' roll space (provisionally) employed narratives from earlier spatial constructs, it was of itself without a singular defining narrative; it refused to locate itself definitively in relation to "the outside," just as it refused to locate its internal elements definitively in relationship to one another. Its participations remained discrepant, asystematic. Gene Vincent pointedly provides no explicit closure to his story of the race with Satan. That is the one place he would not go. Even Chuck Berry's most explicitly happily ending teen-love narrative ("You Never Can Tell," 1964) ends with a firmly stated inconclusiveness: "'C'est la vie,' said the old folks, 'it goes to show you never can tell!'" (And even this is uttered by outsiders—"the old folks"—rather than the teen lovers.) The one thing for which there is little room in the synchronic ecstasies of rock 'n' roll is speculation about the future. What became of Billy Lee Riley after his interactions with the Little Green Men? What finally became of Warren Smith, endlessly dancing the Ubangi stomp somewhere in the African jungles? What happened when Berry's juke joint finally closed up for the night? There is no answer to any of these questions.

The spaces of classic rock 'n' roll were excised from temporal trajectories. The diachronic was eschewed in favor of limitless synchronic. Time and life might move on, and the current participants might go with it, but the fact of musical space–making, of territory-creating (rather than the specific attributes of any particular territory), once discovered, was there to be rediscovered and reinvented by others, in other places, at other times, for other purposes.

Notes

Chapter 1. Introduction (pp. 1–37)

1. The term *hammering on* usually refers to the banjo and guitar technique of sounding an open (i.e., unfretted) string and then quickly and forcefully stopping the string at the first or second fret, in such a way that the string continues to sound.

2. Marcus 1991.

3. *Mystery Train* (1989), directed by Jim Jarmusch.

4. The title track of Paul Simon's *Graceland* being a well-known instance.

5. It is notoriously difficult to talk of the aural perception of space without resorting to visual metaphors, and neologisms such as "soundscape" entirely fail to break away from dependence on the visual sense. For reasons of simplicity and ease of communication, however, the present work will make use of visual metaphors.

6. That is, a single, rapid repeat of the source sound, spaced with sufficient delay time to make the repeat clearly audible, but near enough in time to source to provide a rhythmic effect.

7. See, for example, Middleton 1990, 103–126; Shephard and Wicke 1997, 2–6; and Walser 1993, 38–39.

8. See Middleton 1990, 34–63.

9. McClary and Walser 1990.

10. McClary and Walser 1990, 285.

11. McClary and Walser 1990, 284–285.

12. Walser 1993, 39.

13. Walser 1993.

14. Brackett goes on to invoke Gino Stefani's five-part model of musical competence, which ranges from (a) *general codes* (the basic conventions through which we perceive and understand sound experience), to (b) *social practice* (culture-specific institutions such as language, religion, and musical practices such as concert, ballet, and so forth), to (c) *musical techniques,* to (d) *styles,* finally through to (e) the single musical work, or *opus.* (Stefani 1987, 7–22). Different listeners (or the same listener on different occasions) may attend to a greater or smaller numbers of these levels simultaneously, giving rise to a split between "high" competence and "popular" competence. A maximum "signification effect" would occur when a piece is interpreted on all levels, while a relatively weak effect would occur if a work were perceived solely in terms of the broad, general code. (Bracket 2000, 12–13).

15. Deleuze and Guattari 1987, 311.

16. Deleuze and Guattari 1987, 312.

17. Deleuze and Guattari 1987, 312.

18. Deleuze and Guattari 1987, 317.
19. Murphie 1996.
20. Murphie 1996, 19–20.
21. Murphie 1996, 20.
22. Keil 1994, 210.
23. Keil 1994, 211.
24. Keil 1994, 214.
25. Keil 1994, 213.
26. Schafer, quoted in Keil 1994, 258.
27. In Keil 1994, 258–259.
28. See also Mowitt 1987; Eisenberg 1988; and Middleton 1990 for applications of Benjaminian ideas to the study of recorded popular music.
29. Attali 1985.
30. Baudrillard 1975, 1981.
31. In Keil 1994, 265.
32. Bateson 1972, 109; quoted in Keil 1994, 265.
33. Bateson 1972; quoted in Keil 1994, 265.
34. Barfield 1965, 32; Lévy-Bruhl [1910] 1966: 62, quoted in Keil 1994: 97.
35. Keil 1994, 98. For Keil, participation is something which occurs "in the flesh," when music makers and participants share the one physical space. "The social moments where I get these 'oneness' and 'urge to merge' feelings most forcefully are when I'm dancing at polka parties . . . or salsa parties, swept up in a black church service, or when making music" (98). But there seems to be no intrinsic reason why the concept of participation should not be extended to apply to other, perhaps less literal types of copresence.
36. Escott 1992, 1994, 1996.
37. Gillett 1975, 1983.
38. Guralnick 1981, 1989, 1994.
39. Lomax 1993.
40. Malone 1985, 1993.
41. Murray 1989, 1999.
42. Oliver 1967, 1984.
43. Palmer 1981, 1991, 1996.
44. Tosches 1977, 1989, 1991.
45. Russell 1970.
46. Published as a collection in 1991 under that name.
47. Guralnick 1981.
48. Guralnick 1986.
49. Guralnick 1989.
50. Guralnick 1994.
51. Guralnick 1999.
52. Marcus 1991, 63.
53. Although the reverse situation often applies: recordings, rather than live appearances, were frequently southern music's main currency, its medium, even in its "legendary" pre-rock phase. Muddy Waters, for example, in interviews repeatedly stressed that for all his stylistic debt to Robert Johnson, he knew his work primarily from records.
54. Murray 1989.
55. Zak 2001, 13.
56. Although he is sensitive to the differing sonic effects of delay in early Elvis Presley recordings (72–73).
57. Moore 1993.
58. Moore 1993, 6.

59. Moore 1993, 105.

60. Moore 1993, 105.

61. Moore 1993, 105.

62. Moore 1993, 106.

63. Moore 1993, 56.

64. Although many if not most then current playback media in use—jukeboxes, AM radios, portable record players, and so forth—may only have been capable of mono reproduction.

65. Moore 1993, 106.

66. Moore 1993, 107.

67. Moore 1993, 109.

68. Moore 1993, 108.

69. Moore 1993, 108.

70. Wishart 1985, 79. Wishart's work, not cited by Moore, had earlier laid out a painstaking formulation of sonic spatialities, in which he carefully examines many possible dispositions, fixed and mobile, of sound objects within various real and sonically constructed virtual spaces. He specifically includes a situation not dissimilar to that described above, in which "real" sounds are deployed in nonrealist "positions." Wishart uses his construct to schematize and aid discussion of experimental music pieces by Stockhausen, Schaeffer, himself, and others, and to aid in the building of new compositional techniques. Like Moore's, Wishart's constructs are stereo-dependent, and thus of limited applicability here.

71. Although certain vertically located bodily sensations appear to attend to the singing of higher or lower notes. We seem to sing "from the head" for high notes or "from the chest" for lower, even though all sound is produced in the throat.

72. Moore 1993, 106. The tendency to overlook prestereo popular music recording is widespread. Evan Eisenberg in *The Recording Angel* (1988) gives a single paragraph to Sam Phillips, makes no mention at all of the Chess brothers and blithely declares Phil Spector to be "the first *auteur* among producers" (103).

73. Moore 1993, 106.

74. Cunningham 1996.

75. Lubin 1996.

76. Lubin 1996, 61.

77. Lubin 1996, 62.

78. Lubin 1996, 77–78.

79. Palmer 1991. Palmer substantially revised and enlarged this piece for inclusion in his *Dancing in the Street* (1996), the book that accompanied the BBC television program of the same name, written by Palmer and Charles Shaar Murray.

80. Palmer 1996, 193.

81. This particular quote did not survive in the revised version of the piece; indeed, many of the more journalistic turns of phrase have been toned down. However, the basic point that electric guitar is uniquely capable of invoking much deeper mystical responses remains.

82. Palmer 1991, 657.

83. See also Palmer 1981 for a similarly evocative, but ultimately nonexplicit treatment of some of the "hoodoo" sites of country blues: deserted railway stations, lonely crossroads, thumping juke joints out in the sticks, and so forth.

84. Lacasse 2000. The phrase here quoted is the work's subtitle.

85. Lacasse 2000, 4.

86. Lacasse 2000, 5.

87. Lacasse 2000, 70.

88. Lacasse 2000, 109.

89. Lacasse 2000, 21.

90. Bruce Johnson's investigation of female vocal technique also works with the notion of vocal "staging," weaving details of recorded texture and vocal effects into a broader discussion of cultural change in early to mid-twentieth-century Australia. Johnson is particularly concerned with the new expressive capabilities that were afforded by the microphone and the public address system, and how these both reflected and enacted subtle but important shifts and tensions in the gender politics of the time. These ensembles in turn he sees within a context of the coming of modernism to Australian urban society in the 1930s and 1940s. (B. Johnson 2000).

91. Shea 1990.

92. Gelatt 1977.

93. Read and Welch 1976.

94. A great deal of information is available on editor Tim Gracyk's home page: http://www.garlic.com/~tgracyk/. This page links to one on essential reading, in which Gracyk says of Read and Welch and Gelatt:

> Most of the best books about our hobby are in print. Yes, there are plenty of books out of print, but I am not sure we are missing much. For example, Roland Gelatt's out-of-print history called *The Fabulous Phonograph* is really just a mediocre history by the standards of 1999 (it was first published fifty years ago), and I never consult my copy. Likewise, the big 2nd edition of *From Tin Foil to Stereo* by Oliver Read and Walter L. Welch was impressive when that was just about the only book available in the 1970s, but I feel the book is so outdated and problematic (the pro-Edison, anti–everything else bias is ridiculous) that I would never quote from it. People who do quote it discredit themselves as authorities, I believe. (http://www.garlic.com/~tgracyk/essential_books.htm).

Gracyk's *Encyclopedia of Popular American Recording Pioneers: 1895–1925* (2000) is the most exhaustive book-length treatment to date of pre-electric popular music recording artists in the United States.

95. Read and Welch 1976, 377.

96. Read and Welch 1976, 377.

97. Hurst, quoted in Read and Welch 1976, 356.

98. Wallis, quoted in Read and Welch 1976, 385.

99. Read and Welch 1976, 387.

100. Read and Welch 1976, 388.

101. Cabrera 1997.

102. Cabrera 1997, 110.

103. Cabrera asked his subjects to rate sounds on a succession of thirty-three bipolar continuous semantic scales, divided roughly into four categories: evaluation, literal description, metaphorical description and emotion. The evaluation scales included such binaries as like/dislike, interesting/uninteresting, beautiful/ugly. There were also literal descriptors, such as loud/quiet, high-pitch/low-pitch, even/uneven. Metaphorical descriptors included clear/hazy, cold/warm, dull/bright, full/thin and so forth, while the last category—emotional—included alive/dead, happy/sad, nostalgic/novel, peaceful/violent (125).

104. Les Paul's "sound on sound" recording, made on direct-to-acetate discs (before magnetic tape was available), involved a "sedimentary" aggregating of successive tracks (see chapter 6) but Paul was at pains to keep the sound as "clean" as possible, and to keep extraneous room noise (Cabrera's "resonance") to a minimum.

105. Beranek 1962.

106. Beranek 1962, 421.

107. See Doyle 1999.

108. Beranek 423.

109. Quoted in Cunningham 1996, 25.

110. Hoggart 1957, 135.

111. Hoggart 1957, 136.
112. Hoggart 1957, 190.
113. Schafer 1980, 118.

Chapter 2. Harnessing the Echo (pp. 38–63)

1. Rasmussen 1964, 224.
2. Quoted in Bagenal and Wood 1931, 338.
3. Quoted in Weis and Belton 1985, 143.
4. See Pierce 1992, 144–146.
5. See Rasmussen 1964, 224–237.
6. See *Chiron Dictionary of Greek and Roman Mythology* 1997, 97.
7. See Ovid, "Echo and Narcissus" in *Metamorphoses,* trans. Ted Hughes, in Hughes 1997, 74–84.
8. This particular telling of the relationship between Echo and Narcissus and its unhappy outcome appealed greatly to ancient Roman taste; fifty murals depicting the story have been uncovered in Pompeii alone. It is not, however, the only version: in the poet Conon's telling, the rejected suitor is male, for example; see Price and Kearns 2003, 368.
9. Bulfinch's *Mythology* 1970, 101–104.
10. In his study of mystical states and the perception of visual depth Aaronson (1967) hypnotized subjects so that they would experience alternately a greatly enhanced sense of visual depth and a complete negation of visual depth. The subjects under heightened depth perception experienced states akin to mystical revelation: "Lines seemed sharper, colors intensified, everything seemed to have a place and be in its place, and to be aesthetically satisfying" (247). Later he says: "The usual perception of objects in the environment as things in themselves, independent of their surroundings, seems replaced by a perception of objects as being in interaction with their surroundings and with the active properties of the space around them. The account of the simulator suggests that necessary to the development of these conditions is an interest in and investment of the self in the objects of the environment" (251).
11. See *Chiron Dictionary of Greek and Roman Mythology* 1997, 97.
12. Grant and Hazel 1957. See also Hollander (1981, 7–22) and Loewenstein (1984, 1–56) for extended examinations of the figure of Echo in Greco-Roman mythography.
13. Wrightson and Wrightson 1998, 7–8.
14. Schafer 1980, 207.
15. Schafer 1980, 89.
16. Eisenberg 1988, 41–42.
17. Campbell 1974, 254–268.
18. See Lacasse (2000, 32–70) for a broad overview of the archeology and anthropology of "vocal staging," in which he draws attention to the resonant, echoic and reverberant properties of sacred, magical or ritually significant natural and architectural spaces. Lacasse's survey is wide-ranging in temporal terms—covering prehistory, classical antiquity, the Middle Ages and early modernity, right up to the advent of electrical recording and amplification—and global in scope, citing examples from Western Europe, the Mediterranean and the Levant, Africa, North America (including the Arctic), Melanesia and Mongolia. In virtually all of Lacasse's instances, reverberation and echo are associated with the magical, the mythic, the mystical or the hallucinatory; in particular, they accompany psychic and/or physical transformations.

19. Campbell 1974, 254–268.

20. Krautheimer 1975, 42.

21. Schafer 1980, 52.

22. Bagenal and Wood 1931, 364.

23. Bagenal and Wood 1931, 365.

24. Mowitt 1987, 189.

25. Bagenal and Wood 1931, 365.

26. Bagenal and Wood 1931, 380.

27. Bagenal and Wood, 1931, 369–370.

28. Bagenal and Wood 1931, 372.

29. Levine 1988.

30. Levine 1988, 186.

31. Levine 1988, 190.

32. Levine 1988, 195–196.

33. Elias 1994.

34. Levine 1988, 199.

35. Although the terms *phonograph* and *gramophone* are applied in an inconsistent and contradictory manner, for convenience I shall here use the term *phonograph* to denote the early Edison cylinder-type recording devices, which had their heyday in the United States and Britain roughly up to the turn of the twentieth century (but remained in production for many years after that); and *gramophone* to indicate flat disc–playing devices, which assumed prime importance at the end of the 1890s and into the early twentieth century; see Gelatt 1977, 17–73, 83, 134. "Phonograph," however, became the generic term in the United States for all domestic record players, and that usage will also be observed here when referring to the United States.

36. Gelatt 1977, 204.

37. Gelatt 1977, 47.

38. Gelatt 1977, 29.

39. Gelatt 1977, 44.

40. Gelatt 1977, 45.

41. Coin-operated machines were largely limited to the United States. By 1898 there was still an "utter absence" of coin-operated machines in England and Scotland, for example (Gelatt 1977, 101), a result of high costs outside the United States. A unique coin-operated system was to be found in Paris however, at Pathé's Salon du Phonographe:

> The salon was a palatial emporium, beautified by thick carpeting, red plush and polished mahogany, in which top hatted boulevardiers could be found day and night, sampling the latest tunes. There were rows of richly upholstered easy chairs, each facing an ornate mahogany cabinet from which protruded a pair of hearing tubes, a coin slot and a dialing device. When the customer had chosen the title from the catalogue, he dropped a fifteen-centime token in the slot, dialed the desired record number and put the tube to his ears. A minion below ground would scurry to the record bins for the appropriate cylinder and put it on a phonograph connected to the ear tubes. (Gelatt 1977, 103)

42. Gelatt 1977, 48–57.

43. Gelatt 1977, 72. No date given for this recording beyond "the Nineties."

44. Gelatt 1977, 73.

45. Quoted in Obrecht 1995 (unpaginated).

46. It was by no means unusual in nineteenth- and twentieth-century vaudeville, music hall and variety entertainment for performers to make a career out of as little as one or two songs, a few acrobatic tricks, or one short comedy routine or recitation. The vaudeville/variety/music hall/tent show practice of presenting

a large number of artists in the course of one show, with each performer taking the stage for only a short period to deliver the most guaranteed crowd-pleasing item in their repertoire, provided a natural training ground for early popular recording artists.

47. Quoted in Gelatt 1977, 88. At the time of writing, "Morning on the farm" can be accessed online at the U.S. Library of Congress, *http://memory.loc.gov/ammem/ammemhome.html.*

48. Of another early descriptive record, Fred Gaisberg (1943) writes:

But the star turn during the Boer War was a descriptive record entitled 'The Departure of the Troopship' with crowds at the quayside, bands playing the troops up the gangplank, bugles sounding 'All ashore,' farewell cries of 'Don't forget to write,' troops singing 'Home Sweet Home,' which gradually receded in the distance, and the gradual far-away hoot of the steamer whistle. The record became enormously popular and eventually historic. It bought tears to the eyes of thousands, among them those of Melba, who declared in my presence that this record influenced her to make gramophone records more than anything else. (45)

A grimly authentic bellicose descriptive record appeared after the Great War. However, unlike the fabricated "Departure of the Troopship," the so-called Gas Shell Bombardment Record was, according to the HMV catalogue of 1924:

the actual reproduction of the screaming and whistling of the shells previous to the entry of the British troops into Lille. It is not an imitation but was recorded on the battlefront. The report of the guns and the whistling of the shells is the actual sound of the Royal Garrison Artillery in action on October 9th, 1918. No book or picture can ever visualise the reality of modern warfare just the way this record has done . . . it would require only the slightest imagination for one, by means of this record, to be projected into the past, and feel that he is really present on the battlefield witnessing this historic chapter of the war. (From Rust 1975; quoted by J. Raymond, e-mail correspondence, January 22, 1999)

49. For detailed histories of sound recording in this period. see Gaisberg 1943, 40–65; Gelatt 1977, 83–99; and Read and Welch 1976, 119–136, 151–176.

50. Gaisberg 1943, 32–38, 53–65.

51. See also Farrell 1998 for an account of Gaisberg's travels in India.

52. Lesser lights from the French *Opéra* and *Opéra Comique* regularly recorded for Pathé in Paris (Gelatt 1977, 102) and members of Milan's various opera companies, without international reputations, recorded similarly for Anglo-Italian Commerce Company (104).

53. Gaisberg 1943, 40.

54. Gelatt 1977, 119.

55. Gaisberg 1943, 86–88.

56. Gaisberg 1943, 51. Soprano Emma Calvé also visited the premises of the Gramophone Company's London Maiden Lane recording studio in 1902, transported there in queenly style by luxurious carriage, only to declare upon arrival: "Never in my life will I enter such a place. It is a tavern—not a manufactory. I shall be robbed there. You have brought me to a thieves' den" (Gelatt 1977, 116).

57. Indeed, there is little difference between Gaisberg's (1943) telling of his encounters with opera stars and his encounters with royalty such as his attempt to record the voice of the Russian tsar (33).

58. Gelatt 1977, 29.

59. Gelatt 1977, 145–146.

60. Gelatt 1977, 148–149.

61. Gelatt 1977, 149.

62. Gelatt 1977, 158–171.
63. Sanjek 1988, 25.
64. Sanjek 1988, 25.
65. Sanjek 1988, 25.
66. Sanjek 1988, 27.
67. Gelatt 1977, 197–198.
68. Gelatt 1977, 200.
69. Gelatt 1977, 202.
70. Mackenzie 1966, 243.
71. Gelatt 1977, 191–192.
72. Gelatt 1977, 220.
73. Gelatt 1977, 222.
74. Gelatt 1977, 223.
75. Sanjek 1988, 77.

76. The term *voice* is used here and henceforth in its more general musicological sense to mean a line or separate strand of music in a harmony or counterpoint.

77. Coffman; quoted in Fischer 1980, 190.

78. Handzo 1985, 396; Cameron 1980, 211.

79. Read and Welch 1976, 377.

80. Read and Welch 1976, 377. The terminology here is potentially misleading. "Romantic" recording tended to create a sense of a real space, while "realist" recording sought to be aspatial.

81. Gelatt 1977, 229. Columbia's own publicity claimed that 4,850 voices were captured on the record.

82. Gelatt 1977, 232.

83. Schafer 1980, 104.

84. See, for example, Mumford 1963, 202.

85. Mumford 1963, 203.

86. Just as the opera singer was allowed to behave "like a prima donna," willfully indulging his or her own emotions in public, completely contrary to the late nineteenth-century notion of bourgeois "good manners."

87. While it is difficult to know precisely how people felt about the enhanced spatial properties of the new phonograph, the coming of television to Australia is within this author's memory. The modern-day offhandedness toward the device, and toward particular channels' programming plans stands in contrast to the reverential gathering around the box and the entranced, awestruck respect shown toward the apparatus by Australian suburbanites in the late 1950s. The power of the device to reorganize domestic space and impose strict disciplines on the bodies therein was manifestly great; looking back now, one can detect a scarcely submerged religiosity to the experience. Gathering in the dark at a neighbor's place, sitting quietly in a semicircle around the set, watching the advertisements with the same rapt attention as the main programs, certainly no channel surfing—the experience had something of the séance about it.

88. Eisenberg 1988, 38.

89. A related phenomenon (although one to which Mackenzie himself was not a party) was the rise of "techno-buffism": the positioning of the gramophone as the domain of the technically able middle-class male. With the introduction in the 1920s of the "closed" radio receiver, which discouraged tinkering by the owner, the gramophone gradually began to replace the radio receiver as the newest instance of domestically deployed technological "magic"; while its owner may have been unable to dismantle and reassemble it, he could if he was so inclined, familiarize himself with frequency responses, degrees of wow and flutter, the properties of woofers and tweeters, the merits of different makes of component and so on.

The literature of gramophone recording largely operates between the poles of this technical fetishism on the one hand and an awed reverence toward the traditions of European classical music on the other. In magazines such as *Audio* and *Gramophone,* or books such as Read and Welch's (1976), an unstated but ever present assumption is that "involved" gramophone ownership is the domain of the middle-class, technically literate male. As Eisenberg says:

"Instrument" was the word enthusiasts used in the 1920s and 1930s when referring to their phonographs. . . . Grown men seriously interested in music did not want to be thought of as playing with toys.

The phonograph is a scientific instrument for the reproduction of sound; it is also a musical instrument that the amateur must play, not play with. (144)

The ultimate goal of this style of gramophone ownership concerns the correct use of the technical apparatus in order to accomplish the "trick" of exemplary sound reproduction (of a piece of canonical Western music). If the apparatus was correctly used, the owner/listener would effect a kind of territorial appropriation, whereby he might enjoy the privilege of private re-creating of a special kind of public event. The buff aspired not so much to possess public space—the space of the classical concert hall—but to enjoy privileged possession of the means of access, the apparatus itself. This full, conscious, involved possession of the apparatus might be likened to having a private box in a concert hall.

Mackenzie himself was ever careful to point out his own lack of technical expertise, and occasionally admonishes against obsessive buffism. James in his *Hi Fi for Pleasure* (1955) talks of the "nowadays universally popular hobby of high fidelity reproduction," for example, but warns owners against becoming obsessed with the apparatus: "A good gramophone ought to be self-effacing" (9). Mackenzie wrote the introduction to James's text, commending it to listeners who were, like himself, technically inexpert.

90. Even though recordings of sermons, recitations and hymns composed a large segment of the recorded corpus of the time, apart from the high-flown advertising rhetoric that often accompanied them, there is little to suggest that these commanded any special respect from record buyers.

91. The persona(e) of the recording suggested a respectful sobriety. Even in the case of "rube" comedy, blackface minstrelsy, "Irish" recitation and other "low" acts, the demeanour of the performer lurking behind the stage persona was unfailingly correct, respectful, at the beck and call of the entertained.

92. Indeed, the "roominess"/"dryness" dichotomy in sound recording provides a close counterpart to Walter Benjamin's distinction between "auratic" and "nonauratic" art. Reverb, echo, room provide a neat material enactment of Benjamin's notion of "aura," which he applies primarily to visual art.

93. In the main, popular recording in the United States and in Britain remained strictly in the depthless, nonreverberant "realist" mode. One significant exception however is Paul Whiteman's recording of "Rhapsody in Blue" (1927). Here the dynamic plane is given a specifically spatial caste, in direct and conscious imitation of "romantic mode" classical recording. The clarinet slide up that opens the piece is reverberant, suggesting a haunting, "off-camera" quality, and the various solo piano and string passages that occur throughout the piece are all carefully (and differently) located by means of varying degrees of reverb. The effect is to re-create the exaggerated dynamic plane of romantic classical orchestra. Indeed, Whitman and composer Gershwin's aim was to show the world that "jazz music" could aspire to the complexity and polish of Western classical orchestral music.

94. Indeed, collectors report that modern listeners frequently describe acoustically recorded hot dance recordings as "cartoon music."

95. In some senses acoustically recorded hot dance might be likened to house, techno and contemporary dance music, in that the "manic clockwork" sound of hot dance became a sort of sonic signifier of the cocaine- and bootleg liquor–driven "jazz age," just as contemporary dance musics might be associated with an amphetamine-ecstasy culture. But for all the popularity of hot dance, audiences quickly opted for the more sonically and emotionally varied palette offered by orchestras and singers of the late 1920s, and the most "driven" hot dance dated very quickly.

96. Keil and Feld 1994, 96.

Chapter 3. "Way Out There" (pp. 64–93)

1. A notable exception to this recording placelessness was the practice of deliberately "setting" a recording in a putative or imagined location. Such releases as "A Night With Paul Whiteman" at the Biltmore, or the two recordings "Jimmie Rodgers Visits the Carter Family" (putatively in Virginia) and "The Carter Family Visit Jimmie Rodgers" (putatively in Texas, but like its predecessor recorded in Louisville, Kentucky) (Porterfield 1992, 411). The Whiteman recording is aping, I believe, a then current radio broadcasting notion of mise-en-scène, whereby radio programs were in fact broadcast live from such places as the Biltmore, and listeners were invited to vicariously imagine themselves part of a "make-believe ballroom." The Carter Family–Jimmie Rodgers recordings are attempts to evoke a preexisting romance of the south and the west respectively (examined in greater detail in chapter 7).

2. Radio broadcasting studios, at least until the coming of television, were frequently grand establishments, with large auditoriums, impressive foyers and porticos, executive offices and boardrooms; recording studios, on the other hand, have always tended to be places of technical/industrial enterprise, rather than of architectural excellence. Indeed, there almost seems to be a trade-off between the drab smallness of the actual recording studio and the "largeness" of the sonic product.

3. Nick Tosches (1985) suggests that the verbal interlude on "KC Blues" was wholly unplanned: "To Hutchison's mind the song is ended. There is a small silence as the men from Okeh signal that he must continue, that the record must be longer than the minute and fifty seconds he has given them. Hutchison's solution is to speak" (177).

4. See Malone 1985, 31–76; Porterfield 1992, 84–103; Sanjek 1988, 64–66; Shelton and Goldblatt 1966, 23–53.

5. Sanjek 1988, 72.

6. Conte 1995, 5.

7. As well as Conte's liner notes to the CD series *The Secret Museum of Mankind* (Yazoo), see also the website Secret Museum of the Air at http://www.megasaver.com/sma/sma.html.

8. Which is not to discount the influence or importance of other, less well known, regional music makers. Indeed, the major difference between, say, a near immediate global hillbilly superstar such as Jimmie Rodgers and any number of "obscure" ethnic musicians might ultimately simply be the shape and duration of their "arcs of influence." Recordings of hitherto obscure back-catalogue artists, such as klezmer bands or Caribbean calypso singers recording in New York in the 1920s, or Tex-Mex groups or blues guitarists of the 1930s, are now of great interest to many contemporary listeners and musicians. Unlike that of their more spectacular contemporaries though, their contribution to the dialogue has been subject to a fifty-, sixty-, seventy- or even eighty-year "delay."

9. Goffman 1969, 141.

10. Neil Rosenberg warns, however, that Hutchison's interjection might be less revolutionary than it appears; spoken introductions and even midsong commentaries like Hutchison's were by no means unique in hillbilly music of the time, he says. And rakish references to liquor drinking, such as Hutchison's, were also commonplace in 1920s hillbilly recording, exemplified by such popular skits as "A Corn Licker Still in Georgia." Furthermore the interjection itself might not be so spontaneous as Tosches assumes it to be (see note 3). At that session, his second to last, Hutchison was near the end of what Mark Wilson (editor of the Rounder reissue of Hutchison's recordings) describes as a limited repertoire; "KC Blues" is in fact simply an instrumental version of Hutchison's hit of a few years before, "The Train That Carried The Girl From Town."

A rather different scenario . . . suggests itself: the A & R man heard the piece, noted the small amount of variation in it and recognized it as a repeat of a piece already in the catalogue by the same performer. Consequently he advised, probably coached a break in the middle with a slightly racy spoken interlude—one that combined regionalism and politics and was congruent with Hutchison's image as white man who played black music, with all that implied to his southern listeners—to add some regional spice to the recording. (Letter to the author, September 29, 2001)

In this context, Hutchison's utterance, rather than a move that attempts to subvert a rapidly hardening recording protocol, is in fact simply "shtick" of a higher order, an early, highly sophisticated instance of faux authenticity. For this listener, however, while the tempo and picking pattern of "KC Blues" is not wholly dissimilar to "The Train That Carried The Girl From Town," the changes are different: the former moves twice to the IV chord, which is more or less absent from the latter, and there is a different opening lick on the top string in each song. And the interjection itself is spoken in a decidedly relaxed, "unstagey" manner; even if contrived, it was seemingly contrived for that recording, rather than being a piece of established performance patter.

11. Although contemporaneous blues, jugband, hillbilly and ethnic recording frequently featured dexterous and arresting guitar work, I know of no examples that quite share the reverberant sonic authority of Rodgers' guitar on this and his other recordings.

12. See Porterfield 1992, 47–65.

13. Porterfield 1992, 42.

14. Porterfield 1992, 42.

15. The Carter Family's recordings demonstrate an assertion of self that is in many ways the opposite of Hutchison and Rodgers, but no less effective. Their resolutely nonfancy, deadpan southern delivery, their complete refusal to put on an act, their sometimes awkward but always unmistakable recorded (and photographic) presence, asserts a powerful "plain-folks" sense of self that is radically without "folksiness," apparently without stage artifice. There is a kind of "documentary realness" to the Carters' recorded presence that in its own way stands as an implicit critique of "entertainment industry" conventions. But as Richard Peterson (1997) points out, this "authenticity" quickly became a major part of "country music's" marketing strategy.

16. Indeed, Ralph Peer's budget for his first recording trip to the south for Victor (he estimated it would cost twenty-five dollars per song recorded) was angrily rejected by recording director Nat Shilkret as being far too low for recordings on Victor (Porterfield 1992, 100, 104).

17. Porterfield 1992, 120.

18. Whitburn 1994 (unpaginated); Hardy and Laing 1990, 27–28.

19. Porterfield 1992, 140, 151–152.

20. The visual semiotics of photographs of Rodgers reinforce these effects. The "polish" evident on mainstream popular recordings was usually replicated in visuals: hair was slicked, faces were made-up and subjects assumed elaborate, nonnaturalistic poses for photo sessions. Photographs were often later touched up and printed in high-contrast tones, rendering subjects at an even further remove from the everyday. The most widely distributed (in his day) images of Rodgers on the other hand display a relaxed carriage, a broad, apparently unforced smile. Perhaps the best known was a picture of Rodgers in linen suit, bowtie and hat, photographed from slightly below. Rodgers is holding his lapels, leaning back slightly, smiling down at the camera, sporting the customary smile (see Porterfield 1992, between pages 226 and 227). The suggestion is overall one of great casualness. He is not leaning forward deferentially to the viewer, but his posture suggests a welcoming, inclusive openness and approachability. There is a close match between the photos, the voice qualities on record and the legendary "real life" Rodgers charm (which enabled him to "get away with" often highly questionable practices) reported by virtually all of biographer Porterfield's informants.

21. At the 1999 International Association for Popular Music Studies (IASPM) Conference in Sydney, Australia, Paul Oliver, one of the most influential researchers of prewar southern country blues expressed bemusement at the extent to which Robert Johnson had come to be the blues icon non-pareil. Researcher and record producer Peter Lowry takes an even more iconoclastic position, stating "there is no such thing as Delta blues," insisting that the notion of "Delta blues" has become a marketing and labeling shorthand for a range of musical practice and styles that have little or no exclusive or essential connection with that region, nor any defining property unique to the region (conversation with the author).

22. Here, as elsewhere in this work, it is near impossible to declare anyone conclusively to be an originator of any particular technique, be it musical or technical, and such is not my aim. The techniques that Johnson employed may have been used earlier, elsewhere; given the range of field and studio recordings made during the early electric period, in the Americas, Europe, Africa, the Indian subcontinent, Oceania and elsewhere, it is impossible to say conclusively that such eccentric and innovatory recording practices were the sole domain of (some) U.S. recording artists. But what can be pointed to is a widening range of recording possibilities that in the 1930s resided primarily within an American tradition. The Robert Johnson records clearly signal the availability of an expanded set of recording options, regardless of whether Johnson himself originated the techniques.

23. See for example unattributed liner notes to *King of the Delta Blues Singers,* Columbia, 1961.

24. Obrecht 1990, 78.

25. See booklet to *Robert Johnson: The Complete Recordings,* Columbia CD.

26. A point made by Cooder elsewhere in the same interview already quoted above. Steve Waksman (1999) identifies Cooder's idea—that Johnson's corner loading was a kind of anticipation of the sound of an electric guitar with its midrange boosted through a Marshall amplifier—as an instance of a particular "cultural fantasy surrounding the blues, a fantasy primarily held by white critics and musicians," involving "the insistent celebration of black musicians as technological innovators and conspirators who drew upon their cultural resources to open new avenues of sonic experimentation via electronic means" (116). (Robert Palmer's "Church of the Sonic Guitar" [1991] is cited as another instance.) Waksman, while conceding that this privileging of earlier African American guitar acts as an important corrective to the common tendency to hold up the 1960s as the most innovative of musical eras (a presumption which also tends to cast African American musicians in mere supporting

roles), draws our attention to the parallel and contemporaneous nonblues electric experimentations of Les Paul and Chet Atkins.

27. See Lacasse (2000: 32–41) on reverberant cave sites and sacred spaces.

28. Palmer 1981, 124–125.

29. Johnson's complex and active relationship to his immediate built environment recalls other examples of performances in dystopian places, in which special use is made of surroundings: doo-wop groups (and later hip-hoppers) harmonizing on street corners or in reverberant tenement and project block stairwells; basketball players in vacant city lots, skaters making sport of the hard surfaces of public plazas—in all cases, the performers use the qualities of the physical walls, reconfigure harsh and ungiving physical surfaces, making them partners in their work. The game, whether it is singing, declaiming, bouncing a basketball, maneuvering a skateboard, involves continual, almost obsessive physical testing and retesting of the surface itself, until the precise interaction, the bounce of the ball, the quality of the sound reverberation and amplification is exactly known, felt. Spaces are temporarily mastered, even though they may remain in the political and proprietorial sense hostile to the performer. For a time though, despotic architectures are remade, reterritorialized.

30. Ry Cooder plays the guitar piece, in what must be one of the most "authentic" cinematic re-creations of a "classic" music performance. The filmmakers' pains to "get it right" stand in contrast to the great majority of earlier music-bio films. In films such as *Lady Sings the Blues* and *Your Cheating Heart,* the subject of the bio is used as a theme around which to display the talents of a contemporary star (Diana Ross and George Hamilton, respectively). In films like *Crossroads* (at least in its early stages), *Coal Miner's Daughter,* and to a certain extent *Bird,* more diligent attempts have been made to access the historicized moment of the diegesis, to reach "the place." This is most evident in the opening scenes of *Crossroads,* which tacitly acknowledge the latter-day fetishization of much "classic" blues recording, particularly Delta blues. Within *that* style, nothing stands as more "sacred" perhaps than Johnson's recordings, and none have more cachet than "Cross Roads Blues." The song has a little of everything that Johnson is remembered for: the performance is one of his most angular and innovatory in feel; the guitar playing demonstrates Johnson's radical slide technique and fearless dynamic control; and the song itself hints at Johnson's alleged demonic encounter. Cooder here performs his own fan devotion to the "magic moment." It is the only case in Cooder's oeuvre that I know of in which he plays a true "cover," a faithful, "photographic" re-creation of a canonical piece; part of the enjoyment of this particular moment, for me at least, was the sense of having Cooder "wink at" the audience. In this case the exactitude of the musical quotation serves to further sacralize the original recording moment. In an interview in *Guitar Player* (Forte 1988, 38) published to coincide with the release of the film, Cooder expressed reservations about performing such a close copy.

31. The term *itinerant* is used here to be distinct from Deleuze and Guattari's notion of the "nomadology" (1987, 351–423), which is integrally tied up with the "war machine." Unlike Deleuze and Guattari's nomad, the itinerant here is essentially an unaccompanied, and therefore a mostly nonbellicose traveler.

32. Obrecht 1990, 78.

33. Obrecht 1990, 78.

34. Goffman 1971, 28–61.

35. Goffman 1971, 28.

36. Goffman 1971, 33.

37. Goffman 1971, 34.

38. Goffman 1971, 34–35.

39. See Palmer 1996, 46–77, for a perceptive overview of the ecstatic religious traditions in American secular popular music, including notably his discussion of the influence of one "Whirling Willie" on Lionel Hampton's original formulation of hard-driving swing.

40. Read and Welch 1976; 1959 edition cited.

41. Barthes 1981.

42. Zak 2001, 20.

43. Palmer 1996, 46–77.

44. See for example Chilton (1992) on Louis Jordan's band.

45. But sometimes white groups were also recorded with a similar sense of physical "locatedness": recordings by Bob Wills and his Texas Playboys often manifest a similar sonic emplacement (see especially that group's radio transcriptions on the Tiffany label) as do the various small groups built around guitarist Eddie Lang and fiddler Joe Venuti.

Chapter 4. "Blue Shadows on the Trail" (pp. 94–119)

1. See Green 2002; Malone 1985, 137–175; 1993; Shelton and Goldblatt 1966, 145–177; Tosches 1989, 108–117 and 162–217; Townsend 1976; Morthland 1984, 95–135; information on Australian hillbillies in Watson 1975 and 1983. See also Devitt and Doyle 2000 and Green 1996.

2. See Slotkin 1985.

3. A version of the group, obviously with different personnel, still performs.

4. Although at least one cowboy song, Bob Wills's version of Cindy Walker's "Dusty Skies" speaks of expulsion from the cattle range—"So git along little dogies, we're moving off this range / never thought as how I'd make a change" and "'Cause the blue skies have failed / And we're on our last trail"—it clearly speaks to and of the experiences of dispossessed Dustbowl farmers rather than ranchers. Wills's usually playful "deconstructive" interjections to Tommy Duncan's "straight man" singing are here uncharacteristically sober, indicating the true seriousness of the song.

5. O'Brien 1979, 61.

6. See O'Brien 1979.

7. W. J. Cash 1956.

8. See Malone 1985 and 1993; Morthland 1984; Tosches 1989.

9. Quoted in Malone 1993, 71–72.

10. Kirby 1986.

11. The crime fiction of John D. McDonald has made much use of the brutal Georgia "cracker" villains; more recently Elmore Leonard and James Lee Burke have written in white-trash villains. Robert De Niro showed he was well conversant with the stereotype in his characterization of Max Cady in Martin Scorsese's *Cape Fear*. And in writing about southern music, Peter Guralnick's (1989) portrait of singer Charlie Feathers in *Lost Highway,* and Roger Williams's (1981) biography of Hank Williams, *Sing a Sad Song,* both have strong elements of gothic, as does Myra Gale Lewis's (1982) biography of her ex-husband Jerry Lee, *Great Balls of Fire*. Perhaps the most enthusiastic quest for southern gothic is to be found in the writing of Nick Tosches, in both his celebratory biography of Lewis, *Hellfire* (1982), and his treatment of country music, *Country: Living Legends and Dying Metaphors in America's Biggest Music* (1985).

12. Malone 1985, 151–152.

13. Malone 1993.

14. Malone 1993, 79–80.

15. Malone 1993, 80.

16. Malone 1993, 81.

17. Malone 1993, 82.

18. Malone 1993, 83

19. Malone 1993, 84.

20. Quoted in Malone 1993, 92.

21. See Devitt and Doyle, 2000.

22. Exact date not known, but Watson (1983, 7) suggests it was recorded in 1951 or soon after.

23. Watson 1983, 7.

24. The faces of the American presidents carved in the rockface at Mount Rushmore acknowledge this connection between mountains and patriarchal power.

25. See Aaronson (1967) in which he argues that "mystic experience seems associated with increased depth suggestions, schizophreniform states with no depth" (246). He also notes William James's observation that mystic experience tends to occur outdoors, in mountain or desert places.

26. Director Walsh used a high mountain location again for the opening scene in *White Heat* (1949) which, like both *Shane* and *High Sierra*, locates the protagonist's final moment of truth—the decisive encounter with the law—in a spectacularly elevated place. Ridley Scott's *Thelma and Louise* "telegraphed" the hint to its viewers right at the outset that the action would inevitably draw to a showdown with the forces of law and order by reprising in its opening scene a look-alike to Walsh's opening scenes from *High Sierra* and *White Heat*.

27. Davidson 1989, 52–55.

28. Davidson 1989, 55.

29. Sanjek 1988, 235.

30. See Moore 1993, 106–110; and Middleton 1990, 89, for discussions of the notion of "texture."

31. The narrator in "Rider in the Sky" speaks at a greater remove from the events he describes than his counterpart in "Blue Shadows": the events of which he tells happened to an unnamed "old cowpoke," in contrast to the narrator in "Blue Shadows" who presumably is narrating an exegesis in which he is a participant. Or is the narrator in fact the same "old cowpoke," here using the sermon / parable-telling device of the third-person account, to be resolved at the finish with a trick-reveal along the lines of "And friends, this story is true, because you see, I *was* that cowpoke"?

32. Kawin 1978.

33. Echoes and reverberation also seem to figure prominently in other popular adventure fiction. In the course of researching the imagination of indigenous musics of the Pacific, says Phil Hayward, he read "a huge stack of popular fiction from the 1880s–1930s. . . . I was surprised at how often descriptions of sound, echoes etc. in landscapes (many of them melodramatic and/or impossible) occurred" (e-mail to the author, October 16, 2000). I am grateful to Phil Hayward for alerting me to this important literary forerunner to recorded echo and reverb.

Chapter 5. "And as the Sun Sinks Slowly in the West . . ."
(pp. 120–142)

1. Kanahele 1979, 45.

2. Whiteoak and Scott-Maxwell 2003, 314.

3. Kanahele 1979, 46.

4. Kanahele 1979, 254.

5. Kanahele 1979, 256.

6. Kanahele 1979, 290–291.

7. Kanahele 1979, 120.

8. Kanahele 1979, 120.

9. See Kanahele 1979, 109.

10. See Kanahele 1979, 387.

11. Ruymar 1996, 70–71.

12. See Coyle and Coyle 1995, 34.

13. Kanahele 1979, xxiv.

14. Kanahele 1979, xxv, 53.

15. Kanahele 1979, xxv.

16. Kanahele 1979, xxv. See also Gurre Ploner Noble's biography of bandleader Johnny Noble, the so-called Hawaiian King of Jazz for an early account of the emergence of *hapa haole* and jazz and big band–inflected Hawaiian popular music (Noble 1948).

17. Hawaiian guitar shares this quality with the slide or bottleneck guitar styles originally of the U.S. south (although "bottleneck" players often—but not exclusively—hold the guitar in the more conventional "Spanish" position, rather than flat on the lap). Unfretted stringed instruments possibly have an African pedigree, and there are nineteenth-century reports of black children in the south nailing a piece of taut wire to the side of a shack and using a bottle, steel or even a rock as a slider—sometimes called a "diddley bo." By the late nineteenth and early twentieth century, black guitar players were occasionally using bottlenecks or penknives to fret conventional Spanish guitars, and the practice may have been already established when Hawaiian guitarists first toured the vaudeville circuits in the early 1900s. See Palmer 1981, 46, and Nick Tosches (1989, 173–185) for informed overviews of slide, Hawaiian and steel guitar. See also Robert Mugge's film *Deep Blues* for a demonstration of diddley-bo playing, and further elucidation from Robert Palmer onscreen. Accounts of slide and Hawaiian styles most frequently locate the origin of the style in Hawaii. Black players adopted the bottleneck style after seeing touring Hawaiians or Hawaiian-styled vaudeville acts, it is said; see, for example, Kanahele 1979, 20–21. David Evans (1970, 238) posits that the process may well have worked the other way: Hawaiians quite likely were introduced to non-fretted guitar playing by U.S. Negro seamen crewing the freighters that visited the Hawaiian Islands in the nineteenth century. See also Ruymar 1996, 54.

18. In many cases, but for the presence of steel guitar and the use of Hawaiian words or place references, many modern listeners might be hard pressed to identify anything intrinsically "Hawaiian" about much Hawaiian music of the time. Nonetheless, numerous harmonic, melodic and textural musical features *are* identified with Hawaiian music. See, for example, Kanahele 1979, xvii–xxix, 2, 58, 59, 133–138, 194, 215, 223, 230, 269, 271, 272, 357–359, 371–372.

19. Kanahele 1979, 112.

20. Kanahele 1979, 215. Staccato phrasing, brisk ensemble singing and "peppy" march tempos were all mainstays of early twentieth-century Hawaiian music, so presumably this was not the kind of "pep" to which King was objecting. Whether King's was an objection to broadly modernist "Jazz Age" ideas and cultural views or a more specific rejection of fast tempos, staccato playing, "blue notes," or even a rejection of audience-centered dynamics (expressed in terms of volume, "showmanship" or the use of improvisation) remains unclear.

21. See in particular Said 1978; 1993.

22. See in particular Born and Hesmondhalgh 2000; Radano and Bohlman 2001.

23. Ralph P. Locke 1991, 263; quoted in Born and Hesmondhalgh 2000, 8. In Locke's analysis, Saint-Saëns knowingly complexifies the construct.

24. Born and Hesmondhalgh 2000, 8.

25. As argued by Richard Taruskin 1992, 255; quoted in Born and Hesmondhalgh 2000, 9.

26. Born and Hesmondhalgh 2000, 9.

27. Kanahele 1979, 234.

28. Kanahele 1979, 46, 254.

29. Kanahele 1979, 113.

30. Middleton 2000.

31. Middleton 2000, 62.

32. Middleton 2000, 66–68.

33. Middleton 2000, 70.

34. Middleton 2000, 71.

35. Buck 1993, 174. We might wonder at the extent to which the "pep" versus "sweet" opposition reflected class fault lines in Hawaiian society. The patrician bandleader and composer Charles Edward King was of mixed Hawaiian and Caucasian extraction, and had been brought among the *aili'i*, the old royal caste. He was at one time a Republican territorial senator, was an esteemed educator and a successful businessman. His musical and social roots were very much with the waltzes and parlor songs favored in genteel Hawaiian social circles in the late 1800s. Sol Hoopii on the other hand—the "peppiest" of Hawaiian guitarists—was born into modest circumstances. At age seventeen he stowed away on a Matson liner for San Francisco. He did not return to live in Hawaii for any extended period, remaining on the West Coast until his death in 1953.

Despite the traditionalist cast of Charles King's public utterances, he composed songs for the steel guitar, mostly waltzes, but also some syncopated *hapa haole* songs, and songs with ragtime influences. He also wrote numerous songs in English (Kanahele 1979, 216). Sol Hoopii and other "hot guitar" masters always included older-styled songs of almost infinite languor in their programs. At the time of writing, there is still no major investigation in print of the racial and cultural politics of early twentieth-century Hawaiian music and the international Hawaiian craze.

36. The idea of the island, cut off by the sea, limited in area, stands in contrasts to the seemingly endless expanses (and possibilities) of the continent. The word "paradise" itself is derived from an Old Persian root, *pairidaeza,* meaning "enclosure" or "park," from the words, *pairi,* "around" and *diz,* "to mould" or "form" (*Oxford English Dictionary,* 2nd ed., 183).

37. No recording date available.

38. Indeed, it is a truism among (necessarily speculative) accounts of the origins of music that it began as mimesis; humans strove to sonically copy or to at least reference the animate and inanimate aspects of their lived reality. But the act of rendering the world inevitably alienates it as well. Rituals of participation counterbalance what R. Murray Schafer calls *schizophonia:* the splitting of sounds from their sources (Schafer 1977, 88). Although Schafer applies the term to electroacoustical means of sound recording and reproduction, in a sense any mimetic musicality (not simply the commodified sound products of the industrial age) is intrinsically alienating. Again the myth of Echo and Narcissus speaks to this alienation and implicitly laments the absence of compensating participatory regimes that may maintain or repair the bonds between humanly reproduced sounds and their sources in nature.

39. See Sallis 1982, 101.

40. In 1957 and 1958 Chuck Berry would release electric slide instrumentals under the names "Deep Feeling" and "Blues for Hawaiians" respectively, both of which were clearly indebted to "Floyd's Guitar Blues" of nearly twenty years earlier.

41. Or the guitarist might move away from the amplifier during his performance—a device perhaps best exemplified by Guitar Slim, who in his chitlin circuit

stage show of the early 1950s, with a 350-foot lead plugged directly into the band's public address system, would be carried around the hall by valets, out into the parking lot and back again while soloing (Palmer 1991, 665).

42. Or chose deliberately to overdrive their amps for sonic effect; see Palmer 1991.

43. Palmer 1996, 197.

44. The guitarist on this session, Jerry Byrd, became famous for this heightened rubato-style, and used it frequently on his considerable corpus of Hawaiian recordings through the 1950s, up to the present day.

45. Russell 1970.

46. Tosches 1985.

Chapter 6. "How Near, How Far?" (pp. 143–162)

1. See Shea 1990; Lacasse 2000, 125; and Cogan and Clark 2003, 127. The term *echo chamber* was used in the literature of the time more or less generically to describe any manufactured reverb or echo effect, with little regard for how the effect might have been generated.

2. Quoted in Cogan and Clark 2003, 127–128.

3. The recording was used as theme for Dennis Potter's television series *The Singing Detective* (directed by Jon Amiel, 1986), and the accompanying visuals—dark back streets, a pool of light beneath a streetlamp—were well complemented by the recording.

4. R. Sanjek 1988, 239.

5. Lacasse 2000, 121. Lacasse refers this device back to a suggestion made in the 1930s by sound engineer Rudolph Arnheim that a conversation "between a man and himself" might be effected by representing each voice as coming from a different room, the tempter's coming from a narrow cabin, the warning voice of conscience from a resonant room (Arnheim 1936, 104). It is perhaps no surprise that the moral voice should have churchlike or "institutional" acoustics.

6. See Waksman 1999, 60, referring to Lucy O'Brien 1995, 37, 42–43.

7. Sean Cubitt 1984, 212–213.

8. We might further add Tina Turner's partnership with Ike, Kylie Minogue's association with Stock, Aiken and Waterman, and various performers with Phil Spector.

9. Tosches 1985, 1–21.

10. See Daniel Pick (2000) for a discussion of the Svengali figure in modern culture.

11. Sievert 1977 (at time of writing this interview is accessible online at Guitar Player Magazine's archives at http://www.guitarplayer.com/archive/artists/lespaul 77.shtml).

12. Shaugnessy 1993.

13. Waksman 1999.

14. Sievert 1977, 58. See also Waksman 1999, 58.

15. Sievert 1977, 59.

16. Indeed, when I first encountered the Les Paul–Mary Ford recordings twenty five years after they were made, I had difficulty believing that they in fact dated from the very early 1950s, so contemporary-sounding and bright was the production, notwithstanding that the musical styles so clearly seemed to belong to the pre–rock 'n' roll era. Even the earlier disc-recorded songs such as "Little Rock Getaway" display a degree of clarity unmatched by other recordings of the time. Paul was able

to achieve astonishing clarity by using extra-large discs, recording at 78 rpm. Using 17-inch discs he was able to use just the outside of the disc, where the highs were better recorded. "That gave me a lot of room, and I was burnin' up those discs. That's why the quality was so great. I was going at 78 with the EQ of 33⅓, so when my records came out, they were hotter than a skunk" (Sievert 1977, 61–62).

17. Anderton 1985, 34; cited in Lacasse 2000, 134.

18. Laurence and Rypinski 1978, 38.

19. Sievert 1977, 58.

20. Laurence and Rypinski 1978, 37.

21. Laurence and Rypinski 1978, 56.

22. Laurence and Rypinski 1978, 56.

23. See chapter 1.

24. Sievert 1977, 61–62. See chapter 2 for a medieval instance of the perception of a virtual extra voice,

25. Sievert 1977, 62. It is a strange conceit. The early postwar years in the United States and elsewhere were a period of widespread faith in technological marvels, as military technology entered the mainstream in the form of consumer goods and industrial technology. Many people returning from the services possessed a practical knowledge of electronics and military technology in general, and Paul enjoyed a reputation as both musician and inventor. The device of the spectral second voice offstage was a kind of guessing game, or like a trick of an illusionist or mentalist.

26. Hillman 1990, 47.

27. Waksman 1999, 65–66.

28. Brackett 2000, 7.

29. Bakhtin 1984, 78–85; quoted in Bracket 2000, 7.

30. Bakhtin 1984, 78–85; quoted in Bracket 2000, 7.

31. Shaugnessey 1993, 148.

32. Shaugnessey 1993, 150.

33. It remains the case that female pop singers are frequently represented in popular music mythologies as being under the dominion of powerful male producers. See for example the near biopic *Glitter* (2001, directed by Vondie Curtis-Hall), in which Mariah Carey's character is seen as the (uncomplaining) property of one unscrupulous deejay/producer or another.

34. Shaugnessey 1993. 196.

35. Waksman 1999, 59–60.

36. Writes Shaugnessey (1993): "Mary contributed a lively chorus of harmonies as well as the singular sound of her pulsating rhythm guitar (though to this day Les refuses to give public credit to Mary's splendid strumming on this or any of their joint recording ventures" (186).

37. The highly public Paul-Ford marriage ended in acrimonious divorce in the early 1960s. In an ironic twist, Foy Willing, the "cowboy" singer of "Blue Shadows on the Trail" referred to elsewhere here was named as correspondent. After the divorce Ford toured with Willing for a period, performing "a knockoff of the Les Paul/Mary Ford act" (Shaugnessey 1993, 251).

38. Toop 1999, 106.

39. Kienzle 1999 (unpaginated).

40. Kienzle 1999 (unpaginated).

41. In the film *The Girl Can't Help It* (directed by Frank Tashlin, 1957) a drunken Tom Ewell hallucinates London sitting next to him at the bar, singing to him alone. As the music fades in deepening reverb, so the image of London fades into the ether. Both the sonic and visual fade-out enact mythic Echo's wasting away.

42. Toop 1999, 106.

43. In early 1951 Ingle and his then band, the Frantic Four, toured the United Kingdom, with Peter Sellers as a support act. One wonders to what extent Ingle's stage act and recordings influenced the craziness of *The Goon Show*.

44. See Toop 1999, 137–141 for a discussion of ahbez.

45. Samuelson 1997 (unpaginated).

46. Similar interjections and mock arguments between singers and accompanists can be heard on Spike Jones's recordings; see, for example, Spike Jones and the City Slickers' "Riders in the Sky" (1949), in which the lead and backup singer converse: "When do I come in old timer?"/ "In this song it don't matter, partner! Go ahead, sing!" Later, after the lead sings the phrase "on horses snorting fire," the backup singer asks, "Is that *possible*?" and later asks rhetorically, in heavily accented English, "*This* is a cowboy legend? Oy!!" As with Red Ingle's "Serutan Yob," the backup singer enacts a kind of "disobedient Echoic" to the lead.

47. See Hayward 1999a for a discussion of the deterritorializing, interplanetary aspects to this particular recording and its ability to destroy airborne alien invaders in the film *Mars Attacks*.

48. The strict "whiteness" of Whitman's recording persona is even more pointed when it is considered in context: his label Imperial recorded mainly R & B music and later introduced Little Richard and Fats Domino to international pop audiences. Whitman himself was from the Deep South, and his name, for all that it suggested the cowboy persona, could just have readily belonged to a southern R & B performer (think of Lightnin' Slim, Guitar Slim, or pulp writer Iceberg Slim). Indeed, while Whitman's vocalizing displays an effortless quality, it is markedly without swing inflections or blue notes of any sort. In the context of postwar West Coast pop music, Whitman's work stands out as a throwback to pre-jazz, pre-blues styles. It should be noted too that the spatial derangements of Whitman's "Indian Love Call" are by no means unusual in his 1950s work: his "Cattle Call" and "Love Song of the Waterfall," for example, both similarly make sport of western spatialities.

Chapter 7. "Off the Wall" (pp. 163–177)

1. Date unknown, taped interview with Phil and Marshall Chess, broadcast on US public radio; transcription taken from WGBH website, http://www.wgbh.org/, March 1, 1998.

2. See Gillett 1983 and other works cited in chapter 1.

3. Evan Eisenberg (1982) traces three generations of producer in the field of Western classical music recording. The first generation is typified by Fred Gaisberg, who recorded the likes of Caruso, Chaliapin, Elgar, Menuhin. A combined engineer and businessman, his aim was primarily to get "the best musicians to record and to [see] to it that the discs were without serious blemish"(95). The next generation is typified by Walter Legge, who recorded Elisabeth Schwarzkopf and Herbert von Karajan. Legge saw himself as being in the Gaisberg tradition, but as a much more interventionist producer. He put Schwarzkopf on a "super-rich diet of historic discs," and rehearsed her through pieces of music "bar by bar, word by word, inflection by inflection." With Karajan, similarly, he worked through collections of discs, borrowing promiscuously to assemble ideas prior to making recordings. The recordings themselves would then be assembled from a large number of takes. The successor to Legge is John Culshaw, active in the late nineteen sixties, and who "was condemned by some for a production technique that brazenly (by classical-music standards) pulled out the stops of the studio apparatus. Where Gaisberg was content to take a sound photograph, Legge to extract an impossibly perfect performance,

Culshaw wanted to make something new: a record that was deeply and unabashedly a record" (98).

4. See Gillett 1983, 413.

5. See Dixon and Godrich 1970, Porterfield 1992; and Oliver 1984 (especially chapter 9).

6. N. Cohen 1972: "'I'm a Record Man,' Uncle Art Reminisces," *John Edwards Memorial Foundation Quarterly*, no. 8:18–22; quoted in Oliver 1984, 265.

7. See Guralnick (1981) for interviews with Charlie Rich, Charlie Feathers and Carl Perkins as well as Guralnick (1989) for interviews with Charlie Feathers, Jack Clement, Charlie Rich and Phillips himself.

8. See Palmer 1981, 233–235; and Guralnick 1989, 330–332.

9. Guralnick 1989, 334–335.

10. Guralnick 1989, 328.

11. J. R. Cash 1997, 71.

12. Dirty guitar sounds were not restricted to the players at Phillips's studio. John Lee Hooker, then in Detroit, Muddy Waters and Elmore James in Chicago, Goree Carter in Houston and Guitar Slim in New Orleans were all playing electric guitar in juke joints and clubs using, for the time, unprecedented volume levels with extremely "thick" distortion. Palmer credits Willie Johnson and Pat Hare—both Memphis Recording Studio/Sun artists—as being the originators of the power chord, "one of the most basic gambits in the rock 'n' roll guitarist's arsenal" (1991, 661).

13. See Kloosterman and Quispel (1990), who argue that blacks in the south in particular were obliged by overt and covert racism to refrain from acts and behaviors that might be felt as "impudent" or "uppity." Such things as a good job, the ownership of land or the possession of any special personal capabilities were likely to be considered as threats by racist whites and might well lead to retaliatory violence.

14. From W. C. Handy, *Father of the Blues* (New York: Macmillan, 1941); quoted in Palmer 1981, 45.

15. Palmer 1996, 200–201.

16. Palmer 1981, 158, gives the date as "early in 1948," while Campbell and White place it in November, 1947 (http://hubcap.clemson.edu/~campber/aristocrat.html, 8/1/2001).

17. Palmer 1981, 160.

18. Regarding the reverb arrangements at Chess, researcher Robert Campbell writes:

Universal Recording, which was the studio that Aristocrat and Chess relied on in most cases (up until the construction of the Termar/Chess/Sheldon Recording Studio in 1957—three names, one studio) had an echo system operating as early as 1946. It involved playback and re-recording in the bathroom next to the studio!

Leonard Chess also had a homemade echo/reverb setup by 1950. It consisted of playback into one end of a length of concrete sewer pipe and re-recording from the other end. At least I have heard this from a number of sources. "All Night Long" by Muddy Waters has been put forward as the classic example. "Blues at Twilight" (the echo-fied version of an earlier recording titled "Slumber" by Tom Archia) seems to be another. (e-mail to the author, March 16, 1999)

19. Pop and jazz electric guitarists tended to play in the middle and upper registers, using mostly the top four strings of the guitar. Significant exceptions were to be found in hillbilly and related music including Arthur Smith's instrumental "Guitar Boogie" and in the playing of Zeke Turner, whose simple bass-string figures lent such character to Delmore Brothers recordings, including the influential "Blues

Stay Away From Me." Porky Freeman began adapting boogie bass patterns to the electric guitar in the mid-1940s, and Junior Barnard, guitarist with Bob Wills's band through much of the late 1940s used a particularly "grungy" sound on passages that worked their way down to the low registers (which would prompt the exultant commentary from Wills, "Nasty!" perhaps in unconscious acknowledgment of the genital or scatological associations of the low register).

Country acoustic players, both black and white, had frequently favored the bass strings. Jimmie Rodgers's only recorded guitar solo (on "Muleskinner Blues"), and Hank Williams's solo on "My Bucket's Got a Hole in It" both favor the bottom strings. Maybelle Carter's distinctive bass-string runs on Carter Family records crucially influenced the country and bluegrass picking that followed. Among country blues players, Blind Blake, Fred McDowell, Lonnie Johnson, Blind Willie McTell and Son House did some of their most effective, atmospheric work on the bottom strings.

The combined efforts of all these players served to push guitar sounds away from the "stringy," organic sound of acoustic guitar, and equally away from the muted tones favoured by jazz and jazz-pop electric players.

20. Around this time, 1950, we begin to see representations in movies of recording studios as places of concentration, of this very inwardness. The performer sits in a semidarkened studio, watched through the glass by engineers and onlookers in the control room. *Young Man With a Horn* (directed by Michael Curtiz, 1950) may be the first of many films that feature a key moment in a recording studio. In later films, such as *Jailhouse Rock* (directed by Richard Thorpe, 1957) the musician hero suffers an initial failure in connecting with some inner quality. The moment is usually marked by the manifest indifference of the engineers or backing musicians. Eventually he or she succeeds, and there follows a run on discs in the record store. "We've got a hit on our hands!" says the promoter/manager figure. Variants of this scene have become set pieces of the music biopic, and continue to crop up in films right up to the present.

Chapter 8. *"Train I Ride" (pp. 178–212)*

1. "Walkin' the Boogie" was released on Chess. Charles Shaar Murray implies it was recorded in Detroit, either with Bernie Besman or Joe Von Battle (1999, 525), but Cohodas (2000) firmly locates the recording at Chess itself: "[Hooker] didn't consider himself bound to any one company, and he made records for a number of labels at once, changing his name as needed. . . . Leonard [Chess] signed Hooker to make some records in Chicago, and one of his tunes was a variation on the successful 'Boogie Chillen,' 'Walkin' the Boogie'" (67).

2. Palmer 1981, 210.

3. Palmer 1981, 210.

4. Palmer 1991, 210.

5. Other Chicago blues and R & B recordings roughly contemporaneous with "Juke" also make use of delay. Robert L. Campbell writes:

Some echo effects not achieved by such crude means as Leonard's sewer pipe can be heard on United States recordings by Tab Smith, the Four Blazes, and others. For instance, "The Perfect Woman" by the Four Blazes (recorded 1952) has both echo and overdubbing. You can hear an alternate version on the recent Delmark CD that was rejected at the time because of a mismatch in the echo between the basic Four Blazes recording and the overdubbed tenor sax by Eddie Chamblee that makes them sound thoroughly bizarre in combination. These sessions were recorded at Universal, by the way—perhaps still using the bathroom in 1952. (e-mail to the author, March 16, 1999)

6. "Juke" might suffice as a landmark rock recording for other reasons: the song does not have a "take-off" solo featuring extended sequential improvisation; rather, each verse establishes a different, but basically simple riff that is worked throughout that particular verse. Indeed, each verse could be the "head" for a separate song. The textural/dynamic/spatial regime does continually change throughout the song, however, and as noted above, the song becomes more "animate" as it progresses. The title of the song, "Juke" is also fitting, given the importance of the charged sonic space of juke joint and the jukebox.

7. There is a strong tendency to view landmark recordings strictly within their *generic* contexts (as located within a jazz, country or blues lineage, say) while ignoring contemporaneous happenings in Tin Pan Alley—as though the recordings were made without reference to or awareness of sounds and practices elsewhere. It would seem unlikely, however, that in the making of "Juke," Jacobs, Chess and especially Putnam would not have mentioned, or at least have had somewhere in the back of their minds the million-selling, also heavily sound-processed harmonica antecedent provided by The Harmonicats.

8. These tunes might be grouped in a larger category of jukebox hits from the late 1940s and early 1950s that includes Pee Wee Crayton's "Blues after Hours," Sonny Thompson's "Long Gone," the Delmore Brothers' "Blues Stay Away From Me," Willie Dixon's "Walkin' the Blues," Jimmy and Walter's "Easy" and others. Each features a distinctive "lazy" walking bass or guitar figure and a "low down" vocal or reverberant instrumental lead (sometimes with the addition of deeply reverberant footsteps). The suggestion is of a lonely urban figure walking home late at night, maybe half drunk, through deserted city streets. The flip side of Les Paul and Mary Ford's original "How High the Moon" single, "Walkin' and Whistlin'" was one such tune. They may also be related, more distantly, to the Harmonicats' pop hit of 1947 "Peg o' My Heart" (see chapter 6).

9. Paul clearly distinguished between reverb and delay. He described his long wrestle with the problem: "I'd discussed this with a lot of people, and they said, 'Well, why doncha put a speaker on the one end of the room and the mike on the other end?' and I said, 'Now look. That's reverb . . . I've already got that.'" At a drinking session with buddies in 1944, Paul was still preoccupied with the delay problem. Finally he was invited by his engineer friends to air his thoughts:

I says, "If you were on top of the Alps and you were to yell out and you'd say, 'Hello there' and 'hello there' would come back. Now that's what I want."

The guy says, "You mean if you put the playback arm behind the record arm?"

I says, "That's it!" (Laurence and Rypinski 1978, 54)

Paul rushed directly to his studio.

We had taken that arm off and I heard the engineer holler at me, "It won't work, you're going into oscillation." . . .I said, "It's gonna work . . . we can get 'tock *tock*' or we can get 'tock tock tock tock tock tock' . . . we can run these boxcars all the way round that 16-inch disc . . ."

. . . so when we picked up on this echo delay, this just turned the world upside down . . . you got a sound coming that was just not normal. It's repetitive, but there's a delay *and* a decay. The amount of delay is varied, by the distance of each boxcar that you put on. (Laurence and Rypinski 1978, 54)

Paul was easily able to translate the multiple playback head principle—the "boxcars"—to magnetic-tape technology.

10. See Escott 1992, 15.

11. Escott 1992, 54.

12. Guralnick 1994.

13. Iain Chambers in a brief discussion of Sun-period Presley writes:
Listening to the recordings that Elvis made for Sam Phillips in Memphis in the mid-1950s and comparing them with those made a little later for the same Sun label by Carl Perkins, the magisterial power of Presley's performance is unmistakable. With Perkins . . . the . . . country and blues elements remain less integrated; his voice tends to cut across and over the instrumental backing. Presley's voice has a "voluptuous" presence within the music. This is particularly evident if we compare the two singers' versions of "Blue Suede Shoes". . . . It is an aural difference that permits us to appreciate Presley's fundamental importance in white popular music and Roland Barthes' point that in the "grain" of the singing voice it becomes possible to locate a cultural sense. (1985, 37)
In fact, Presley's "Blue Suede Shoes" was recorded after he left Sun, at RCA Studios in New York City, under the guidance of Steve Sholes, RCA's head A & R person (Guralnick 1994. 246). Presley doing "Blue Suede Shoes" was in the tradition of the hastily released cover record, whereby performers on major labels with access to more effective distribution and promotion networks cover promising regional and/or independent hits. Carl Perkins's original version of "Blue Suede Shoes" (which he wrote) was in fact Sun Records' first million-seller, *prior* to Presley's first release on RCA. Presley's major-label cover version was given a huge (accidental) boost when Perkins's career was stalled by a serious car accident—which also kept him off national television programs (on which he had been booked to perform "Blue Suede Shoes," also prior to Presley's celebrated television appearances).

It could indeed be argued that Presley's "Blue Suede Shoes" represents a normalizing of the democratic, anarchic, decentered textures of Sun, by means of an aggrandizement of the centrally located human voice. Presley's singing here, notwithstanding the "voluptuousness" Chambers finds in it, is in the mannered, "boogified" mode and relates just as much (or more) to the mainstream popular tradition of singers like Dean Martin as it does to the Sun Records traditions. The perceived "presence within the music" is arguably more the result of the producer's skillful use of reverb to construct the "romantic," intimate crooner spatiality on a twelve-bar, R & B-like song that cannily combined both teen-oriented and "down home" lyrics. But the purpose here is not to declare any particular recording as better than another—although for this listener, Perkins's "Blue Suede Shoes" outclasses Presley's (an opinion also held by Presley, according to Guralnick [1994. 246]).

14. This may or may not be the first time Phillips used the effect on a lead vocal. Reverb and echo is certainly present on Harmonica Frank Lloyd's vocal on "Rockin' Chair Daddy," released just days before Presley's first Sun session.

It is possible that Phillips borrowed the slapback idea from Dewey Phillips, the Memphis deejay and friend of Sam's (though no relation) who was instrumental in launching Presley's first record. According to Guralnick (1994, 97) Phillips broadcast recordings using a twin turntable arrangement, playing two copies of the record simultaneously, "creating a phased effect that pleased Dewey unless it got so far out of line that he took the needle off both records with a scrawk and announced that he was just going to have to start all over again." This is in essence not dissimilar to how Sam Phillips created his slapback using dual tape recorders.

15. See chapter 6.

16. See Escott 1992, 78; Guralnick 1994, 236.

17. Marcus 1991. Marcus finds the song to be a "hard," "fatalistic" song about the futility of action, in which "there is no protest . . . no revolt, only an absolute almost supernatural loneliness" (171). Presley must confront the bleakness of the "song's point: the uselessness of action, the helplessness of a man who cannot understand his world, let alone master it . . . Presley had his job cut out for him if he was to make the song his own" (173).

18. *Mystery Train* (directed by Jim Jarmusch, 1989). The song appears on the soundtrack, accompanying the train journeys into and out of Memphis that bookend the film.

Both Marcus's and Jarmusch's uses of the song revolve around repeated, intensive listenings to the record. Marcus uses the tools of the literary critic, one who has deeply considered the object over time and Jarmusch's Japanese couple are rockabilly fans travelling to Memphis in order to immerse themselves in the spirit of the place, to access, if possible some residual essence. Again the sensibility is a long-after-the-event phenomenon, and part of the joke of the film is that people from such an apparently remote cultural launching pad should want to or be able to access the Memphian "soul." The *Mystery Train* of the title is a much mediated object; nonetheless, it still holds a magic for the visitors. The couple appear satisfied with what, to the viewer, seems an oddly deserted Memphis. In fact, the tourists are in a privileged position to apprehend the place. They alone can ride the Mystery Train. Its "meaning" is as inescapably historicized for them as it is for Marcus.

19. See Tosches 1985, 58.

20. Indeed, Les Paul first conceived of echo effects as a sequence of boxcars; see note 9.

21. See Mumford 1963.

22. See for example Odum 1936; W. J. Cash 1956; M. O'Brien 1979; Slotkin 1980; Kirby 1986.

23. Guralnick 1989.

24. Marcus 1991, 60–66.

25. Marcus 1991, 64.

26. Marcus 1991, 65.

27. Marcus 1991 65.

28. Marcus 1991, 65–66.

29. Guralnick 1989, 328.

30. Guralnick 1989, 330.

31. Quoted in Guralnick 1989, 332.

32. Guralnick 1989, 333.

33. Leppert and Lipsitz 1990, 266.

34. Leppert and Lipsitz 1990, 267.

35. Mintz and Kellogg 1988.

36. Leppert and Lipsitz 1990, 267, citing Mintz and Kellog 1988, 155.

37. Leppert and Lipsitz 1990, 268.

38. Ehrenreich 1983.

39. Indeed, Escott's (1994) biography of Williams resoundingly confirms and details what was hinted at in earlier biographies (Roger M. Williams 1981; Flippo 1981): that whatever his artistic achievements, in his personal life Williams was a desperately unhappy, largely disempowered alcoholic and sometime drug addict, a battered subject (as well as perpetrator) of considerable physical and psychological abuse.

40. See especially Guralnick 1994.

41. May 1988.

42. May 1988.

43. Guralnick 1989, 333.

44. Guralnick 1989, 338–339.

45. Guralnick 1989, 334.

46. Unlike Presley, Perkins was a seasoned juke joint player *before* he recorded, and unlike most rockabillies, he had developed his unique singing style *before* he ever heard Presley; see Escott 1992, 129.

47. Rosalind Williams 1990.

48. Hugo 1987, 983; quoted in Rosalind Williams 1990, 47.

49. Rosalind Williams 1990, 47.

50. Rosalind Williams 1990, 48.

51. The metaphor of subterraneity is implicitly employed by Dick Hebdige in his subcultural theory and by Grossberg, who sees rock 'n' roll and rock as "[incorporating] itself into the 'belly of the beast.' It is 'internalised but unintegrated,' included within the dominant culture but alien to it, inaccessible; . . . *enclosed, entombed, encysted inside*" (emphasis mine; Grossberg 1984, 235, quoting from Nelson 1978, 57–58.

52. Escott 1992, 130.

53. See, for example, Guralnick 1989, 334.

54. Guralnick 1989, 330.

55. Another version of the same transformation was replayed in the film *Jailhouse Rock* (directed by Richard Thorpe, 1957), in which the singer at first fails in the studio, then succeeds after being told that he should sing from the heart. *Young Man With a Horn* (directed by Michael Curtiz, 1950) may be the first of many films to feature such a key moment in a recording studio.

56. Keil and Feld 1994, 96.

57. Indeed, through the late 1940s and early 1950s Walter and Waters, Rogers and the Aces were known in the Chicago club scene as "the headhunters": appearing at jam sessions with their electric instruments and amps, they had a reputation for repeatedly humiliating jump bands and other blues players in cutting competitions. Walter with his custom-made amp and built-in reverb in particular was able to produce a louder, gutsier and newer sound than entire horn sections. Electric bassist Louis Myers of the Aces told an interviewer:

now you imagine we gone all amplifiers and here's these cats playing the old style, just sitting up there playing drive-along-jimmy no amplifiers. . . .

How could a small four piece group do harm to a big band? . . .We had amplified music . . . we would chop them bands—Walter was playing like forty horns, man. His amplifier would sound like that sometimes, put his echo on and God! Music was hittin' the walls and bouncing back to us and they'd say "them cats sound like a giant band and there ain't but four of them." (quoted in Waksman 1999, 127)

58. Sievert 1977, 62.

59. Keil 1994, 105.

60. Guralnick, 1994, 237.

61. Guralnick 1994, 237.

62. Guralnick 1994, 237.

63. Guralnick 1994, 237.

64. Guralnick 1994, 238.

65. Guralnick 1994, 239.

66. The song also bears resemblance's to Chuck Berry's heavily reverberant "Down Bound Train" of 1955, which in turn recalls "Riders in the Sky" in feel. But like the latter, Berry's song is a stern cautionary tale, drawing directly on nineteenth-century sermonizing traditions. The grim vision of damnation that the drunkard witnesses is heeded; unlike Vincent's unrepentant hot-rodder, the drunkard changes his ways.

67. Perhaps no verbal rendering of frenzied vibration quite rivals Carl Perkins's description of his girlfriend who, when "she gets that rockin' beat" can "shake the polish off her toes" ("Put Your Cat Clothes On" [1958/1974]).

1. Ry Cooder's soundtrack to *Paris, Texas* drew much of its power from invoking precisely this tradition, counterpointing the "haunting" music against the images of down-at-heel Harry Dean Stanton stumbling out of the wilderness.

2. See note 8 to chapter 8.

3. Sanjek 1997, 149.

4. Gillett 1983, 28; quoted in Sanjek 1997, 139.

5. Sanjek 1997, 139.

6. Sanjek 1997, 161.

7. Tosches 1991, 66.

8. Charline Arthur, interview with Bob Allen, quoted in liner notes to "Charline Arthur: Welcome to the Club," Bear Family CD, BCD 16279 AH.

9. Charline Arthur, interview with Bob Allen, quoted in liner notes to "Charline Arthur: Welcome to the Club," Bear Family CD, BCD 16279 AH.

10. Chuck Berry's "Little Queenie" (1959) is an instance, comparatively rare, of a male singer enacting in turns an inner monologue and an "outward" address to a prospective partner. Berry deftly switches between private and public domains through the use of dynamic shifts and verbal clues and by alternately reciting and singing the lyrics; he further emplaces the whole by starting the song well into the story. "There she is *again* [emphasis mine] standing over by the record machine," he sings. (Again? There's a back story here for the listener to impute.) At this point, Berry might be talking to a friend or to himself, although with the famous, "Meanwhile, I was thinking . . ." it becomes clear that the monologue is primarily inner. As with Charline Arthur's "Hamletian" meditation, the issue is largely whether to act or not; when Berry finally comes out, he does much more than simply declare his interest in Little Queenie, performing instead a triumphant call to the broad constituency of the rock 'n' roll faithful, with the "Go! Go! Go, Little Queenie!" The song's territorial range begins with the most intimately private and ends with the global.

11. See Komorowski 1997, 7. See also Escott 1992, especially their chapter 10, "Those who would be king" (169–187).

12. Sanjek 1997, 141.

13. Women rock 'n' rollers, many of them now even more obscure than Charline Arthur, were an important part of touring rock 'n' roll shows. For example, "Alys Lesley" (one of many since forgotten "female Elvises") accompanied Little Richard, Eddie Cochran and Gene Vincent on their legendary 1957 tour of Australia, while Barbara Pittman, though without a hit record to her name, toured with high-powered Sun shows at the height of the rockabilly craze.

Bibliography

⊨◇⊣

Aaronson, B. 1967. Mystic and schizophreniform states and the experience of depth. *Journal for Scientific Study of Religion* 6, no 2:246–252.

Academy of Motion Picture Arts and Sciences, Research Council. 1938. *Motion Picture Sound Engineering*. New York: Van Nostrand.

Allen, Bob. 1984. *George Jones: Saga of an American Singer*. New York: Doubleday Dolphin.

———, ed. 1994. *The Blackwell Guide to Recorded Country Music*. Oxford: Blackwell.

Altman, Rick. 1985. "The evolution of sound technology." In *Film Sound: Theory and Practice*, edited by Elisabeth Weis and John Belton. New York: Columbia University Press.

Anderton, Craig. 1985. *The Digital Delay Handbook*. New York: Amsco Publications.

Arnheim, Rudolph. 1936. *Radio*. Translated by Margaret Ludwig and Herbert Read. New York: Arno Press.

Attali, J. 1985. *Noise: The Political Economy of Music*. Translated by Brian Massumi. Theory and History of Science, vol. 16. Minneapolis: University of Minnesota Press.

Bacon, Tony, ed. 1981. *Rock Hardware: the Instruments, Equipment and Technology of Rock*. Poole, U.K.: Blandford Press.

Bagenal, H., and A. Wood. 1931. *Planning for Good Acoustics*. London: Methuen.

Bakhtin, M. 1984. *Problems of Dostoevsky's Poetics*. Edited and translated by Caryl Emerson. Minneapolis: University of Minnesota Press.

Balazs, Bela. 1985. "Theory of the film: sound." In *Film Sound: Theory and Practice*, edited by Elisabeth Weis and John Belton. New York: Columbia University Press.

Barfield, Owen. 1965. *Saving the Appearances: A Study in Idolatry*. New York: Harcourt Brace Jovanovich.

Barthes, Roland. 1981. *Camera Lucida: Reflections on Photography*. Translated by Richard Howard. London: Fontana Paperbacks.

Bateson, G. 1972. *Steps to an Ecology of Mind*. New York: Ballantine.

Baudrillard, Jean. 1975. *The Mirror of Production*. Saint Louis, Mo.: Telos.

———. 1981. *For a Critique of the Political Economy of the Sign*. Saint Louis, Mo.: Telos.

Bellman, J. 1993. *The Style Hongrois in the Music of Western Europe*. Boston: Northeastern University Press.

———, ed. 1998. *The Exotic in Western Music*. Boston: Northeastern University Press.

Benjamin, W. 1969. *Illuminations*. New York: Schocken Books.

———. 1986. *Reflections: Essays, Aphorisms, Autobiographical Writing.* Translated by Edmund Jephcott. New York: Schocken Books.

Beranek, L. L. 1962. *Music Acoustics and Architecture.* New York: Wiley.

Berry, Chuck. 1989. *The Autobiography.* London: Faber and Faber.

Beville, M. 1980. "Extra facilities." In *Sound Recording Practice,* edited by J. Borwick. London: Oxford University Press.

Bisset, A. 1987. *Black Roots, White Flowers: A History of Jazz in Australia.* Revised ed. Sydney, Australia: ABC Enterprises.

Blacking J. 1973. *How Musical is Man?* Seattle: University of Washington Press.

Born, G. and D. Hesmondhalgh, eds. 2000. *Western Music and Its Others: Difference, Representation and Appropriation in Music.* Berkeley and Los Angeles: University of California Press.

Borwick, J. 1977a. A Century of recording: part 1, the first 50 years. *Gramophone* 54, no. 647:1621–1622.

———. 1977b. A Century of recording: part 2, the second 50 years. *Gramophone* 54, no. 648:1761–1765.

Brackett, D. 2000. *Interpreting Popular Music.* Berkeley and Los Angeles: University of California Press.

Broven, J. J. 1974. *Walking to New Orleans.* Bexhill-on-Sea, U.K.: Blues Unlimited.

Buck, Elizabeth. 1993. *Paradise Remade: The Politics of Culture and History in Hawai'i.* Philadelphia: Temple University Press.

Bufwack, M. A. 1995. "Girls with guitars—and fringe and sequins and rhinestones, silk, lace and leather." In *Readin' Country Music: Steel Guitars, Opry Stars and Honky Tonk Bars,* edited by C. Tichi. *South Atlantic Quarterly* 94, no. 1:173–216. Durham, N.C.: Duke University Press.

Bullfinch's Mythology. 1970. New York: Crowell.

Cabrera, Densil. 1997. Resonating sound art and the aesthetics of room resonance. *Convergence* 3, no. 4:108–137.

Cameron E. W., ed. 1980. *Sound And The Cinema: The Coming of Sound to American Film.* New York: Redgrave.

Campbell, Joseph. 1974. *The Masks of God: Occidental Mythology.* London: Souvenir.

Cash, John R., with Patrick Carr. 1997. *Cash: The Autobiography.* New York: HarperCollins.

Cash, W. J. 1956. *The Mind of the South.* New York: Doubleday Anchor.

Cateforis, T. 1993. "Total trash": analysis and post-punk music. *Journal of Popular Music Studies* 5:39–57.

Chambers, I. 1985. *Urban Rhythms: Pop Music and Popular Culture.* London: Macmillan.

Charles, Ray, and D. Ritz. 1978. *Brother Ray: Ray Charles' Own Story.* New York: Dial.

Chernoff, J. 1979. *African Rhythms and African Sensibility.* Chicago: University of Chicago Press.

Chilton J. 1992. *Let the Good Times Roll: The Story of Louis Jordan and His Music.* London: Quartet Books.

Chion, M. 1994. *Audio-Vision: Sound on Screen.* Edited and translated by Claudia Gorbman. New York: Columbia University Press.

Chiron Dictionary of Greek and Roman Mythology. 1994. Translated by E. Burr. Wilmette, Ill.: Chiron.

Cogan, J., and W. Clark. 2003. *Temples of Sound: Inside the Great Recording Studios.* San Francisco, Calif.: Chronicle Books.

Cohodas, Nadine. 2000. *Spinning Blues into Gold: the Chess Brothers and the Legendary Chess Records.* New York: St. Martin's.

Cohn, Nik. 1989. *Ball the Wall: Nik Cohn in the Age of Rock.* London: Picador.

Coker, J. 1964. *Improvising Jazz*. Englewood Cliffs, N.J.: Prentice Hall.

Connell, J., and C. Gibson. 2003. *Sound Tracks: Popular Music, Identity and Place*. London and New York: Routledge.

Conte, Pat. 1995. Liner notes to CD *The Secret Museum of Mankind*. Vol. 1. Yazoo, 7004.

Coyle, R., and J. Coyle. 1995. Aloha Australia: Hawaiian music in Australia (1920–1955). *Perfect Beat* 2, no. 2:31–63.

Cremer, L., and H. Muller. 1978. *Principles and Applications of Room Acoustics*. Vol. 1. London: Applied Science.

Cronin, P. 1994. The Sun King: Interview with Scotty Moore. *Country Guitar* (winter): 59–64.

Cubitt, S. 1984. "Maybellene": meaning and the listening subject. *Popular Music* 4: 207–224.

———. 1997. "Rolling and tumbling: Digital erotics and the culture of narcissism." In *Sexing the Groove: Popular Music and Gender*, edited by S. Whitely. London: Routledge.

Culshaw, J. 1980. "The role of the producer." In *Sound Recording Practice*, edited by J. Borwick. London: Oxford University Press.

Cunningham, Mark. 1996. *Good Vibrations: A History of Record Production*. Surrey, U.K.: Castle Communications.

Davidson, L. S. 1989. "Frontiers and Femininity: Dreams and the Twelfth-Century Renaissance." Ph.D. diss. University of Sydney.

Davis, Miles, with Q. Troupe. 1990. *Miles: The Autobiography*. New York: Touchstone.

Deleuze, G., and F. Guattari. 1987. *A Thousand Plateaus: Capitalism and Schizophrenia*. Minneapolis: University of Minnesota Press.

Devitt, R., and P. Doyle. 2000. "Lost riders of the empire: Non-US singing cowboy music." In *Changing Sounds, Proceedings of International Association for the Study of Popular Music Annual Conference, 1999*. Sydney, Australia: UTS. 145–149.

Dixon, Robert M. W., and John Godrich. 1970. *Recording the Blues*. New York: Stein and Day.

Doane, Mary Ann. 1985. "The voice in the cinema: the articulation of body and space." In *Film Sound: Theory and Practice*, edited by Elisabeth Weis and John Belton. New York: Columbia University Press.

Doyle, P. 1999. Flying Saucer Rock 'n' roll: the Australian press confronts early rock 'n' roll. *Perfect Beat* (July).

Duby, G. 1986. *History of Medieval Art, 980–1440*. New York: Rizzoli.

Ehrenreich, B. 1983. *The Hearts of Men: American Dreams and the Flight from Commitment*. London: Pluto.

Eisenberg, E. 1988. *The Recording Angel: Music, Records and Culture From Aristotle to Zappa*. London: Picador Pan.

Eliade, M., ed. 1987. *The Encyclopedia of Religion*. New York: Macmillan.

Elias, Norbert. 1994. *The Civilizing Process: The History of Manners*. Translated by Edmund Jephcott. Oxford: Blackwell.

Ennis, P. H. 1992. *The Seventh Stream: the Emergence of Rocknroll in American Popular Music*. Wesleyan University Press; Hanover, N.H.: University Press of New England.

Epstein, J. 1985. "Slow motion sound." In *Film sound: Theory and Practice*, edited by Elisabeth Weis and John Belton. New York: Columbia University Press.

Escott, C., with Martin Hawkins. 1992. *Good Rockin' Tonight: Sun Records and the Birth of Rock 'n' Roll*. London: Virgin Books.

———, with G. Merritt, and W. MacEwen. 1994. *Hank Williams: The Biography*. Boston: Little, Brown.

———. 1996. *Tattooed on their Tongues: A Journey through the Backrooms of American Music*. New York: Schirmer Books.

Evans, D. 1970. Afro-American one-stringed instruments. *Western Folklore*, no. 29:229–245.

Farrell, G. 1998. "The early days of the gramophone industry in India: historical social and musical perspectives." In *The Place of Music*, edited by A. Leyshon, D. Matless and G. Revill. New York: Guilford.

Fast S. 2001. *In the Houses of the Holy: Led Zeppelin and the Power of Rock Music*. New York: Oxford University Press.

Feld, S. 2000. "Anxiety and celebration: mapping the discourses of world music." In *Changing Sounds: New Directions and Configurations in Popular Music, Proceedings of the International Association for the Study of Popular Music 10th International Conference, 1999*, edited by Tony Mitchell and Peter Doyle. Sydney, Australia: University of Technology.

Fischer, Lucy. 1980. "*Applause*: the visual and acoustic landscape." In *Sound and the Cinema*, edited by E. W. Cameron. New York: Redgrave.

Flippo, Chet. 1981. *Your Cheatin' Heart: A Biography of Hank Williams*. New York: St. Martin's.

Forte, D. 1988. Ry Cooder: in search of the big note. *Guitar Player* 23 (March): 32–35.

Fox, Aaron A. 1992. The jukebox of history: narratives of loss and desire in the discourse of country music. *Popular Music* 11, no. 1:53–72.

Frith S., and H. Horne. 1987. *Art into Pop*. London: Methuen.

———. 1988. *Music for Pleasure: Essays in the Sociology of Pop*. Cambridge: Polity Press.

———. 1990. What is good music? *Canadian University Music Review* 10, no. 2:92–102.

Gaisberg, Fred. 1943. *Music on Record*. London: Robert Hale.

Gelatt, R. 1977. *The Fabulous Phonograph*. London: Cassell.

Gillett, C. 1975. *Making Tracks: The Story of Atlantic Records*. London: Panther.

———. 1983. *The Sound of The City: The Rise of Rock and Roll*. Revised ed. London: Souvenir.

Ginell, Cary. 1994. *Milton Brown and the Founding of Western Swing*. Champaign: University of Illinois Press.

Goffman, Erving. 1969. *Presentation of the Self in Everyday Life*. Harmondsworth, Middlesex, Eng.: Penguin.

———. 1971. *Relations in Public: Microstudies of the Public Order*. New York: Harper and Row.

Gordon, R. 2003. *Can't Be Satisfied: The Life and Times of Muddy Waters*. London: Pimlico.

Grant, M., and J. Hazel. 1973. *Gods and Mortals in Classical Mythology*. Springfield, Mass.: Merriam.

Green, Douglas B. 1996. Liner notes to *Stampede! Western Music's Late Golden Era*. Rounder CD 1103.

———. 2002. *Singing in the Saddle: A History of the Singing Cowboy*. Nashville, Tenn.: Country Music Foundation Press and Vanderbilt University Press.

Grey, Zane. 1988. *Riders of the Purple Sage*, Bath, U.K.: Chivers Press.

Grissim, J. 1970. *Country Music: White Man's Blues*. New York: Paperback Library.

Grossberg, L. 1984. Another boring day in paradise: rock 'n' roll and the empowerment of everyday life. *Popular Music*, no 4:224–258.

———. 1992. *We Gotta Get Out of This Place: Popular Conservatism and Postmodern Culture*. New York: Routledge.

———. 1996. "The space of culture, the power of space. In *The Post-Colonial Question: Common Skies, Divided Horizons*, edited by I. Chambers and L. Curti. New York: Routledge.

Guralnick, P. 1981. *Feel Like Going Home: Portraits in Blues and Rock 'n' Roll.* New York: Vintage Books.

——, (1986) *Sweet Soul Music: Rhythm and Blues and the Southern Dream of Freedom.* New York: Harper and Row.

——. 1989. *Lost Highway: Journeys and Arrivals of American Musicians.* New York: Harper and Row.

——. 1994. *Last Train to Memphis: The Rise of Elvis Presley.* Boston: Little Brown.

——. 1999. *Careless Love: The Unmaking of Elvis Presley.* Boston: Little Brown.

Handzo, S. 1985. "Appendix: a narrative glossary of film sound technology." In *Film Sound: Theory and Practice,* edited by Elisabeth Weis and John Belton. New York: Columbia University Press.

Hannusch, J. 1985. *I Hear You Knockin': The Sound of New Orleans Rhythm and Blues.* Ville Platte, La.: Swallow Publications.

Harbison, R. 1989. *Eccentric Spaces.* London: Secker and Warburg.

Hardy, P., and D. Laing, eds. 1976a. *The Encyclopaedia of Rock,* Vol. 1. London: Panther.

——. 1976b. *Encyclopaedia of Rock,* Vol. 2. London: Panther.

——. 1990. *The Faber Companion to 20th-Century Popular Music.* London: Faber and Faber.

Harker, D. 1980. *One for the Money: Politics and Popular Song.* London: Hutchinson Group.

Hayward, P. 1999a. Interplanetary soundclash: music, technology and territorialisation in *Mars Attacks. Convergence* 5, no. 1:47–58.

——, ed. 1999b. *Widening the Horizon: Exoticism in Post-War Popular Music.* Sydney, Australia: John Libbey.

——. 2000. Exotica, ambience and pacificism: a dialogue with Mike Cooper. *Perfect Beat* 5, no. 1:81–88.

Hebdige, D. 1979. *Subculture: The Meaning of Style.* London: Methuen.

Hesmondhalgh, D., and G. Born, eds. 2000. *Western Music and Its Others: Difference Representation and Appropriation in Music.* Berkeley and Los Angeles: University of California Press.

Hewitt, R. 1983. Black through white: Hoagy Carmichael and the cultural reproduction of racism. *Popular Music,* no. 3:33–50.

Higham, C. 1961. *Teenbeat.* London: Horwitz.

Hill, T. 1991. The Enemy within: censorship in rock music in the 1950s. *South Atlantic Quarterly* 90, no. 4:675–707.

Hillman, J. 1990. *The Essential James Hillman: A Blue Fire.* Introduced and edited by Thomas Moore. London: Routledge.

Hoggart, R. 1957. *The Uses of Literacy.* London: Chatto and Windus.

Hollander, J. 1986. *The Figure of Echo: A Mode of Allusion in Milton and After.* Berkeley: University of California Press.

Hosakawa, S. 1984. The Walkman effect. *Popular Music,* no. 4:165–180.

——. 1999a. "Martin Denny and the development of musical exotica." In *Widening the Horizon: Exoticism in Post War Popular Music,* edited by P. Hayward. Sydney, Australia: John Libbey.

——. 1999b. "Soy sauce music: Haruomi Hosono and Japanese self-orientalism." In *Widening the Horizon: Exoticism in Post War Popular Music,* edited by P. Hayward. Sydney, Australia: John Libbey.

Hoskyns, B. 1991. *From a Whisper to a Scream: the Great Voices in Popular Music.* London: Hammersmith.

Hughes, Ted. 1997. *Tales From Ovid: Twenty-four Passages from the Metamorphoses.* London: Faber and Faber.

Hugo, V. 1987. *Les Miserables: A New Unabridged Translation*. Translated by N. MacAfee. New York: Signet Classics.

Humphrey, M. 1977a. Playboy days, part 2. *Old Time Music*, no. 24:17–20.

———. 1977b. Playboy days, part 3. *Old Time Music*, no. 25:25–27.

I'll Take My Stand: The South and the Agrarian Tradition. 1977. By Twelve Southerners. [Louis D. Rubin, John Crowe Ransom, Donald Davidson et al]. Baton Rouge: Louisiana State University Press.

James, B. 1955. *Hi Fi for Pleasure*. London: Phoenix House.

John, Dr. [Mac Rebennack], with Jack Rummel. 1995. *Under a Hoodoo Moon: The Life of Dr John the Night Tripper*. New York: St Martin's Griffin.

Johnson, B. 2000. *The Inaudible Music: Jazz Gender and Australian Modernity*. Sydney, Australia: Currency Press.

Johnson, M. 1987. *The Body in the Mind: The Bodily Basis of Meaning, Imagination and Reason*. Chicago: University of Chicago Press.

Jones, S. 1992. *Rock Formation: Music, Technology and Mass Communication*. Newbury Park, Calif.: Sage.

———. 1993. Sound, space & digitization. In *Media Information Australia*, no. 67 (February): 83–90.

Kanahele G. S., ed. 1979. *Hawaiian Music and Musicians: An Illustrated History*. Honolulu: University Press of Hawaii.

Kawin, Bruce F. 1978. *Mindscreen: Bergman, Godard and the First Person Film*. Princeton, N.J.: Princeton University Press.

Keil, Charles. 1994. *Music Grooves: Essays and Dialogues / Charles Keil & Steven Feld*. Chicago: University of Chicago Press.

Keillor, G. 1974. Onward and upward with the arts: at the Opry. *New Yorker* 50, no. 11:May 6.

Kennedy, R., and R. McNutt. 1999. *Little Labels—Big Sound: Small Record Companies and the Rise of American Music*. Bloomington: Indiana University Press.

Kienzle, Rich. 1999. Liner notes to *Swingin' on the Strings: The Speedy West & Jimmy Bryant Collection*. Vol. 2. Razor and Tie CD.

Kirby, J. T. 1986. *Media-Made Dixie: The South in the American Imagination*. Athens: University of Georgia Press.

Kloosterman, R. C. and C. Quispel. 1990. Not just the same old show on my radio: An analysis of the role of radio in the diffusion of black music among whites in the south of the United States of America, 1920 to 1960. *Popular Music* 9, no. 2:151–164.

Komorowski, A. 1997. Liner notes to *Barbara Pittman: Getting Better All the Time*. Charly CDCP 8319.

Kraft, J. P. 1996. *Stage to Studio: Musicians and the Sound Revolution, 1890–1950*. Baltimore, Md.: Johns Hopkins University Press.

Krautheimer, R. 1975. *Early Christian and Byzantine Architecture*. Harmondsworth, Middlesex, Eng.: Penguin.

Lacasse, S. 2000. *"Listen to My Voice": The Evocative Power of Vocal Staging in Recorded Rock Music and Other Forms of Vocal Expression*. Ph.D. diss. University of Liverpool.

Lamb, A. 1991. Metaphysics of wire music. *New Music Articles*, no 9:3–6.

Laurence, P. and B. Rypinski. 1978. Interview with Les Paul. *Audio* (December): 36–60.

Leppert, R. 2002. "Cultural contradictions, idolatry and the piano virtuoso: Franz Liszt." In *Piano Roles: A New History of the Piano*, edited by J. Parakilas. New Haven: Yale University Press.

Leppert, R., and G. Lipsitz. 1990. "Everybody's lonesome for somebody": age, the body and experience in the music of Hank Williams." *Popular Music* 9, no. 3:259–274.

Levine, L. W. 1988. *Highbrow/Lowbrow: The Emergence of Cultural Hierarchy in America* Cambridge, Mass.: Harvard University Press.

Lévy-Bruhl, Lucien. 1910. *How Natives Think.* New York: Washington Square Press.

Lewis, Myra, with Murray Silver. 1982. *Great Balls of Fire: The Uncensored Story of Jerry Lee Lewis.* New York: Morrow.

Leyshon, A., D. Matless, and G. Revill, eds. 1998. *The Place of Music.* New York: Guilford Press.

Locke, R. P. 1991. Constructing the Oriental other: Saint-Saëns's *Samson et Dalila. Cambridge Opera Journal* 3, no. 3:261–302.

———. 1993. Reflections on Orientalism in opera and musical theatre. *Opera Quarterly* 10, no. 1:49–73.

Loewenstein, J. 1984. *Responsive Readings: Versions of Echo in Pastoral, Epic, and the Jonsonian Masque.* New Haven: Yale University Press.

Lomax, A. 1968. *Folk Song Style and Culture.* Washington, D.C.: American Association for the Advancement of Science.

———. 1993. *The Land Where the Blues Began.* New York: Pantheon.

Lord, A. B. 1964. *The Singer of Tales.* Cambridge, Mass.: Harvard University Press.

Lord, P., and D. Templeton. 1986. *Architecture of Sound: Designing Places of Assembly.* London: Architectural Press.

Lubin, Tom. 1996. The sounds of science: the development of the recording studio as instrument. *NARAS Journal* 7, no. 1:41–101.

Mackenzie, C. 1966. *My Life and Times, Octave 5, 1915–1923.* London: Chatto and Windus.

———. 1967. *My Life and Times, Octave 6, 1923–1930.* London: Chatto and Windus.

Malone, Bill C. 1982. "Honky Tonk: the music of the Southern working class." In *Folk Music and the Modern Sound,* edited by W. Ferris and M. L. Hart. Jackson: University Press of Mississippi.

———. 1985. *Country Music, U.S.A.* Revised ed. Austin: University of Texas Press.

———. 1993. *Singing Cowboys and Musical Mountaineers: Southern Culture and the Roots of Country Music.* Athens: University of Georgia Press.

Marco, Guy, ed. 1993. *Encyclopedia of Recorded Sound in the United States.* New York: Garland.

Marcus, G. 1990, *Lipstick Traces: A Secret History of the Twentieth Century.* London: Secker and Warburg.

———. 1991, *Mystery Train: Images of America in Rock 'n' Roll Music.* London: Penguin.

———. 1992. *Dead Elvis: A Chronicle of a Cultural Obsession.* London: Penguin.

———. 1997. *The Invisible Republic: Bob Dylan's Basement Tapes.* New York: Henry Holt.

Marre, J., and H. Charlton. 1985. *Beats of the Heart: Popular Music of the World.* London: Pluto Press.

May, E. T. 1988. *Homeward Bound: American Families in the Cold War Era.* New York: Basic Books.

McClary, S. 1991. *Feminine Endings: Music, Gender and Sexuality.* Minneapolis: University of Minnesota Press.

———. 2000. *Conventional Wisdom: The Content of Musical Form.* Berkeley and Los Angeles: University of California Press.

McClary, S., and R. Walser. 1990. "Start making sense! Musicology wrestles with rock." In *On Record: Rock, Pop and the Written Word,* edited by S. Frith and A. Goodwin. London: Routledge.

McLean, D. 1997. *Lone Star Swing: On the Trail of Bob Wills and his Texas Playboys.* London: Jonathan Cape.

Melly, G. 1971. *Revolt Into Style.* London: Pan.

Mencken, H. L. 1920. "Sahara of the Bozart." In *Prejudices: Second Series.* New York: Knopf.

Middleton, R. 1990. *Studying Popular Music.* London: Open University Press.

———. 2000. "Musical belongings: Western music and its low-other." In *Western Music and Its Others: Difference, Representation and Appropriation in Music,* edited by G. Born and D. Hesmondhalgh. Berkeley and Los Angeles: University of California Press.

Millar, B. 1974. *The Coasters.* London: Star Books.

Miller, D. 1995. The moan within the tone: African retentions in rhythm and blues saxophone style in Afro-American popular music. *Popular Music* 14, no. 2 (May): 155–174.

Miller, J., ed. 1976. *The Rolling Stone Illustrated History of Rock & Roll.* New York: Random House.

Mintz, P. 1985. "Orson Welles' use of sound." In *Film Sound: Theory and Practice,* edited by Elisabeth Weis and John Belton. New York: Columbia University Press.

Mintz, S., and S. Kellog. 1988. *Domestic Revolutions: A Social History of American Family Life.* New York: Free Press.

Moore, Allan F. 1993. *Rock, the Primary Text: Developing a Musicology of Rock.* Buckingham, Eng.: Open University Press.

Morrison, C. 1996. *Go Cat Go!: Rockabilly Music and Its Makers.* Champaign: University of Illinois Press.

Morthland, J. 1984. *The Best of Country Music.* New York: Doubleday Dolphin.

Mowitt, John. 1987. "The sound of music in the era of electronic reproducibility." In *Music and Society: The Politics of Composition Performance and Reception,* edited by Richard Leppert and Susan McClary. Cambridge: Cambridge University Press.

Mumford, Lewis. 1961. *The City In History: Its Origins, Its Transformations and Its Prospects.* London: Secker and Warburg.

———. 1963. *Technics And Civilization.* New York: Harcourt, Brace and World.

Murphie, Andrew. 1996. Sound at the end of the world as we know it: Nick Cave, Wim Wenders' *Wings of Desire* and Deleuze-Guattarian ecology of popular music. *Perfect Beat* 2, no. 4 (January): 18–42.

Murray, Charles Shaar. 1989. *Crosstown Traffic: Jimi Hendrix and Post-War Pop.* London: Faber and Faber.

———. 1999. *Boogie Man: Adventures of John Lee Hooker in the American Twentieth Century.* London: Viking.

Nelson, C. 1978. "The psychology of criticism, or what can be said." In *Psychoanalysis and the Question of the Text,* edited by G. H. Hartmen. Baltimore: Johns Hopkins University Press.

Nisbett, A. 1974. *Technique of the Sound Studio for Radio, Television and Film.* London: Focal.

Noble, G. P. 1948. *Hula Blues: the Story of Johnny Noble, Hawaii, its Music and Musicians.* Honolulu, Hawaii: Tongg.

Oakley, G. 1974. *The Devil's Music: A History of the Blues.* New York: Taplinger.

Obrecht, J. 1990. Talking country blues with Ry Cooder. *Guitar Player* (July): 74–85.

———. (1994) Muddy Waters: The life and times of the Hoochie Coochie man. *Guitar Player* (March): 30–48.

——. 1995. 'George W Johnson: African American Recording Pioneer' http://garlic. com/~tgracyk/johnson1.htm.

O'Brien, Lucy. 1995. *She Bop: the Definitive History of Women in Rock, Pop and Soul.* New York. Penguin.

O'Brien, Michael. 1979. *The Idea of the American South, 1920–1941.* Baltimore, Md.: Johns Hopkins University Press.

Odum, Howard W. 1936. *Southern Regions of the United States.* Chapel Hill: University of North Carolina Press.

Oliver, P. 1967. *The Story of the Blues.* London: Barrie and Rockcliff.

——. (1984) *Songsters and Saints: Vocal Traditions on Race Records.* Cambridge: Cambridge University Press.

——. 1989. That certain feeling: blues and jazz . . . in 1890? *Popular Music* 10, no. 1:11–19.

Ostransky, Leroy. 1978. *Jazz City: The Impact of our Cities on the Development of Jazz.* Englewood Cliffs, N.J.: Prentice-Hall.

Palmer, R. 1981. *Deep Blues.* London: Macmillan.

——. 1991. The church of the sonic guitar. *South Atlantic Quarterly* 90, no. 4 (fall): 649–673.

——. 1996. *Dancing in the Street.* London: BBC Books.

Paris, M., and C. Comber. 1977. *Jimmie the Kid: The Life of Jimmie Rodgers.* London: Eddison.

Pearsall, R. 1976. *Popular Music of the Twenties.* Lanham, Md.: Rowman & Littlefield.

Peterson, R. A. 1990. Why 1955? explaining the advent of soft music. *Popular Music* 9, no. 1:97–116.

——. 1995. "The dialectic of hard-core and soft-shell country music." In *Readin' Country Music: Steel Guitars, Opry Stars and Honky-Tonk Bars,* edited by C. Tichi. *South Atlantic Quarterly* 94, no. 1: 272–300. Durham, N.C.: Duke University Press.

——. 1997. *Creating Country Music: Fabricating Authenticity.* Chicago: University of Chicago Press.

Pfeil, Fred. 1988. "Postmodernism as a 'Structure of Feeling.'" In *Marxism and the Interpretation of Culture,* edited by C. Nelson and L. Grossberg. Urbana: University of Illinois Press.

Phillips, Stacey. 1991. *The Art of the Hawaiian Steel Guitar.* Pacific, Mo.: Mel Bay.

Pick, D. 2000. *Svengali's Web: The Alien Enchanter in Modern Culture.* New Haven: Yale University Press.

Pierce, John R. 1992. *The Science of Musical Sound.* New York: Freeman.

Pope, Edgar W. 2001. Exotic reflections. *Perfect Beat* 5, no. 2:91.

Porterfield, Nolan. 1992. *Jimmie Rodgers: The Life and Times of America's Blue Yodeler.* Urbana: University of Illinois Press.

Price, S. and E. Kearns, eds. 2003. *The Oxford Dictionary of Classical Myth and Religion* Oxford: Oxford University Press.

Radano, Ronald, and Philip V. Bohlman, eds. 2000. *Music and the Racial Imagination.* Chicago: University of Chicago Press.

Rasmussen, S. E. 1964. *Experiencing Architecture.* Cambridge, Mass.: MIT Press.

Raynor, Henry. 1972. *A Social History of Music: From the Middle Ages to Beethoven.* London: Barrie and Jenkins.

Read, O. and W. L. Welch. 1976. *From Tinfoil to Stereo: Evolution of the Phonograph.* Indianapolis, Ind.: Howard Sams and Bobbs-Merrill. (Originally published 1959.)

Reig, T., with E. Berger. 1990. *Reminiscing in Tempo: The Life and Times of a Jazz Hustler.* Studies in Jazz, no 10. Metuchen, N.J.: Scarecrow.

RE/Search no. 14. 1993. Incredibly strange music. Vol. 1.

RE/Search no. 15. 1995. Incredibly strange music. Vol. 2.

Reynolds, S. 1990. *Blissed Out: The Raptures of Rock.* London: Serpent's Tail.

Riesman, D. 1950. Listening to popular music. *American Quarterly* 2:359–371.

Rosenberg, N. V. 1985. *Bluegrass: A History.* Urbana: University of Illinois Press.

Russell, T. 1970. *Blacks, Whites and Blues.* London: Studio Vista.

———. 1971. Frank Hutchison, the pride of West Virginia. *Old Time Music,* no. 1 (summer): 4–7.

———. 1977 ReDECCAration. *Old Time Music.* no. 25 (summer): 30–34.

Rust, Brian. 1975. Introduction to *Gramophone Records of the First World War: An HMV Catalogue, 1914–1918.* The Gramophone Company, Newton Abbot, North Pomfret, Eng.: David and Charles.

Ruymar, L. 1996. *The Hawaiian Steel Guitar and Its Great Hawaiian Steel Musicians.* Anaheim Hills, Calif.: Centerstream.

Said, Edward. 1978. *Orientalism.* New York: Pantheon.

———. 1993. *Culture and Imperialism.* London: Chatto and Windus.

Sallis, J. 1982. *The Guitar Players: One Instrument and Its Masters in American Music.* Lincoln: University of Nebraska Press.

Samuelson, Dave. 1997. Liner notes to *Red Ingle—Tim Tayshun,* Bear Family CD, BCD 16 115 AH.

Sanjek, D. 1997. "Can a Fujiyama mama be the female Elvis: the wild, wild women of rockabilly.: In *Sexing the Groove: Popular Music and Gender,* edited by S. Whitely. London: Routledge.

Sanjek, R. 1988. *American Popular Music and Its Business: The First Four Hundred Years.* Vol. 3, *From 1900 to 1984.* New York: Oxford University Press.

Schafer, R. Murray. 1980. *The Tuning of the World: Towards a Theory of Soundscape Design.* Philadelphia: University of Pennsylvania Press.

Schivelbusch, W. 1986. *Railway Journey: The Industrialization of Time and Space in the Nineteenth Century.* New York: Berg.

Schwarz, D. 1997. *Listening Subjects: Music, Psychoanalysis and Culture.* Durham, N.C.: Duke University Press.

Scott-Maxwell, A. 1997. Oriental exoticism in 1920s Australian popular music. *Perfect Beat* 3, no. 3 (July): 28–57.

Shaugnessy, M. A. 1993. *Les Paul: An American Original.* New York: Morrow.

Shea, W. F. 1990. Role and function of technology in American popular music, 1945–1964. Ph.D. diss., University of Michigan.

Shelton, R. and B. Goldblatt. 1966. *The Country Music Story.* Indianapolis, Ind.: Bobbs-Merrill.

Shepherd, J. and P. Wicke. 1997. *Music and Cultural Theory.* Cambridge: Polity.

Sievert, J. 1977. Les Paul. Interview in *Guitar Player* (December): 34–36ff.

Sklar, R. 1984. *Rocking America, An Insiders Story: How the All-Hit Radio Stations Took Over.* New York: St. Martin's.

Slobin, M. 1992. Micromusics of the West: a comparative approach. *Ethnomusicology* 36, no. 1 (winter): 1–87.

Slotkin, R. 1985. *The Fatal Environment: The Myth of the Frontier in the Age of Industrialization, 1800–1890.* New York: Atheneum.

———. 1993. *Gunfighter Nation: The Myth of the Frontier in Twentieth-Century America.* New York: HarperCollins.

Small, C. 1994. *Music of the Common Tongue: Survival and Celebration in Afro-American Music.* London: Calder.

Smith, S. G. 1992. Blues and our mind body problem. *Popular Music* 11, no. 1:41–52.

Specht, Joe W. 1980. An interview with Hoyle Nix, the West Texas Cowboy. *Old Time Music,* no. 34 (summer–autumn): 7–11.

Spottswood, R. 1982. "Ethnic and popular style in America." In *Folk Music and the Modern Sound*, edited by W. Ferris and M. L. Hart. Jackson: University Press of Mississippi.

Stearns, M. W. 1956. *The Story of Jazz*. New York: Oxford University Press.

Stefani, G. 1987. A theory of musical competence. *Semiotica* 66:1–3, 7–22.

Stratton, J. 1992. *The Young Ones: Working-Class Culture, Consumption and the Category of Youth*. Perth, Australia: Black Swan Press.

Stambler, I., and G. Landon. 1969. *Encyclopedia of Folk, Country and Western Music*. New York: St Martin's.

Struthers, S. 1987. "Technology in the art of recording." In *Lost in Music: Culture, Style and Musical Event*, edited by A. L. White. London: Routledge and Kegan Paul.

Swiss, T., J. Sloop, and A. Herman. 1997. *Mapping the Beat: Popular Music and Contemporary Theory*. Malden, Mass.: Blackwell.

Tagg, P. 1979. *Kojak—50 Seconds of Television Music*. Göteborg, Sweden: Musikvetenskapliga Institutionen.

———. 1982. Analysing popular music: theory, method and practice. *Popular Music* 2:47–62.

Taruskin, Richard. 1992. "Entoiling the Falconer": Russian Musical Orientalism in Context. *Cambridge Opera Journal* 4:253–80.

Taylor, C. 1992. *Exploring Music: The Science and Technology of Tones and Tunes*. Bristol, Eng. IOP.

Taylor, T. D. 1992. His name was in lights: Chuck Berry's "Johnny B. Goode." *Popular Music* 11, no. 1:27–40.

Theberge, P. 1997. *Any Sound You Can Imagine: Making Music, Consuming Technology*. Wesleyan University Press; Hanover, N.H.: University Press of New England.

Toop, David. 1995. *Ocean of Sound: Aether Talk, Ambient Sound and Imaginary Worlds*. London: Serpents Tail.

———. 1999. *Exotica: Fabricated Soundscapes in a Real World*. London: Serpents Tail.

Tosches, N. 1976. Al Dexter. *Old Time Music*, no 22 (autumn): 4–8.

———. 1977. *Country: The Biggest Music in America*. New York: Stein and Day.

———. 1978. Nick Tosches interviews Ted Daffan. *Old Time Music*, no. 30 (autumn): 6–8.

———. 1982. *Hellfire* New York: Dell.

———. 1989. *Country: Living Legends and Dying Metaphors in America's Biggest Music*. London: Secker and Warburg.

———. 1991. *Unsung Heroes of Rock 'n' Roll: The Birth of Rock in the Wild Years Before Elvis*. London: Secker and Warburg.

———. 1993. *Dino: Living High In The Dirty Business Of Dreams*. New York: Dell.

Townsend, C. R. 1976. *San Antonio Rose: The Life and Music of Bob Wills*. Urbana: University of Illinois Press.

Van Der Merwe, P. 1989. *Origins of the Popular Style: The Antecedents of Twentieth-Century Popular Music*. Oxford: Clarendon Press.

Vale, V., and Andrea Juno, eds. 1993. *Incredibly Strange Music*. Vol. 1. San Francisco, Calif.: RE/Search Publications.

Van Leeuwen, T. 1991. Sociosemiotics of Easy Listening Music. *Social Semiotics* 1, no. 1: 67–80.

Waksman, Steve. 1999. *Instruments of Desire: The Electric Guitar and the Shaping of Musical Experience*. Cambridge, Mass.: Harvard University Press.

Walser, R. 1993. *Running with the Devil: Power, Gender and Madness in Heavy Metal Music*. Wesleyan University Press; Hanover, N.H.: University Press of New England.

Watson, E. 1975. *Country Music in Australia*. Sydney, Australia: Rodeo Publications.
———. 1983. *Country Music in Australia*. Vol. 2. Sydney, Australia: Cornstalk Publishing.
Weis, Elisabeth, and John Belton, eds. 1985. *Film Sound: Theory and Practice*. New York: Columbia University Press.
Whitburn, Joel. 1994. Liner notes to *Billboard Pop Memories—the 1920s*. Rhino CD R2 71575.
White, C. 1985. *The Life and Times of Little Richard, the Quasar of Rock*. London: Pan.
Whitely, S., ed. 1997. *Sexing the Groove: Popular Music and Gender*. London: Routledge.
Whiteoak, J. and A. Scott-Maxwell, eds. 2003. *The Currency Companion to Music and Dance in Australia*. Sydney, Australia: Currency House.
Williams, Roger M. 1981. *Sing a Sad Song: The Life of Hank Williams*. Urbana: University of Illinois Press.
Williams, Rosalind. 1990. *Notes on the Underground*. Cambridge, Mass.: MIT Press.
Wishart, T. 1985. *On Sonic Art*. York, U.K.: Imagineering.
Wilson, M. N.d. Liner notes to Frank Hutchison, *The Train That Carried my Girl From Town*. Rounder LP 1007.
Wolfe, Charles K. N.d. Liner notes to *Classic Country and Western, the Rarest Radio Recordings of all Time*. Radiola LP, 4MR2.
———. 1973. 'The discovery of Jimmie Rodgers: a further note. *Old Time Music*, no. 9 (summer): 24.
Wrightson, Patricia, and Peter Wrightson. 1998. *The Wrightson List*. Sydney, Australia: Random House.
Zak, Albin. 2001. *The Poetics of Rock: Cutting Tracks, Making Records*. Berkeley and Los Angeles: University of California Press.

Discography

All cited items are on compact disc, unless stated otherwise.

Arthur, Charline. "The Good and the Bad." On *Welcome to the Club*. Bear Family CD BCD 16279.
———. "The Good and the Bad." on *Welcome to the Club*. Bear Family, 1998.
Austin, Gene. "My Blue Heaven." On *Billboard Pop Memories, the 1920s*. RCA/BMG/Rhino, 1994.
Bechet, Sidney, and His Orchestra. "Chant in the Night." On *The Electric Guitar Story, 1935–1945*. Jazz Archives no. 84, 1996.
Berry, Chuck. "You Can't Catch Me." On *Rock 'n' roll Music*. Roots 33008, n.d.
Big Maybelle. "Gabbin' Blues." On *The Complete Okeh Session, 1952–1955*. Sony 1994.
Cochran, Eddie. "Summertime Blues." On *The Very Best of Eddie Cochran*. UA LP, 1975.
Cline, Patsy. "Walking After Midnight." On *Hillbilly Fever*. Rhino, 1995.
———. "Wayward Wind." On *The Patsy Cline Collection*. MCA, 1991.
Clooney, Rosemary. "Hey There." On *Songs from the Girl Singer: A Musical Autobiography*. Concord 1999.
Diddley, Bo. "Bo Diddley," "Down Home Special," "Pretty Thing" and "Who Do You Love." On *Jungle Music*. Orbis, 1993.
Doctor Ross. "The Boogie Disease." On *The Sunbox*. Charly LP, 1980.
Duncan, Tommy. "Gambling Polka Dot Blues." On *Swing West!* Vol. 3, *Western Swing*. Razor and Tie, 1999.
Ford, Tennessee Ernie. "Mule Train." On *The Ultimate Tennessee Ernie Ford Collection*. Razor and Tie, 1997.
Green, Al. "Jesus is Waiting." On *Call Me*. Hi Records LP, 1973.
Holiday, Billie. "Swing Brother Swing." On *Lady Day Box*. New Sound Planet, 1989.
Hooker, John Lee. "Walkin' the Boogie." On *Walkin' the Blues*. Roots RTS 33016, n.d.
Howlin' Wolf, "Moanin' at Midnight" and "Smokestack Lightnin.'" On *Howlin' Wolf* / *Moanin' at Midnight*. MCA, 1986.
Hutchison, Frank. "KC Blues." On *A Whiter Shade of Blue: White Country Blues (1926–1938)*. Columbia/Legacy, 1993.
Ingle, Red, and the Unnatural Seven. "Serutan Yob." On *Tim-Tayshun*. Bear Family, 1997.
Isham Jones Orchestra. "Swingin' Down the Lane." On *Billboard Pop Memories, the 1920s*. RCA/BMG/Rhino, 1994.

Jackson, Wanda. "Fujiyama Mama" and "Let's Have a Party." On *Vintage Collections*. Capitol, 1996.

Jim and Bob, the Genial Hawaiians. "Song of the Range." On *Hawaiian Steel Guitar Classics, 1927–1938*. Arhoolie, 1993.

Johnson, Robert. "Come in My Kitchen." On *King of the Delta Blues Singers*. Columbia/Legacy, 1998.

Kirk, Andy, and His Clouds of Joy. "Floyd's Guitar Blues." On *The Electric Guitar Story, 1935–1945*. Jazz Archives no. 84, 1996.

Little Walter. "Blue Lights," "Juke," "Sad Hours" and "A Quarter to Twelve." On *Blues With a Feeling*. Roots RTS 33006, n.d.

London, Julie. "Cry Me a River." On *Julie Is Her Name*. London LP, HA-U2005, n.d.

Louis, Joe Hill. "Treat Me Mean and Evil." [Also known as "When I'm Gone."] On *The Sunbox*. Charly LP, 1980.

Mendelssohn, Felix, and His Hawaiian Islanders. "Bali Hai." On *Serenade to Hawaii*. Encore LP 142, 1951.

Monroe, Vaughn, and His Orchestra. "Riders in the Sky." On *Stampede! Western Music's Late Golden Era*. Rounder, 1996.

Morse, Ella Mae. "House of Blue Lights." On *The Very Best of Ella Mae Morse*. Collectables, 1998.

Morton, Tex. "Crime Does Not Pay." On *The Tex Morton Regal Zonophone Collection*, Vol. 2. *1938–1943*. EMI, 1993.

Murad, Jerry, and his Harmonicats. "Peg O' My Heart." On *Greatest Hits*. Collectable CD, 1999.

Page, Patti. "Confess." On *All My Love*. AV Living Era, 2003.

Paul, Les, and Mary Ford. "How High the Moon." On *The Very Best of Les Paul and Mary Ford*. EMI CD 7243 8 57396 2 0, 1997.

Perkins, Carl. "All Mama's Children" and "Gone, Gone, Gone." On *The Best of the Sun Sessions*. Music Club, 1994.

Pittman, Barbara. "The Voice of a Fool." On *Getting Better all the Time*. Charly CD.

Presley, Elvis. "Baby Let's Play House," "Blue Moon of Kentucky," "Good Rockin' Tonight," "Milkcow Blues Boogie," "Mystery Train," and "That's All Right." On *Sunrise*. RCA, 1999.

———. "Heartbreak Hotel." On *The Complete Fifties Masters*. RCA, 1992.

Riley, Billy Lee. "Flying Saucer Rock 'n' roll." On *Red Hot Rockabilly*. EMI, 1991.

Rodgers, Jimmie. "Blue Yodel No. 1 (T For Texas)." On *The Essential Jimmie Rodgers*. RCA, 1997.

Shepard, Jean. "A Dear John Letter." On *Melody Ranch Girl*. Bear Family CD, 1996.

Smith, Warren. "Ubangi Stomp." On *Red Hot Rockabilly*. EMI, 1991.

Vincent, Gene. "Race with the Devil." On *The Bop That Just Won't Stop*. EMI [Australia] LP, 1974.

Waters, Muddy. "All Night Long." On *The Chess Rarities, 1947–1966*. MCA, 1996.

———. "I Can't Be Satisfied." On *Blues*. Disc 3. Universal [Australia] 1997.

———. "I Feel Like Going Home." On *Rare and Unissued*. MCA, 1995.

———. "Still a Fool." On *She Moves Me, Muddy Waters*, Vol. 2. Roots, 1992.

Watson, Johnny. "Guitar," "Space Guitar." On *Blues Masters: The Very Best of Johnny "Guitar" Watson*. Rhino, 1999.

West, Speedy, and Jimmy Bryant. "West of Samoa." On *Swingin' on the Strings: The Speedy West and Jimmy Bryant Collection*, Vol. 2. Razor and Tie, 1999.

Whiteman, Paul, and His Ambassador Orchestra. "Changes," "Three O'Clock in the Morning," "Whispering." On *The King of Jazz*. ASV Living Era, 1996.

Whitman, Slim. "Indian Love Call." On *Greatest Hits*. Curb, 1990.

Williams, Hank. "I'm So Lonesome I Could Cry." On *40 Greatest Hits*. Polydor, 1988.

——. "My Sweet Love Aint Around." On *Low Down Blues*. Mercury, 1996.

Willing, Foy, and the Riders of the Purple Sage. "Blue Shadows on the Trail." On *Foy Willing and the Riders of the Purple Sage*, Vol. 1. Cattle Records LP 18/19, n.d.

——. "Stampede." On *Stampede! Western Music's Late Golden Era*. Rounder, 1996.

Witherspoon, Jimmie. "When the Lights Go Out." On *Blues, Disc 1*. Universal [Australia] 1997.

Wray, Link. "Rumble." On *The Original Rumble Plus 22 Other Storming Guitar Instrumentals*. Ace, 1989.

Index

Jarmusch, Jim, 3, 188

Jazzed-up Hawaiian music, 124–25, 126–27

Jazz music: Basie and Holiday, 62, 63, 87–93; and deterritorialization, 54; Ellington, 89–90, 127, 128, 129; influence on western swing, 137; jungle themes and innovation, 127–29

Jerry Murad and the Harmonicats, 143–44

"Jesus Is Waiting," 152–53

Johnson, Robert, 3–4, 75–87, 246–47nn21–30

Jones, George, 142

Jones, Jo, 88

Jose, Richard, 49

"Jubilee Stomp," 89–90, 91

"Juke," 179–81, 257nn6–7

"Jungle Band," Ellington's, 127

Kanahele, George, 122, 125

Kawin, Bruce, 115

"KC Blues," 64–65, 244n3, 245n10

Keil, Charles, 18–19, 20, 62, 205–6

Kellogg, S., 195

Kienzle, Rich, 156

Kincaid, Bradley, 102

King, B. B., 166

King, Charles Edward, 124, 251n35

King of the Delta Blues Singers, 75, 76

Kirk, Andy, 135

Krautheimer, R., 43–44

Lacasse, Serge, 29–31, 144

Landforms: and echo in western films, 107, 110, 111; and hillbilly stereotypes, 102–3; mountains as sacred spaces, 108, 110

"Land of My Boyhood Dreams," 96

Lap (table-style) electric steel guitar, 123

"Leader of the Pack," 221

Lennon, John, 203

Leppert, R., 194–96

"Let the Jukebox Keep Playing," 199

Levine, Lawrence, 46, 47

Lévy-Bruhl, Lucien, 20

Lewis, Jerry Lee, 224

Leyshon, A., 15

Lipsitz, G., 194–96

Listeners/listening: and affective experience, 12–14, 35–36; classical music connoisseurs, 55; classical vs. popular music roles of, 60; competence of, 12–14, 235n14; cultural background of race music, 165; immersion in recorded musical space, 77, 81, 91; live vs. recorded

performance, 23; overview, 8–9; post–rock 'n' roll pop music, 225; power of recorded music for, 52; producer as listener for studio artist, 164; and reverence for classical music, 59; and shared experience of social change, 192–93; shared space with performers, 9, 170, 176–77; teen fans of Presley, 183; teen identification with rock 'n' roll message, 203; territorial dichotomies vs. performer, 85. *See also* Intimacy of popular recorded music; Participation

"Little Lies," 26

Little Richard, 211–12, 224

Little Walter, 157–58, 179–81, 206

Live vs. recorded performance: and high vs. low art, 35–36; listener experience of, 20, 23; Matassa's preference for live replication, 211–12; performer's position in, 78; and Presley as recording artist first, 183–84; recordings as main southern music source, 236n53; replication of recording on stage, 150–51; schizophonia of, 19; and "Swing, Brother, Swing," 88

Locke, Ralph P., 125

Lomax, Alan, 20, 21

London, Julie, 158

Loner icon, 106, 108–9, 110, 111, 215–16. *See also* Itinerancy, mythos of

"Looking the World Over," 218

Lost Highway (Guralnick), 21, 191–92

Louis, Joe Hill, 168–73, 181

"Love Bites," 26

"Love Song of the Waterfall," 26

Low vs. high art. *See* High vs. low art

Lubin, Tom, 27–28

Lyric content: and cowboy song spatiality, 114; and immersion invitation, 88; and inner dialogue with multiple voices, 145, 219–20; and Presley's direct adoption of blues space, 185; and reverb effects, 158, 161, 176–77, 188–89; spoken vs. sung words, 64, 80–81, 221–22, 245n10; and underground metaphor for rock 'n' roll, 201–2; and undermining of feminine self, 223–24; Williams's establishment of country music themes, 140–41

Mackenzie, Compton, 55, 59–60, 243n89

Magnetic tape technology: Paul's use of, 147–48; and signal processing, 28; and

Mysticism. *See* Religion and spirituality
"My Sweet Love Ain't Around," 138
Mythological sources for echo, 40–41. *See also* Echo and Narcissus myth

Narcissus, 40, 132, 138
Nelson, Ken, 210
Neotechnic vs. paleotechnic industrial phases, 191
New Sound, 151, 155
New Zealand, 103, 104–5
Nighttime space, authority over, 215–16
Nolan, Bob, 103
Nonconformity in 1950s, 197–98
Novels and southern/western stereotypes, 95–96, 99, 109, 117–18

Obbligato accompaniment, 137–38
Oceanic mode of musical apprehension, 77, 130. *See also* Immersion of self
Odum, Howard, 98
Oedipal perspective on social relationships, 195–98
Off-mic vs. on-mic recording: classical vs. pop music aesthetic, 57, 72–73; in Hawaiian musical space, 133; Muddy Waters's style, 174, 176–77; and sonic spatial depth, 26, 105, 113; and vocal-instrument dynamics, 105, 148, 168–73
Okeh records, 64–65
"Old Faithful and I," 104–5
Oliver, Paul, 20
Opera and phonograph development, 51–52, 55
Orientalism and Hawaiian music, 124–25
Orpheus myth and power of producers, 146
"Other" spaces: and amplified instrumentation, 136; and black jazz-swing music, 91–92, 127–29; confluence of self and other in blues artists, 171–72; dialogue with self and multiple voicing, 145, 152–54, 155, 219–20; in Echo and Narcissus myth, 139; in Hawaiian music, 124, 125, 126, 129, 130–31; hillbilly invitation to backstage space, 68, 74; Johnson's blues invitation to, 80–81; merging of self and other in rock 'n' roll, 184–85, 187–88, 210, 232; reverb as signifier of, 221; rock 'n' roll as home for social outsiders, 222; and uncanny spaces, 229–30
Overdriven guitar sounds, 137–38, 168

Page, Patti, 30, 144, 146, 152
Paleotechnic vs. neotechnic industrial phases, 191
Palmer, Robert, 20, 28–29, 80, 173–74, 179–80, 194
Paris, Texas (film), 13–14
Parker, Junior, 186, 189
Participation: as anthropological concept, 20, 22, 236n35; and dance, 53–55, 199–200, 243–44nn94–95; freedom of rock 'n' roll, 234; and human alienation from nature, 40–41; and immersion in recorded experience, 77; rock 'n' roll's invitation to, 186–87, 199–200, 205–6, 221–22, 231–32; in "Swing, Brother, Swing," 88
Participatory discrepancies in band instrumental roles, 62–63
Patriarchy, western loner as escaping from, 109
Patti, Adelina, 51
Paul, Les, 33, 35–36, 146–55, 156, 168, 181
"Paulverizer," 151
Paul Whiteman Orchestra, 54–55
Pedal steel guitar, 123
Peer, Ralph, 68, 102
"Peg o' My Heart:, 143–44
Peirce, C. S., 14
Penniman, Little Richard, 211–12, 224
Performers: and discipline of sliding steel guitar, 124; freedoms of marginality, 72; glorification over recording itself, 22; in hillbilly music spatiality, 73, 74; and intimidation of traditional recording culture, 67–68; and live vs. recorded performance, 78; as originators of spatial effects, 28; and producers, 22, 82, 146, 153–55, 163–65, 194, 198, 203–6; recorded visibility of, 68; and restrictions of early recording equipment, 49–50; as secular mystics, 46; shared space with listeners, 9, 170, 176–77; territorial dichotomies vs. listeners, 85. *See also* Gender
Perkins, Carl, 142, 167, 186, 198–203, 258n13, 259n46
Perry, Edward Baxter, 47
"Peter Gunn," 215
Phillips, Sam: importance of innovative role, 163; interpersonal skills, 193–94, 203–6; neglect of women performers, 223; on nonconformity, 197–98; vs. Les Paul, 181; pre-rock 'n' roll developments, 165–73. *See also* Sun records

Paul's R & B innovations, 149–50; Presley's direct adoption of, 184, 185–86; reverb in early R & B, 158–59; and studio relationships, 6; and vaudevillian stereotyping, 122. *See also* Blues music; Jazz music

"Race with the Devil," 210, 232

Radio broadcasting: and country music development, 102; *Hawaii Calls* program, 121; influence on early pop music recording, 56; physical environment of, 244n2; and realism vs. romanticism, 32, 33; and western iconography, 97

R & B music, 149–50, 158–59. *See also* Blues music; Race music

RCA records, 183–84

Read, O., 31–32, 151

Realism vs. romanticism: and classical vs. popular music aesthetics, 58–59, 228; hillbilly disregard for realist aesthetic, 65; and Johnson's blues spatiality, 81; Matassa's realist approach, 211–12; overview, 8; and popular music development, 62–63; and recording development, 32–33, 57, 62, 243n93; research issues, 33; and singing cowboy spaces, 2, 3–4, 8, 168–69; and Tin Pan Alley songwriting, 72–74; Williams's realist style, 141. *See also* Echo and reverberation effects

Reappropriation of stereotypes by marginalized groups, 127, 192

Rebel Without a Cause, 196

Recordings: Australia/New Zealand western sonic spatiality, 104–5; autonomy of, 18; birth of recording artists, 70–71; resources for history of phonograph, 31–33; spatial sense in, 2; women's conflicting roles in, 217. *See also* Live vs. recorded performance; Phonograph development

Red Ingle and the Natural Seven, 159–60

Red Seal Records, 53

Reed, Jimmy, 225

Refrain concept and spatiality in music, 16, 17

Regional marketing of early recordings, 51, 66–67

Religion and spirituality: echo as invitation to transcendence, 180–81; echo/reverb as divine voice, 97, 108–9, 113, 175; echo/reverb as sacred space, 29, 42–46, 110–11; and Hawaiian mystical discon-

nection from reality, 133; and nature as mystical experience, 108, 110, 118–19; and sentimental popular songs, 36–37; and studio as retreat space, 204–5. *See also* Echo and Narcissus myth; Immersion of self

Remington, Herb, 137

Renunciatory space, rock 'n' roll as rejection of, 233

Resonance: and performance intensity, 77–78; vs. reverberation, 34

Resonator (steel) guitar, 134. *See also* Steel guitar

Reterritorialization of music after initial rock 'n' roll revolution, 225, 232–33

Reverberation effect. *See* Echo and reverberation effects

Revill, G., 15

Rhythm section, spatiality role of, 89, 112

"Riders in the Sky," 8, 111–14

Riders of the Purple Sage (band), 1–4

Riders of the Purple Sage (Grey), 117–18

Riley, Billy Lee, 214

Rock, the Primary Text (Moore), 24–27

Rockabilly music, Williams's legacy to, 142. *See also* Rock 'n' roll/rockabilly music

Rock music, 23, 27, 142

Rock 'n' roll/rockabilly music: analytical neglect of, 31; and chaotic manifestation of spatiality, 14; at Chess, 179–81, 206–8; demise of first wave, 224–25; deterritorialized nature of, 213–15; gender issues, 215–24; importance of echo and reverb to, 8; introduction, 178–79; and participation in recorded vs. live music, 20; and performers' confidence in recording studio, 67; Presley at RCA, 208–9; and social changes, 191–97; spatial contribution of, 225–34; spread of reverb effects, 210–12. *See also* Sun records

Rodgers, Carrie, 71

Rodgers, Jimmie: deterritorialization by, 68–72, 74, 78, 85; and Hawaiian music, 121; spatiality of, 229; as western icon, 96

Rogers, Jimmy, 179

"Rolling Stone," 176–77

Romanticism vs. realism. *See* Realism vs. romanticism

Roots music, 7, 21. *See also* Blues music

"Roundabout," 26

Royal Hawaiian Band, 124

"Rumble," 215

Running with the Devil (Walser), 11

Rural-to-urban migration, 191, 192

Russell, Tony, 20, 140

"Sahara of the Bozart, The" (Mencken), 99

Said, Edward, 125

Saint-Saëns, Camille, 125

Samson et Dalila, 125

Sanjek, David, 216, 217, 224

Sanjek, Russell, 113, 144

Satherley, Art, 165

Satirizing of reverb, 214–15

Scalar renderings for vertical space, 58

Schafer, R. Murray, 19, 37, 42, 44

Schismogenesis, 19

Schizophonia metaphor, 19–20, 34

"School Day," 233–34

Schools for Hawaiian music, 121–22

Searchers, The, 196

Self, psychic: dialogue through multiple voicing, 145, 152–54, 155, 219–20; in Echo and Narcissus myth, 40–41, 139; and echo as divine inner voice, 109; and Johnson's spatial intensity, 77; merging with "other," 171–72, 184–85, 187–88, 210, 232; and reality as displaced self, 140; reverb role as underminer of feminine self, 223–24; and spatiality, 7; territory of, 86–87. *See also* Immersion of self

Self-audiencing, 77

Semiotic approach to musicology, 12, 31, 71

Sensuality and exotic other, 125, 126, 129, 130–31

Sergio Leone westerns, echoic soundtrack in, 215

"Serutan Yob," 160

78 Quarterly, 31

Shane, 107–9, 196

Shangri Las, 221

Shared space of listeners and performers, 9, 170, 176–77

Sharp, Cecil, 99

Shea, William, 31

Shepard, Jean, 220–21

Signal processing, echo and reverb as, 27–28

Simon, Paul, 188

Sinatra, Frank, 177

Singing cowboys: and existential spatiality, 73; vs. hillbillies, 94, 95–98, 101; international appeal of, 103–5; movies for, 106; and "Riders in the Sky," 112; romanticism vs. realism, 2, 3–4, 8, 168–69

Singing Cowboys and Musical Mountaineers (Malone), 102

Singleton, Shelby, 167

Single plane aesthetic in early recording, 61

Slapback echo and reverb: Chess's use of, 179–80; definition, 235n6; on lead vocal, 186; overview, 6; pre–rock 'n' roll use of, 144, 147–48; and rock 'n' roll signature sound, 166; at Sun, 181–83, 258n14

"Sleepy Eyed John," 167

Slide guitars, 121, 123, 250n17

Sloop, J., 15

Small ensemble jazz, spatiality of, 87–93

Smith, Floyd, 135–36

Smith, Warren, 214

"Smokestack Lightnin'," 157

Snow, Hank, 103

Social factors: black influences on hillbilly music, 140; and deterritorialization of high art music, 71; industrial culture and music development, 59, 132, 134, 191–97; musicology neglect of, 11–12; nonconformity in 1950s, 197–98; Oedipal perspective on relationships, 195–98; overview, 14–15, 36–37; in phonograph development, 51–52, 242–43n89; post-WWII mobility, 230; reverb as sonic signifier of black struggles, 170–71; and rock 'n' roll innovations, 191–97, 200–202, 216; and romance of itinerancy, 84; and secular spirituality in music, 46–47; shared experience of social change through music, 192–93; and spatial devices in recording, 23–24; strength of, 6–7; and western vs. southern myths, 94–105. *See also* Cultural issues; "Other" spaces; Race music; Religion and spirituality

Sonic spatialities, 5–6, 237n70. *See also* Spatiality

Sons of the Pioneers, 95, 96–97

Sound art, 34

Sound-box construct and depth, 26–27

Sound in film. *See* Film industry

Sound Tracks (Connell and Gibson), 15

Sousa, John Philip, 49–50

MUSIC/CULTURE

A series from Wesleyan University Press

Edited by Robert Walser and Susan Fast

Originating editors, George Lipsitz, Susan McClary, and Robert Walser

Popular Music in Theory
by Keith Negus

*Upside Your Head! Rhythm and Blues
on Central Avenue* by Johnny Otis

*Singing Archaeology:
Philip Glass's Akhnaten*
by John Richardson

*Black Noise: Rap Music and Black
Culture in Contemporary America*
by Tricia Rose

*The Book of Music and Nature: An
Anthology of Sounds, Words, Thoughts*
edited by David Rothenberg and
Marta Ulvaeus

*Angora Matta: Fatal Acts of
North-South Translation*
by Marta Elena Savigliano

*Making Beats:
The Art of Sample-Based Hip-Hop*
by Joseph G. Schloss

*Dissonant Identities: The Rock 'n' Roll
Scene in Austin, Texas*
by Barry Shank

*Banda: Mexican Musical Life across
Borders* by Helena Simonett

*Subcultural Sounds: Micromusics
of the West*
by Mark Slobin

Music, Society, Education
by Christopher Small

*Musicking: The Meanings of
Performing and Listening*
by Christopher Small

*Music of the Common Tongue:
Survival and Celebration in African
American Music*
by Christopher Small

*Singing Our Way to Victory: French
Cultural Politics and Music During the
Great War* by Regina M. Sweeney

*Setting the Record Straight: A Material
History of Classical Recording*
by Colin Symes

*False Prophet: Fieldnotes from the Punk
Underground* by Steven Taylor

*Any Sound You Can Imagine: Making
Music/Consuming Technology*
by Paul Théberge

*Club Cultures: Music, Media and
Sub-cultural Capital*
by Sarah Thornton

*Running with the Devil: Power, Gender,
and Madness in Heavy Metal Music*
by Robert Walser

*Manufacturing the Muse: Estey Organs
and Consumer Culture in Victorian
America* by Dennis Waring

*The City of Musical Memory: Salsa,
Record Grooves, and Popular Culture in
Cali, Colombia* by Lise A. Waxer